REPUBLICAN GERMANY

A POLITICAL AND ECONOMIC STUDY

BY

HUGH QUIGLEY

AND

R. T. CLARK

NEW YORK

Howard Fertig

1968

First published in 1928 by Methuen & Company Ltd., London

HOWARD FERTIG, INC. EDITION 1968
Published by arrangement with Associated Book Publishers, Ltd.

Library of Congress Catalog Card Number: 67-24592

PRINTED IN THE UNITED STATES OF AMERICA
BY NOBLE OFFSET PRINTERS, INC.

REPUBLICAN GERMANY

PREFACE

WHILE a number of special studies have appeared in this country on the subject of contemporary Germany, no effort has yet been made to examine in detail those political and economic factors which have gone to the formation of the German Republic. It is not sufficient to attach a concluding chapter to a history of Germany covering the contemporary epoch. While, of course, no history can be interrupted at any particular point, Germany has undergone so many difficult and critical experiences since the conclusion of the War that one is justified in regarding her as almost a new State ; an immensely complicated work of adjustment in practically every phase of national life has been carried out during the last nine years, and such an adjustment has its own interest, its own significance and its own value. We have, therefore, decided to begin our survey with the revolutionary period which took place towards the end of the War, and devote attention wholly to political and economic factors. It may be possible in a later study to deal with philosophical, literary, artistic, musical, and other elements which are expressive of the contemporary German spirit.

The book falls into two parts clearly defined : the first part is almost purely historical and describes the formation of the German Republic, the constitution, the consolidation and the strengthening of the central executive ; the second part does not lend itself to pure historical narration, owing to the fact that production, finance, industry and labour are all forces with their own sphere of activity ; it would be dangerous to mix them together and, out of this mixture, arrive at some conception of the new German economic State. In the political, as well as in the economic, sphere, certain salient characteristics appear, certain forces have been active in both, and it has been our desire to explain some of these characteristics and assess at their true value many of the forces which have linked up all activities within the German State.

The political section does not pretend to be a formal history of the first nine years of the German Republic ; it is rather an attempt to create an historical background, in front of which the spiritual and intellectual forces of the new Germany may be seen more clearly.   The standpoint adopted has been that of Republicanism, since we believe that a German Republic is more useful to the world than a German Empire, and that democracy in the long run is the only form of government worthy of men with any claim to freedom in thought or in action.   Certain critics may consider this attitude as one of bias and question the accuracy and the balance of the analysis, but no political history can be entirely impartial if it is to be something more vital than a bald record of fact.   The inter-pretation is, therefore, individual, but there is no attempt to introduce theory into historical narration ; individuality lies only in method of approach.   There has been no manipulation or distortion of historical facts or tendencies.   In spite of this, there will be disagreement no doubt as to many points in the general interpretation and in the judgments implied in the choice of events, but there is always room for the play of per-sonal opinion, even in the most scientific disquisition, and if we have been able to explain the development of the German Republic clearly and convincingly, we may find in that sufficient justification.

In the economic sphere, there is a danger of going too deeply into statistical comparisons, with neglect of theory and of connecting narrative.   To give some unity of purpose and treatment to the survey, selection has been carried out with a view to eliminating those characteristics and those develop-ments which may not be regarded as specially Republican. Thus, in the chapters devoted to industrial production, we have concentrated attention on those industries which were affected by the Treaty of Versailles, and described changes which have taken place in other industries since the conclusion of the War. This observation applies especially to the section on electricity and super-power.   In the case of reparations, no elaborate detail has been given regarding the negotiations between the Allies and Germany or the various schemes put forward by the Allies in dealing with the question.   We have been concerned more with the principle of reparations and its place in the eco-nomic development of Germany.   It is difficult to strike the balance between what is and what is not significant, especially in labour problems and in the organization of industry, and the objection may be raised that generalization should be based more adequately on detailed analysis.   Such a detailed analysis would, however, entail a separate monograph for each main subject discussed in the economic section, and break up the unity of the book.

The book has one theme—the origin, definition and consolidation of the German Republic. The period, 1917–1927, represents one great phase in the political and economic history of the German people, almost wholly self-contained, with few unfinished elements. Its conclusion can be seen in the Conference held between the *Reich* and the *Länder* regarding the unitary State at the beginning of 1928 and in the elections to be held in the same year. A new phase begins with the first full year of the Dawes payments and with the revival of normal trading agreements between Germany and other countries ; in finance, in politics, in industry and trade, the strength of the Republic has been restored and the return to normal conditions ensured.

Some hesitation was felt about employing the word " Republic " in connection with Germany, owing to the fact that Germany has adhered consistently to the word " Reich " and has shown unwillingness to adopt unhesitatingly the word " Republican " in legal and other documents. Nevertheless, Germany is a Republic as far as a constitution can make her a Republic. She is not, however, a centralized Republic like France, for her component " Lands " have their defined autonomy. Although the word " Land " was adopted to indicate that these component parts were not " States," we have for reasons of easy comprehension and, to avoid the use of an unfamiliar word, translated " Land " as " State ", except in the section dealing specifically with the German Constitution. There the term has a particular legal significance and has no real equivalent in English. Elsewhere in the book, " Land " has been abandoned in favour of " State ", since it is not, in these cases, a question of the legal distinction but of a territorial unit. The whole question of the relationship between the central executive and the various States or *Länder* has been under discussion for many years, and the feeling is growing that Germany should be a single united State, with greater power vested in the Government. Under these reservations, we have adhered to the terms, " Republic " and " Republican ", throughout the book.

We would, in conclusion, like to express our indebtedness to the German journalists, who never record a political event without prolonged and instructive comment, and to Professor Hohlfeld for his wholly admirable and stimulating "*Geschichte des deutschen Reiches.''*   We should also express our admiration for the remarkable work which is being carried out in Germany in the sphere of economic research by institutions like the Federal Statistical Bureau and the *Institut für Konjunkturforschung* ; they have brought the art of statistical analysis to a very high level indeed, and made the work of examination of modern industrial tendencies in Germany much less exacting than it would otherwise have been.   We have also to thank Mr. F. Hall for his assistance in correcting the proofs and in verifying statistical data.

H. QUIGLEY
R. T. CLARK

LONDON ⎫ *May, 1928*
MANCHESTER ⎭

CONTENTS

ix

MAPS

DIAGRAMS IN THE TEXT

REPUBLICAN GERMANY

REPUBLICAN GERMANY

INTRODUCTION

CONTEMPORARY GERMANY

Difficulty of an historical survey—assessing factors of permanent value—a dramatic theme—the rise of the new democratic State—an inspiring subject—democracy on trial—Ebert and Hindenburg—industrial adjustment—the conception of the German mentality—philosophic doctrines and personalities—three great thinkers—literary and artistic criticism—" Thomas Paine "—the art of the film—contemporary art movements and tendencies—the Expressionists—industrial architecture—decorative principle—conclusions.

THE bare chronicle of fact may be, in itself, of sufficient interest to keep alive a modern history, but such a chronicle can have little value outside of the facts that it gives ; it may be used as a source of reference and it may supply romantic story-tellers with certain hard details sufficient to rescue otherwise vague narrations from the danger of unreality. When the object of survey is an immensely complicated industrial State like Germany, the mosaic presented by a mere record of what has taken place in every branch of activity must be more bewildering even than those decorations which have been built into the baroque palaces of Vienna. There is a feeling that each detail must have its own significance, but what that significance is lies beyond comprehension ; there must be some connecting link, some general plan which will give dignity and meaning to the architectural mass, and, where such a meaning can be found and placed in true perspective, the effect is one of a complex and even stimulating beauty. On the other hand, it may be possible to concentrate on ideas alone, develop a thesis, bring elaborate arguments into line, and evolve principles which appear to carry with them a satisfactory interpretation of what has occurred. In this case, one may assume a certain degree of conscious or unconscious assimilation of fact without the necessity for minute statement or close representation. There is here, however, a

1

danger of interpretation becoming unsubstantial and unreal ;
there may be too many assumptions and too many points of
view.   The basis of criticism may be subjective, and thus a
wholly individual conception be expressed, which has no significance outside of the mind of the critic.

Again, there are fashions in philosophy, in the theory of
history, in historical method, in æsthetics and in ethics, which
may decree at one time a certain method of approach and a
certain arrangement of values, but there is no certainty that
fashion will coincide always with truth or with the lasting elements in criticism which survive the most revolutionary and
the most extreme phases of opinion.

What, then, remains to be done in the case of a country like
Germany ?   The way of safety lies, of course, in an immensely
voluminous narration of fact, without commentary and without interpretation, but, even in this case, the presentation
of the subject or the arrangement of the material may lead
to greater distortion of the truth than the most perfervid
eloquence.   Yet, any survey of contemporary Germany must
depend above all on the intelligent use of fact   One may, of
course, content oneself with selection of a few movements
already clearly visible, and by the study of such movements
arrive at some conception of what Germany means in the
international political and economic spheres.   Such a selection
suffers from incompleteness, but it leads to a clear understanding of the principal forces making for national development,
and such forces are in themselves the results and the origins of
historical events.   The ideal arrangement would be, therefore,
the grouping or the selection of facts leading to and illustrative
of those creative forces, with elimination of unnecessary and
purely superficial phenomena.

What method can be adopted of assessing such forces at
their proper value, or even of interpreting events in such a way
that recognition of a creative force at work will be possible ?
Against that difficulty every student of contemporary Germany
has to strive.   In the case of histories with a perspective hun-
dreds of years before the present time the passage of the centuries has usually been sufficient to arrange values and facilitate
interpretation, so that a certain objectivity is possible in criticism and, with it, a fair degree of accuracy.   With Republican
Germany, however, no such assistance can be expected ; we
are still too close to events to be able to size up the picture as a
whole and to decide which are its salient features ; we run the
danger perpetually of admiring the embroidery instead of the

cloak, of singling out secondary characters while the hero escapes our attention. The developments on which we now lay great importance may, in a few years, look grotesquely insignificant. In the case of Germany, for example, the inflation period occupied all minds during 1921, 1922 and 1923, and gave rise to an immense volume of theory and of economic journalism mixed with a little inspired musing. Now, however, the whole subject has faded into the background and has left practically nothing behind ; prophecies have proved unfruitful and jeremiads singularly hollow of meaning. The inflation years made, undoubtedly, a great impression on the German people, but, historically, they represent a period which, in the evaluations of a century hence, will probably be as nothing. In the same way, one can look back on the enthusiastic ideals of the revolutionary period and marvel at the optimism of those who were responsible for Socialistic Utopias drawn on paper. Even at this distance of time, we can see how inconstant the most solidly rooted doctrine was and how enormous the forces of opposition were to changes in the social complex of Germany.

Some effort can, therefore, be made to place values in a perspective different from that which held the scene nine or seven or six or five or three years ago, and perhaps to determine the relation between such values from the point of view of their contribution to the formation of contemporary German mentality and the contemporary German State. Whether such evaluation will be recognized in the future as even approximately correct lies in the lap of the gods. To the historian of fifty years hence, all the difficulties which have arisen round reparations and the Dawes Plan may appear singularly uninviting objects of discussion—symptoms of a widespread disease, the very name of which might be distasteful.

There are complications which must serve to make the most careful record almost a speculation. Yet we have in Germany what is lacking in other countries during the post-war period—namely, a theme. The consolidation of the German Republic is in itself a theme of the most absorbing interest ; it lends itself to dramatic presentation with the leading characters active at moments with a real dramatic force. The first act had all the vivacity and strength and suggestive force of a great play—the collapse of the German armies and the outbreak of the revolution, with Ebert emerging as the character dominating the stage. The second act, if we may continue the simile, was less interesting than the first, and represented a period of preparation, when new characters were introduced and new dramatic *motifs* were being evolved—the Treaty of Versailles and the early reparations discussions terminating in that eventful Conference of the Reparations Commission in 1921, when Germany's total indebtedness was finally agreed. The third act had all the elements of tragedy in it, and at one time (when the collapse of the Republic came very near) catastrophe could be visualized. Yet the dramatic action moved much more rapidly at this time ; against a background of destitution and despair, rapid changes of scene took place, with eagerly gesticulating characters discussing artistic, literary and social events. There were strong contrasts and strong colours with a suggestion of future greatness of a fine, inspiring quality. This act closes with the collapse of passive resistance, on the part of the German Government and the industrialists, to the French and Belgian occupation of the Ruhr. The fourth act was less interesting in its play of character and of event ; it represented the destruction of certain characteristics which had previously almost led to tragedy and the emergence of new motives closely related to those which had gone to the proclamation of the Republic in the early years. Capital and labour were working together and the State was deriving fresh strength from their union. The reparations problem had ceased to be an object of dissension and of perpetual duelling ; it reached a temporary solution in the elaboration of the Dawes Plan and in the report by the Commission of Experts. This act illustrated the first period of consolidation of the German Republic after a time of disturbance. The fifth and probably the last act is now being played, and promises something more heartening than a catastrophic ending. There may be scenes of conflict, world-shaking events, accompanied by the possibility and dangers of war, but the real consummation will probably be reached—namely, the recognition of the German Republic as a permament feature in German history and in economic and political relations, and, with it, the opening of a new era of international prosperity.

The dramatic theme is present, therefore, and only requires illumination and, to some extent, interpretation. Such an interpretation would only receive justice at the hands of a poet like Hardy intent on creating a modern version of *The Dynasts* ; it lends itself to the finest qualities of vison and of sure delineation ; the scene is not dominated by a colossus like Napoleon, but, on the other hand, it is not crowded with a mass of insignificant and irresponsible characters. The decorations are not conceived in a spirit of bravado with an immense flourishing of tinsel draperies and papier-mâché statues ; artistic *motif* is couched in a chaster phraseology and expressed in more vivid and more intimate colouring and line ; the impression of reality and of throbbing life is never obscured by a display of pyrotechnics or magnificently empty gesture. We may have a tendency to regard such things as the development of a democratic constitution as outside the range of literary and artistic effect, but even the struggles of a State forcing its way into a new conception of social, economic and cultural values may have in it all the greatness and all the tragic pettiness of the human spirit. There is certainly in this subject of Republican Germany the possibilities of a fine drama or of a world-embracing novel similar to Tolstoy's *War and Peace*. It is in this spirit that the study of contemporary Germany should be undertaken ; otherwise there is a danger of too absorbed attention to detail, which may become tedious in the extreme and ultimately unsatisfactory through sheer insignificance.

The main problem confronting the German Republic from the day of its birth was, in essence, that which confronts every modern democracy. Only, instead of a democratic constitution and a democratic view of life being developed over many decades and even many centuries, the act of conversion had to take place within a very short period. The Reich prior to the Great War was almost wholly an absolute monarchy, with the concentration of responsibility and the sources of power in a certain class, which, in turn, was dominated by a few outstanding personalities. It is true, of course, that, as a modern nation, with a full knowledge of social, economic and political movements in the world, the tendency towards assertion of the democratic standpoint was inevitable, even in the pre-war years. The point at issue is, however, that the very constitution of the German Reich precluded the assumption of power by the democracy itself ; there were no tribunes of the people to maintain some balance of power against the aristocracy and the patricians. The German revolution destroyed this elaborate system, overturned the machinery of government and responsibility, and forced democracy to undertake its own salvation and its own direction.

From the beginning, therefore, it was on trial, without traditions, without previous experience, and possibly without any real vision of future expansion. In any other country, as Italy and Russia have shown, democracy would not have survived the trial, and there would have been a restoration of the old

absolutism, without any modifying qualities whatever. The
German temperament was a temperament attuned to authority ; it was unwilling to experiment and to embark on hazardous adventure ; it was willing to concur with any government
which promised a fair measure of stability and of peace ; it was
definitely unwilling to be convulsed by perpetual changes in
the form and in the policy of the constitution. The new democracy had, therefore, a fair guarantee of life, even at its most
critical moments. Relations had to be adjusted between all
the elements composing the State—between the central executive and the executives of the individual States, between the
State and industry, between industry and labour, and between
the State, industry, labour and finance together. Much of
this work of delicate adjustment had already been carried out,
and was inherent in the economic and political development of
the State. The greater part of the task lay, therefore, in the
definition and in the grading of values.

A central motive existed, which was in itself a powerful
factor making for unification—reparations; the necessity of
recovering lost ground, of maintaining a strong position against
the hypercritical body of the Allies, of resisting excessive
demands and of creating a solid national front against the political manœuvres of France and her satellites, did much undoubtedly to consolidate the new democratic *régime* and make
it operate with satisfactory efficiency. It was largely a shak-
ing-down process, with the discarding of many elements in the
old *régime* which might at one time have been deemed important, and the discarding of such elements was not unattended
by political and social disturbances. The Kapp revolt and
the Hitler disturbance were political phenomena actuated by
reactionary and conservative elements, even as much as the
Spartacist and Kurt-Eisner revolutions were phenomena of
extremism from the Left, which, in turn, had to be broken up
and discarded.

We should not forget also the rôles played by the first two
German Presidents—namely, Ebert and Hindenburg. They
contributed immensely to the success of the new *régime* ; their
sincerity, their keen sense of duty and their consistency of character were, in themselves, an inspiration to the rest of Germany.
Ebert passed through much the most critical period, and his
policy was more subject to disastrous comment and perhaps
disastrous result, but on practically no occasion did the German Republic or the German Constitution suffer any real
weakening of authority or any loss of prestige, either at home

or abroad.   Hindenburg came at a time when the first definite movement towards consolidation of the German Republic had begun ; the Ruhr adventure was over, and the economic recovery of the country was assured.   Yet there was still danger of a movement away from the Republican form of government towards royalism—not necessarily the restoration of the old *régime*, but the adoption of some constitution not far removed from that of a monarchy.   The close attention to the duties and the responsibilities imposed on him by the Republic, without any question and with an almost instinctive justice in application, made Hindenburg an even more admirable defender of the new democracy than Ebert.   It is perhaps significant that neither Ebert nor Hindenburg was a professional politician ; they stood outside of politics and were, therefore, able to keep clear of the petty intrigues and the little acts of dishonour and compromise which enter into a politician's life ; they were able to see the big things and measure at their value the efforts made by the professional politicians to strengthen their position or exact one further ounce of power.

Industry went through much the same process as the political democracy, but, in its case, both causes and results were purely economic.   It depended on organization more than on personalities.   It was perhaps more exposed to the hostile action of the Allies than the German Constitution ; the occupation of the Ruhr represented for it a much more disastrous event than anything which took place in the political sphere, and the process of recovery told more on the resources of the country than political changes or the revolutionary efforts of a few individuals.   In this case, the inspiring motive was wholly one of consolidation and of substitution.   The Ruhr-Lorraine-Luxemburg economic unit had been broken up by the Treaty of Versailles, and on the maintenance of this unit had depended in the past much of the prosperity of the heavy industries. The organizing genius and the administrative capacity of the industrialists were taxed to the utmost to make good dislocations caused by the disruption of this unit, and they were confronted with difficulties, both financial and political, not of their own choosing.   Their task lay clear before them, and it appeared to be merely a case of adjusting resources to an immensely increased demand on them, but innumerable complications crept in—inflation, reparations, the collapse of the mark, stabilization, and the Dawes Plan—all containing possibilities of depression or even of disaster.

The constitution of industry itself changed to meet the new

economic conditions, and it had no set definition. In this, at least, it was different from politics, where, of course, the form of government had been decided by the revolution and elaborated in the Constitution of Weimar. We cannot find any dominant personality at work during all this period of experiment with vertical combines, horizontal trusts and selling syndicates ; the imperialism of Stinnes came to a conclusion very soon and died out without leaving many traces behind it, while the theories of Rathenau remained in a state of suspended animation, largely owing to the inability of Rathenau himself to apply them to the great industrial concerns under his own control. Although administrative capacity was present to a notable degree, the forces of character and of vision were not always in the ascendant, and it is difficult now to single out individuals in whom might be glorified all those qualities which made for the recovery of German industry and for the consolidation of the new German economic State. Yet the part played by industry, however less spectacular and less vivid with human values it might have been, had intrinsically dramatic possibilities, which only required a touch to become as profoundly exciting as political or human drama. Both politically and economically, all the forces of the new Germany were coming into action to strengthen the State and bring it into its due position among the great industrial countries of the world.

Other factors of profound significance enter into the composition of the contemporary German State ; they comment on and expound many of the leading characteristics disclosed by political and economic investigation. One cannot ignore the influence of philosophy, criticism, art, literature and music on the German mentality, but the study of such aspects would involve in itself an enormously complicated work, much beyond the range of the present book. Yet the political and economic phases must be brought into line with the intellectual, philosophic and artistic, if one is to understand the real achievement of Republican Germany. It is possible, of course, to isolate each section and devote to it a minutely detailed study, and perhaps create out of a group of such studies what may be regarded as a full statement of the aims and ideals and strength of the German nation. In doing so, however, one would have in opposition practically every thinker of significance in Republican Germany ; pragmatism and empiricism are no longer greeted as magic formulae for the perception of truth. The exact registration of phenomena as carried out by the natural sciences, the classification of ideas, even as of facts, according

HEINRICH RICKERT

to a rigid system incapable of modification, and the codification of mental impressions and even emotions are almost wholly repugnant to the modern German spirit.   The one conception held to be valid is that throughout every manifestation, whether it be political, economic, literary, artistic, or musical, there pulses a nerve force, a vitality which derives its origin from a central nerve complex, a central source of power, which is what we understand by the German nation and the German spirit.

The work of investigation becomes, therefore, highly intuitive and at times highly speculative.   Can we find those essential characteristics which link up one manifestation with another and together form one conception ?   What basis of evaluation and criticism is to be adopted ?   Should theory be confined within the limits of what is actually discovered or postulated from the evidence supplied by fact, or should there be some effort made to define the nature of the theory which should be applied to the evaluation of material developments ? These are questions which have agitated contemporary thinkers in Germany, and they are problems which go far beyond the scope of a merely philosophical discussion ; they affect the mentality of the German people and their capacity to conduct life and follow out the process of material existence.   In other countries, there would be less preoccupation with such questions, owing perhaps to the instinctive feeling that some natural and unseizable historical process is at work which will smooth out difficulties and ensure the continued prosperity and the continued progress of the human race.   But in German philosophy, as in German industry, the doctrine of *laissez-faire* has never had much influence.

We find three men active above all in the expression of the modern German spirit—Ernst Troeltsch in the sphere of religion and ethics, Heinrich Rickert in the sphere of pure speculation and scientific investigation, and Max Weber in the sphere of sociology and economics.[1]   All three belonged to the same school of thought, and, in common with thinkers of less extensive range—namely, Natorp, Husserl, and Lask—were interested more in the mental perception of the historical process than in the search after reality itself ; they had abandoned to

[1] Although Heinrich Rickert's principal work, *Die Grenzen der naturwissenschaftlichen Begriffsbildung*, appeared originally in 1902, it only reached a second edition in 1913, eleven years after, whereas, in 1921, two editions appeared, with considerable alterations and extensions—sufficient almost to make of it a new book.   His second great work, *System der Philosophie*, appeared in 1921, and his *Philosophie des Lebens* in 1920.   Ernst Troeltsch produced his main studies

a very large extent the search after some system which would
explain reality and give it a definite value for the spirit ; they
were interested not so much in the question whether reality
could be understood and truth be defined with reference to a
higher power such as God, as in the spirit itself. They felt
that some connection existed between an individual mind, the
mind of a mass of individuals such as a nation, and the universal
mind, and they strove to discover what form and what functions such a spirit under all its aspects would assume.   With
the purely logical extremists, the task of bringing philosophy
closer to reality, or rather of fusing reality into one act of perception and of knowledge, was abandoned at once, and attention concentrated on the abstract investigation of mental
perceptions.   Their science of the mind was confined purely to
the mind and to the creation of a logical system, which should
act later as a basis for approaching material existence.   They
worked from the mind outwards, and perhaps some of their
success as creators of systems has been due to this deliberate
exclusion of the complicated problems inherent in material
existence.

   In the case, however, of the humanists, such as Weber and
Troeltsch, the conviction that mere theorizing was of little
consequence beside the social mission implied in any real
philosophy did much to widen their outlook and to strengthen
their influence on the German mentality. With Troeltsch,
religion represented the vital force active throughout the history of the human mind, and it meant to him what sociology
meant to Max Weber, with exactly the same problem implied,
—the reality of the human spirit and its movement through
history, and the progress of the human spirit towards a universal mind and the fundamental reality which governs the uni-
verse.   The task of speculation lay in determining what bonds
united the spirit of the present to the immense progression of
the human spirit through time and space ; the eternal halted
to the ever-present contemplation, and we passed to a future
which became, in turn, the present ; the present lived in the
power and beauty of the spirit, picking up from the inexhaustible spirit its own inspiration and its own food.

on the history and philosophy of religion before the War, but his
principal work in pure philosophy, *Der Historismus und seine Probleme*, written during the period 1916–1922, was published in 1922.
In influence, therefore, these thinkers belonged to the post-war generation and touched on deeper issues for the contemporary German
mentality than writers like Oswald Spengler, Max Scheler and Graf
v. Keyserling, who enjoyed a much more fashionable vogue.

There is an inspiring quality in such a perception, since, instead of the absolute being recognized as something unattainable and something which should not be investigated, there is a pure idealism of the spirit as eternally active and eternally capable of progress. For all three philosophers, the essential article in any creed was exactly this belief in the domination of mind, of reason, of the ever-active spirit. In a world depressed economically and politically, such a doctrine was in itself a vitalizing force ; it brought the future always before the vision and acted in this way as a source of inspiration.

In addition to this, the efforts of this modern school to clear up mental processes and to elaborate some clear definition of the relations between the sciences as controlled by and expressive of the human spirit meant that clear thinking should be applied to the investigation of ordinary, every-day developments. Rickert alone of the three great philosophers has definitely evolved a system which is designed to present his ideas to the world, but it is doubtful whether, in future years, a few sentences and a few magnificent paragraphs scattered through Troeltsch and Weber may not be worth all the elaborate speculative systems evolved. All three writers strove to attach their conception of mind and of human existence to a more fundamental conception of the purpose and reality of history : the lesson of history was a lesson for humanity even in the face of providence, which appeared to be dissociated entirely from any historical perception ; there was a meaning behind and within all human activity sufficient to give to it its position and its reality. In the words of Goethe, " It is a characteristic of mind that it should always stimulate and inspire mind "—and in this power to awaken thought and deepen motive lie the great contributions of these three thinkers to the idealism of their time. The power of thought was for them the power to reconcile and bring human activity into the ideal of harmony and peace.

The contribution of the philosophers to the interpretation of the German outlook on life has been no inconsiderable one, and we can trace their influence through political and economic movements, which otherwise would be difficult of interpretation. It is necessary to remember that the capacity of the German people to absorb philosophic doctrine is greater than that of almost any other people in the world, and from the time of Kant onwards, the political influence of philosophic theory has never been insignificant. With a school which would have advocated mere preoccupation with details and not with the great problems of human existence, with a school which would have contented itself merely with the study of the past without any constructive ideals for the future, the will to victory and to economic recovery might have been less strong in Germany than it was, and certainly less effective in its methods of expression.

Similar movements took place in the sphere of literary criticism, which is not radically distinct from philosophy itself. In the hands of critics like Georg Simmel, Gundolf, Heinrich Rickert and Dehio, the discussion of the literary and philosophic achievements of the great figures of German history became an illustration of the philosophic movement actually in progress. The great figures were creators not so much of literary and philosophic works intrinsically valuable, as of the German spirit active at certain periods of time. Simmel, like Gundolf, whose *Stefan George* and *Goethe* belong to the finest and most suggestive the modern German school has produced in criticism, moves from the interpretation of the individual through his work. The artist stands alone as a creator, and in him alone the motives and impulses underlying creation must be found : the examination of sources and contemporary records, biographical or philological, are as nothing in the actual creation, which is a complete and perfect thing in itself, four-square, unassailable. It is possible to trace exquisitely and delicately to this source every manifestation of the spirit, and the sum of these manifestations is the spirit itself. The creative spirit gleams through the work of art like rays from a central flame. The success of such a theory must depend absolutely on the power of the critic to achieve unity of vision in his criticism ; and the various studies which Simmel devoted to the great figures in literature and art, Kant, Schopenhauer, Nietzsche, Goethe, and Rembrandt, show in their varying degree the strength and weakness of the underlying philosophical conception.

Other critics, chief among them Heinrich Wölfflin, move in an entirely opposite direction ; they are concerned less with the spirit active in the work of creation than with the registration of periods and of styles shown in the work of art. Their criticism is purely formal, and as such has had little effect outside the narrow range of students and experts. Other critics again, like Emil Ludwig, float gracefully over the surface, carrying out attractive studies in one plane ; the characters they draw appear before us in a beautiful and moving fresco, but we cannot feel that in the flesh they could have represented anything more fundamental than one individual active in an enormous crowd of individuals. The vital energy, which makes their work so notable for us in our efforts to meet contemporary problems, has escaped definition.

In philosophy and in criticism we can find elements at work which have gone towards the development of the spirit pulsating through Republican Germany, and, from many points of view, their contribution will probably be regarded as one of the lasting things in the progress of German civilization. In literature, poetry and the drama there is less evidence of creative forces at work. If we except novelists, dramatists and poets like Thomas and Heinrich Mann, Stefan George, Franz Wedekind, Richard Dehmel, Reiner Maria Rilke, and many of the writers active during the revolution period, the work carried out by Germany in the literary sphere has not been at all comparable with that of Britain, or even France, and the preoccupation of the German reading public with translations of Russian and British writers, principally novelists and dramatists, does show that there is a gap to be filled. Economic conditions may be the explanation for the lack of creative energy in the sphere of pure literature since 1921. Literature demands a background of leisure and of wealth : a work of art cannot as a rule be executed in intervals of leisure after strenuous labour, and the general impoverishment of the German people, with the necessity for every individual to become active in some bread-winning occupation or other, has undoubtedly reduced the ranks of potential literary geniuses. Such a state of affairs will undoubtedly be remedied in future, since the activity recorded in the economic, political and philosophical spheres will probably be extended to the literary, artistic and dramatic. The domination of the economic motive has certainly been a factor tending towards neutralization of literary inspiration and towards elimination of a background sympathetic to the efforts of the artist, whether in words, in colour, or in line.

Yet certain features assume an extraordinary interest through the light they cast on national aspirations and the national mentality. During 1927, perhaps one of the most highly eulogized dramas performed on the German stage was the tragedy of " Thomas Paine ", written by Hans Johst, who has already acquired some distinction as a writer of plays and novels. " Thomas Paine " describes the struggles of the American democracy, led by George Washington, to free itself from the domination of Britain ; it also gives expression, through Thomas Paine, to many sentiments inspired by the noblest form of Republicanism—sentiments which shine out all the more brightly in contrast with the brutality and materialism rampant during the French Revolution.   Paine is honoured in the new American Republic and thrown into prison in the new French revolutionary State.   Yet, on his return, unknown, to the United States after many years' imprisonment, he finds incredulity and indifference ; much of the splendour and idealism of the early Republican days has already disappeared.   The play, as such, has many fine dramatic qualities, but it had intrinsically few claims to popular success.   One would be inclined, therefore, to attribute the interest of the German public in it to its glorification of the Republican form of government and to its ennoblement of the Republican spirit and its advocacy of freedom.   These sentiments were calculated to appeal to a country overshadowed by reparations, and struggling to strengthen and consolidate a new form of government—the new State which had been ushered in at the revolution.

In other directions we can find similar reactions, and they show that a definite change has taken place in the German spirit.   In art, in architecture, and in the cinema especially, certain manifestations can be recorded of more than passing interest.   The German genius came to expression more vividly in the art of the cinema than even in literature or the drama. The film constitutes in itself one of the most inspiring and, socially, one of the most significant, developments of recent times ; its justification is primarily social, since it opens up a new world of human interest to the public generally and provides a form of pleasure which is the modern equivalent of the Greek or Roman theatrical representations.   In the hands of geniuses of the quality of Fritz Lang, Murnau, and Dupont, supported by actors like Emil Jannings, Conrad Veidt, Werner Kraus, as well as Mady Christians [in light society dramas], the film obtained recognition as one of the highest forms of art, and it is a distinctive contribution of the German producers and the German public (which, of course, made it possible for the producers to carry out their work) that they should have raised the film to an artistic level not inferior to that already achieved by literature, the drama, pictorial and plastic art.   Their influence has been such as to cause a radical change in the whole conception of the nature and the power of the film, and although at times American financial penetration and perhaps excessive preoccupation with purely popular success may have dimmed and distorted the original vision of the great

German film producers, the work they have carried out must always retain an historical and æsthetic significance as part of the contribution of Germany to the development of modern culture.

The inspiration within the films has been derived almost wholly from the treasure-house of the German mind as shown in history and in art. Thus, in films like " The Nibelungs ", " Faust ", and its modern counterpart, " The Student of Prague ", we find great dramatic themes enshrined in the history of the German spirit transferred to the screen without any loss of power or of beauty. In " The Nibelungs ", the imagination displayed in the arrangement of the scenes and in the conception of the atmosphere and of the historical setting bears comparison easily with the musical conceptions of Wagner and the dramatic power of Friedrich Hebbel : there is the same perception of an immense background of human destiny and of human fate, granting to every figure in the legend the magnificence and the glory of a symbol active in the human spirit ; there is the same perception of a beauty, which is not plastic or pictorial or purely verbal alone, but æsthetic and soul-stirring ; there is direct community of interests and inspiration between the artists and the public viewing the work of art. This criticism applies especially to " The Nibelungs " of Fritz Lang, and, to some extent, also to " Metropolis ", which, even although technical experts may question the design and the functions of the wonderful machinery installed in the mechanical city of the future, does impress the spectator with highly dramatic suggestion. The vision shown in " Metropolis " bears many points of resemblance to the vision shown in " The Nibelungs ". In each case, human characters are struggling against forces beyond their control and beyond their conception : in " The Nibelungs ", these forces are supernatural, and may be identified with the great historical movements and changes enshrined in legend, while, in " Metropolis ", the civilization of the future is undoubtedly man-made without real control by man himself. This mechanical cosmos assumes all the dreadfulness of a Frankenstein, and, in the end, may overwhelm civilization itself.

In these four films and in the screen dramas of a mysterious and purely philosophical nature, such as " Doctor Caligari ", we can trace an affinity between the romantic mentality of the early nineteenth century and the ideas of the present ; they are in the tradition of Novalis and Tieck. In other films, such as " Vaudeville ", " The Last Laugh ", " The Waltz Dream ", the interplay of characters in the modern world has brought them closer to the novel pure and simple, where action depends on psychological changes and reactions, on the adjustment of the human element to change in surroundings and the assertion of personality through a series of complicated motives terminating in a dramatic crisis.   These elements are less distinctively German, and they show more of the German humour and sentimentality than " Faust " or " The Student of Prague ", but they are notable through the amazingly vivid impression of reality they convey.   The sense of intimacy between the audience and the characters active on the screen is closer, and every action of even the most trivial type assumes dramatic significance and a compelling attraction.   In one film especially, " The Secrets of the Soul ", which is a dramatic version of a Freudian theory, the whole theme is held together by the magnificent acting of Werner Kraus, and it is acting which depends on significant touches and vivid projections of personality from the screen to the audience.

In these films, certain qualities have been illustrated, which are universally recognized as German, and yet we cannot define those German characteristics which distinguish them from American or British qualities ; we know that the world as shown to us is not the world that can be reproduced or even paralleled in Great Britain or in the United States.   The action and reaction of characters within that world, the setting of the scenes, the development of atmosphere, the accumulation of dramatic motive, are not beyond the range of the British or American producer, but the result is something purely German and yet universal in its appeal.   Such an imaginative power extends even to historical dramas devoted to the life of Frederick II, the German musicians and episodes such as can be found in great profusion during the Thirty Years War and the Napoleonic campaigns in Germany, while a less significant range of activity is to be found in elaborate fantasias, short didactic allegories and screen versions of fairy tales. Variety is infinite, and almost every film, where some conception of artistic and dramatic values is present, bears a significance not merely for those enamoured of the screen-world, but also for those who would desire to penetrate to the modern German mentality through its manifestations in literature and art.   It is essential to recognize now that a film must take its place as a great art midway between the drama and pictorial or plastic representation, and the contemplation of the achievements of the German producers and actors during the last six years must strengthen the impression that in this, at least, Germany has given to the world something of lasting significance.

In pictorial and plastic art, achievement is more difficult to find since their very nature is such that few revolutionary changes really take place ; changes in style and in method may cause what is tantamount to a new method of artistic represent-ation, but the fundamental conception remains unchanged. The preoccupation of the artist may lie in the photographic reproduction of reality, in the realization of rhythmic sensation-alism on canvas, or in the expression of a definite attitude towards colour and towards form, but the limitations imposed on art re-duce it finally to reproduction—representation infused with the personality and the genius of the artist. The War might have given rise to a new school of painters intent on recording, as far as colour and line would allow, the ideals and the visions of a gener-ation to whom war was an abhorrence, and to whom the problem of existence presented itself under gloomy and fugitive colours. But we cannot find any such school in action, and to understand contemporary movements in German art we must go back to the nineties of last century, when the first exhibition of the great French painters, Manet, Degas, Puvis de Chavannes and Sisley, were held in Berlin. Before that time, a number of German artists, whose work still commands respect, had already introduced elements of an Impressionistic and wholly modern nature into German art. Side by side with this older school, which still occupies an imposing part of the stage, one can place those artists who are influenced, first of all, by the French Impressionists and later by Renoir, Vincent van Gogh, Céz-anne, Manet, Matisse, and, later still, by Georges Bracque and Pizarro. Other French artists had a modified influence on contemporary German painting, chief among them, Bonnard, Vuillard, Denis, Rousseau and Roussel. Another group should be distinguished, namely, the Expressionists and the Cubists and purely rhythmic painters, who correspond perhaps more vividly to the contemporary German spirit than the other groups. Yet even in this last case we find that the Expres-sionist programme, as elaborated by Nolde, Pechstein, Schmidt-Rottluff and Heckel, dates from 1910.

It is difficult, therefore, to trace any movement which may be regarded either as specifically German or so modern in inspiration that it can be placed within the period of the German Republic. It is true, of course, that art in its finest manifestations must be a growth as well as a complex ; no one movement and no one period ever dominates the scene. There is a perpetual flux of ideas, a swirl of emotions, a rich confusion of colours and forms, a struggle between tradition and ultra-modernity, a contrast of personalities, of ideals, and even of technical systems. In the light of purely æsthetic criticism, all these movements, all these personalities, all these conceptions, coherent and incoherent, may appear singularly pale and undistinguished. If an effort is made to gather up all these artistic manifestations, and force out of them some essential meaning, some deeply imbedded emotion, some eternal vision and knowledge of beauty, and bring them into the vivid illumination of the age, disappointment and disillusionment may well result. The German mentality is not easily satisfied with pictorial or plastic representation. Its achievement in this sphere is not to be compared with its achievements in the economic or industrial spheres, but it has originality and a vitality of its own.

The older school of artists and sculptors can still be appreciated and the beauty of their work be felt even in an age of Futurism and Impressionism. The perfection of line and mass shown in the sculptures of Adolf von Hildebrand, where an almost classical theory of form and ideal has predominated, the vivid naturalism of Max Liebermann, Walter Georgi and Bartels, where Dutch influence has been at work, the lush symbolism of Franz von Stuck, where colour and shadow have been used to convey a symbolical and almost statuesque meaning to historical scenes, the social *expertise* of Habermann, and the living portraiture of Max Slevogt or Leo Samberger, are all elements which have entered into the contemporary German art mentality, and even the most extreme representations of the Futurists, the most violent declarations of war against them on the part of the younger generation have not been sufficient to weaken their influence or break down their authority. The modern French individualists, such as Cézanne and Van Gogh, have inspired almost the whole of the work of the new generation of painters like Hans Purrmann, who form a transition from the older German school to portraiture as represented by Leibl and Trübner. Contemporary sensationalism in paint is quite clear, while, in other artists, such as Breitner, Robert, Steinmetz, Hüther, Puttner, Schrimpf, Hufer and Pascin, the imitation, conscious or unconscious, of contemporary French models can be seen.

Five artists, other than the Expressionists, may be singled out as representative of the definitely original and definitely

German artistic genius—first of all, Eduard Munch, who, before Cézanne and Van Gogh had penetrated into Germany, was already working out his own problems of form and colour and light and shadow. There is an affinity of interest and of conception between him and Paul Gauguin, but there is no reason to believe that Gauguin had any influence on the formation of the art of Munch. Two artists specializing in drawings and in etchings—Rudolf Grossmann and Robert Engels—and, with them, to a less degree, Richard Seewald, come very close to expression of what we generally regard as the essentially German spirit. All three have a keen sense of the humorous and the grotesque ; Grossmann has a tendency towards artistic shorthand reminiscent of the Expressionists, but Seewald and Engels, in the innumerable illustrations they have drawn for German classics, have a pleasure in life and in dramatic motive which is almost Rabelaisian ; their humour is of the romantic blend, strong, obvious and palpitating with life ; æsthetics, with a delicate appreciation of *nuance* and inner meaning, have no significance for them ; they work out illustrative and, in some cases, decorative themes solely with reference to their human qualities and to the impression they are designed to make on the spectator. In sculpture, Hermann Haller is in direct line of descent from Adolf von Hildebrand, but he has been able to impart a certain individuality to his bronze models of the human figure and a certain decorative symbolism which stamps him as original ; their beauty has vivacity and a sly quality of humour.

The Expressionist group of painters occupies a place apart in the history of contemporary German art, and at one time, namely, the four years 1918–21, there was every possibility of a general revival of art on Expressionistic or Futuristic lines. The spirit of the time, with its uncertainties and its sudden enthusiasms, was sympathetic to anything of an eclectic or even erratic nature. Material existence during the years of inflation had assumed all the character of a speculation, the outcome of which was doubtful, and this speculative element penetrated into art. The Expressionistic movement had qualities destined to attract minds insecure and apprehensive of the future ; mysticism, symbolism, emotionalism and innumerable other " isms " could be found in it. It proposed a rhythmic abstraction which was in itself an escape from reality ; it dealt with subjects which lent themselves to fantastic and highly poeticized treatment, such as religion and the representation of the new architecture as well as imaginary landscapes. In the hands of colourists like Josef Eberz, Seewald, and Dauring-hausen, who had also a sure grasp of form and rhythm and composition, Expressionism rose to a high level of art, and introduced something vital and strangely beautiful into pic-torial representation conceived as poetry or as the expression of human emotion.   In a long series of paintings devoted to the illustration of the story of Christ, Eberz accomplished a work of illustration of a rare magnificence in colour and unity of in-spiration.   He had reduced dramatic incident, as shown in the New Testament story, to abstraction, which, however, had an emotional significance and æsthetic justification.   In this sense, at least, he came close to El Greco ; in other directions, namely, in landscape and *genre* scenes and in portraits, he was rather less successful.

In other directions, Expressionism was able to produce work of more than contemporary significance : the architectural abstractions of Feininger, which can serve as illustrations of the mechanical city of the future, the strange visions of Ehmsen shown in colour abstractions suggestive through decorative power alone, the more restrained portraiture carried out by Emil Nolde, the distorted anatomy of Schwalbach and Ewald, the strongly imaginative and even repellent pastels done by Weinzheimer as an illustration for the " Divine Comedy ", all form part of the distinctive contribution of this new movement to contemporary German art.   In woodcuts, as experiments carried out by Dulberg, Heckel, Pechstein, Lange, Schmidt-Rottluff and Seewald showed, the force and the crudely imagin-ative qualities of the German spirit can find expression in art and give it a compelling attraction.

Since 1921, however, the influence of the advanced school of artists has waned, and much of their extremism has been soft-ened down and a compromise made with naturalism.   Yet the influence of Futurism or Expressionism was not confined to the actual work of the artists ; it caused a change in decorative art generally, and was instrumental in developing a higher conception of decoration, especially in the art of book-pro-duction.   As the exhibition at Leipzig in 1927 proved, the new German book-production has been suffused with many of the ideas, both technical and æsthetic, of the more advanced artistic schools, and in the art of the films, as shown in " Metropolis ", Expressionism has had fruitful results.

In architecture, many of the qualities inspiring contemporary art movements have also been at work, especially in the con-struction and in the design of industrial buildings.   It is only necessary to enter the main hall of the new railway station at Stuttgart to understand the distinctly modern, and even revolutionary, character of much of the architectural activity now going on in Germany.   In this hall, we stand as in a temple devoted to modern industry, with every detail of the structure simplified to give this impression.   The great windows rising almost from floor to roof of the main façade, the lofty roof held on beams, a feeling of immense space and the deliberate use of the texture of the stone and of the wood to give a decorative effect—are all characteristics which stamp this new architecture as something original and impressive.   In the same way, we can look at the great offices built for the United Steel Works in Düsseldorf, for the *Gutehoffnungshütte* at Oberhausen, the Wilhelm-Marxshaus in Düsseldorf, and similar structures carried out in Hamburg.   A special style has been evolved for industrial purposes, where simplicity and subdued colour strike the dominant note ; bricks and tiles are used for decorative purposes in the most skilful manner.   The plane is always horizontal in the sense that each main decorative section in the building is drawn on horizontal lines, but the tendency of the mass itself is upwards, and this struggle between the horizontal decorations and the upward striving of the building constitutes some part of the value and significance of contemporary industrial architecture.   The interiors have been carried out in strange and startling colour schemes stimulated through the use of bricks of a certain type with a glaze of colour which takes the light and reflects it from wall to wall. The decorative scheme depends on light as a principal factor in intensifying and giving new value to colours.   The effect of this can be seen at its best in the Planetarium constructed at Düsseldorf, where there is a vaulted passage round the main hall conceived in dark green glazed brick, with windows casting light at close intervals from one side, the central window closing up the end.   The effect of the vaulting, of the coloured bricks and of the lighting is one of mystery and a slightly harsh beauty.   In the same group of buildings, the use of mosaic built into a purely Expressionistic design is singularly effective and stimulating, through the contrast between the purely horizontal decorative scheme carried out without elaboration in line and the tumultuous colours thrown together in the mosaic.

A characteristic also of the new architecture is the employment of statuary which has ceased to have any connection with naturalism.   It is highly stylized and even distorted to suggest and strengthen the decorative motive. This use of statuary is not, of course, an absolutely contemporary development ; it may be seen in the great buildings owned by the Tietz Company in Cologne and Düsseldorf, while it can be seen also in whole streets of towns like Stuttgart and Leipzig. In this architecture, which bears many points of resemblance to the more advanced forms of art, we may perceive the beginning of a movement towards a closer relationship between industry and art, which would bring the economic development of Germany into line with the artistic and cultural.

One can prolong the survey indefinitely, since the elements composing a modern State, expressive of the mentality of a people like the German people, are infinite, but even this inadequate survey may suffice to introduce a subject of intense interest and very great significance. Germany, politically and economically, has moved out of the depths and has become again one of the Great Powers : that is a great achievement after seven years' difficulty ; everything else is subordinated to that fact, but full comprehension of what this means is only possible after we have become aware of the atmosphere surrounding the principal tendencies and movements in contemporary Germany. The appreciation of atmosphere, as such, must be an instinctive process, and the best one can do is to create the conditions favourable to such an instinctive appreciation. There are links joining up all those manifestations recorded in politics, in economics, in literature, in art, and in philosophy, and they come together in one conception of the German mentality and the German spirit. The justification of a survey, however closely detailed it may be, lies in the effort it makes to recapture this spirit and show exactly where it has been active and what its finest achievements have been. We have indicated lines of approach to this engrossing and exceedingly difficult subject ; they may serve to guide appreciation and excite a desire for direct investigation—in itself, a contribution to the history and expansion of culture.

BOOK I

BUILDING THE GERMAN REPUBLIC

CHAPTER I

FROM AUTOCRACY TO REPUBLIC

The work of the autocratic *régime*—the struggle between the government and the democratic parties—the influence of the Russian Revolution—the resignation of Bethmann-Hollweg and its consequences —towards revolution—the policy of Hertling—concession to democracy —the Cabinet of Prince Max of Baden—the Kiel revolt—the choice before the Majority Socialists.

ON August 4, 1914, the Imperial *régime* in Germany reached its zenith. For the first time since the foundation of the Empire, the whole nation, an insignificant fraction excepted, stood solidly behind the Imperial Government and the Emperor, and when the latter, with his usual and not always unfortunate sense of the dramatic, declared " I know no more parties," he expressed fairly accurately the sense of unity with which the German nation confronted the peril its statesmen had brought upon it. On August 4 the German democracy in the Reichstag virtually abdicated its function ; the sole protestor, Karl Liebknecht, a man whose courage verged on mania, did not make his protest vocal.

The completeness of the abdication may be explained as the chivalrous surrender to patriotism, but it also gives the measure of the democracy's weakness. It confined its action to acquiescence. It is true that the abdication could have been foreseen, although the theory to explain it—that the German is by nature non-political and non-democratic, so assiduously propagated by the Right in Germany and the uncritical abroad—will not bear examination in the light of history. There was an exceedingly powerful democratic movement in Germany comprising the conventional type of continental Liberalism and the equally conventional type of continental Socialism. It had been extremely critical of the Imperial rule ; it had made its voice heard effectively on numerous occasions—the *Telegraph* interview of 1908, for instance, and the Zabern incident of 1913 ; it had agitated sincerely for constitutional and social reform, for Parliamentary government in the Reich, for electoral reform

25

in Prussia, for the democratic control of foreign policy and the like. Its action had, however, never borne much fruit. The mutual hostility between Liberalism and Socialism prevented the elaboration of common action ; the Imperial rule, however undemocratic, had been, economically and militarily and, so far as was known, politically, a brilliant success. From a disjointed collection of weak States, Germany had risen to be the greatest power on the Continent ; her commercial expansion had been phenomenal and showed no signs of flagging ; politically and economically, she was on the way to world-empire. The *régime* was efficient and fundamentally the people were content and happy. Democracy was an academic creed ; even Socialism was touched with the academic blight because it could promise little more of vital purpose to the average citizen than he already enjoyed. The discontent voiced in the political literature of the pre-war years latterly became almost theoretical, and the agitation for reform and change lacked the solid basis of hardship and profound sense of grievance. The programmes of the German parties were confessions of belief far more than the announcement of truceless war against the *régime* and, even where passion crept into them, it was powerless against the indifference of the many and the hostility of the few. It was unable to use the one unassailable argument for change that the *régime* to be supplanted had failed. The greatest asset of the Socialists was that the *régime* persisted in treating them as a pariah party, but, on August 4, that asset, like so many other things, disappeared.

The root cause of the collapse of the *régime* was that it absolutely failed to read the lesson of the abdication of August 4. It was incapable of realizing that the democracy expected to be paid for its sacrifice. The dramatic declaration of unity— a declaration which had involved on the part of a compact mass of the nation the uneasy surrender of cherished principle— had to be translated into a state of fact. That could only be achieved by modifying the Government on the lines demanded, and by a unifying act on the part of the Government recognizing at last the position of the Socialists within the state—a position which they had hitherto obstinately denied them. That modification was never voluntarily attempted ; that unifying act was never made. Even if brilliant success had attended Germany's war effort, the attitude of the *régime* at the crisis would in the end have destroyed it, but the destruction was made absolutely certain when it gave failure instead of success. The *régime* had claimed and had been given the credit for Germany's remarkable achievement ; without delegating or sharing its power, it could not escape having to bear all the responsibility for destroying that achievement. The successive shocks administered first by the failure of Imperial diplomacy, second by the failure of the military machine, third by the breakdown of the economic life with the consequent disappearance of prosperity, the beginning of hardship and the menace of starvation, did more to convince the masses of the people that change was necessary than fifty years of theoretical demonstration, and explain the fact that, when change did come, it met with no resistance.

The reaction to the inability of the *régime* to act in the spirit of August 4 began before the war was a year old. The failure of the *attaque brusquée*, whose success had long been held as essential to ultimate victory, and the prolongation of the war gave the democracy time to reflect, and the Government did nothing to distract that reflection. It is significant that the first symptom of disaffection came from the uneasy consciences of the Socialists and took the line of least resistance in opposition to the war. The first opposition, that of the Left Socialists, took the form of peace propaganda.

To trace the history of the revolt against the *régime* is outside the compass of this work ; it must suffice merely to sketch it in the broadest of outline.

The movement of resistance strengthened in direct proportion to the increase in hardship and to the realization that decisive victory was impossible. That being so, it followed that the war must end either in decisive defeat or in peace by compromise. To avoid the former might demand a national effort ; to secure the latter a declaration on war-aims according to the later fashionable formula " peace without annexations or indemnities " was urgently necessary. Neither the one nor the other could be expected from the *régime*, and hence the opposition to it took the character of a peace movement plus advocacy of such constitutional reform as would realize national unity. In the appeal to the masses, the former aspect was much more important than the latter. In January 1916, the extremists founded the Spartacus League which aimed at sabotaging the war, and, six months later, came the first strike— that of the metal workers, a strike fomented and directed by the extremists and definitely of a political character. It was not supported by the official trade-union leaders nor generally by the rank and file of trade unionism, but, for the Government and for the trade union and Socialist leaders, it was the writing on the wall ; the latter read it, the former did not.   Defeatism of a revolutionary type had definitely made its appearance.

The peace polemic at Christmas 1916 and in January 1917 brought the question of war-aims to a head.   It revealed the well-defined character of the Entente policy that was lacking in the German, but, in that definiteness, was a revelation of Imperialist designs which could have been used to Germany's advantage.   The attempt to do this encountered a resistance which virtually sealed the fate of the Imperial *régime*.   While the Chancellor Bethmann-Hollweg shared the view of the opposition (now concentrating itself into a solid bloc), that decisive victory was impossible, that it was important to state Germany's war-aims in a manner calculated to influence favourably neutral opinion and that peace with America, above all, must be maintained, the military leaders were still confident of victory.   Ludendorff believed that, with intensive submarine warfare, the war could be ended in three months.   So confident indeed were the military leaders that they accepted cheerfully the risk of adding the United States to the ranks of Germany's enemies, and were chock-full of annexationist schemes.   The *régime* was divided against itself.   Between the two, the Chancellor with great courage held stoutly on, losing influence daily but maintaining himself in power with no little dexterity of compromise.   The struggle suddenly resolved itself into one between a military dictatorship and a parliamentary rule with Bethmann and the politicians who shared his view vainly trying to maintain the Bismarckian system, as it was in 1914.

Into this charged atmosphere came the bombshell of the Russian revolution.   The most amazing thing about the revolution from the European point of view was that, although everyone expected and confidently prophesied its coming, it took everybody by surprise when it did come, and it triumphed in forty-eight hours.   Its effect was all the greater and all the swifter.   To Europe the fall of Tsardom was what the fall of the Bastille was to France ; there is no mistaking the genuineness of the thrill that went through the nations, and that thrill was felt not least violently in Germany, for the March revolution left the Central Powers the last stronghold of autocratic reaction on the Continent.   Within a month, revolutionary strikes broke out, and the Socialist Left at last broke definitely with the party and formed a new organization whose peace policy was nearer to a revolutionary policy than that held by any recognized party.   But it was the course of the Russian

revolution that exerted the most sinister influence. Russian
Liberalism went from victory to a disaster. Supported by all
the democratic elements, it was challenged at once by a ridiculously tiny Socialist minority with a clear-cut programme.
The fight between Liberalism and reaction gave place to the
fight between the Liberal revolution and the Communist revolution, and the Communists won because of the failure of their
opponents to translate the revolution into political act. The
end of revolution was thus seen to be the victory of extremism
which preached world revolution to its adherents, and summoned the proletariat of the world to rise. The extremists in
Germany had at last a concrete basis to work on and a definite
end to gain.

The revolutionary challenge could not be mistaken, but it
was accepted very differently by the three anti-revolutionary
sections into which the nation was now divided. The Right,
grouped round Imperial Head-quarters, believed, despite
strikes, propaganda in the army and mutinies in the fleet, that,
whatever menace there was, could be dispersed by a whiff of
grape-shot and denounced the Government for its failure to take
drastic measures against external and internal foes. They still
considered the Russian revolution, with some reason, as a
military and political gain to Germany, and they saw no need
to secure national unity at the price of concessions. The democratic opposition began to close its ranks ; it realized that
peace took precedence over reform and its efforts culminated
in the creation of a democratic front which, in July 1917, presented to the Reichstag the famous peace resolution in the
name of the Majority Socialists (so-called to distinguish them
from the seceding Socialists called since April the Independent
Socialists), the Centrum, the Progressives and the parties which,
despite diversity of aims, combined to form a Reichstag majority. The Government, between which and Imperial Head-
quarters the Kaiser wavered pathetically while it lasted, had
no illusions as to the seriousness of the situation ; as a sop to
the democracy, it extorted from the Kaiser the Easter declaration from the Throne that the work of constitutional reform
should be taken in hand. But it would not accept the peace
resolution, and so Bethmann drew upon himself the hostility of
both sides. The odds were too great, but it was Imperial
Head-quarters which forced his resignation.

The disappearance of Bethmann left the militarists the sole
support of the *régime* which now became identified with Imperial Head-quarters and the Right. Two solutions suggested

themselves. One was the proclamation of a military dictatorship ; the other, the acknowledgment of the parliamentary situation by the appointment of a ministry based on the new Reichstag majority. The Kaiser would consent to neither ; he appointed to the Chancellorship a Prussian official whose function was to represent Imperial Head-quarters, but who was still to be a constitutional minister. Whatever dictatorship there was, had to be carefully veiled.

The advent of Michaelis meant a decided defeat for the democracy, but that was largely the democracy's fault. The majority had issued the word " Bethmann must go " because they fancied that, if they forced a statesman so much in sympathy with them to resign, the *régime* would have to capitulate to parliamentarism. They did not realize that, in the circumstances, such a capitulation would have been an abject confession of the *régime's* failure, and the time for that was not yet ripe. Instead of forcing Bethmann to resign as an opponent of Liberalism, Imperial Head-quarters got rid of him because he was not conservative enough. Thus passed the one statesman acceptable to the Kaiser who might have steered Germany from an absolute to a constitutional monarchy.

Naturally the war against Bethmann was carried on with redoubled vigour against Michaelis. The democratic opposition smarted under the snub administered to it, especially when they found that the peace resolution, which they regarded as vital, meant nothing to the new Chancellor. Michaelis lasted one hundred and ten days. These hundred and ten days saw a definite bid on the part of the Reichstag majority for the leadership of the nation. Time had come to take some such step, for anti-war and revolutionary propaganda was steadily making headway. The troops in Russia were being inoculated with the virus of Bolshevism, and the recruits to the western armies obtained from the great " comb-out " of the sheltered trades in the autumn introduced the revolutionary element to the front line. Imperial Head-quarters pressed for repressive measures, and Michaelis permitted the general indictment of the Independent Socialists as a revolutionary body on the ground of subversive activity in the fleet. The Reichstag majority rose to defend their colleagues, and they received the important addition of the National Liberals, who demanded from the Kaiser a Chancellor in harmony with Parliament. Imperial Head-quarters did not sustain their nominee and Michaelis fell. The situation of July was repeated.

But there were differences. This time a military dictator-

ship was mentioned and it was clear that the reaction now
lacked a leader. The elements supporting the Imperial *régime*
looked towards Head-quarters and the latter, with the liquidation of Russia in sight and the great bid for a decision preparing, were too much preoccupied with military affairs. The
Kaiser appeared to be little better than a puppet ; the Crown
Prince was half suspected of resenting the tyranny of Head-
quarters ; the junker and officer class was restrained by discipline and etiquette from taking an initiative which Hindenburg-Ludendorff renounced, and, of that class, the best representatives felt uneasily that catastrophe was approaching and
that it could not be averted by the policy of the *régime*. It is
probable that the vast majority of the nation would have welcomed the appointment of a Chancellor who would have announced, as his mission, the smooth transition to democracy
outlined in the Easter declaration and a statement of war-aims
on the lines now adopted by democracy throughout the world,
but again they were disappointed. At the same time, Imperial
Head-quarters must have felt equal disappointment, for, if the
Reichstag majority did not get a parliamentary Chancellor,
Head-quarters did not get another Michaelis. The new Chancellor was the Kaiser's nominee, the aged Catholic premier of
Bavaria, Count Hertling.

Hertling's task was merely to delay. For the moment, all
the efforts of Imperial Head-quarters were directed to military
ends. The Bolshevik revolution took Russia out of the war,
an invaluable military and political success soon to be sealed
by the peaces of Brest and Bucharest. There was even confidence in the success of the gamble for decisive victory in the
West. Hertling had only to hold the home front together.
The home front needed no holding ; it only required to be
given responsibility. It was not the home front that collapsed.
but the front at Imperial Head-quarters, while the German
nation generally was still prepared to defend German soil
against the ever clearer intentions of the Allies to impose a
Carthaginian peace. The revolutionary movement, despite
the steady reinforcement of the Spartacists—now aspiring to
be the Bolsheviks of Germany—and the Independent Socialists,
now working in closer union with the Spartacists, had still no
firm hold either on the intellect or the imagination of the
masses. In January, the great munitions strike, organized
with great skill by the Spartacists and Independents, was
sabotaged by the trade unionists themselves, who appealed to
the Majority Socialists to take charge and save their leadership

of the working class. They did so, to the intense disgust of the extremists, and the strike fizzled out. It represented a most dangerous blow to the prosecution of the war, delivered at a critical hour ; it was averted solely by the patriotism of the German workers.

The Reichstag majority was placed in a distinct quandary by Hertling's appointment. It indicated that the *régime* was not yet prepared to yield to parliamentarism, but, at the same time, the majority, as represented by Payer, was included in the Government ; it was understood that Hertling had taken office on the condition that Imperial Head-quarters did not interfere in politics and that, while the decisive battle was now impending, the renunciation of Belgium was made part of the Government policy. The majority therefore had to mark time. The promise to abstain from political interference was not kept. Kuhlmann, the Foreign Minister, speedily came to loggerheads with Imperial Head-quarters on the Russian peace terms. Hindenburg-Ludendorff demanded his dismissal, but the Government stood firm. Head-quarters demanded a reaffirmation of annexationist policy in Belgium ; in June Payer was permitted definitely to announce that this should not form part of Germany's policy. Consequently the majority had no reason to fight Hertling as they had fought Michaelis, and when they had, when Kuhlmann's adherence to the peace resolution caused his fall and it was again evident that the Cabinet was in the hands of the Militarists, the great crisis of the war had arrived and men were too anxious to fight.

The great offensive achieved a great triumph and then wore itself out : the gamble had failed and Ludendorff passed to a strategy of exhaustion. The great defeat of August 8 meant a further transition to a dogged defensive. The transition from anxious hope to the contemplation of disaster had a devastating effect on the German nation, but it did not yet despair. Despite the triumph of the extremists, despite the ominous appearance of unrest in the army, the national morale held. It was Imperial Head-quarters that broke down. By September, Ludendorff recognized that the fighting value of the army had been so lowered by casualties and defeat, and the position so compromised by the collapse of Germany's allies, that even a dogged defensive was impossible. Characteristically, he took a view of extreme pessimism and, in a nervous crisis, sent a despairing appeal for immediate overtures for an armistice.

It was not open to the politicians to question the military necessity of the request, but they must have felt that the anxiety of Imperial Head-quarters lay in avoiding responsibility and in forcing the statesmen to accept the burden of liquidating the war. Head-quarters, having practically ruled the country, suddenly abdicated. Their rule had destroyed alike the prestige of the Throne, the *régime* and the Government. There was no leader left except the Reichstag to take control. For that body, there was as yet no question of playing the rôle of the Duma in March 1917. It did not, save on the meagre benches of the Independents, desire a revolution. All it wanted was to secure a democratic *régime*. To that end, Prince Max of Baden formed a parliamentary Cabinet which depended on a Reichstag majority inclusive of representatives of the Majority Socialists. A popular Government, appointed by the Kaiser but responsible to the nation, it was to conduct the peace negotiations and transform Germany into a constitutional Monarchy. Prince Max did not despair of the peace negotiations. He reckoned the situation less desperate than did Ludendorff when his pessimism was lowest and less favourable than that general when his optimism was in the ascendant ; he still believed it possible for a national effort to be made sufficient to give the enemy pause, for if it did ruin Germany it would probably ruin Europe with her—a risk the Allies, he felt, dare not take.

The victory of democracy had been won. Without revolution, the *régime* had discredited itself and had fallen unregretted and unregarded. Germany might be expected to rise in defence of her new-won liberties against foreign domination. But the leaders in closest touch with the people may well have felt that the time for a national effort was past. It required organization and that organization, in face of exultant extremism, would have been difficult. Till it was organized the fighting line must hold ; there was no reason to hope that it would come from the army leaders. The sole generals, with whom the new *régime* could have co-operated, were pessimists to a man. They saw nothing but the need to save the German army from disgraceful rout and dissolution. All that Prince Max could do was to busy himself with the formalities of surrender ; till that issue was settled, it was impossible to proceed to constructive work.

At that moment, the Government had the vast majority of the nation at its back. The official class stood solidly true to it and, with it, the majority of the officer class, including Hindenburg himself. When Ludendorff resigned its last dangerous enemy disappeared ; there was nothing to fear from the Right, which, willy-nilly, had to support Prince Max lest a worse fate overtake it. Even the Left confined itself to growling and grumbling ; it could not create a revolutionary situation. But the Government did not fully realize that this overwhelming support of the nation was passive and not active. That passivity left Germany at the mercy of an incident and characteristically enough that incident came from the Right.

The extremists had been spurred to new activity by the collapse of the Imperial *régime* ; the task incumbent upon them, and long prepared, was to turn a March into a November revolution. They had been greatly strengthened by the release of political prisoners, notably Liebknecht and Eisner who, at Berlin and Munich, conducted frenzied propaganda for a revolution on Bolshevik lines. But if their aims were clear, the means of attainment were not ; and their appeals fell on deaf ears.

Then came the crash. The Admiralty determined to make a last effort. In spite of the fact that armistice negotiations were in progress, they resolved to fight a general action—a last " death-ride " of the German battle fleet. They acted on their own authority, although they could claim that, in Prince Max's policy of appealing for a national effort, a *levée en masse*, such as an action of the fleet, was a necessary part. On October 28, when part of the fleet was already in battle position, the crews of three battleships refused to weigh anchor. The mutiny was the work of a minority, but the officers did not grapple with it. They referred the issue to the High Command and, next day only, were the mutineers arrested. On the 30th, the plan of the Admiralty became known and mutiny broke out throughout the fleet at Wilhelmshaven. The civil population took the side of the mutineers ; officers who attempted to use force were shot down and by November 3 the movement had gained Kiel and Hamburg. The revolutionary situation had arisen.

Despite the participation of the civil element, the Kiel movement was in essence a military revolt. There was no revolt against the Government—its representative, Noske, had little difficulty in getting control of the movement—but, on November 7, Kurt Eisner, using his unrivalled talents as agitator and orator to inflame the populace of the Bavarian capital with an adroit blend of particularism and revolutionism, proclaimed the Bavarian Republic. This was revolution, for the Government had made no pronouncement on the *régime* ; it was a definite appeal to force and a challenge to the whole German system. It was also the signal for the release of forces long pent up. Once the step had been taken the revolutionary fever spread the more quickly as it was seen that no action would be taken against the revolutionaries. The movement gained all the German cities as well as the army. Generals lost their authority ; princes fled ; governments resigned ; self-appointed rulers took over control ; soviets began to be formed and the workers' and soldiers' republic became a possibility. All that was needed was leadership, but the revolutionary chiefs were not ready. The revolution took them too by surprise and, before they had recovered, the moment for decisive action had passed. Whatever might ultimately have happened to it, the workers' republic was a possibility during that week of confusion, but the Spartacists had had no Lenin to turn them into a corps of professional revolutionaries, and lead them into action.

The effect on the Government was immediate. The outbreak of revolt ended at once any possibility of making a last desperate national effort : the war was lost ; it remained only to save Germany from chaos. But a government, intended merely to secure a transition, is not a government for a crisis. The victory of Liberalism had too academic a sound to soothe the masses and it was clear that hourly the latter were getting out of control, hourly the number of extremists was increasing ; at that rapid rate of progression, a revolutionary leader might appear. The sole solution was to head the revolution and endeavour to guide it. That the Government could not do. The Majority Socialists could and did.

For that party it was literally all power or downfall. They had co-operated loyally with the bourgeois parties, and they had seen their supporters pass at a steadily increasing rate into the ranks of the Independents. They were now faced with the possibility of general defection. The support of many loyal Socialists for Liebknecht's abortive attempt at an immediate Bolshevik rising was a plain indication of the way things were going, and it was known that the attempt had only been postponed and not abandoned. In the rapidly growing confusion it might be successful, and the Majority leaders would find the revolution proclaimed over their heads and themselves treated as merely bourgeois like their Liberal colleagues.

The choice was not so much between fighting the revolution with a risk of reaction and leading the revolution with a risk of Bolshevism, as between leading the revolution and being extinguished in the ultimate fight between White and Red extremists. They chose to lead. It was a desperate choice, but it was the only way that promised hope that the democratic Germany, just come painfully to birth, would survive ; Germany has reason to be grateful that the Majority leaders were patriotic enough, able enough and strong enough to take it.

There only remained to find a procedure capable of facilitating the transition from the parliamentary government of a coalition to the revolutionary dictatorship of a party.   Luckily, a pretext was available for the disruption of the coalition.   On October 28 Herr Scheidemann, the Socialist representative in the Government, had addressed to Prince Max a demand from the party that the Kaiser should abdicate ; on November 7 the demand was transformed into an ultimatum.   The Kaiser returned no answer to the Government's inquiry and next day the Socialists resigned from the Cabinet.   Automatically they placed themselves and their party at the service of the revolution.   On November 9, their leaders went to the Cabinet then in session and informed it that " the people " desired to take power into its own hands, and Prince Max, having informed them of the Kaiser's abdication, resigned.   His transference of power to Ebert was an act without meaning.   Ebert by a revolutionary act had assumed the rôle of dictator ; his proclamation of it did not even assume it as an act willed by the people. The Imperial *régime* had yielded to democracy ; before constitutional democracy could be established, it was forced aside by a revolutionary dictatorship.   A saddler sat on the throne of the Hohenzollerns and possessed their heritage.

CHAPTER II

THE MENACE FROM THE LEFT

The policy of the Majority Socialists—a united Socialist party—
the first revolutionary ministry—moderate character of ministry
—dissensions in the Government—between the old *régime* and the
workers' and soldiers' councils—the First Congress of Workers' and
Soldiers' Councils—results of the elections—suppressing Communist
revolts.

ALTHOUGH the assumption of power by Ebert was a
revolutionary act, its significance is lost if it is not
realized that it was also a tactical move. There was
little exultation about the German revolution. It was the
culmination of a long process consciously worked out ; there
were no scenes reminiscent of those of March 1917, when a
nation was literally drunk on liberty, and there would have
been no revolutionary act had the culmination of the process
not coincided with defeat in the field and a crisis at home.
The first democratic Government could not hope to control the
forces thus unleashed ; a revolutionary dictatorship might.
It is untrue to say that the Majority Socialists usurped power
to sabotage the revolution, but they certainly did so to prevent
a Bolshevik revolution. With a far-sightedness that does
them credit, they realized that, in a highly developed, educated
country like Germany, such a revolution meant a bloody civil
war ending with the victory of reaction, whether Left or Right.

Their aim was to hold power till the nation could pull itself
together, till the democracy could concentrate its forces, till a
majority of the nation within a democratic *régime* could be duly
organized. And it was time indeed to take control, for everywhere there reigned an orgy of abdication. All that the *régime*
and its supporters sought was to escape responsibility for the
collapse that was imminent. Everywhere the Governments
had disappeared, and self-appointed committees under the
guidance of irresponsible leaders held most of the German
towns. Unless some central authority took control and at
once, they would fall an easy victim to the extremists. It

37

was the Bolshevik parties and leaders, and not the dispirited, disorganized remnants of the Imperial *régime*, that constituted the most serious menace, both internally and internationally. Ebert had seized power to parry this menace.

The Left movement was split, at the moment, into three sections, with a tendency to merge imperceptibly one into the other. It was possible to unite the movement, either in a Right or in a Left sense, and thus form either a democratic or a Bolshevik Republic. For the moment, the Socialists held the field ; their decision meant the decision of the nation. The first stage obviously was the reunion of the two Socialist parties. There existed little difference between the leaders of the rival groups. None of them were statesmen, they were all party men of ability and character who had never been called upon, save in a few cases a few weeks ago, to fill positions of risk and responsibility. The Independents had attracted the brilliant, the Majority retained the able ; the Independents had greater driving power, the Majority greater stability ; the Independents were under the influence of words, the Majority under that of facts. There were few illusions on the subject of each other, for the leaders on both sides had known each other in union and disunion for years, and, if doubtful of the strength of the other, each realized quite clearly the other's weaknesses. But both realized also their failure to attain the picturesqueness and appeal, actual, historical and moral, of the darlings of the truly revolutionary elements—Liebknecht, Rosa Luxemburg, Radek and the like, who were even then as much legend and inspiration as flesh and blood, and whose hold on the general mass of the workers might well be far greater than could be supposed.

The Majority took the initiative and never lost it. Ebert's dictatorship was not twelve hours old ere he offered to share power with the Independents by offering them an equality of seats in a revolutionary Government. It was the obvious policy. If the offer was accepted, it closed the ranks of Socialism ; the united party could evolve in one direction or the other and the power of the extremists, who had adopted Leninist tactics against " a March revolution ", would be put at once to the test. The apparent magnanimity of the offer made it easier for the Majority to offer but more difficult for the Independents to accept. There were the long and bitter quarrels with the Majority, the revolutionary activity of past months, the close connection with the Spartacists and the genuine hold on many of the leaders of Bolshevik principles and, at least, their desire to push revolution to its farthest length. Germany was, according to Marxian thought, the one country where a workers' republic could be carried through ; it was difficult to renounce a task that seemed possible, as difficult as to work with men who had been stigmatized as traitors and whose policy had not been to their liking. The choice before the Independents was either to hold no relations with the " social patriots " and to push on to the proletarian dictatorship—the course eloquently advocated by Liebknecht—or to join the " social patriots " and influence their conception of a Socialist State—in other words, to abandon revolutionary and go back to evolutionary work with the possibility of returning to revolution if evolution proved too slow. The possibility of capturing the whole movement by union no doubt influenced the Independents when they chose the second alternative, just as it influenced the Majority in making the offer, but, at the same time, the choice was also due to a desire to serve the nation and save it from anarchy. There were social patriots even on the extreme Left whose internationalism was not yet complete.

On November 10, therefore, the first revolutionary ministry was announced—Ebert, Scheidemann and Landsberg for the Majority, and Haase, Dittmann and Barth for the Independents. It was a revolutionary ministry in strict accuracy ; actually it was a Socialist Cabinet supported by a majority of the nation. It held its power from the people even if the people had not been formally consulted. Although the Independents had made it a condition of their participation that the workers' and soldiers' councils, everywhere established on the Russian model, should be regarded as the source of the Governmental power, no steps were taken to give effect to the condition ; a mass meeting of council delegates had the formation and composition of the new Government announced to it and recorded an approval valuable only as a sign that the extremists did not control a majority of the councils actually in being. The Cabinet indeed described itself as "the Council of People's Commissaries" and announced its intention of carrying out a Socialist programme, but these were only concessions to the spirit of the hour.

The formation of the ministry was a distinct blow to the extreme Left, which still dreamed of a November revolution. That the dream was not mere fantasy is shown by the fact that, only a few hours before the decision of the Independents was taken, Barth had pleaded vigorously for the summoning of a workers' and soldiers' congress to elect a Cabinet. Now this champion of the idea of " All power to the Soviets " was a member of the Government, and he and the wing of his party which he represented had agreed to the summoning of a Constituent Assembly to decide the future form of government of Germany. They may have thought that they could pack that Assembly, but the revolt from Bolshevik practice was plain. The extreme Left had, as a matter of fact, hopelessly miscalculated the extent to which Leninism had penetrated the German masses. They remained in the majority true to democracy ; in spite of appeals, some of them by men of almost heroic stature, in spite of defeat, starvation and ruin, they were not yet disposed to pass out of the Western European tradition to try the fortune of a Communist experiment. And in reliance on that sense of reality in the workers, the whole of the bourgeois classes, with but few exceptions, fell in behind the Socialist Government. The official class had not been disturbed by the revolution ; it had gone on functioning as a truly official class always does, apparently reckless of Cabinet changes, of revolutionary outbreaks, of self-elected workers' councils ; it kept the machinery of the State going. It was a remarkable achievement and one of supreme importance, for it minimized the seriousness of the revolution to the class which in a highly organized State is always ready to fight revolution by force, and which is apt to gauge the importance of things by the degree to which they affect its routine. The fact that the reaction did not at once coalesce into a fighting power is due indeed to the Government and its conception of its duty ; it is also due to the bureaucracy which kept those services going whose importance we realize only when they cease.

For the moment Germany was personified by six men, once the despised leaders of the ragged proletariat ; against it and them stood a minority of extreme Socialists, angrily conscious that they had been outmanœuvred and prepared to go any lengths to recover the ground which they felt they never should have lost. They had no alternative to acquiescence save the carrying out of a *coup de main* on the Leninist model. Through its recognized leaders, the extreme Left declared uncompromising war on the new Government ; they realized only partially that they were declaring war on the German nation.

The first essential for the Government was to get control of the country and liquidate the war. The country offered no difficulties, nor did the Allies. On November 11 the armistice was signed ; Germany scarcely examined the conditions ; she trusted blindly to the magical fourteen points and the peace conference.

The discussion of these terms belongs to military history, but the German signatory is significant of the new Germany ; he was the bourgeois politician Erzberger. The Socialist dictators had simply co-opted the bourgeois leaders. They looked after the country, and experts—Solf at the Foreign Office, Schiffer at the Treasury, Preuss at the Home Office—formed a Cabinet and looked after the government. And indeed the Council of Commissaries had its hands full. It was not a harmonious body ; old enmities are not wiped out in a day, and many of its adherents were not to be trusted. Against its programme of a democratic Republic which could become Socialist only by will of the people, the Spartacists formulated their ideal of a Soviet Republic and began the formation of a Red guard. The Commissaries were responsible for the maintenance of law and order. They had several regiments at hand who had adhered to the Republic and officers to lead them, but to use them might have caused a revulsion in the minds of their supporters. Eichhorn, an Independent, appointed Chief of Police in the capital, had raised an armed force, but Eichhorn was more than half a Communist. Wels, the Majority Socialist military commander of Berlin, had likewise raised a Republican guard. All the forces were well armed and all were not entirely reliable. The same held true of other towns and, to add to the difficulties, the legions from west and east were marching home, some quietly demobilizing themselves, others retaining, thanks to the patriotic sacrifice of Hindenburg—now undergoing his greatest humiliation—and his colleagues, their old discipline. The disciplined presented as great a problem as the undisciplined.

The rival tendencies in the Government soon showed themselves. On the one hand, the Majority wanted to hurry on the Constituent Assembly and turn over responsibility to a Constitutional Government ; the Independents desired to delay the Assembly and get the Socialist *régime* on a firm basis. Their representatives in the Land-Governments did their best. But the Majority stood obstinately by their guns and the Independents did not press their case ; they knew their followers too well. It is difficult to overestimate the difficulties of the Cabinet. They had not unnaturally got rid of the parliaments of the Imperial *régime*, which clearly did not reflect the opinion of the new Germany, but, at the same time, they refused to take orders from the workers' and soldiers' councils. They had therefore no real connection with the electorate save through the party organizations, and the lack of such connection was not atoned for by the willingness of all the bourgeois parties to make things easy for them. That alone supplied a glorious argument to the Communists and sowed doubts in the minds of many Independents as to the wisdom of their renunciation. Were the bourgeois merely rallying their forces while the Left movement, rent by faction, exhausted itself in a struggle whose fruits the victors would not be permitted to enjoy ? The extreme Independents were so convinced of the answer that they had already passed over to the Bolsheviks, whose tactics in penetrating the workers' councils were daily gaining them adherents.

The loyalty of the Independents was indeed sorely tried. There had been collisions in the streets of Berlin in which soldiers—their old enemies—had fired on Spartacists nominally but also on honest workers. No progress had been made towards establishing Socialism, and more than one Independent must have asked himself, as did Eisner, the head of the Bavarian revolution, when his adherents declared for a Constituent Assembly, if the fruits of the revolution were not slipping away. There was still time to save the councils from dying a natural death and some of the Independents resolved to use it.

On December 16 there met the first Congress of Workers' and Soldiers' Councils. The five weeks that had elapsed since the Berlin councils had approved the Socialist Council of Commissaries had been well used by the Spartacists. All they required was an organized body to maintain a balance of power against the Government, as had been done in Russia, and in the Congress they hoped to find it. The councils for the most part had worked well ; they had been guided by the officials and they had always listened to the expert ; if their management of the food supply created much difficulty locally, their handling of demobilization was a real service to the nation. They had largely been appointed by the two Socialist parties and the majority of them had no political aims. They wanted to co-operate, to feel that they, the representatives of the pariah class, were necessary to the State, but they did not want to rule. "All power to the Soviets" was no slogan of theirs, and the Spartacists suffered a humiliating and crushing defeat at the outset ; the Congress declined to invite Liebknecht and Rosa Luxemburg to join its councils. The defeat was decisive and the extremists transferred the battle to the streets.

Inside the Congress, however, it came to an open conflict, not only between the coalition parties, but between the Commissaries. The Spartacist sympathizers poured out their wrath on the Cabinet for betraying the people's revolution, and demanded a clear affirmation of loyalty to the workers' Republic. Young, hotheaded and inexperienced, but desperately sincere, Barth joined in the criticism of his colleagues. The opposition, thus reinforced, carried their point that the councils should be recognized as the source of power in the State and that a central committee to be elected by the Congress should supervise, with the right of appointment and dismissal, the German Cabinet. Such a plan made the councils or their representative committee the supreme authority in the State, but all meaning was taken from the act by the fact that the Independents abstained from joining the Committee because they thought that it had not power enough and only Majority men were elected to it. When the Congress agreed to elections for the Constituent Assembly being held on January 19, the victory of the Socialist Right, despite the pious constitutional opinion expressed in the resolution on the Councils' Committee, was complete.

But the Congress had revealed the serious rift in the ranks of the coalition, in which a growing number of the Independents supported Liebknecht's campaign against the Constituent Assembly, and the Independent leaders, especially after Barth's revolt, began to feel their position compromising. A revolt of sailors forming part of the Berlin command, which was suppressed by regular troops with a good deal of bloodshed, gave the Independents the excuse they needed. They saw counter-revolution raising its head and left the Government. The Majority cleverly left the filling of the three vacancies thus caused to the Congress Committee, and that body promptly elected three Majority Socialists, including "the *saboteur* of the Kiel revolution," Noske.

The Independents' tactics had not been particularly ingenious and they reduced themselves to impotence, leaving the Government and the Spartacists face to face. The former at once took action. On January 4 it demanded the resignation of Eichhorn—a Left wing Independent—from the office of Chief of Police. Eichhorn appealed to the party which joined the Spartacists in declaring a general strike A revolutionary committee was formed, but it talked instead of acted, while, among its enemies, was Noske, who acted and did not talk. He appealed to the officers of the old army, formed a fighting force and proceeded to put down the revolt by force. The

soldiery were not over tender in their methods ; there was
much unnecessary killing and, in the confusion, Liebknecht and
Rosa Luxemburg, who had been arrested, were brutally murdered by their guards.   The lesson was a bloody one, but it
was approved by the nation, and on January 19 the elections
to the National Assembly were held in perfect order.   The
Majority Socialists polled 37·9 per cent. of the votes and the
Independents 7·6 per cent. ; the Socialist parties secured only
thirty-six seats short of an absolute majority ; the Radical
wing of the bourgeois polled 18·5 per cent., its centre 4·4 per
cent. and its right 10·3 per cent.   The Centrum polled 19·7 per
cent.   The result was a striking victory for German Radical-
ism ; a setback to the extreme Left, a defeat for the Right, and
an overwhelming victory for constitutionalism.

Berlin was thought too stormy a place for peaceful discussion
and the Assembly met at Weimar, the classic home of the old
German culture.   The Cabinet at once handed power over to
it—no more was heard of the councils—and it proceeded to
elect Ebert to the Presidency of the German Republic, and he
entrusted Herr Scheidemann with the formation of a ministry.
The new ministry was formed on a broad basis in view of the
national significance of its task, and was composed of Majority
Socialists, Centrists and Democrats, representing three hundred,
and twenty-six members in a house of four hundred and twenty-
one.

While the Assembly worked at the fashioning of a constitution, the Cabinet, at last a regular, constitutionally functioning Government, took over the difficult problems left by the
revolutionary ministry.   The Spartacus menace was scotched
but not killed.   Men were now recovering from the shock of
revolution and surrender and beginning to realize the nature
of the economic and political difficulties confronting them ;
the Allied blockade was only partially lifted and there was
widespread unrest.   The extremists had good material to work
on, but they were never able to give their agitation a national
aspect.   The outbreaks were sporadic, and as the nation
steadied itself and the anti-revolutionary elements recovered
courage the more and more useless did sporadic attempts become.   A demand for the socialization of the Westphalian
mines, backed by a general strike, proclaimed equally by the
Majority Socialists, was ended by the intervention of Government troops ; in the Rhineland, in Thuringia, in Saxony, in
Bavaria (where Eisner was murdered by a counter-revolutionary on February 21), strikes and *émeutes* were constant,

necessitating a further enrolment of troops, and, still more, a further employment of army officers by the Government.   The troops were ably handled, but every suppression raised up new enemies for the ministry, and especially caused grave suspicions to grow in the minds of the rank-and-file Socialists.   The storm came to a head in Berlin on March 5.   The trade unions called a general strike to force attention to the economic difficulties of the workers.   The strike was ineffective and the extremists declared it extended to the public services, whereupon the Majority Socialists called their members off and, to avoid a fiasco, the strike was cancelled.   The crowds in the Berlin streets got out of hand ;   shots were exchanged between the police and the " rowdies " ;   a portion of the volunteers enrolled in the November days and the sailors' corps, already wavering in their allegiance to the Government, seized the Lichtenburg suburb.   The Government seized the opportunity and with allegations, subsequently proved false, that the Spartacists had murdered numbers of policemen, sent in troops who suppressed the movement with brutality and bloodshed sufficient to arouse fierce criticism even in the Democratic and Centrist Press and almost to unite the workers against the Government.   Even bloodier reverses were suffered by the Spartacists in Magdeburg, Leipzig, Dresden, Brunswick, and Munich.   In Munich, after Eisner's murder, the Socialists of all shades demanded a Workers' Republic ;   it was proclaimed and was then overthrown by the Communists, whose rule, maintained by terror, was ended in a blood-bath worthy of the best traditions of White reaction.   There was bloodshed at Magdeburg ;   in Dresden, a Red dictatorship murdered the Socialist Minister for Defence and was suppressed by force ;   at Leipzig and Brunswick, the movement collapsed.   There were sporadic outbreaks till the end of May and then the Peace Treaty put an entirely new complexion on the whole struggle.

With the crushing of the extremists by the old army, the chances of a Bolshevik revolution passed definitely away. They were rendered precarious by the decision of the Independents to take the national line, and they were doomed by the failure of the extremist leaders to take advantage of the confusion preceding the election of the Constituent Assembly. It is more than doubtful if the ablest revolutionary could have done more than give considerably more trouble than Liebknecht did, for the odds would have been fatally against him, and his enemies were men who had nothing to learn even from Lenin in ruthlessness and decision.   It is well indeed that Germany was spared a successful Bolshevik revolution, but, at the same time, the internecine strife of the Socialist elements had disastrous effects on the future history of Germany. While the extremists later formed the Communist party and became, under the rigid discipline imposed by Moscow, a far more formidable though smaller force than Liebknecht could have controlled, the rift between Independent and Majority Socialists came to open rupture, the benefit of which the Independents reaped. The workers were unpleasantly awakened when soldiers under officers of the old *régime* shot down members of their class. They sensed the approach of counter-revolution and a state no better than in days of autocracy ; in great numbers, they passed to the Independents, who, despite their faults of indecision, had not shed the blood of their own class. The result was to cripple the Socialist power and to throw the Government more and more under the control of the bourgeois parties, among whose less radical members the idea of sharing power with the Socialists—always repugnant—now seemed unnecessary. The way was paved for the fall of the Socialists from governmental power, and on the Right the counter-revolution raised its head. The crushing of the menace from the Left created the menace from the Right. It was a menace consciously risked, and possibly justifiably risked, for no member of the Scheidemann Government, when he was asked, dreamed that the Allies were to supply the reaction with its best weapons.

CHAPTER III

THE WORK OF THE CONSTITUENT ASSEMBLY AND THE PEACE TREATY

The Constituent Assembly at Weimar—the grouping of political parties—the national background—a democratic charter—the German State as laid down in the Constitution of Weimar—the *Reich* and its relations with the *Länder*—the rights of the President—social and labour clauses—the effect of the Peace Treaty—disillusionment and reaction.

THE revolutionary period in the history of the German Republic ends with the meeting of the Constituent Assembly, the election of the President and the appointment of the first coalition Government. There are revolutionary outbreaks in the succeeding years, but there is no revolutionary period. At no time did constitutional government see itself forced to abdicate. The foundations of the new Germany were too firmly laid by the Assembly, and its work remains a turning-point in German history.

When it met in Weimar its mere appearance must have seemed a guarantee of stability to the nation, for that appearance differed extraordinarily little from that of the Reichstag which it had replaced. Most of the old faces appeared again ; the party strengths were, proportionately, much the same, in spite of the fact that the elections had been absolutely free. But a closer examination would have shown significant changes of name, and an examination of the party programmes might have suggested that all the German parties had taken a pace to the Left. Elected on a proportional representation system by universal suffrage, the Assembly was far more representative of national opinion than the old Parliaments, and yet the respective strengths of the parties were little more than the normal evolution of German democracy might have produced after a normal victory of democracy over the *régime* expressed in constitutionally won reform. Only the fact that all the bourgeois parties had reconstituted themselves indicated that something abnormal had occurred. There were no Communists,

but the Socialist party had split into Independent and
Majority Socialists. The Progressives had become the Democrats and had attracted to their ranks the left and centre of
the National Liberals, whose right element now called itself the
German People's Party. The Centrum had become the Christian
People's Party—it speedily reverted, however, to its old name
—while the Conservatives appeared as the German National
People's Party. The fact that a change of name was thought
wise is significant, but it implied little drastic change in the
policy of the parties, and, except in one or two cases more important in promise than in fact, the Constitution contains little
that had not been part of the stock-in-trade of progressives of
all shades during the long period of constitutional discussion.

The Constitution is a compromise, but a compromise in
which the Right lost heavily. The winners in the elections
were the Majority Socialists, and the Democrats who, for
national reasons, notably the necessity for acceptance on a
national basis of the Peace Treaty when it came, had formed a
coalition with the Centrum. The Cabinet and its majority
were Left Centre and the Constitution is a compromise between
the Left Centre parties fairly representing the views of the
voters supporting them. Its broad lines represent agreement ;
its details compromise, and one can often detect the party
victories by the mere wording of the text without reference to
the debates.

The basis was the draft constitution drawn up by one of the
ablest constitutional lawyers in Germany, Hugo Preuss, and
published to give the nation an idea of what appeared in the
mind of a good Democrat to be a suitable constitution for a
democratic Republic. There was no doubt that, whatever the
extremists on either side might say, Germany was going to be a
democratic Republic. The autocracy had been crushed ; the
attempts to establish a proletarian dictatorship had failed ;
and neither the Anti-Republican nor the Anti-Democratic
opposition had any opportunity of uttering more than a feeble
protest. All they could do was to use the dissensions of the
Republicans to colour some of the clauses, and even so they had
little success. All the broad principles laid down by Preuss
were translated into law and, if the Constitution as passed
differs from the draft submitted to the Assembly, the differences do not affect broad general principles. The debates were
prolonged and often acrimonious, for, to many in the House,
one clause or another meant a defeat of principle amounting to
destruction of a political ideal, a sacrifice of what had made the

old Germany great or a rejection of what alone could give political power to the worker, but there was also displayed an amazing amount alike of goodwill and of faith, and the Weimar Constitution remains a great charter for a democratic nation at once Conservative and Radical, and capable of constant modification as the wheels of history go forward or reverse.

The post-war mood of Europe under the inspiration of the Wilsonian ideal, which became something far greater than the limited academism its author had originally intended, was one of exaltation, and that exaltation inspired even a nation crushed with defeat. A new era of class and national co-operation appeared perfectly possible to minds in all countries, and the constitutions of 1919 and 1920 are inspired with that conviction, even although the exaltation had begun to sink. The war was the *via dolorosa* to liberty ; after being sent like sheep to the slaughter, the peoples had come into their own and they alone were the power in the State. The formula enshrined in the German and other constitutions that the source of power is the people is not empty rhetoric ; it is expressive of a new popular conception of the relation of the State to the people. In the German Constitution it meant a clear break with the past. The old German Empire had been virtually a league of princes and its emperor had condescended to give legal form to a desire to co-opt the nation, through elected representatives, to the Government of the country, but the source of all authority remained the prince, who derived his authority from supernatural sources. The Weimar Assembly, having seen all the princes abolished, had to find new authority and it expressed its opinion of the origin of the power conferred upon it by the notable words : " The German People, united in all their branches and inspired by the determination to renew and strengthen their commonwealth in liberty and justice, to preserve peace both at home and abroad, and to foster social progress, have adopted the following Constitution." The Assembly was building for more than the Government of Germany ; the Constitution was not merely a summary of the governmental *status quo* ; it was a basis for the development of a future of national progress and international co-operation.

Whatever local patriotism may say, the Weimar Constitution struck at the roots of German particularism. It is profitless to go into the interminable controversy on the nature of German federalism ; it is sufficient to note that the federalism implied in the Constitution is a concession rather than an affirmation. The insistence on the German people indicates

the conception dominating the Assembly, although even that
is a retrograde step from the unitary State which Preuss envisaged, and it is quite clear that it intended to signify that
the old federalism was dead.   It was in its nature a federation
of princely houses under the guidance of Prussia ; the princely
houses had gone ; the German people remained and the existence of " Lands "—the successors of the kingdoms and duchies
—derives from the will of the German people as a whole.   Apart
from the Reich, the Lands have no existence ; they are virtually
administrative divisions and the ruling tendency of contemporary German thought is to make them actually so.   Germany to-day ranks as a federal State and her Constitution is a
federal one, but it is so ordered that the federal aspect has
less vital importance than the unitary aspect.   Not merely
has the Reich exclusive authority over foreign relations, citi-
zenship, defence, coinage, customs and posts, but it has supreme
authority over a score of other things (art. 7), including civil
and communal judicial procedure, public health, social legislation, insurance, railways, and the like.   In cases of emergency, it is the exclusive authority.   Jurisdiction is left to the
Lands only " so long and in so far as the Reich does not
exercise jurisdiction " (art. 12), and any laws passed by the
Lands may be questioned by the Reich if the general welfare is
affected, while, in all cases of difference in dispute, Reich laws
take precedence over Land laws.   The nature of the Lands'
constitutions and the principles they embody are laid down
for them by the Weimar Constitution (art. 17), and no insistence
on local rights can prevent the alteration of Land boundaries
if national interests and the will of the people concerned desire
it.   The Reichsrat represents the Lands, each Land having at
least one vote, the votes of the larger Lands being computed at
one vote per 1,000,000 inhabitants, but no State, however great,
being able to have votes exceeding two-fifths of the whole—a
provision which militates against the realization of a unitary
state by the creation of a greater and greater Prussia.   It is
not the Bundesrat from which it derives, but it may become an
instrument of unification.   It was dislike of Prussia far more
than dislike of unity that rendered, and still renders, particularism so strong.   The small States of Central Germany
formed the Land of Thuringia rather than be absorbed in
Prussia and, since 1919, only Waldeck has consented to lose
its identity as a Land and become part of Prussia.   Lands like
Hesse to-day are convinced of the need of a unitary State, but
they refuse to seek the road to it via Prussia, and, although

Prussia is, for administrative purposes, itself a federal State—an arrangement that facilitates its easy disappearance in Germany—a Prussian sentiment responds to the violent particularism of the South German Lands. But here the logic of facts is against romantic history, and the practical difficulties presented by the existing federalism are convincing the mass of the nation that the sooner the map of Germany can be printed in one colour the better. The unitary Germany is within reasonable distance of realization because of the gradual spread of the conviction that it is necessary, but the basis of it was laid in the Weimar Constitution as an act of political faith. When the Council of the Lands became merely a consultative and revisionary body in contradiction to the old supremacy of the Bundesrat, the victory for unity was won and the Germany of to-day has only to exploit it and gather in its fruits.

The Lands disposed of and the essential unity of Germany asserted, the Constitution simply ignores them when it comes to deal with governance of the nation except to assert their inferiority. It concerns itself solely with the establishment of popular rule. Here the Assembly was faced with its most difficult task. It was brought up against old and established custom and new and dangerous prejudices. It had been elected definitely to prevent the establishment of any type of dictatorship and yet it had to create a strong Government which would be able to maintain itself against such dictatorship as threatened it. The form that emerged is a compromise, but it is a compromise that has stood the test of nine stormy years. That compromise is based on the balancing of the powers between President, Chancellor (*plus* his Cabinet) and Parliament, with Parliament in every case the supreme authority, which in the circumstances means the electorate. The President is the head of the State with wide powers, but in practice he is compelled to co-operate with Parliament. He can dissolve a Parliament in the event of disagreement if he cares to, but he cannot dissolve the next Parliament for the same reason. If the election succeeding the dissolution gives him reason he has but appealed to the sovereign people ; if it does not, he can be removed as a result of a popular vote proposed by two-thirds of the deputies. He is given (in art. 48—one of the most hotly-debated articles in the Constitution) dictatorial powers in case of emergency envisaged as rebellion on the part of a Land or a party and can then govern by decree, but the decrees can be revoked by Parliament. The need for authority to take urgent measures, e.g. during a dissolution or in the absence of the majority of ministers and deputies, is obvious, but the control is so carefully laid down that dictatorial power could hardly be abused unless the President were deliberately meditating unconstitutional actions of some kind, i.e. appealing to force. The risks of that are evident, but they are risks that an educated democracy need rarely run. In all other respects the President seems little more than the constitutional signatory authority of Parliament, and all other authority he possesses at home and abroad must be extorted by his own personality.

The right of the President to dissolve Parliament has been mentioned. He has also a further right : he appoints the Chancellor who in turn appoints the Ministers, but as the Chancellor, and the Ministers depend individually on the confidence of Parliament, the right is only formal. The Chancellor (art. 56) determines the general course of policy and assumes responsibility therefore to Parliament. Normally he or a Minister initiates legislation, but the individual deputy also has the right of initiation. Here, the Reichsrat, viewed as part of the legislature, has an important right ; its consent must be demanded before a Bill is introduced into Parliament as a Government measure, although the refusal of consent does not prevent introduction ; but it can force the Cabinet to introduce a Bill against the Cabinet's will, though the Cabinet can state its dissent while so doing. Parliament is the supreme authority on legislation, and no Bill can come into law without parliamentary approval save in circumstances (detailed in arts. 72–74) where a referendum is ordered. The sovereignty of the people in Parliament is complete even if there should be conflict between Parliament and people, but everything is done by a balancing of powers to prevent such conflict and to make the Constitution easily workable by men of goodwill, and it has proved workable, although on occasion certain men were not of goodwill.

The Assembly, in its zeal for justice, decided on an elaborate system of proportional representation as the method of election for Parliament, and, except for small and local minorities, the result does give a remarkably accurate picture of the mind of the nation. For that very reason, it creates a state of things which so far has rendered government by coalition unavoidable and has led to peculiar methods of forming Cabinets which the Assembly scarcely envisaged. The President does not send for a party leader as such ; he sends for a statesman who can persuade a sufficient number of parties to co-operate under

PRESIDENT EBERT

his leadership, and the parties share the Cabinet posts in proportion to their strength or to the value of the support they
bring.   The result has been that not always the best men have
received the posts, that there has been a series of weak
Cabinets who have existed only because foreign affairs were of
such paramount importance, that controversial legislation of
the normal parliamentary type has been impossible, that
Cabinet adhesion is weak and that non-party and even non-
political persons have been co-opted into Cabinets, not always
with happy results.   Now that the foreign situation is regular-
ized and home affairs are paramount, the system is at last
being severely tested and the makeshifts of the years between
Versailles and Locarno will yield to a more rigid and stronger
system of government.   Parliament has more than won its
spurs ; the Cabinet has still to win them.

   But the most notable part of the Constitution is perhaps the
treatise on the rights and duties of German citizens which
forms Part II.   Under the guise of legal provisions it is a political tract which plainly illustrates the mind of the Assembly.
It declares the responsibility of the Government for the governed and of the governed for the Government, laying down for
everybody in Germany collectively and individually a sort of
Terentian *nil alienum*.   It is not merely an abstract statement
of equality before the law, of sex equality in rights and duties,
of freedom of the person, of speech, of the written word, of
thought, of religion and legal protection therefore, but it
embraces nearly the whole of life in its details.   It outlines the
whole policy of a democratic State on the general life of the
nation from the cradle to the grave.   It begins with the protection of motherhood, lays down the basis for marriage in a
modern community, protects the child, legitimate or illegiti-
mate, and insists on its education.   It protects youth against
exploitation and against neglect of its moral, mental and phy-
sical welfare.   To the grown man or woman it guarantees
religious, political and economic freedom.   There is no State
Church, but all education is supervised by the State.   Private
property is protected, but the right to private property is subordinated to the welfare of the community.   The distribution
and use of land is supervised by the State to the deliberate end
of creating the city and the house beautiful.   Labour, says
art. 157, is under the special protection of the Reich, and socialization to the farthest extent is legal under art. 158.   Naturally, the right of the worker to combine is recognized, though
the legislators of Weimar were not so bold as those of Reval and

refused to recognize the right to strike as a constitutional one. Instead they laid down the very important provisions for local and national Workers' Councils and for a National Economic Council which would be virtually a vocational parliament.

All this part is worth detailed and careful study as a fine expression of national will to attain a new and better social state. It is true that it is prophecy rather than legislation, true also that it is sometimes confused prophecy. Morality, liberty and Socialism—the watchwords of the three Government parties—are the occasionally conflicting ideals that inform it and they are not always successfully reconciled. The important thing is that the reconciliation is attempted and attempted along practical lines. It may be an essay in political philosophy ; it is also a basis for political practice, and it finally disposes of the idea of the non-political German. There is nothing about it of the naïve idealism of which Germany has been and still is so prolific ; it is emphatically the work of practical politicians who were no Utopians but were wise enough to reject the extremes of anti-Utopianism and to recognize the necessity of an idealist basis for development. The form of that development is variously conceived, but the end is the same—the harmonious development to full stature of every individual by the subordination of the individual to the community through his willing recognition that liberty, happiness and moral goodness are perfected only when they are universally enjoyed. It is the work of men whose ideal of the State and of the citizen is service, and who honestly sought to build a new Germany. It is the swan-song of the enthusiasm of the democratic revolution. The succeeding years gave no chance for it to be translated into legislation, except in bits, and much of its fine precepts have been silently neglected. Power has passed from the men who framed it and the enemies of the ideal it embodied have so far prevailed, but it remains as a monument in German history and the basis on which the Germany of the future must be built if it is to continue true to the ideal laid down at Weimar. Swan-song it is ; it is also a challenge.

In any circumstances the Constitution would be a remarkable document, but in the circumstances of 1919 it is more than remarkable. It is the failure to appreciate these circumstances that makes so much of the political—as opposed to the legal—criticism of it really irrelevant. The passing of the Constitution took from February 19 to August 11, and during that period Germany passed through a long crisis which began in hope and ended in black despair.   The struggle against the Left extremists has already been described, but that was only part of the crisis.   Germany was still in a state of war with the Entente powers and the blockade had not yet been raised when the Weimar Assembly met.   The enemy indeed seemed deliberately playing into the hands of the Republic's enemies, for the food shortage was the strongest ally of the Spartacists. In the east actual war existed with Poles and Russians and large portions of German territory were in enemy possession. Demobilization proceeded with difficulty ; industry was disorganized ; foreign trade had disappeared ; the national strength was physically and mentally exhausted.   The men who met at Weimar might well have despaired of their country ; instead they were full of faith, and the significance of the Constitution is missed unless its character as an act of faith is recognized.

For half-way through the deliberations of the Assembly came the shattering blow of the Peace Treaty.   The history of the Peace Conference is irrelevant here ; let it suffice to say that it missed, and missed disgracefully, the greatest opportunity in history.   The severity of the blow lay in the fact that the German democracy had expected it not to miss it.   It is at once difficult and easy to understand the incredulity with which that democracy received the Treaty of Versailles.   It was not ignorant of the fact that the vanquished has to pay for defeat. It was resigned to the loss of Alsace and Lorraine, to paying for the devastations its armies had caused, to a reduction of its armaments and, in view of the declared acceptance of the rights of the peoples to self-determination, to loss of territory. Territory was already lost as a result of the Polish revolt and the forcible expulsion from Polish-inhabited territory of German troops and officials.   But it expected such losses to come as a result of a general European agreement and that the Peace would bury the war.   Instead a Carthaginian peace was imposed on it.   Its territorial losses surpassed expectation, in cases, lacked all justification, and the Treaty appeared but a measure, not so much punitive as intended to serve the ends of French hegemony in the establishment of a girdle of encircling States each secured to French policy by having earned the undying hostility of Germany.   The disarmament ordered was paralleled only by the devastations of early history, the military system which had led Germany to within an ace of world power and was essentially a domestic affair was compulsorily changed, the mercantile marine was crippled, vast stretches of territory lay under a long enemy occupation, the colonies were all lost, the union with Austria so proudly voted at Weimar was forbidden, and an undefined burden of war indemnities masking under the name of reparations was imposed, which paralleled political impotence by economic servitude. Now the German democracy had come to victory under the Wilson inspiration. It clung with earnestness that was not all selfish to the declaration that the Allies warred not with the German people but with the Empire. It had wrecked the Empire and it claimed to rank with the other democracies of Europe. It did not claim preferential treatment, but it claimed recognition of the fact that an epoch-making change had been accomplished. Instead of being admitted into the comity of nations, it was expressly marked out as a pariah and its people saddled with the total guilt of causing the war. There was no reconciliation ; the war was still being carried on. There was certainly *naïveté* in the thought that the miscellaneous collection of individuals whom the fortune of war had placed in control of Allied policy were capable of taking the long historical view and resisting the pent-up passions that with victory found expression ; there was *naïveté* in the over-estimation of Wilson and in the trust in the Allied democracies, but there was enough evidence in the words of the Allied statesmen to save the *naïveté* from being culpable. The Peace Treaty tore the last mask from the war. With its promulgation the last defence of the war fell as the last appearance of generous idealism vanished.

The disillusionment was bitter, the sense of injustice very deep ; men began to regret the surrender, for the terms, if the Allies had had to fight their way into Berlin, could scarcely have been worse. A dangerous revulsion of feeling took place all over Germany, and the men who dreamed of a new Europe at Weimar had to face a difficult situation. The indignation and horror at what was regarded as a betrayal were not confined to a section ; they were universally felt. The first impulse undoubtedly was to reject defiantly the terms. At the great protest meeting at Berlin, the Chancellor Scheidemann struck at once the note of defiance. The treaty was " inacceptable ", and speaker after speaker agreed. It seemed as if the Cabinet might place itself at the head of the national resistance. Now, whatever excuse there was for the nation in its touching faith in the new spirit, there was less excuse for the Cabinet, for it had been repeatedly warned that a punitive peace was intended. It had either remained unconvinced or had feared to enlighten the nation, and was now in a difficult position. The majority held that the treaty meant the collapse of Germany and refusal to sign could make no difference ; a minority held that nothing is so bad that it could not be worse and that in acceptance lay more hope than in resistance. Statesmanship was on the side of the minority and the event has given them reason, though, in view of the panic fears in some Allied quarters, resistance might have produced unexpected results. The Chancellor, however, had burned his boats and the Cabinet resigned. The Assembly was divided. The Nationalists and the People's Party declared for rejection, the Independents for acceptance ; the other parties remained in anxious debate before painful alternatives. The Democrats refused to collaborate, but the Centrists and Majority Socialists formed a Cabinet under Gustav Bauer which secured a majority for acceptance with reservations on the war-guilt question and the surrender of the so-called " war-criminals ". The realist views had triumphed, but only by a small minority. Even with the reservations only two hundred and thirty-seven deputies supported acceptance.

Relying on the view of Erzberger—the signatory of the armistice who had been in close relation with the enemy powers—that the reservations would be accepted, the Assembly had begun to disperse, when there arrived an Allied ultimatum refusing the reservations and demanding unconditional acceptance. All was once more consternation. Bauer had no mandate for unconditional acceptance ; he had equally no mandate for refusal. The parties pledged to refusal would not form a Government and accept responsibility, but eventually, as the minutes of the ultimatum were running out, they agreed to allow the previous vote to be interpreted as authorizing the Government to sign, and the Bauer Cabinet sent to Paris a telegram of unconditional acceptance. A Majority Socialist Hermann Müller and a Centrist Johannes Bell were the actual signatories. Their courage and sacrifice give them a sure place in the history of the German Republic.

The difficulties of the surrender are not realized to-day, and for long it was a fatal disadvantage to the Republicans. One would ascribe far too much intellectual power to the Allied statesmen if one assumed that they realized what would follow, but had they desired to strangle German Republicanism they could scarcely have found a better way. Many Germans had accepted the Republic because they felt a Republican Germany would receive decent treatment ; they now found that the sacrifice they made had been in vain. More than the surrender, the establishment of the Republic and the disorders that ensued had effectually deprived the German nation of the power of resistance. Inevitably they blamed the Republic for the terrible humiliation inherent in the nation having to confess publicly that it was a justly punished criminal. From toleration they passed to open opposition, and it was the knowledge that many of the German citizens would not lift a finger to preserve a Republic that had brought them shame, that encouraged the extremists of the Right. Defeat, surrender, starvation after all are more endurable than insult, and the Allies knew it. For the events of the next years they must bear a heavy responsibility. Nationally each can make out a good case that before 1914 was perfectly valid. In 1919 the case had to be made out internationally, and it never has been made out yet.

CHAPTER IV

THE MENACE FROM THE RIGHT

The policy of the Allies and the movement towards the Right—Separatism—the provocation from France—the Kapp-Lüttwitz rebellion—the flight of the Government to Dresden—the elections for the first Republican Reichstag—the defeat of the Government—reparations discussions—the Conference of London.

IT was a sullen resentful Germany which greeted the passing of the Weimar Constitution, a Germany which was not in the mood to do anything, much less seek to realize the ideals expressed in that document.   The national morale had been gravely shaken, and the nation as a whole concentrated on chewing the cud of its own hatred while the social fabric went to ruin.   Instead of zeal of work came apathy ; instead of co-operation came disunion, instead of solidarity came selfish individual effort.   Mutilated and crushed, the German nation, in depressed exhaustion, threatened to be as dangerous to Europe as to itself.

From the national point of view the succeeding months were largely wasted.   The statesmen sought to use the danger as a political weapon and so embarked on a sullen passive resistance to the peace terms.   It is true that a loyal and prompt execution of the peace terms would not necessarily have caused any alleviation of them, but it would have permitted the statesmen to make political use of the dissensions of the Allies, now apparent in Europe, Africa, and Asia.   Their attitude imposed on the Allies the necessity for solidarity and on Germany unnecessary burdens by inviting foreign interference and wrecking the chances of those abroad who rightly saw that the salvation of Europe lay in reconciliation.   The mistake is obvious, but it was practically impossible to avoid making it.   No nation can tamely submit to being branded as a pariah, and in the absence of the power of retaliation the most attractive policy is to act like one.   That alone would have rendered difficult the loyal execution of the treaty, but execution became impossible when a large section of the nation felt that it, at least, was not bound

59

by the treaty and performed a national duty by preventing its being carried out. Besides, the terms themselves inflicted so crippling a blow on German industry that execution demanded a fiercer national effort than the nation could for the moment achieve.

The Assembly adjourned in August with a definite cleavage in the nation. To crush the Bolshevik menace, the Government had appealed to the servants of the old *régime* and to these the signature of the treaty appeared base betrayal. Such it appeared to so many of the nation that, round the supporters of the old *régime*, rallied the elements of a strong party which in the nature of things was anti-Republican. That the Imperial *régime* would have incurred no less a humiliation was obvious, but not so obvious as to prevent large sections laying all the blame of it on the Republic and those who had created it, and declaring roundly that the Republican system was incapable of organizing Germany for the recovery necessary to revenge. The modern world is not capable of the "never speak ; always think " policy ; it is needlessly vociferous, and in the savage denunciation of the Right and the open expression of a *revanche* policy, the Allies saw all their fears confirmed and their policy of repression justified. When Germans talked of recovering the lost territory, the French militarists felt they had now an unanswerable case for the " security " policy, and the best security was to keep Germany divided and helpless. The result was that they played so directly into the hands of the German Right that it took years to recover enough common sense to escape from the vicious circle so created. The utter lack of statesmanship in post-Versailles Europe will appear ludicrous to the historian of the future ; only by a miracle did it escape from being a tragic disaster to the generation that had to suffer it.

At no time had the Anti-Republicans a majority and they never succeeded in finding a great leader. The one man whose name might have rallied them into a great party, whose loyalty to his troops and chivalrous bearing in the face of disaster had been worthy of the greatest traditions of the German army, refused. Hindenburg was no Republican, but he loved Germany more than he hated the Republic and refused to lend himself to the cause of civil strife. For leaders, the fighting Anti-Republicans could produce only Ludendorff, discredited and rapidly losing his mental balance, and obscure officers and officials whose names meant nothing to the public. All was in their favour except their leaders. Sporadic outbursts of

Bolshevism still continued to terrify the bourgeois ; Munich, scarred and bloodstained after her Bolshevik experience, was the seat of violent reaction and arming as if an enemy were at her gates ; Poles and Germans were fighting in Silesia in anticipation of the plebiscite and, in the Rhineland, intriguers like Dorten and Haass were proclaiming the independent Republics of the Rhine and the Palatinate under the direct protection of the commanders of the French army of occupation.   The population, overwhelmingly loyal, dealt with the Separatists precisely as they deserved and were maltreated by the gangs of ruffians in Separatist pay under the complacent eyes of the French soldiery who had disarmed the loyal police.   From the occupied territory came a long tale of brutality and violence, much of it exaggerated, but enough of it true to cause the whole of Germany to seethe with indignation.   Nothing helped the enemies of the Republic more than the criminal folly of the French High Command.   The surrenders of material, the untactful attitude of commissions of control and inquiry, the constant humiliations and privation were nothing compared to the fact that black troops could with impunity insult German women in the Rhineland and that the German Government could do nothing.

The Republican leaders were not unaware that the forces of reaction were growing, but they seem to have tried to deceive themselves with the thought that the swing to the Right meant only the formation of a constitutional opposition.   They depended for their security on elements that were by nature reactionary and they underestimated altogether the feeling in the country which, neither violently reactionary nor Anti-Republican, merely sought relief for its feelings.   Still they were not blind to what was going on—the formation of Anti-Republican clubs and secret societies, the tampering with officers in Government service and the plotting of a *coup d'état*.   In October, the Democrats re-entered the Cabinet and so restored the " Weimar coalition " and, some weeks later, Scheidemann, in an impressive speech, warned the country that " the enemy is on the Right ".   Germany lived half in eagerness, half in terror on the edge of counter-revolution.

Constitutional and democratic government was still a novelty.   It had no prestige and the average German found it difficult to believe that it could give him the reasonable security of life and property that he desired.   What he wanted was a strong government of the sort he knew and there is little doubt that the nation would have accepted with little demur a strong dictatorial *régime* under one of the few men, Noske, for instance, who had proved themselves capable of decisive action. The extremists of the one side were as little popular as those on the other. Even the members of the Right did not conceive of the dictatorial *régime* as composed solely of Conservatives ; they would have consented to share power, and even to abandon Monarchism, if constitutional government, as established at Weimar, were abolished in favour of a *régime* approximating to the old autocracy. Such a *régime* might have functioned as well and perhaps better than the successive Republican Cabinets, but the time had passed for it. Between Republicanism and autocracy, between democracy and reaction, there could be no compromise.

On January 10, 1920, the treaty of Versailles had come into force, and for two months it was a melancholy tale of evacuation. The Rhine was entirely in enemy hands. Flensburg, Danzig, Memel, the Corridor, Upper Silesia, the Saar saw the last of the German flag. There were moving manifestations and Allied representatives were insulted so that the Government had to issue a special warning against " Hurra patriotism ". In the same month, the Independent Socialists staged a huge street demonstration, which ended in a riot, against the Government's Bill establishing Works' Councils. Government troops fired on the crowd and caused one hundred and forty-seven casualties. The Independents called a general strike, but the response was so poor that it was abandoned. Yet it confirmed the bourgeois in their fears. The surrender of the railways to Reich control was made the occasion for intemperate speeches on the need for a unitary State and alarmed South Germany ; the wide taxation schemes of Erzberger threw the comfortable citizens into a panic and alienated both finance and industry. On January 19 a reactionary shot at and wounded the Finance Minister. On March 9 the Nationalists demanded a dissolution and the motion was defeated in the Assembly only by sixty votes.

To the conspirators of the Right it may have appeared that the popularity of the Government was melting away, and that a bold stroke might easily succeed. They knew that the Nationalists and People's Party, despite their bitter hostility to the Government, would not be implicated in counter-revolution officially, but they had reason to believe that neither would raise a finger to resist, and so a *coup d'état* was decided. The moving spirit of the little group was Ludendorff, but it was agreed that he should take no public part in the plot in the meantime. The leadership fell to an obscure Prussian official called Kapp—a hireling of the militarist opposition to Beth-mann-Hollweg—and under him to Jagow, the notorious Wilhelmian chief of police in Berlin. Associated with them as military experts were Col. Bauer, once Ludendorff's Chief of Staff, and the Commander-in-Chief of Berlin, Lüttwitz, two able soldiers who were supposed to have the army devoted to them. Their supporters were recruited mainly from disbanded officers and professional men whom the fall in the currency was hitting particularly hard and many of whom were already organized in Anti-Republican societies. The plan adopted was perfectly simple. Outside Berlin lay two strong bodies of troops composed of the troops nominally employed until lately in the Baltic provinces in defending the Baltic States against Russia and supporting the Russian Monarchists in their feeble efforts to take Petrograd. They were a fine type of mercenary, and were at the moment in a fury of passion at the decision for their disbandment forced by the Allied Commission of Control on the Government, who found them useful as police troops. The whole of the army was honeycombed with anti-Government propaganda and no resistance was anticipated.

On March 10, Lüttwitz presented himself before President Ebert with what he alleged were the demands of the army. Why he did so is a mystery. It may have been that he felt that the first demand—for a general election—were it granted, would give the Right a constitutional victory. The second demand for a presidential election by plebiscite was not in itself unconstitutional ; the third, a Cabinet of experts, probably not obnoxious, but the fourth—the cessation of the disbandment of troops which was the real arm of the military conspirators —was not in the power of the Government to grant, and a Right Government, which did grant it, would at once have been involved in a conflict with the Allies. There is no evidence that the conspirators wanted that ; the mere warning of the Allied High Commissioners that a movement to overthrow the Republic would meet with Allied resistance showed plainly what consequences such a conflict would have If Lüttwitz hoped to terrify the Government into resignation he failed, for he encountered his chief, Noske, who told him that if he used force the Government would meet it with all the force it could command. All Lüttwitz accomplished was to convince the Government, already well-warned but incredulous, that something serious was being planned and to receive an unwelcome intimation of its intention to resist. The resistance indeed began at once, for, on the 11th, Noske dismissed Lüttwitz.

He had ascertained that the army as a whole would not support a *coup d'état*, but equally that it would not proceed to deal firmly with the conspirators. An attempt indeed to arrest the leaders failed owing to the obstruction of the military and police officials. The result was that the conspirators had to act long before they were really ready. They made the same mistake as the Bolshevik leader ; they misinterpreted the spirit of the country. They expected that, once the banner of revolt was raised, the nation would rally to it and carry the revolt through to a victorious issue, while all the nation was prepared to do, was to accept the rebels if and when they were successful. When it came to action, they found themselves a small minority. On March 12, the corps outside Berlin prepared to march on the capital. The troops in Berlin were called out, but it was clear that they would not resist the invaders by force and, after convincing themselves that the defence of the capital was impossible, the Cabinet fled to Dresden leaving one of their members, Schiffer, in charge of Berlin. The garrison evacuated Berlin.

It was not a heroic action, but it was probably wise. After the events of the spring the Government did not dare arm the population of Berlin, which was ready and even eager to meet the reactionaries, but which might quite conceivably have refused to be disarmed and been supported in its refusal by a considerable body of the Socialists. Early on the 13th the first brigade of the counter-revolutionary force marched into Berlin unopposed, and the leaders found the Government and President fled. There was no chance of a compromise. The Government refused to enter into negotiations ; the politicians of the Right held aloof and Kapp had to nominate himself Chancellor.

The Kapp Cabinet dissolved the Assembly, but its President, Fehrenbach, summoned it to meet at Stuttgart, where it was joined by the Government. Not a single leader of note came in to the Kappist camp and the Lands simply ignored the rising altogether. Nowhere did it obtain popular support and it did and could do nothing to obtain it. Its fiat did not run beyond the quarters held by its troops, and when the trade unions called a general strike the Kappists were as much cut off as if they were formally besieged. A strong leader might have turned the situation to his advantage because the general strike created again a revolutionary situation and produced disorder of which the Spartacists were quick to take advantage. But there was no leader and, when Kapp, within two days, sought to come to terms with the Government, the game was up. Despite the proud words of the terms he offered, his ultimatum was really a surrender. The Government treated it as such and demanded unconditional surrender and Kapp, confronted by a Berlin seething with hostility, lost his nerve and fled. It remained only to round up the rest of the conspirators, who surrendered unconditionally, and General von Seeckt, ablest and coldest of the Prussian officers, took over command of the army and, with a peremptoriness that betrays his disgust at men with whose aims he was not out of sympathy, ordered the rebel army to retire to its camps. As it left Berlin it fired into a demonstrating crowd of youths, killing many of them. That was the only time during the rebellion that the Kappist corps were in action.

Conspiracy and conspirators alike simply faded away and the strike was at once called off. The decision to call it, accepted by the union leaders, had been Noske's, that man of stern decisions, but the leaders had never liked it. Yet it was easier to call than to call off, for Bolshevik agitators had been busy during its short existence. The unions therefore endeavoured to get something definite from the Government on nationalization and on wages before resuming work. Their demands were accepted by the Government, but it was a mere case of rhetoric on either side and the strike in Berlin died out. Minor disturbances caused by the Communist leaders were quelled with unnecessary brutality by the troops, whose attitude effectually prevented the bringing to justice of the minor military members of Kapp's conspiracy.

Outside Berlin, as has been said, little notice was taken of the coup, but in the all-important Ruhr district, where conditions were very bad, the Bolshevik agitator had had an easy task. The news of the Kapp coup was the signal for a formal rising. Essen was made the head-quarters of the rebels ; quantities of arms of every kind were distributed to a hastily enrolled Red Guard and a sort of administration set up. The moment the Kapp coup was liquidated, Government troops moved hastily west. Almost a regular campaign followed, but the Red Guards were hopelessly outmatched and, although they fought more than once with splendid courage, it was massacre rather than war. The middle of April saw the revolt crushed completely, but, while the Kapp leaders flaunted their crime of rebellion in the faces of the Berliners or enjoyed the admiration of Munich society, the gaols of the Ruhr were crammed with luckless workers whose crime was a lesser one and who were punished with a savage vindictiveness that showed the real extent by which the old *régime* of repression and class distinction had returned.

The Government realized the position perfectly clearly, and the moment the Kapp rising was at an end had striven to ingratiate itself with the general mass of the nation by yielding to the demands made on it before the rising took place.   The Cabinet was reformed, Hermann Müller taking his comrade Bauer's place as Chancellor and Noske being sacrificed to the Socialist protests against the brutality of the " Noske guards ". The Assembly was dissolved and elections for the first Republican Reichstag ordered for June 6.   The members of the Müller Government were not altogether ingenuous in their sudden yielding to the desire for an election.   They were well aware of their unpopularity and the dissension even in the parties nominally supporting them, but the swift liquidation of the Kappist revolution seemed a useful election cry.   Unfortunately the nation was not interested in the Kapp adventure. It was interested in the peace treaty and the Red menace ; the Right were as hostile as ever and the Left greatly shocked by the difference in the treatment meted out to officers and workers alike guilty of active treason to the Constitution.   Whatever hopes the Government parties may have cherished were speedily blasted when the full force of the national indignation fell upon them.   Even the Centrum suffered—through dissensions—and were reduced to sixty-eight seats from eighty-nine.   The Majority Socialists fell from one hundred and sixty-three to one hundred and twelve, while the Independents rose from twenty-two to eighty-one.   The Democrats fell from seventy-four to forty-five, the People's Party rose from twenty-two to sixty-two and the Nationalists from forty-two to sixty-six.   The verdict was quite plain.   All the blame of the events of the past months fell on the parties which had made the revolution and signed the peace treaty.   The losses of the Majority Socialists were the judgment of the workers on the failure to realize Socialism and the acquiescence in repressive measures against the workers.   The defeat of the Democrats was due to the revival of the Right and the reaction from the revolution, while every vote for the two Right parties was a vote against the treaty.   The Government parties no longer had a working majority.

At first sight, the result showed a victory for extremism and the various types of extremism and their national and international backers were jubilant, but in fact it was far more a defeat for the Government than a victory for anybody. The nation was simply wreaking its ill nature on the parties in power, not recording a vote of confidence in their enemies. These enemies had showed neither resolution nor ability, very largely because, knowing only vaguely what they wanted, they had no definite programme. On the Left, the Independents were already splitting into two parties, and the extremist wing knew its own impotence in face of the hostility of all the rest of the nation and the military strength of the Government. Their programme was mainly rhetorical and, as they had no possible chance of governing save as the result of a successful revolution, could hardly be taken seriously. On the Right, the hostility against the Government was negative rather than positive. Like the Left, the Right was remarkably vague about what it wanted. The Simon pure Monarchists were a small minority and were by no means agreed on the nature of the monarchy to be restored ; the rest started from the basis that they should have far more power than they had and desired " a restoration of the old *régime* ", which may be interpreted simply as restoring the old Junker officer and official class to its former position of class prestige. How that was to be attained they did not explain : even Kapp had been vague and hesitating in his proclamations On neither side was there active work for a violent overthrow of the Weimar *régime*. The mass of the workers had let the Ruhr Communists fight alone ; the mass of the Right let Kapp fail ridiculously in Berlin. The *régime* survived literally because its adversaries shrank from assuming the responsibility of overthrowing it. Apart from the handful of thorough extremists who believed in bombs, murder and armed rebellion, there was no active sedition with a movement towards realization of a clearly defined aim. The difficulty of presenting a clear-cut programme which would be attractive to the nation is obvious, but greater difficulties have been overcome by resolute men, and it is impossible to escape the feeling that, in the hesitations that prevented the success of rebellion against the *régime*, there was a bigger element of patriotism than the partisan chronicler is willing to admit. The German never suffered the denationalizing process that made Russia for so long a battlefield. The few traitors to Germanism, which the years of trouble revealed, were only ordinary hirelings ; they neither headed a party nor upheld an ideal.

After so dramatic a vote of no-confidence, the Müller Govern-

ment resigned and, consequent on difficult negotiations, the
Centrist politician, Fehrenbach, formed a new coalition of
Centrists, Democrats and Populists. It had no majority and
was a compromise ministry which could initiate no controversial legislation. Formed from the definitely Republican
Democrats, the Centrists, who varied from violent Republicanism to violent Monarchism, and the Populists, then avowedly
" Monarchist " (with careful avoidance of too clear a definition
of the word), the Cabinet depended on playing off the Socialists
against the Nationalists. By securing the vote of either, it
could defeat the other and only a radical defection of its own
followers or what was then thought an unnatural alliance of
Right and Left would defeat it. But there was no real desire
to make things too difficult for it. The Right had given host-
ages to the Government through the presence in it of the
Populists : the union of Independents and Majority Socialists
was still in the future, and the extremists could busy themselves
with murder and conspiracy, but the bulk of the nation had no
wish for change unless it was proved to it that only by change
could any alleviation of its lot be secured. A dead weight of
indifference had ruined Kapp and the lesson had not been lost
on the enemies of the Weimar Constitution.

But, to the Cabinet, the position may well have seemed desperate. Germany was still in the dark regarding what reparations she must pay. She had lost land of inestimable worth ;
she had already made big deliveries of material ; she was ready,
though unwilling, to make the heroic effort necessary for restoration, but no effort was possible until she knew what her
enemies required of her. Meantime the economic system was
going to wreck and the steady fall in the mark was confronting
whole sections of the nation with ruin. The first essential towards facing the gloomy future was to know the facts, even
the worst of them, and it was just these facts that could not be
ascertained.

Characteristically enough, the Allies did not know the facts
themselves ; equally characteristically neither collectively nor
individually had they any clear policy, except the noisy proclamations of French Chauvinists supported by irresponsible
elements in Britain, who simply wanted Germany to break up.
These knew well that it is impossible to keep a great nation
permanently in subjection, but, with their fine sense of the
realities of history, they knew that such a nation can cease to
be a great nation by civil war, starvation and disruption.
Their policy was to do nothing to prevent these three agents

of destruction doing their work. The official Allied policy had been elaborated in a series of conferences and was communicated in principle to the Germans in July at Spa—the first occasion since the treaty that the Allied Governments had condescended to speak in public with German ministers. The speech was, it is true, one-sided and the method of it a fresh humiliation, but it was a beginning of the admission that the Allied statesmen needed German co-operation if they were to achieve any positive result, and the need for achieving some sort of positive result was being rapidly brought home to them by their respective electorates. Three months later, the Brussels conference of experts met to put into concrete form the principles communicated at Spa. It was prevented by the politicians from doing all it might have done, but it performed two valuable tasks, it supplied adequate data on the European financial situation and made no bones about its seriousness and it indicated methods to meet it. Above all, it established beyond dispute by any reasonable being the impossibility of restoring Europe when the key State of Europe was held to be merely an object of policy. That was a great step forward, but the Allies did not take immediate advantage of it. The story of the reparations problem in the latter half of 1920 is an unpleasing record of politics, where intrigue usurps the place accountancy should have filled.

In fairness it must be said that Germany did not really materially help towards a solution. Her Right parties, including even supporters of the Government, openly professed to be conducting a campaign of resistance to the treaty ; the Government itself, in response to its masters, was sullenly unresponsive and its experts consumed much paper and eloquence in demonstrating that, whatever Germany was asked to pay, she could not pay it. The problem was still being almost entirely envisaged nationally by the statesmen and, till some change came in that attitude, the atmospheric deadlock could not possibly be broken.

Eventually, however, the Allies did get together a series of demands. Vitiated though they were by being drawn up far more to suit French politics than European economics they did at least provide a basis and they did condescend to concrete figures. But, in addition to fixing the total amount of reparations at the colossal sum of £11,300,000,000—a figure quite meaningless to all but the most expert of experts—and suggesting a plan for its payment, the Allied terms included a whole series of demands for the accomplishment of German disarm-

ament. Politically, these were the important things. The
German army was to be reduced at once to 100,000 men : the
civic guards and the various police and military forces, established because of the alleged danger from the Left, were to be
at once disbanded ; the dismantling of the fortresses and the
completion of the surrender of material, and the reduction of
armament plant were to be accomplished with the least possible
delay. The demands were formulated as an ultimatum : if
there was any failure further German territory would be occupied. The authorship of the ultimatum is written all over it
and, in proof thereof, there is not lacking that touch of humour
with which the Allies rarely failed to enliven the dullest of their
productions—as a final punishment for non-fulfilment, Germany was to be permanently excluded from the League of
Nations !

The terms were announced at the end of January 1921, and
German representatives were summoned to receive them at
London on March 1, the ultimatory tone of the communication
being softened slightly by describing the demands as a basis for
discussion. This it was that was seized upon by the Fehrenbach
Cabinet in accepting the summons, but all that Germany saw
was the ultimatum. The indignation was universal, but it was
differently expressed. The Left had no reason to complain of
the demand for the dissolution of the irregular police forces,
although they saw that it would apply equally to Red guards,
but they resented the manner of it. The Right relied entirely
on these forces to protect themselves against a Red rising,
for there were ominous signs that the patient docility of the
German worker, wage-earner or salaried employee, was wearing
very thin under the starvation *régime* forced on him by the
economic collapse, and still more they regarded them as indis-
pensable to their hopes of transforming the *régime* into a Right
oligarchy. The army had its own particular indignation.
The curious thing is that it was at that time perhaps the most
efficient military force in Europe and the fears of the French
Chauvinists were not unjustified. Had a united nation risen
behind it in a wild revulsion of national anger, it could, in the
then state of Europe, have presented a very formidable problem to the French. But the conditions for such a rising were
absent. The army was under severe discipline ; under its
new chief, it would only move on orders, and the statesmen had
no intention of pushing matters so far. But it had developed a
strong *esprit de corps* aided by the economic advantages of service and a move to reduce it was certain to arouse strong oppo-

sition. The opposition existed outside the army not merely
because of national prestige but because of the widespread
conviction that, in 1920, the Russians would walk through
Poland—they nearly did—and enter Germany. Whether they
came as allies or as enemies the need for a strong army was
obvious. The same consideration applied to the irregular
forces, but here local interests also were involved. Apart from
the formations of old regulars, who had resisted disbandment
and whose presence was considered necessary by the authorities, all the States and most of the cities had forces of their
own either directly under local authority or loosely controlled
by the Reich. Their existence was at once a reply to the
defederalization of the army and a guarantee of public order.
Both considerations applied with special force to Bavaria,
which resented the disappearance of the old Bavarian army and
lived still in the shadow of its Communist revolution. The
armed forces of all kinds in Bavaria were estimated at about
400,000, of which a considerable part was controlled by private
organizations. They were well armed and enjoyed public
support, so that the problem of suppressing them was no light
one. There were French intriguers at Munich and the fear
that Bavaria would proclaim her independence as a reply to
force was clearly visible among the statesmen at Berlin.

All these considerations impressed the Government. The
German delegation went to London with the feeling that it was
impossible to admit dictation and they should count on the
fact the Allied demands were only a basis of discussion. In the
circumstances, agreement was impossible. With considerable
skill and force, the Germans made the retention of Upper
Silesia—about to suffer a plebiscite—a *sine quâ non* of fulfilment. It was good propaganda, but it took no account of the
real situation. The condition was brushed aside and, after
much futile discussion, the Allied demands were formally presented as an ultimatum, while, to prove how much in earnest
the Allies were, the French forces, to the great glee of the French
militarists, marched into Düsseldorf, Ruhrort and Duisburg—
a step of dubious legality. The anger in Germany was intense
and, to complicate the situation, the Communists engineered
a serious rising at Halle. It was defeated by the refusal of the
workers to support it, but its initial success and the notorious
fact that it was controlled and financed by Russian Bolsheviks,
lent colour to all the tales of the Red menace.

To the ultimatum, the Government returned neither yea nor
nay till Allied patience was exhausted. A final demand—

which incidentally reduced the reparations demanded to
£6,600,000,000—was put forward for unconditional acceptance
by May 12 and, in the event of such refusal, the French troops
would, it was stated, at once occupy the Ruhr. The debates
in Berlin were anguished and protracted. The opponents of
surrender pointed out, on the one hand, that obstructive pro-
crastination had secured a considerable reduction already and,
on the other, that, as it was impossible to pay the amount
asked, surrender would not avoid the Ruhr occupation. Those
in favour of acceptance urged the paramount necessity to save
the Ruhr now that Upper Silesia was in jeopardy and that
surrender would render the Allies more reasonable. Both
agreed almost unanimously that Germany was ruined in any
case, but, while there was only a moral value in no surrender,
there was a glimmer of hope of practical results from surrender.
The Populists stuck to their guns for no surrender and, on May 4,
the Cabinet resigned. Seven days later Wirth, at the head
of a Cabinet of Majority Socialists, Democrats and Centrists,
accepted the ultimatum. Once again the Weimar coalition
had been a coalition of surrender, and the rift between Right
and Centre was widened. No fraction of the Right had any
responsibility in the decision, and that circumstance was to
have many consequences in the new period begun by the
Wirth ministry. All that had been achieved was that the
project of definite resistance had been abandoned. The
struggle against the Allies was to be continued no less
fiercely, but by less obvious means, and, in the meantime, the
advance of the French was prevented.

CHAPTER V

FROM RESISTANCE TO FULFILMENT

Reparations and security—the Rathenau-Loucheur agreement—the Government and armed resistance—the assassination of Erzberger—the Genoa Conference—the Russo-German alliance—the murder of Rathenau—the Cuno Government—the occupation of the Ruhr—inflation and the collapse of the mark—Stresemann—disorders in Bavaria and Saxony—Monarchism and Fascism in Bavaria—combating Separatism—political consequences of stabilization of the mark—reshuffling of parties—the Dawes Plan and the elections—towards political stability—the nomination of Hindenburg as President.

ALTHOUGH the Wirth Cabinet had accepted the Allied ultimatum and had therefore taken office with a nominal programme of fulfilment, the day of resistance was not yet over. The whole reparations problem was clouded over with politics, and, on neither side, was it faced in the proper spirit. Reparations bulked less largely in French eyes than did security—they even appeared to be part of the security problem ; in German eyes they appeared as economic, arising from political vindictiveness—a prolongation of the war to be met in the war spirit. There was an element of reality in both views which rendered them difficult to refute, but the truth had long been evident to practical men on both sides, that, as long they prevailed, the reparations problem was incapable of solution. Whether a solution was desirable in the interests of Europe, was a question that had not occurred to anyone other than the disinterested spectator and it has not yet been faced properly, although the evils of the existence of reparations are apparent in abundance. But it was becoming evident that others than politicians were taking the matter in hand. The German industrialists had long since recognized that the payment of reparations could only be made by increase of trade, and that that increase could only be obtained at the expense of other States. They had never lost their grip on trade and, with the fall in the stock of Socialism, they did not anticipate any radical interference with the reorganization of industry which, with most skilful use of

73

apparently adverse circumstances, they were busily engaged in effecting.

The inclusion in the Wirth Cabinet of Walther Rathenau, the head of the great electrical trust, as Minister of Reconstruction, was significant of a change of attitude. His broad views of economic principle, his grasp of detail and the hardiness of his conceptions made him the ideal negotiator on the reparations question and, in Louis Loucheur on the French side, he found a counterpart. Almost at once, they reached an agreement as to deliveries in kind while, by superhuman efforts and at the cost of a heavy fall in the exchange, Wirth and the Treasury officials raised enough foreign currency to pay in time the first instalment of £7,500,000 of the £50,000,000 demanded in the ultimatum. Had the Cabinet been given a fair deal, the reparations moneys might have been found without trouble, for in spite of the loss of national morale, German industry had preserved its position as far as the international market was concerned, but, once again, politics supervened.

The old cleavage of parties became intensified, especially as only a small defection from the ranks of Wirth's dispirited majority would mean the fall of the Cabinet. That majority was neither homogeneous nor friendly. The conditions of the Socialists that the necessary additional burdens should be laid on capital irritated the right wings of the Democrats and the Centrists and, as the abstention of either in face of the united hostility of the Right meant a heavy defeat in Parliament, it was difficult to avoid a patchwork policy of compromise. From the Right, no aid could be expected. They had wrecked the Fehrenbach Cabinet deliberately. The Populists had left that ministry because of their refusal to accept the London ultimatum without the guarantee of the return of the whole of Upper Silesia. Their attitude was justified, they believed, by the results of the plebiscite which had shown a gratifyingly large majority for Germany. The avowed intention of the Allies to partition the plebiscite area was easily interpreted as a dishonourable evasion of the result, and the anger aroused by the delay in announcing the Allied decision was so great that the Cabinet was forced to countenance the raising of a local force for the defence of German interests—a step which ruined at once any hopes of amicable agreement with France.

That country, true to her secular policy, was far more concerned with disarmament than reparations and, in the state of German disarmament, some of her statesmen saw the means of promoting that disruption of Germany which had been pre-

DR. WIRTH (on left)

vented by what was held to be the premature granting of the armistice. The separatist tendencies of Bavaria were notorious. The South German State was an armed camp. In addition to a formidable National Guard, there were numerous other organizations for military training and (what was more deadly) secret societies in morality and mentality far more akin to the worst traditions of mediaevalism than to those of the twentieth century. The leaders of the Kapp revolt were among the most active of the chiefs of the movement dominated by the military element, and it was illumined by the names of Ludendorff and Hitler. In vain the Reich authorities sought to have an end put to the plain violation of the disarmament clauses. They shrank from coercion, even if the alternative to coercion were the seizure by the Allies of more German territory. Coercion would probably not have been sabotaged by the Right politicians whose Prussian majority disliked the Bavarians, nor by the Reichswehr who resented the anti-Prussianism of the Bavarian societies, but it was not certain that it would not be so sabotaged. The sight of Germans coercing a German State—especially when it was not ruled by Communists, would have shocked all but those who considered, and rightly, the reactionary gangs of the South every whit as bad as the international ruffians who had ruled Munich under the Red flag. The Allied pressure at Berlin was severe, for apparently the French hoped to see civil war result from coercion. These hopes might have materialized since the bombastic Herr von Kahr, the Bavarian Prime Minister, was completely in the power of the societies and obstinately and volubly stuck to his guns. But wiser counsels prevailed and the Allies suddenly addressed themselves directly to Munich, whereupon the resistance collapsed.

The only result was that numbers of the disbanded guards were enrolled into one or other of the illegal organizations, all the more illegal in that official resistance to the Allied demands and Allied supervision of the execution of the disarmament clauses had ceased. The situation favoured a grave development of ruffianism, and Bavaria, always famous for manifestations of sadistic ill-temper, smirched her name by a series of cowardly assassinations of individuals, mostly humble, who were suspected of giving information, as it was their duty to do, about concealed arms and munitions. The Government made not the slightest effort really to check the murder campaign, although it raged with impressive severity against all suspected of designs against reaction, and, with apparent sincerity, believed Bavaria a land of order and discipline in contrast to the socialistic anarchy in Prussia. Berlin did indeed present in these days the picture of a great city in dissolution, of lust, debauchery and waste in which the foreign element was the leading spirit, but it was at least free from political murder.

It was the sympathy of the German reactionaries generally that had let the murder gangs practise their trade so long with impunity. For all practical purposes Bavaria was lost to the Republic and the Reich Government let her alone, with the inevitable result that, pent up in their prison-house of crime and sedition, the gangs determined to carry the war into Germany and, by means of faithful Bavaria, purge the Fatherland of the infidel. In August 1921 two selected assassins shot Erzberger dead in the Black Forest. The choice of victim was significant : of all the bourgeois politicians, Erzberger had done most to make the Republic inevitable and he it was who had signed the armistice which ended the German army as pre-war Europe knew it. There were many politicians, not all of them on the Right, who cordially hated the murdered statesman ; there were even many who applauded the deed in secret, but the public explosion of wrath was unmistakable. The Socialists, already savage at the murder of their adherents in Bavaria, had reason on their side when they cried " The Republic is in danger " and, to the amazement of the heads of the reaction in Bavaria, who represented themselves to themselves as liberators, Germany refused liberation in no uncertain terms. The Cabinet, despite the Right, was able to suspend the constitutional guarantees by an emergency law for the protection of the Republic, and announced its intention of having the emergency law carried into force at Munich itself and by force if necessary. The struggle was avoided by the announcement of the partition of Upper Silesia, an event that no student of Allied policy could have failed to foresee. It caused a fierce outburst of wrath in Germany, not from the Right alone, and the passions thus stirred up made it impossible for the Cabinet to take drastic action against Bavaria. It also caused, what was much more serious, a disastrous fall in German credit and the mark in its descent began to come in sight of astronomical figures at a perilous rate. The Wirth Cabinet resigned, but no one would step into the gap, and Wirth accepted office, again relying on the same coalition. But his prestige had suffered a severe blow and the mark continued its headlong course. Bankruptcy and chaos faced the nation—a much more serious thing than a certain default in reparation payments—and the difficulties of the Government became so great that it was clearly evident to practical men that only international action could save the situation. Even the German industrialists who had skilfully used the earlier fall in the mark to improve their position, were thoroughly scared and economists alarmed the world with prophecies of a general crash. The Allies summoned the nations to Cannes for a preliminary conference to a great economic congress, world-wide in its representation and its scope—Mr. Lloyd George's last attempt to bring on the delayed millennium.

The Cannes Conference was, however, but a preliminary fiasco to the greater fiasco at Genoa. The Germans expected to have a full discussion of the financial situation and, in view of Budget and exchange difficulties, to obtain a moratorium and even a reduction in payments. Their resistance to the Allied demands had stiffened, for they felt that the Allies must see that the financial chaos which Germany was fast approaching might well render all hopes of reparations illusory. But the times were not yet ripe for co-operation. The financial plight of Germany was roundly denounced in France as calculated evasion ; and the admission of the German delegates to equality in the endeavour to hammer out a solution was impossible alike for the French and the Germans, each holding that victory was to him who would hold out longer. Briand, with that sense of reality which gives importance to his chequered career, saw the reparations problem in its proper light as only a phase of the Franco-German problem and, for the first time, raised the question of security by the suggestion of a guarantee pact between the two States. The conclusion of such a pact would clearly have placed the discussion of less vital problems on a different basis, but the idea was premature. French opinion took alarm ; the President, M. Millerand, intervened, the Government fell, and Poincaré replaced Briand. The arrival of Poincaré meant that not an iota of the letter of the treaty would be surrendered and that the relations between France and Germany would be placed once more on a war footing. Retrogression, not progression, was to be the order of the day and Briand had to wait long for his day to return.

The immediate effect of the change of Cabinet in Paris was to sabotage the Genoa Conference. Although it was virtually a world conference and was attended by Russia, and although it offered a chance for discovering a plan for the recovery of Europe, the Poincaré Government showed itself hostile from the first, for it had been placed in power not to concern itself

with Europe, but to keep Germany in subjugation. Poincaré
made no secret of his intentions, but it was the fashion in 1922
to believe anything but the facts and the usual rhetoric was
poured out in streams. It did not deceive Germany. There
was no question of a Franco-German pact ; there was no question of a French compromise or even of a reasonable French
attitude, and the German delegates concluded, not without
reason, that their hands were free. They used the conference
to conclude a treaty with Russia. The treaty had been long
under discussion. It was fundamentally commercial, an
attempt on Germany's part to stake out an impregnable position in the Russian market of which great things were generally
expected in the near future, and was political only in so far as
it was an attempt to forestall other Powers as Russia's intermediary with the West.

The failure of the treaty was due to miscalculations on the
possibilities of the Russian situation ; its intention was perfectly sound. It had even a useful moral effect in convincing
Germany that, even under an unstable Republican Government, it was possible for her to pursue an independent policy.
Looked at in that light, it seemed evidence of Germany's return
to independence again, and, in view of the clear indications
that, so far as Germany was concerned, the Genoa Conference
was to be a failure, its justification both commercially and
politically was easy. But, in view of the strained relations
between Germany and the Allies and between the Allied
Powers, it was a diplomatic *faux-pas*. It was too sharp a
reminder to old competitors, who were casting covetous eyes
on Russia, that their most dangerous rival was as formidable
as ever—hence the naïve, but quite genuine, surprise displayed
by the Allied delegations at Genoa when the signature was
announced—and it was tactless, just when their bitterest enemy
had become Premier of France, for the Germans to assert so
dramatically their right to the status of a Great Power and to
summon up the bogey of a Russo-German alliance. With
Germany disarmed and helpless, with every point of military
importance heavily garrisoned, the French were still more nervous about the Rhine than ever. The mere thought that the
Russian hordes might appear on that river, not as allies but as
enemies, sent the militarists into a panic and supplied that
shrewd Lorrainer M. Poincaré, who never got into a panic, with
a basis for a policy lasting through two years that was as dangerous to Europe almost as the war.

From the internal point of view, the treaty was regarded

with far more favour by the Right than by the Left, which had a shrewder sense of the European situation than its opponents and it was regarded and claimed as a Nationalist triumph. That in itself was sufficient to arouse Allied distrust and, as it was impossible for the Wirth Cabinet to dissociate itself from the Nationalist jubilation, it was impossible for it to reach ground for equal negotiation with the Allies. This was the period of Nationalist ascendancy and of the strengthening of extremist elements whose intemperate language again and again wrecked, or gave the Poincarists the chance to wreck, every attempt on the part of sane people to bring the German problem outside the narrow sphere of Nationalist politics. It equally prevented successive Foreign Ministers from using the differences, at one time amounting to rupture, between the Allies to restore Germany to her old position. Whenever the attempt was made, the sole result was to close the Allied ranks and, in the end, the compromise, which was to solve everything sufficiently to let Europe resume normal life, was brought about by internal crises in the Allied countries and virtually forced on Germany.

Meantime the reaction was never more confident. Genoa had failed and the alliance with Russia seemed to assure Germany, if chaos came, of winning something from it. It therefore lifted not a finger to help the Cabinet, and its gangsters proceeded merrily with the murder campaign as though the exceptional law had never been passed, and the vendetta was declared against all supporters of the Government. Decree of assassination was even issued against Seeckt ; an attempt on Scheidemann's life miscarried and, in June, Rathenau was shot dead near Grünewald by three ex-naval officers. Of the three assailants one was killed resisting capture, the second committed suicide, and the third was caught and heavily sentenced. His statements led to the unravelling of so many threads of conspiracy that the investigation was allowed to fizzle out. Among the public, however, the reaction was similar to that after the Erzberger murder. There were grandiose demonstrations on the part of the Republicans which could convince the observer that the Republicans were still in a large majority, but gave no indication that they were really going to set their heels on the head of the snake of murderous sedition. Their youthful elements indeed formed an extremely numerous Republican society as a counterblast to the innumerable reactionary societies, while the Government made legal the exceptional decrees, stiffened them considerably and, by unearthing proof that the head-quarters of the murder gangs was in Bavaria, did something to create a less tender feeling in the rest of Germany towards the Munich reactionaries, but there was no general rally of the parties of law and order to its support.   It had failed all along the line.   It had humiliated itself and Germany before the Allies and gained nothing.   It had failed to rally a central *bloc* and had let the extremists on Left and Right organize and arm, had failed even to protect the life of its most distinguished member, and in November it resigned.   It is questionable if any other Cabinet could have done better, and it had certainly done one thing.   It had got foreign experts to examine the financial situation and the Keynes-Cassel report had placed the public in possession of accurate facts and of knowledge of the remedies that appealed to distinguished economists.   If the Allies were still unenlightened, the German nation, or what portion of it reads such reports, knew just where it was.

It was inevitable that the next Cabinet should be more reactionary than the last.   It was formed by Cuno, a Populist, from Populists, Centrists and Democrats, but it depended more on the Nationalists than the preceding coalition of the same parties had done.   It was expected to take a much stronger line than the Wirth Cabinet had taken, and it possessed more than its share of the blustering type of diplomat.   Its predecessor had already given as its opinion that Germany must default in her payments and consequently had asked for a short moratorium.   The Cuno Government wanted a moratorium of two years.   The question of the necessity for so long a moratorium is still hotly debated, but, if the Cuno Cabinet were bluffing, they mistook their man.   Poincaré, whose postwar policy is summed up in the panic phrase " Those Junkers will trick you yet ", was not disposed to budge an inch.   Legalist and Lorrainer, he stood on the strict letter of the Carthaginian peace.   No moratorium would be granted without preliminary guarantees to show to the French public.   So he demanded as the price of French complacency the occupation of the Ruhr as guarantee that, at the end of the moratorium, France's complacency would not be mocked.   He even secured the contemptuous rejection of a security pact made by Cuno, apparently in good faith, and in spite of the protests of Britain waited only till the first inevitable formal default late in December was signalled and set the French troops in motion in the first days of 1923.

Whatever the Ruhr invasion may have appeared to the legalist mind of the French Premier, it was in fact a renewal of the war and it was intended to be so. It was simply an assertion that negotiations had failed constantly, that France was not getting her dues and that force would now be used. He had carefully calculated the possibilities ; he considered that Germany could oppose no resistance to the French armies and, if she did, it would be quickly crushed and would afford opportunity for such amendment of the Versailles treaty as would give France, if not reparations, at least eternal security as far as the secular enemy was concerned, and so remedy " the blunder of Versailles ". Whatever happened, he saw great gains for France from the adoption of the strong-hand policy. But he reckoned entirely without the fact that four years had elapsed since the *débâcle* in October–November 1918, that, if the financial and industrial conditions were extremely bad, the national pride had recovered enough to be restored altogether at the cost of a painful shock. Nor did he remember that there are other ways of meeting force than by force or by surrender. The political situation being what it was, it was absolutely impossible for the Cuno Cabinet to surrender to the Ruhr invasion even if—which again is debatable—it could have paid what was demanded. Even its Nationalist supporters, however, realized that armed resistance meant final extinction, and the Cabinet had no difficulty in vetoing such resistance and securing Nationalist support to keep under control the Right extremists. It was the easier in that the news of the Ruhr invasion had caused a unanimous outburst of indignation in Germany. From Left to Right, there was a rally to the Cabinet's support, and Cuno announced amid applause a policy of passive resistance in the Ruhr. Unfortunately, the methods adopted did not meet with universal approval or a national coalition might have been formed, and so the Cuno Cabinet, with no secure majority, had to wrestle with the most difficult situation that had yet confronted a Republican Cabinet.

It is impossible here to follow out the peripatetics of the Ruhr struggle. It was virtually a test of endurance and the dice were heavily loaded against the Germans. The occupation inflicted a crippling blow on German industry, and to carry on the fight successfully meant expenditure which the German nation was not able to meet. The passive resistance, which was met by the French with brutality and oppression, could only be successful if the entire Ruhr population were fed and supported and every legal method used to hamper the enemy

in the work of breaking the resistance. By the occupation
an illegal state of things had been created which, sooner or
later, must call for the interference of other Powers in the
general interest, and it was a question of holding out till the
time for interference arrived or until France's obstinacy was
overcome. But the passive resistance implied two contra-
dictory policies : the need for increased activity and sound
finance to make the resistance economically possible, and the
sullen policy of " ca' canny " to make the French see that their
offensive was killing the goose with the hypothetical golden
eggs. It was in the months following the occupation that the
mark fell to really astronomical figures, and the perfectly incredible figure of 1,000,000,000,000,000,000,000,000,000 marks
became comprehensible to German accountants. Under cover
of inflation financial morality vanished and, while the capitalist
made easy money and profiteers disgusted the not easily disgusted Berlin crowd, the worker was reduced to a sweated
labourer and the black-coated class simply starved. As the
figures for the mark increased with dizzying rapidity, the Budget became a fantastic sort of monstrosity out of a fairy tale
told by a mazochist economist, and it became clear that, unless
drastic measures were taken, bankruptcy, once politically
toyed with, would become an economic inevitability. Another
national effort was wanted, but the whole national effort was
concentrated on the Ruhr struggle, and in any case was paralysed by the loss of that area. The situation for the French
was painful, but it was not so painful as that of the Germans
and, realizing the truth, the Poincaré Cabinet hardened its
heart and refused to let the Ruhr go save on terms of unconditional surrender.

Unconditional surrender, however, was not so easy. The
nation was behind resistance to the enemy, but it was not a
united nation. It was suffering differently according to its
different geography and class. Separatism raised its head in
the Rhineland as a solution of that area's difficulties ; Bavaria
pinned her faith on Monarchism and her reactionaries would
hear nothing of surrender, even of negotiated surrender. Cuno,
who realized, as did his Cabinet and the greater part of the
majority on which he relied, that only a miracle could save
Germany from surrender, sought, as a preliminary step, to make
the coalition broader by including the Socialists. Bavaria at
once and officially threatened secession. At the other end of
the social scale, the ever-increasing number of unemployed
began to show their ugly side, and in Saxony, in particular,

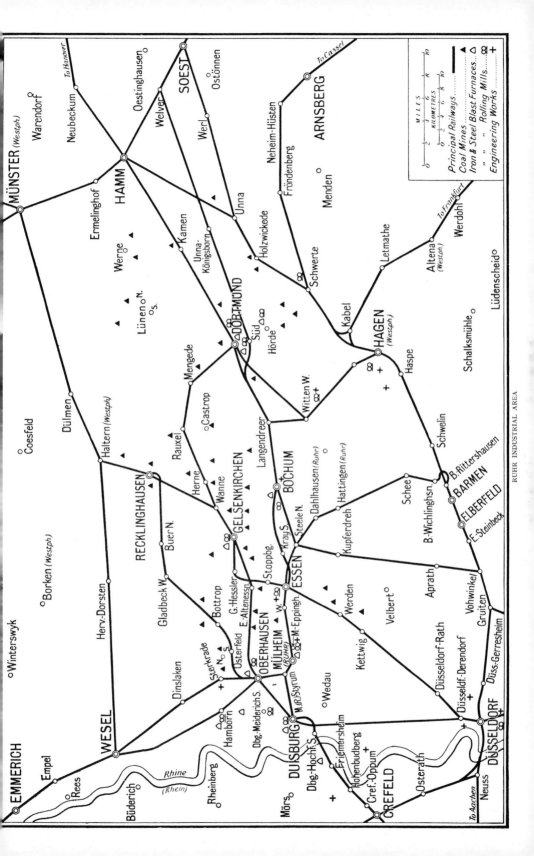

RUHR INDUSTRIAL AREA

the Bolshevik element seemed to be getting the upper hand. Even the Socialists grew restive.

Faced with the failure of his great bluff and unable to adopt the policy he saw to be correct, Cuno resigned in August 1923. He was succeeded by Gustav Stresemann, also a Populist. Whatever in his record may have made him suspect to the Allies, Stresemann at least had no illusions on what he and Germany had to do. He had somehow, and indeed on any terms, to get out of the Ruhr adventure, and he was very doubtful if the nation would let him. He secured the co-operation of the Socialists in a grand coalition which left outside only Communists and Nationalists and, after prolonged negotiations, called off the passive resistance, appealed to the loyalty of the army and the nation and declared the state of siege. Bavaria naturally refused to obey and acted as if she were an independent State, but the rest of Germany was placed practically under armed occupation by the Reichswehr, and Reichswehr generals exercised virtually dictatorial power. Saxony, which was predominantly Socialist, objected to purely military rule. Though the Communists failed to make effective their call for a general strike, mutual hatred of militarism, in spite of the fact that Socialist ministers had approved the extraordinary powers conferred upon the military leaders, brought Socialists and Communists together. The two parties formed a new Cabinet in Saxony which obstructed the military to the best of its ability. It was rumoured that it intended to proclaim a Bolshevik revolution and, taking the rumour as justifying action, the Stresemann Cabinet ordered the Saxon Cabinet to resign. Troops called in to maintain order fired on demonstrating crowds and caused some casualties. The revolutionary leaders hesitated and, ere they could recover themselves, the troops were in possession of Dresden and the Cabinet ministers forcibly ejected from the Diet, while a Government commissioner ruled Saxony with exceptional powers.

The whole procedure was of very doubtful legality, and it had clearly to be followed by equally drastic action against the plotters on the Right if the Government coalition were not to collapse. The Bavarian reactionary leaders, however, did not wait for the menace to materialize. They had resolved to overthrow the Government and believed they could count on the Government troops in their neighbourhood. The Seventh Division was Bavarian and it was now offered and took an oath of allegiance to the Bavarian Government, now virtually Kahr, who had been appointed commissioner extraordinary for the

Land of Bavaria by the Bavarian Government. The commander of the Seventh Division, Lossow, refused to take orders from Berlin and relations with the Central Government were broken off. Bavaria had virtually seceded from the Republic. The Monarchist plot had wide ramifications and nearly all the military figures of the old *régime* were mixed up in it, but the overthrow of the Republic was one thing ; the liberation of Germany under the ægis of Bavaria was something very different. The lack of sympathy with Bavarian patriotism was detected by the right wing of the Bavarian reactionaries led by Hitler. He had organized a movement modelled on Mussolini's and determined to parallel the march on Rome by a march on Berlin in which Ludendorff was to play the rôle of Mussolini. This movement, which had considerable strength in Bavaria, threatened to precipitate both civil war and foreign intervention instead of a peaceful *coup d'état* ; succeeding or failing, it ruined the hopes of the junta ruled by Kahr and Lossow. They tried now to secure Ludendorff, but the only result was to make Hitler realize that an essential preliminary to the march on Berlin was a march on Munich. He decided to act at once, and accompanied by a picked bodyguard, held up Kahr and Lossow at revolver-point and extracted from them a promise to join him. Hitler then proceeded to declare himself President of the Reich and, as such, entrusted Ludendorff with dictatorial powers. But Kahr and Lossow broke the promise forced from them and the Seventh Division declared against the conspirators. There was a short sharp collision and the Hitler rebellion was over. Its sole result was to split and discredit the Monarchist movement. The Central Government, which had moved troops to the Bavarian frontier as a precautionary measure, now gave Seeckt full power to restore order, but there was no need for action. The reactionaries had defeated themselves.

The mass of the nation was willing to see what the Stresemann Government would do and was disposed to give it a fair trial. Its severity to the Left was applauded and, if it had not shown the same severity to the far more dangerous Right, it could plead that the reactionaries had themselves rendered severity needless. They had miscalculated the willingness of the nation to tolerate reaction unless it was clearly synonymous with good government and did not see that their leaders in Munich were regarded only as Bavarian adventurers who had no pretensions to, and never could obtain, national support.

The liquidation of the Bavarian adventure was indeed easier than the surrender of the Ruhr which had ostensibly provoked it. The proclamation by Seeckt, under his exceptional powers, of the Communist and Hitlerite parties as illegal finished the revolutionaries on both wings.

Although the basic opinions of parties had been unchanged, the incidents had effected a welcome clearing of the air. The majority had decided against violent action and was prepared to support a Government which would violently prevent it. The prestige of the Government benefited, and especially that of its head, for it was universally agreed that the vigour of the action was due to Stresemann far more than to the miscellaneous team he led. Another reputation to be enhanced was Seeckt's. He had loyally pitted it against Ludendorff's and had won, and the national army was now as a whole above suspicion of vulgar plotting. The active enemies of the Weimar Republic were seen to be a minority ; the majority of the Anti-Republicans were rather opponents of radical Republicanism than of the Constitution, which after all could be interpreted or amended to bring back an approximation to the old *régime*. They were, however, a minority in the State alike as Anti-Republicans and as Conservatives and, for the moment except for the extreme elements, they were quite content with the Stresemann Cabinet. The strong Government they had asked for they had got and, if its action had fallen on the Right, it had rid the Conservative parties of a set of discreditable adventurers and dangerous particularists. For the net result of this final and successful attempt to cope with sedition and separatism was a striking affirmation of the German nation's will to unity and to constitutionalism.

The financial situation remained to be tackled, but, after the successes of the Government, the conditions for tackling it had altered for the better. Measures which the nation would not have accepted from the Wirth Cabinet became tolerable when presented by the Stresemann Cabinet, and Stresemann took full advantage of his temporary popularity. He knew well that it was only temporary—in 1923 he can hardly have expected three years of power—that he possessed the confidence of few outside his own party. He recognized also that the desperate situation of the Reich as well as the well-founded view of Socialists and Nationalists, that it is better to endure and seek to use the evils one knows than to risk enduring evils one does not know and may signally fail to use, kept him in office. Consequently he was able at once to adopt a policy that would, if successful, give immediate results and it was immediate results that were necessary.

The economic and financial results of the stabilization of the mark and the improvement in the budgetary position are dealt with elsewhere. It must suffice here to indicate the political results. For the measures adopted the Chancellor demanded and obtained special powers. Their necessity was generally admitted and the sole opposition to their granting came from the Left, but the Socialists were satisfied to accept guarantees safeguarding to the extent they believed the necessary minimum conditions and wages. But the application of the measures raised steady opposition and provoked several crises. Neither the opposition nor the crises were, however, formally political although they took political forms, and the Government was able to deal with them with sufficient success to push through the scheme for the financial rehabilitation of Germany which affected too many interests to be accepted willingly or even patiently. The scheme depended on the rapidity with which the stabilized mark ("Rentenmark") was put into circulation, and the Government held to its task until that was accomplished. November 15 saw the first issue of the new notes.

The establishment of the Rentenbank and the issue of the new paper marked the turning-point in the financial struggle. The way to restoration had been clearly shown and, while it was not a popular way, the majority trod it in lieu of a better, and the Allies showed belated appreciation of the situation by accepting the fact that no cash payments were possible and consenting to have the reparations problem examined once again by experts in light of the new financial situation. The decision was inevitable. Default was unavoidable, but the means to repair it had been set in motion. It was important to give these means a fair chance, and the repeated warnings of international finance on the world consequences of a complete German crash forced even the jingoes in the French Cabinet to talk no more of sanctions and little more of demands until the results of stabilization should be seen. The credit of the stabilization scheme has gone to, or has been claimed by, a variety of individuals, but the credit for putting it into operation—a much more difficult thing—rests entirely with the Cabinet. The support it received was so uncertain that its position was consistently unsafe, while the sole contribution of the Reichstag, not an unimportant one, had been the surrender of some of its rights in favour of the Government. Otherwise it had been conspicuous more for the meticulousness than the value of its criticism. But, despite this achievement, the Cabinet realized that in the process of saving Germany—for the political salvation, whatever one may say in criticism from the financial point of view, is undoubted—it had lost all its friends and could not count on a majority in the difficult days to come when once again the Allies and Germany would meet to debate Germany's willingness and power to pay. It had been reconstructed in the course of the struggle and had practically lost the Socialist support, and on November 22 the opposition came to a head. Both the Left and the Right tabled motions of no confidence and then combined with the Government parties to defeat the rival motion. That would not satisfy the Cabinet, which at once put a formal motion of confidence before the House. Only the Government parties voted for it ; all the non-Government parties voted against. The Cabinet at once resigned.

The crisis was perhaps less important than it looked. The next Cabinet could only carry on the policy of its predecessor, and although it was clear that the Reichstag no longer exactly represented the feeling of the nation a dissolution found little favour as a solution. Finally the same parties, with the important addition of the Bavarian Centrists—known as the Bavarian People's Party—who had voted against the vote of confidence, formed a Cabinet. Marx of the Centrum was Chancellor, and Stresemann went to the Foreign Office. The new Cabinet at once proceeded to demand from the Reichstag a new measure conferring on it further special powers which were to be used in consultation with a Reichstag committee of fifteen. The Reichstag, having wreaked its vengeance on the former Cabinet, was complacent towards its almost identical successor and granted the powers asked. It then adjourned and left the Cabinet to carry on the double task of continuing the salvation process and negotiating with the Allies.

Since the abandonment of passive resistance the relations between the Allies had worsened. While the French ministry made every possible difficulty to avoid the logical evacuation of the Ruhr, the London Cabinet had adopted as its formal reparations policy the American idea that the problem should be taken out of the hands of the politicians and put into those of economists. In the middle of 1923, it had formally offered it to its allies as worthy of general adoption ; it was naturally accepted by Germany which, however doubtful of the political, had no doubts whatever on the economic aspect, and the weight of world opinion was such that Poincaréist France could do nothing but accept with several reservations stated and a good many more unstated.   When the Dawes Committee met and began its work of investigation early in 1924 it was universally felt that a new era had begun.   All would of course depend on the extent to which the nations concerned accepted the report when it came.   But, as it chanced, the three nations chiefly concerned—France, Germany, and Britain—all underwent a general election before the real stage of negotiation had been reached.   Left Cabinets under Herriot and Macdonald replaced Poincaré and Baldwin, but, in Germany, the election went the other way.   In Germany, 1924 marks the greatest advance of extremism.

The reasons are not very plain, and the most influential appear to be economic rather than political.   There had been in the days of passive resistance a reshuffling of party loyalties. On the Left, the extremists had formed a proper Communist party directed from Moscow, and the remnant of the Independents had returned to the fold.   Socialists and Communists stood opposed.   The reduction in the combined Socialist vote was certain, for there were bitter critics, among the workers, of the official leaders, who had supported Cabinets which in every case discriminated against the worker and had forced him to make proportionately higher sacrifices than those demanded from any other class.   On the Right, the condition was the same.   The Anti-Republican-Conservative party had split for precisely similar reasons and, in the Racialists or Fascists, had a precisely similar opponent as the Socialists in the Communists.   At the same time, the Conservative element in the country had been reinforced much more than the Socialist. Strong Government of the conservative bourgeois type had been a success and conservatism was inclined to misinterpret the implication of that success.   It was not in any way a success either for Monarchism or reaction ; it was a success for strong government, and the first condition of strong government is constitutional peace.   Had the Right been now content to slough off its extremists, declare for ordered government within a Republican Constitution, there was for a moment the chance of a great party able to impose a conservative policy on the nation.   But there was no bitterer feud than between the clear-sighted economists of the People's Party and the die-hard Prussian landowners of the Nationalists.   The Nationalists put themselves out of the running as a great national party by their obstinate refusal to face the facts of the international situation and refusing to accept any responsibility for a foreign policy which could only be one of obtaining the easiest possible terms from the Allies. While to large sections of the community which would naturally have supported the Right, the Dawes Committee appeared the way of least ultimate sacrifice, it was assailed with unmeasured abuse from the Right and there were unwelcome signs that similar opposition was arising among the workers. The Cabinet, which knew that if the Dawes report, when it came, was accepted by the Allies, there was no chance of refusal by Germany, determined to test the feeling of the country and dissolved Parliament. Seeckt had laid down his exceptional powers in February and, although the existence of the Communists and the Fascists was still illegal, both appeared as contestants at the polls. Incidentally, although the ban on the parties enabled swift State action to be taken against them, it undoubtedly added to their importance and swelled their ranks.

While the campaign was in full swing, the Dawes Plan appeared. It was not so bad as the worst of the prophets had said ; it was perfectly clear that no rejection of it was possible and so the latter stages of the campaign were fought more or less on the report itself. It came too late, however, to cure the evil inherited from the troubles of the past twenty-four months, and the result of the elections only just failed to ruin the chances of international settlement. The Communists won sixty-two seats and the Socialists lost seventy-three, becoming one hundred strong. The Government parties all fell—the Centrists from sixty-eight to sixty-five, the People's Party from sixty-six to forty-four, the Democrats from thirty-nine to twenty-eight, the Bavarian People's Party from twenty to sixteen—a loss of just on 20 per cent. On the other hand, the Nationalists scored a really big victory. In spite of the fact that the Fascists captured thirty-two seats the Nationalists rose from sixty-seven to one hundred and six and were the strongest party in Parliament. The Cabinet resigned on May 26, twenty-two days after the elections, during which time all sorts of fruitless negotiations had been going on. In eight days, it was back in office unaltered.

During these eight days, the Nationalists made a great and important decision. They refused to accept responsibility for the acceptance of the Dawes report ; they even hedged the Cabinet with conditions for its acceptance. By so doing, they disgusted the solid elements on the Conservative side and they completely alienated their own extremists. A proposal, such as they put forward at the crisis, to make Tirpitz Chancellor, indicates the measure of statesmanship in the party which had contributed nothing to saving the State except by being in a minority. Not more than three-quarters of their own followers would have accepted the Grand Admiral and no one else. Their imposition of conditions shows similar lack of appreciation of the issues. It was based on a stupid conception of prestige and not on a knowledge of the tricks in Germany's hands, and it only gravely embarrassed the negotiators who had to take every difficult step with the knowledge of a strong party waiting at home to stab them in the back with no better plea but that the terms they had accepted injured the Junker honour.

As it was, the whole course of the negotiations went in Germany's favour although acceptance appeared in the light of an imposed settlement. The Committee had taken a view of her resources that was nearer to the official German view than to the French view ; it had worked on a purely economic basis and treated the demands of the French budget as irrelevant ; and it had placed its report in the hands of reasonable men who had already agreed amicably to be reasonable together. The Dawes scheme as accepted by the signatory Powers is open to all manner of criticisms, but politically it is a great work. It removed at once the most dangerous problem of the Continent to a position where politicians could not get at it ; it secured for the first time an agreement between the Powers in which the element of honour entered in to enforce legality and it created new atmosphere in international relations. To their credit, the negotiating statesmen saw its possibilities and they ended in agreement simply because they had tacitly agreed that failure to agree could not be permitted.

The German negotiators came back faced with only one fear —would the Nationalists refuse ? The scheme had to be taken bit by bit on the legislation to give effect to it. The debates were heated and the Nationalists consistently voted against the Government, but, as the Socialists rallied to it, the anti-Government vote remained round about one hundred and seventy-five. Then came the decisive vote on August 29 ; for the legislation on the railways a two-thirds majority was necessary as it was a measure involving the Constitution. Would the Nationalists again vote solidly against ? would they abstain ? In either case the Bill was defeated. Four hundred and forty-one members voted, and three hundred and fourteen voted for, one hundred and twenty-seven against the Bill.

The Nationalists had split in two, forty-eight voting for, fifty-four voting against. The scene was memorable ; even the foreign diplomats broke with tradition and applauded vigorously, while the Fascists hissed the minority of Nationalists who made patriotic, if belated, use of the limited common sense which an inscrutable Providence had given them.

The rest of the story of the Dawes Plan belongs to the other part of this book, but its influence on German party politics is decisive. The Nationalists had for the first time accepted responsibility in part for voting a Republican Cabinet measure of supreme national importance. They had in part entered into the framework of the Republic because a strong section of the party, the section which not only possessed the greater sense of reality but the greater hold on the suffrage of the electors, had seen the implications of abstentionism and the danger that, if it continued, the Nationalists would become the anti-Nationalists. Inside the party, great discussions proceeded, but, eventually, it was agreed to negotiate for an entrance into the Cabinet. But Marx was in a far stronger position than in May ; it was not now in their power to make terms and Marx retorted by a proposal for a national coalition to include the Socialists also. He can hardly have expected the slightest success and was concerned mainly to secure a strong position against either party as he depended on one or other for his majority. The negotiations failed and the Chancellor secured a dissolution.

The ensuing campaign was fought with extreme bitterness because there was no great single issue before the electorate. The Dawes report was part of the law of the land, a matter agreed, and the issues were a confused mingling of five-year-old grudges and possible policies for the future. The real issue was one which it was difficult to formulate to the electors— Was Germany to execute the Dawes report as one serving a sentence, or was she to proceed from it to re-enter the European community ? Was she to treat it as a prolongation of the war, or the beginning of peace ? The results showed the immediate stabilizing effect of the economic agreement. The Communists lost seventeen seats, while the Socialists gained thirty-one, the Left showing a net gain of eight. The Fascists lost eighteen seats ; the Nationalists won six, the Right showing a net loss of thirteen.

The Government parties won eighteen seats in all, showing an increase. The actual gains and losses are trifling, but the moral effect was very great. The extremists alone had suffered

seriously, but all the gains worth talking about had gone to the
Government.   It was not a striking manifestation of confidence
in anyone ; it was a sign that Germany was recovering stability
and a clear recognition that the way of recovery lay along the
paths of order and work.   Although the two great parties lay
on the wings, the strength lay in the weaker parties of the Centre, while extremism was in a state of collapse.   The Republican position was unassailable ; the conservative tendency was
for the moment in the ascendant.   These were the two main
deductions from the elections.   According to custom, the
Marx Cabinet, from which the Democrats had formally with-
drawn their support, resigned, and, after negotiations which
were getting more difficult each time a new Cabinet had to be
formed, Luther, the chief negotiator on the Dawes report,
formed an administration early in January.   Luther, at that
time not formally a party man, though Populist in sympathy,
had no mind to try to control a team of politicians.   All he
wanted was a party representative to answer for the security
of a coalition majority and the rest of the Cabinet posts would
be filled by experts.   The Centrists, before joining, frankly
asked him—Would the new Government maintain the Republic
and pursue the foreign policy outlined by the last Cabinet ?
Luther's reply is unknown, but it satisfied the Centrists, and
they entered a Cabinet in which they had only Nationalists and
Populists for colleagues.   They were in fact a guarantee to the
Left parties of the Cabinet's Republican respectability, and the
outline began to appear of a regrouping of parties on the basis
of recognition of the Republic.

Before the Cabinet could really get going, however, another
trial of strength was afforded the parties.   Ebert, who had
occupied the presidency with great ability and distinction since
1919, died suddenly on February 28, 1925.   The electorate had
to provide a successor.   From the Republican point of view
the only point of real importance was that a confessed Republican of tried loyalty should be elected, but the Republicans
could not unite.   The result was that, though the Republican
candidates had a 500,000 majority, the Nationalist candidate—
a Monarchist in sympathies—polled nearly 300,000 votes more
than his nearest opponent, the Socialist.   A second ballot was
necessary, and this time the Republicans took no risks : after
some difficult negotiating all—except the Communists, who
true to Leninism, ran their own candidate—accepted Marx
as the Republican candidate.   The decision was wise, for the
right wing was the doubtful part of the Republican front and

only a Centrist could rally it. The Nationalists and Populists who had supported the Nationalist candidate in the first ballot were in a quandary. So long as there were several candidates in the field there was no direct Republican issue. Now that the Republicans had agreed on a candidate the Nationalist candidate inevitably took on the appearance of an Anti-Republican and would lose the votes of the Republican Populists. They had a brilliant idea—too brilliant though it proved in the long run. They selected Hindenburg and they ran him, not as a Nationalist, hoping he would be mistaken for a national candidate. It was certainly as such that the old soldier stood. He accepted the candidature from a stern sense of duty and prefaced with all sorts of formalities with the ex-Kaiser and the negotiators. All his life had been spent in the service of his country and, if the country needed him in his old age, he regarded the opportunity as an order to serve. The result was never in doubt, and all the surprise there was, was due to the fact that, although over 3,000,000 more persons voted, he had a majority of only 900,000 and, as the Communist polled 1,900,000, was a minority victor.

But the jubilation of the Nationalists was unbounded. They had elected one of the conspicuous figures of the old *régime* to the highest office of the State by nearly an absolute majority and, in their delight, half the viciousness of their Anti-Republicanism vanished. A Republic headed by a Field-Marshal who had once incarnated the whole war effort of Germany was something different surely from a Republic headed by a saddler and a Socialist. It was a typically Nationalist argument, and it pleased them so much that they almost forgot their bitternesses and permitted Stresemann to pursue a foreign policy which, if it succeeded, would knock away the one solid basis of Nationalist influence—the degradation of Germany from her position of a European Power. Nor did the Nationalists see—although perhaps some of them did—that, when the aged Field-Marshal, amid the frenzied acclamations of the crowd which greeted him, not as a Nationalist leader, but a national hero, took the oath to the Republic the triumph was not theirs but the Republic's, and that Hindenburg's act had the significance, not of victory, but of capitulation.

CHAPTER VI

LOCARNO AND THE LEAGUE

The Geneva Protocol—security in France and Germany—a Franco-German pact of mutual guarantee—preparing for Locarno—Germany and the League—negotiations at Locarno—moral strength of Germany—consequences of the Locarno Treaty—the entrance of Germany into the League of Nations—the work of Stresemann.

WHILE Germany, scarcely recovered from the agitation of a general election, was in the throes of a supremely exciting presidential election, German diplomacy was busied with a task of far greater importance than any which it had tackled since the proclamation of the Republic. The positive gain of 1924 had been the settlement of the reparations question and the admission of Germany to the right of discussion with her former enemies. But that touched only one phase of German-Allied relations, and it failed in its diplomatic purpose unless it served as a starting-point for a general settlement. What Herr Stresemann saw with complete clearness was that Germany could not proceed to constructive work unless she was completely free from Allied control and recovered her liberty of action by consent. The general liquidation of the international problem was the necessary preliminary to an attempt to solve the national problem. Parallel to the reparations discussion, an Allied conference had been proceeding at Genoa. The complacency of the Herriot Government in France had caused great alarm in France, and it was clear to the French Premier that, unless he got some political equivalent, the reparations settlement might wreck his ministry. So once again he sought guarantees for French security and, after prolonged arguments, the Geneva Protocol was evolved which used the machinery of the League to make definite the League guarantee of integrity and the League aspiration to perpetual peace. The Protocol, however, by taking its stand on the power to preserve peace by threatening war imposed heavy obligations on a maritime power like Britain without corresponding advantages, and the Conservative successor of

PRESIDENT HINDENBURG

the Macdonald Government lost no time in informing France that it was unacceptable. The Protocol was formally killed in March at Geneva by Mr. Chamberlain.

The beginning of 1925 saw France in a stiffer and more alarmed mood. The Ruhr evacuation was still uncompleted and sufficient grounds of German non-compliance were found to justify a British refusal to evacuate the Cologne zone at the proper time (January 1925). There was even a return to the policy of pin-pricks which caused a fresh outburst of resentment in Germany. But, in this unsatisfactory situation, Stresemann saw a supreme chance. The consistent plaint of " insecurity " by France had raised the whole question of " security ". Every State was " insecure " and some far less " secure " than France. The Protocol had aimed at creating a state of " security ", but the " security " arrived at was rather the " security " of the French continental system than the " security " of national States. All through the discussions, the " security " of Germany had remained undiscussed, yet that country was actually at the moment far more exposed to foreign aggression than any of the others. It almost looked as if the theory of " security " on the anti-German side was that " security " depended on German " insecurity ". With the collapse of the Protocol, the whole question was posed again, but in a far more acute form, and in the circumstances Stresemann saw Germany's chance. He revived the idea put forward by Briand and Cuno before him of a Franco-German pact.

The offer communicated in February put the whole question on a new basis. It at once tested France's sincerity. Did she mean by security what the word meant—security of France within her frontiers—or did she mean the perpetuation of a system whose object was the perpetual subjugation of Germany ? The Treaty of Versailles, despite its severity, held no legal case for perpetual subjugation ; with whatever hopes of that it had been framed, the legal right to disappoint them was undoubted. Did France then want to go beyond the treaty, and did she envisage at all a return to normality in Europe ? Her whole case for security rested on the German menace ; her other neighbours, Belgium, Italy and Spain, were never considered as threatening her security ; her vulnerable flank was on the Rhine. The Versailles settlement protected that flank militarily, but such protection was entirely at the mercy of circumstances. The Stresemann offer placed her in a sad predicament. It offered a joint guarantee of the integrity of the Versailles frontier even to the acceptance of the demilitarized zone on the right bank of the river so strangely valued by military experts. If she accepted that offer, she clearly could not pursue a policy of encirclement, nor insist on continuous interference in German affairs. If she refused, she announced to the world her refusal to make peace with her enemy and, by the open distrust in German good faith, would create at once a reaction in Germany's favour. At the same time, if she accepted, she left Germany free to reconstruct and re-arm till, as was inevitable, the German Republic, or perhaps a German Empire, would confront her with resources infinitely greater than her own, with only " a scrap of paper " to prevent her using them as in 1870 or 1914. The doctrine of the next war is still the basis of French foreign politics. The offer challenged the morality of that basis in the name of humanity, but it envisaged a future when the next war might come upon her robbed of all advantages by its acceptance.

The Stresemann plan was well thought out. Not without irony, it pinned France down to reality by conceiving the proposed pact as a Rhine pact, that is to say the plan was for a guarantee of the French frontier and not of the French system. But it was not merely to be a guarantee of the French but of the German frontier, and the guarantee was to be signed by Britain and Italy as well. That meant no more territorial sanctions and the evacuation of German territory at the time fixed by the treaty. The idea was taken up by Britain, whose brilliant envoy at Berlin, Lord d'Abernon, had been no stranger to its inception, but it was not received particularly favourably in France generally and with fury by the Chauvinists.

Having executed his move and thrown an apple of discord to the Allies, Herr Stresemann waited quietly for his opponents to make the next move. The vicissitudes of French politics brought Briand again to the Quai d'Orsay—a clear gain, for the first proposer of the guarantee pact had become Foreign Minister—and therefore rendered the discussions between the Allies easier. The French insisted on the equal inclusion of Belgium, which was accepted, but a bitter fight raged round the extension of the guarantee to the States in the French system. The guarantee could not be geographical like the Rhine pact, but it could be given in connection with the arbitration treaties, which were an integral part of the German offer and which France suggested should be extended to others of Germany's neighbours. The arbitration treaties, however, did little more than make somewhat more precise obligations assumed under the League Covenant, and it was perfectly clear from the beginning, and no one knew it better than Herr Stresemann, that neither Britain nor Italy would give any guarantees other than those already laid down in the Covenant. They might be bound, if the circumstances defined arose, to defend the integrity of Poland as Poland, but they would never give additional guarantees to defend it as part of the French system. The result was that, baffled by the British refusal to guarantee her system as a system, the French had to bind Germany to the general international guarantee already given by her Allies. As a corollary to the Rhine pact France required Germany to enter the League of Nations.

That was precisely what Herr Stresemann had had in view. He saw clearly that the sole way of escaping from the Versailles prison-house was to get Germany into the League. It was true that the League was intended to be little more than a part of that edifice, but, since its inception, it had become much more and had risen, in spite of some tragic failures, to be the guarantor of the weak against the strong, and the one bulwark of peace in Europe, not by its own sadly faulty Constitution, but by reason of the overwhelming weight of intelligent opinion which was prepared to back it against any and all of its enemies. This weight of opinion had forced Cabinets which loathed it to proclaim *urbe et orbe* that their foreign policy remained within the framework of the League of Nations.

In 1919, Germany had been excluded from the League for unworthiness. German thought had gone to its construction and the international ideal of the young Republic had been a league of free States working for the general interests of the European peoples. The exclusion was an insult, deliberately given and deeply felt, and it made it quite impossible for Germany, however great her needs, to go to Geneva in sackcloth and ashes and, with penitential abasement, beg for admittance. There was no other way unless the invitation came from the Allies, and there is no more brilliant feat of modern diplomacy than the way Stresemann manœuvred the French, who saw themselves Germany's judges, into becoming Germany's suitors. For, however much the Allies maintained the form of a demand, they essentially asked Germany to enter the League from which they had once threatened her perpetual exclusion, and Stresemann emphasized that, when, in his answer to the Allied reply to his offer, he said that he did not regard League membership as a necessary condition of the realization of the German plan, but that he had no objection to the problem of security and the problem of League membership being taken as one.

The diplomatic history of Locarno is the most interesting of all the diplomatic histories of a post-war period, but it cannot be dealt with here. One must indicate its main principles and the triumph it represented for German diplomacy. The offer had been Germany's, and France had been forced to accept. All the quibblings had been French, and the German counter-quibblings had sacrificed nothing essential. In truth the actual form did not matter so much to Herr Stresemann. He was fighting for something far more important than the security of the Rhine frontier ; he was fighting for the return of Germany to the comity of nations without her having to suffer fresh humiliation. He wanted her to return as an equal, and as an equal she did. All the rest of the discussion that was so useful to the journalist and the jurist about general or regional pacts, about the protocol, about guarantees, left Germany for the moment cold. Win or lose in the Rhine pact battle, she had increased her prestige, or rather re-discovered it, and she won. On September 15, she was invited to a discussion with the Allies for the conclusion of a security pact.

The negotiations had been prolonged and they had not been without their unpleasant moments for Germany, but they had on the whole been more difficult between the Allies than between the Allies and Germany, and it was evident that their so far successful course had been due to a very real and not very easy effort of goodwill, which was not regarded with sympathy by a considerable section of the Allied peoples. The truth was that Herr Stresemann had succeeded in establishing Germany in a moral position so strong that the Allies did not dare leave her there and he knew that, when he accepted the invitation to the Conference, that his opponents did not dare let the Conference fail. If it did fail, Germany's actual position would be no worse, but the moral effect of her gesture would be enhanced, while the Allied position would be exposed to severe criticism, and only with great difficulty would Allied unity be preserved. In any case, Germany had asserted her right and her ability to take the initiative in international policy—a circumstance which in itself constituted a defeat for the Versailles policy and a blow at the French hegemonial system. There were moments when the Conference threatened to collapse, and in the end agreement was reached.

The most important result was, of course, the fact that Germany had obtained the admission of her right to an independent policy. It was the theory that she had no such right that had been the real cause of the Allied indignation when

she signed her treaty with Russia during the Genoa Conference.
Now she appeared not only as the initiator of policy but as the
guarantor, on an equal footing, of a fundamental treaty of
which she was not the object but the joint creator.   That position accomplished what all the German Cabinets had striven
for—it made the execution of the Versailles Treaty a matter of
form, and even at need a matter of negotiation.   The spirit of
Versailles and the spirit of Locarno have not been reconciled
yet, but the Locarno Treaties take precedence over the Versailles Treaty whenever there is a definite conflict of principle,
and the Locarno spirit takes precedence over the Versailles
spirit whenever there is a conflict of interpretation.   That is
not to say that the Versailles Treaty is superseded or that the
Versailles spirit inevitably loses, but simply that Germany has
gained the enormous advantage of being able to use a general
opinion that the Locarno agreement marks a great step forward and that a victory for Versailles is a victory for reaction.

Herr Stresemann marked his view that Germany had recovered liberty of action by concluding a treaty with Russia
which occasioned an outburst of indignation in the French
camp, an outburst not less fierce because of the bitter knowledge that indignation was impotent.   There was no doubt a
touch of malice in the conclusion of the treaty, even if it may, as
will be seen later, be ascribed also to considerations of internal
politics, but it is exceedingly important as a demonstration of
the practical consequences of the rehabilitation of Germany
through the Locarno negotiations.   For, although Herr Stresemann and a majority of his countrymen regarded the sacrifices
made at Locarno as sacrifices rather of prestige than of fact,
the fact remains that Germany bought her rehabilitation at a
fairly high price.   It is true that in form it was little more
than an acceptance of the Versailles settlement, but such an
acceptance was a new departure in history.   For the west
Germany substituted a voluntary renunciation for an imposed
peace.   That was a gain, but it involved the moral surrender of
Alsace and Lorraine, Eupen and Malmédy, and absolute sovereign rights on the Rhineland zones, in which she undertook to
erect no works of a military nature.   Such a surrender is not,
in the opinion of many Germans, compensated for by the fact
that the obligation not to go to war (with exceptions that
require no discussion here) is mutual as between Germany and
France and Belgium and that the treaty is guaranteed by Britain and Italy, but the gain is undoubted.   Territorial sanctions are virtually impossible, and isolated French action, as in

the case of the Ruhr, can become an act of war involving foreign intervention on Germany's side. No treaty will avoid war, but, in hedging war with a complicated preliminary procedure which it is to the interest of other States to see punctiliously followed, it goes as far as treaties can to render war impossible. And that for Germany in 1925 was a positive gain.

At the cost of her surrender in the west, Germany obtained a relative freedom of action elsewhere on her frontiers. The course of history shows that France will almost always sacrifice her " system " and the allies who form it if she can obtain directly security on the Rhine. This time France refused altogether to abandon her system, but, at the same time, she was unable to obtain a similar surrender with regard to Germany's eastern frontiers. The territorial settlement in the east still rests on the imposed settlement at Versailles, by which the German people does not consider itself morally bound, and all that France has been able to obtain is a set of arbitration treaties that prevent the upsetting of that settlement by aggressive war on Germany's part. But it leaves Germany free to take advantage of any opportunity to negotiate a change, and it therefore introduces a dissolving element into the French system. The root cause of the failure of French policy here was the impossibility of obtaining the Anglo-Italian guarantee for the eastern frontier and the lack of which prevented the extortion of a moral renunciation by Germany from becoming practical politics.

It is true that, at Locarno, there was, in a very real and European sense, neither victors nor vanquished and that the effort towards peace and settlement was greater than that towards selfish gain, and it is contrary to the Locarno spirit, which, despite its critics, is a real thing, to emphasize gains or losses. But at the same time, it has been necessary to make clear the gain to Germany, especially as the Locarno settlement has fiercer critics there even than in France. The gain was that Germany left Locarno as an equal, and that gain was to be emphasized in a striking and unexpected way. The basic idea of Locarno is the supremacy of the League of Nations and the corollary of the settlement was the entry of Germany into that organization. Procedure demanded that Germany should ask admittance ; at Locarno her former enemies declared that they would support that admission and, although clearly they could not pledge the League in advance, would support her claim to a permanent seat on the Council. Her occupancy of that seat was a legal consecration and a manifestation to the world of the equality she had won and would restore her at once to the comity of nations and to the rank of a Great Power. The application could not be dealt with till the Assembly met in the following March, and ere that body could meet there developed a crisis at Geneva.

It is a difficult crisis to expound, for its elements are many and confused. In one aspect, it was a formal protest by smaller States against the settlement of League business by a private conclave of Great Powers. The Locarno agreement on Germany's permanent Council seat, despite the care with which the Assembly's rights were safeguarded, was clearly an attempt to anticipate an Assembly decision and to add another permanent member to the Council to the detriment of the smaller States. The scepticism with which the smaller States met the current theory of Franco-German antagonism on the Council is a tribute to their sense of reality. They looked beyond the mouthings of pamphleteers and they saw the reality of a combine of Great Powers to settle things in their own interests and turn the League organs into instruments to that end. In the second place, the virtual outlawry of war as between France and Germany and the affirmation implicit in the settlement that Germany felt no moral obligation to admit the intangibility of the territorial settlement in the east caused a genuine alarm in the States which had secured territory from Germany. They felt themselves abandoned, even by France, who had assumed responsibility for the risks they ran when they drew their frontiers to include German populations. They feared a day when these frontiers would be called in question after a Franco-German agreement as Council Powers—a vision that is not nearly so wild as it seems.

Consequently there came a movement, ill co-ordinated but formidable, to secure for States outside the Rhine pact powers to obtain a privilege equivalent to Germany's. Spain, Brazil, China and Poland all claimed a permanent seat on the Council. The Versailles Powers were in a dilemma. They were not committed to the policy that only Germany could have a permanent seat, but, obviously, if permanent seats were to be granted indiscriminately by the Assembly, it not only depreciated the value of the concession won by German diplomacy, but it upset the organization of the League itself. The resulting private negotiations, which might well have gravely injured the prestige of the League by showing plainly how relatively little the interests of the League weighed in comparison with selfish national interests, revealed even more clearly than Locarno the embarrassments of the Versailles Powers. While British diplomacy expended itself in seeking to obtain an agreed solution at all costs irrespective of the merits of the solution agreed, French opinion openly supported Poland, although both Powers sought to bring pressure to bear on the recalcitrant small States. It was perfectly clear that unanimity was impossible and Allied policy was forced to the expedient of persuading the claimant States to withdraw by promises of radical overhaul of the Council's composition. Eventually Poland, Spain and China agreed not to carry things to extremes, but Brazil was obdurate. No argument could move her from interposing her veto when Germany's election to the Council was brought forward, and, after a dignified wait at Geneva, Germany withdrew her application.

The secret of Brazil's obduracy has never been completely revealed, but it did the League no harm. When M. Briand referred bitterly to " the humiliating paralysis of the League ", he only marked more emphatically the diplomatic defeat suffered by the Versailles Powers. They had consoled themselves for the entry of Germany by the comforting thought that in any case they dominated the League and they were publicly and humiliatingly refuted.

More than that, the whole edifice so painfully built up at Locarno threatened to collapse. From the European point of view that collapse would have been disastrous ; from the more selfish point of view, it would have left Germany in the position won by Locarno without the obligations and renunciations imposed upon her by the Locarno agreements. There was only one thing to be done, and the Allies did it : they restored Germany to the concert of Europe. A meeting between the Rhine pact Powers was at once held and a joint *communiqué* issued stating that the Locarno agreement remained the basis of their policy. The signatories—to which were admitted the Poles and the Czechs—called themselves, or let themselves be called, " the Locarno Powers " ; but the *communiqué* specified the discussion only of the Rhine pact Powers, and the fact remained that the crisis had been surmounted by France (*plus* Belgium), Britain, Italy and Germany acting in unison on a footing of perfect equality between themselves and of perfect superiority to all the other European Powers. That was the end of the five years' policy of vindictiveness begun at Versailles ; it faded out under the pressure of facts and Germany re-assumed without question her old place among the nations.

The actual League deadlock took six months to break.

Failure was of course not admitted, and M. Briand, as if to mark that French policy was least innocent of causing it, moved postponement of the German request. After six months' bargaining, arguing and chicanery which was a cause of unholy joy to the League's enemies, of grief to its friends and of serious criticism of Allied policy, Germany was admitted a member on September 8 with a permanent seat on the Council, and six days later the exchange of ratifications of the Locarno agreements marked the formal beginning of a new era in international policy.

Although valuable help had been rendered to him by Dr. Luther in the negotiations, the whole round of two years of foreign policy of a most delicate kind had been borne by Herr Stresemann. The greatness of his achievement cannot be overestimated. It is not so much that it gave actual and immediate results as that it gave promise of a completely new situation. It laid a basis of normal international intercourse and friendship during a period when one State was still undergoing penalties imposed by a treaty inflicted on her by others after defeat in a great war, and it did so by restoring to her equality with her former enemies and liberty to pursue an independent policy within the framework of a Covenant equally accepted by the other European States. Anything more unlike the 1920 position of Germany—legally, politically and morally —than the 1926 position of Germany it would be difficult to imagine, and one might have expected that the German nation would have recognized the value of her achievement. To their credit Herr Stresemann's natural enemies on the Left did recognize it. There were aspects of his policy which they did not like ; it was, in a way, too Nationalist, but they saw quite clearly the tremendous chance it gave of peace and the impossibility of any Left statesman being given a chance to carry through anything similar. And so they played fairly by him. On the contrary the Nationalists, his natural Allies, fought his policy tooth and nail for reasons that are not apparent to the ordinary intelligence and with a reckless ferocity that could hardly have been exceeded in the case of a Socialist Foreign Minister. The history of that fight is the history of Germany during the pre-Locarno period.

The opening of negotiations with the Allies and the German offer was of course a Cabinet decision and the Nationalists have therefore a certain share in the credit of it. Consent was indeed wrung from them simply because the alternative to consent was to leave the Government, and that at the moment they did not want to do. A Right centre coalition was preferable to a Weimar coalition, and the only possibility of maintaining a Right centre coalition with a reasonable majority in Parliament was by their continuance in the Government. The whole aim of Herr Stresemann's policy was to make the Nationalists accept responsibility for the decision which he hoped would be taken to make that policy effective. No doubt he preferred on the whole Nationalists to Socialists, but he saw clearly that no new basis of German-Allied relations was durable unless he could compromise the Nationalists. They had indeed spent their whole political career in evading responsibility, and when it came to life and death decisions less than half of them had had the patriotism to accept a qualified responsibility. Such responsibility was of no use to Herr Stresemann. He had to have full responsibility accepted by the Nationalists for his acts up to the time when it was too late to evade it, or when evasion did not matter.

The significance of Herr Stresemann's achievement is missed unless it is realized that he fought on two fronts, with the Allies and with the Reichstag critics. It is not easy to decide which were the more difficult to handle, but fortune favoured him in having to deal with both in a good humour. There was a real will to peace among the Allied statesmen, and the Nationalists were in a mood of supreme content. They had emerged triumphant from the elections, they had got the Socialist party mixed up in the Barmat scandals, a German Republican equivalent of Panama, they scored another triumph at the first Presidential elections, and they finally elected Hindenburg to the Presidency. Politicians flushed with success are aggressive, but their skill and resolution suffer.

The first symptoms of revolt came from the Pan-German League after the decisive step of making an offer had been made. On March 12, Herr Stresemann, speaking at Cologne, defined Germany's renunciation and emphasized the fact that such renunciation involved security for Germany against French Chauvinism, but the League saw only the renunciation of Alsace and Lorraine and the recognition of the treaty. It characterized the offer as " unhealthy " and called on the German nation to resist " secret diplomacy ". Its protest was echoed by Nationalist spokesmen in the Reichstag, who complained that the party had not been consulted, and that the renunciation had been offered voluntarily and without compensation. Home politics—a new tariff scheme and the question of compensation for losses incurred by the fall of the mark—kept the

DR. STRESEMANN

coalition together, and it survived not only Socialist attacks but a combined attack of Communists, Socialists and Democrats in which, characteristically enough, the Fascists participated. In June, however, the attack on the Stresemann policy hardened, and was aided even by one of his Nationalist colleagues in the Cabinet. In the great debate on July 20, the party accepted the continuance of negotiations with a characteristic disclaimer of responsibility, but the campaign of its extreme wing went on. It was attracting far too much attention in the Allied countries, and Herr Stresemann had to counteract it. When the formal invitation came for a conference, the Nationalists had gone too far to wreck the Cabinet by refusing consent to acceptance, but they insisted on conditions being attached. Herr Stresemann refused to commit the conditions to writing, but had them conveyed verbally to the Allied Powers. The conditions were the securing of the Allied undertaking to evacuate the Cologne zone and the repudiation of war guilt. Both were the objects of a sharp reply from the Allied Governments, with the result that Herr Stresemann could fairly claim to have been forced to expose Germany to an unnecessary humiliation, and the Nationalist blunder was vehemently exposed in the Democratic Press. Their failure made the Nationalists furious, and they eagerly seized a new weapon which the anxiety of Russia placed in their hands. Soviet diplomacy, which suffers intermittently from persecution mania, saw in the attempt to reconcile the Western democracies an attempt to encircle Russia. It appeared to it necessary to ruin the proposed pact and it was warmly seconded by the Nationalists. Herr Stresemann took the wind out of the Nationalist sails by signing the new trade treaty with Russia on the eve of Locarno, but he went to Locarno all the same, and negotiated as if the Nationalist protest did not exist.

When he returned the Nationalists had to decide. They decided speedily. Renunciation of German territory was inadmissible, and they left the Government (October 25). Once again they evaded the last responsibility and refused themselves any share in the rehabilitation of Germany in favour of being able to say " We told you so ", should the day ever come —which to all men of reason appeared unlikely—when Locarno proved a snare and a delusion.

The rump Cabinet decided simply to carry on as a two-party coalition till the final act in the Locarno-League drama. They were soon to have their revenge. In the summer, Germany had been unpleasantly impressed by a rather sharp disarmament note.   On November 16 the Allies sent a new note announcing a considerable reduction in the occupation forces and revision of occupation conditions, an amnesty proclamation for resisters to the occupation authorities, and the evacuation of the Cologne zone contemporaneously with the formal signature of the treaties.   These were gains that no reasonable man could misrepresent and they took half the sting out of the Nationalist attack.   On November 19 the Reichsrat accepted the treaties by a big majority, and on November 27 the Reichstag carried the treaties by two hundred and ninety-one votes to one hundred and seventy-one—the minority being composed of the Nationalists and those quaint brothers in arms the Fascists and the Communists.   Only one constitutional party had voted against.   There was only one hope left for the Nationalists.   Would their idol Hindenburg refuse the Presidential approval ?   Their idol disappointed them.   He had taken an oath and the Nationalists quite forgot that the oaths the grim old soldier took he kept.   The Presidential approval was given automatically and, on December 1, Dr. Luther and Herr Stresemann went to London for the official signing.

There were many Germans and many of the allied peoples who did not understand the significance of Locarno, but no one could miss the significance of London.   While Cologne echoed to the first departing footsteps of the British troops, the German statesmen drove to the Guildhall amid cheering crowds and were fêted with their French and other colleagues as the guests of the British nation.   Before so striking an admission of reconciliation and equality, the war-guilt controversy faded into the historians' background.   It is true more was read into the demonstration than was wise ; it is equally true that its promise has not always been fulfilled and that the pessimists on both sides have a certain reason in denouncing it as a manifestation of deceit.   If that is so, the fault lies with the statesmen ; the peoples have always accepted it for what it was—the end of the war period—and its traducers—Chauvinists, Nationalists, and extremists of all colours—are those who say that the people were right and hated Locarno and all it represented the more bitterly just because of that.   Locarno is very far from being perfect, but the men who made it were on the side of the angels of peace.

CHAPTER VII

GERMANY IN THE CONCERT OF EUROPE

The Luther Cabinet—the claims of the dispossessed dukes, princes and kings—the plebiscite—dispute with Italy over Tyrol—Dr. Held and Bavarian Separatism—the character of the opposition—the Marx Cabinet—the admission to the League of Nations—the resignation of General von Seeckt—the entrance of the Nationalists into the Government—victory of the foreign policy of Dr. Stresemann—the consolidation of the Republican form of government.

ALTHOUGH the first act in the Locarno drama—the appearance of Germany as a League Council Power—was not completed till September 1926, December 1925 is more or less the end of one period and the beginning of another. Germany signalized it by a fresh attempt to create national unity. The rump Cabinet which had borne on its shoulders the task of the last critical weeks now resigned. Its task was over and it felt the need of reconstituting itself on new bases on which its individual parties might or might not be able to stand. German foreign policy was settled for a considerable time to come by the acceptance of Locarno by the Reichstag majority, and whoever assumed the responsibilities of government could not change its course. But, in the weeks to come, it would look better if Germany took the steps still necessary for its completion as a united nation, and efforts were therefore made to restore the grand coalition. The Socialists had steadily voted in the Locarno way, and, with the die cast, it was held not improbable that, for reasons of prestige, the Nationalists, now that there was no responsibility to take, might accept office again. There was no urgent need to form a grand coalition, but it was eminently desirable, if only for purposes of a demonstration. All negotiations were, however, in vain. The Nationalists were obdurate, and the Socialists were beginning to concentrate in preparation for the struggle in home politics which they saw to be the obvious consequence of the settlement of foreign policy. Eventually, therefore, Dr. Luther formed another centre coalition—tech-

nically described as " a neutral government of the Centre "—
of Centrists, Bavarian Populists, Democrats and Populists
which could count only on one hundred and seventy-one votes
in a Reichstag of four hundred and ninety-three. For the
prosecution of business, Luther had to use the old tactics of
playing off Socialists and Nationalists, tactics that gave an
unfortunate sense of unreality to parliamentary proceedings,
although it answered well enough from the foreign political
standpoint. The very first vote showed the farcical unreality
of the situation. The Government won by ten votes, despite
the Socialist abstention, only because the Nationalists and Fascists had not troubled to appear at full strength. The vote,
instead of giving the Government confidence, showed the
urgent necessity of getting somehow a Cabinet able to control a
proper parliamentary majority, and ready to carry a definite
programme. But the political decks would not be cleared of
foreign politics until March—until, as it turned out, September
—and the Government had to wait, despite the realization of
the statesmen that the existence of minority Cabinets, dependent on bargaining and intrigue, tends to bring parliamentary
institutions into disrepute.

It was all the more likely to do so as a score or more of urgent
problems clamoured for solution which could only be disposed
of by a Cabinet whose policy was the policy of a majority.
The history of the attempt to settle accounts—financial
accounts—with the dispossessed dukes, princes and kings, the
majority of whom were now living quietly in their old realms,
and one of whom at least, and not the least worthy, Rupprecht
of Bavaria, was conducting himself as if a royal restoration had
already taken place—illustrates the whole viciousness of the
situation and the impossibility of carrying out a real legislative
programme. The claims were extremely complicated, and involved both Reich and Lands, and the attitude of the nation
towards them varied from the Communists, who simply dismissed them as irrelevant, because kings and such-like were
non-existent, to the extreme Nationalists, who considered them
unnecessary because only kings and such-like had existence in
the true sense of the word. Early in February, after all sorts of
preliminary investigations, the Government tabled a compromise Bill which certainly did not err on the side of severity
to the victims of the revolution. Since the Nationalists had
decided that the duty of an opposition is to oppose, all depended on the Socialists. The moment they showed plainly
their opposition and demanded a plebiscite in conjunction

with the Communists, the Nationalists changed their tactics, but, as it was doubtful if, with such Nationalist support as might be forthcoming, the Government would get its majority, the Government yielded to the Left. The condition for a plebiscite is that a fifth of the electorate must demand one. Nearly 13,000,000 electors backed the demand. The result was unexpected, for it meant in the circumstances that nearly half the electorate were opposed to the Government Bill, and, it was to be presumed, preferred confiscation, since it was unlikely that the Nationalists had voted for the Socialist demand. Yet the Nationalists were equally hostile, so that, although on details the Cabinet could play off Right against Left, the Bill was doomed as a Bill. Yet, to withdraw the Bill was an intolerable confession of weakness, and the preparation of a plebiscite against its own legislation was preferred as an alternative. All the Cabinet could do and did was to delay the holding of the plebiscite as long as it could, and it did so well that it fell before it had fixed the plebiscite date. Even the complete "liberation" of Cologne, however, an occasion of joy to the German people, could not compensate it for the loss of prestige thus incurred. It was well that abroad it spoke for the German nation which declined ever to let it speak for it at home.

Nor did it even escape finding that the power of pursuing an independent foreign policy, however much a source of pride, can be a source of embarrassment. Italy was one of the signatories to the Rhine pact, and one of Germany's sponsors at her candidature at Geneva. Under Fascist rule the German minority in Tyrol had been for long the victim of the senseless tyranny one associates with excitable nationalizers, and of the peculiarly stupid form of it one associates with a dictatorship. Early in the year, Press polemics had become more heated, and there had been demonstrations outside German consulates. In February, a question was asked the Bavarian Landtag, which Dr. Held, the Premier, answered with a violent speech attacking Italy. In the matter, Dr. Held has no *locus standi* whatever, but he called himself Bavarian Minister for Foreign Affairs, and he spoke therefore with authority if his claim was admitted. A serious constitutional difficulty had arisen, but, on such a topic as this, the constitutional aspect bulked far less than the national, and it bulked still less when Signor Mussolini retorted with one of his characteristic mailed-fist speeches in which he seemed to evoke a picture of the legions of the new Roman Empire pouring over the Brenner on a campaign of conquest and vengeance. The excitement in Germany was intense, and, much against his will, Herr Stresemann had to answer with dignity and courage, and to make a definite affirmation that Germany could not be talked to even by the heir of the Caesars as if she were a Central American Republic. The assertion gave Germany satisfaction, but the bitter pill to Herr Stresemann was that just at the moment of the trouble at Geneva he should have been forced into conflict with a friendly State through the absurd pretensions of a South German politician, and prevented from dealing fairly with him because the politician in question had sentiment on his side.

The incident indeed only encouraged Dr. Held to pursue his career as " Foreign Minister ". The failure at Geneva was a welcome chance for the Nationalists, who rarely lost an opportunity to be unpatriotic in the name of patriotism. They could have forgiven Herr Stresemann anything except success, and in spite of the March fiasco he had been successful. So the incidents at Geneva did not seem to them a new reason why Germans should stand shoulder to shoulder with them ; they only afforded occasion for increasing their ululation against the Foreign Minister, and into the chorus Dr. Held thought fit to intrude with a furious attack on the Reich's foreign policy. His first invasion into foreign politics had been, as the Cabinet well realized, part of the campaign of Bavaria to assert her rights. She had already sent a long memorandum on the subject to the Cabinet, and late in March the Chancellor had discussed the whole matter at Munich, but Bavaria had not obtained satisfaction. Dr. Held's outburst was not only an attack on the Foreign Minister, but on the Cabinet. Once again the Foreign Minister was helpless, and all he could do was to administer a sharp constitutional rebuke about minding one's own business, which only stiffened the opposition of Nationalists and Bavarians alike.

The next storm the Cabinet had to weather came from another quarter. In May, it was announced in the Press that the President, in deference to the wishes of Germans abroad, had issued instructions for the Mercantile black, white and red flag, with the Weimar colours in one corner, to be flown on German consulates, and not the black, red and gold of Weimar, and that at the last moment the urgent representations of the Centrists and Democrats had caused the order to be amended to authorize the use of both flags with doubtful precedence to the Republican colours. The news finally roused the Left, already restive at the growing insolence of the Nationalist propaganda. The Socialists promptly tabled a motion of no confidence. The Populists stood by the amended order, the Democrats were against it, and the Cabinet tergiversated, till finally the Democrats—a coalition party—also tabled a motion of no confidence. Not to be outdone, the Fascists tabled a similar motion, apparently because the Republican colours were mentioned at all. The Nationalists gleefully abstained, and the Democratic vote of no confidence was carried by thirty votes. The Cabinet resigned, but its resignation could not mend matters. No other combination could be found ; the Nationalists would not work with Herr Stresemann ; the Socialists held aloof, and the same parties accepted Marx's leadership in another Centre coalition Cabinet, and the miserable story was resumed.

Not one of the constant crises that had oppressed Dr. Luther, and were to oppress Dr. Marx, was necessary, and they could not have caused any difficulty to a strong Cabinet—even if faced with a strong opposition—which had always a dissolution as an alternative to resignation. Only the necessity for preserving Dr. Stresemann at the Foreign Office until the foreign political situation was finally cleared up kept the coalition, not indeed together, but sufficiently friendly to let a coalition Government go on functioning, and only that necessity kept a minority coalition in power for a moment. Even as it was, the necessity being less apparent to the extreme sections, the opposition policy was a series of pin-pricks, which they did not intend to push home as serious attacks, but which, by forcing on the Cabinet a policy of vacillating compromise, destroyed its prestige even more than defeat. That much vaunted device of older *régimes*, the Cabinet of officials, might have been tried with advantage, but it requires for success either an untried or complacent Parliament, and the German Reichstag was neither untried nor complacent, but very conscious both of its rights and duties, and determined to enforce the one and fulfil the other.

Dr. Marx interpreted his mission purely as one of carrying on ; an observer with a military mind might have described it as one of being sniped at. He at least realized that it was not in his power to solve the problems that had vexed his predecessor. The settlement with dispossessed rulers had to go to a plebiscite, but it was varied by a new constitutional issue. The Government stood neutral, although all the parties took up a definite attitude against the Left plan. Asked for a pronouncement, President Hindenburg had very properly said that the President could not constitutionally advocate a policy, but as an individual he did not object to stating that he did not like the plan, and gave a series of such reasons as might be expected from one whose creed had always been blind loyalty. The Socialists promptly turned their guns on the President, accusing him of unconstitutional conduct, with the result that the plebiscite took on a constitutional aspect. The opponents of the Left proposal knew its popularity. They foresaw defeat, and the only way to avoid it was to abstain, and so prevent a sufficiency of votes being polled to satisfy the constitutional regulations. Although the Socialists polled nearly two million more votes, not enough votes were cast to make the poll effective and the proposal therefore lapsed. The result was satisfactory to the Cabinet, but it was no victory for it. Their original compromise lay before Parliament, but it had to face the now united hostility of the Socialists and Nationalists. An appeal to the Socialists failed, and the Cabinet debated whether or not it should resign or ask for a dissolution. In the midst of their discussions came another Presidential intervention. Hindenburg refused a dissolution in advance and begged it to talk no more of resignation. The President was within his rights, but to meet his wishes the Cabinet withdrew their Bill.

The admission to the League of Nations on September 8 came as a welcome relief to the nation, but still more to the Cabinet. That it radically altered the situation was seen in the immediate change of attitude of the Nationalists. They declared that their opposition had been all along a foreign policy, and in truth they had fought every attempt towards the rehabilitation of Germany. Now, in spite of them, it had been accomplished, and, with complete cynicism, they now declared that they wished to see Germany pursue a German policy within the League. The Franco-German *rapprochement* as a result of the Thoiry idyll played by M. Briand and Herr Stresemann was not in the least to their taste, but it was so much to everyone else's that they realized that they could only influence policy from inside the Government, and that, if they failed to get inside, the obvious course of the other parties was to reconstruct the Weimar coalition. They hated Herr Stresemann, but they hated the Socialists worse, and Herr Stresemann, forced to consider them as the necessary part of the Government majority, was preferable to a Socialist Foreign Minister who would make opposing them a pleasure or to Herr Stresemann left as a non-party independent Foreign Minister in a Left coalition.

But, to their amazement, their overtures, couched in their

usual language, were sharply repulsed. Not merely did the Centrists speak plainly but Herr Stresemann, fresh from Geneva and Thoiry, at last permitted himself freedom of speech and told them plainly that co-operation was possible only if their moderate members took control of the party and could co-operate with the coalition parties. He pointed his remarks by a general invitation to the Socialists and ended by a reference to " the spirit of 1848 ". The last reference would have been sufficient, but it was followed by a regrettable incident which added fuel to the Nationalist flame. Their extremists and the party generally had no particular liking for General von Seeckt, but he was undoubtedly the successor of Moltke and Schlieffen. At manœuvres, so ran the story, General von Seeckt had permitted Prince Wilhelm of Prussia, the ex-Kaiser's grandson, to be enrolled in the traditional manner in the First Foot Guards. The story was false, for all that the General had done was to permit the Prince to attend manœuvres with the regimental staff. The Cabinet did little to allay the storm raised in the Left Press, and the General sent in his resignation to the President, which, in a letter of warm sympathy, Hindenburg accepted. But his departure was greeted with so unanimous a howl of joy from the Paris Press that the Nationalists, already roused in his defence, made it a question of foreign policy. They had of course to be sharply reminded that it was not, but the remainder inevitably widened the breach, even when the Socialists intensified their campaign against the Defence Minister (the ex-Democrat Gessler), who from the parliamentary point of view was responsible, and when finally the Socialists tabled a motion of no confidence the Nationalists voted for it. Left and Right had smashed the Centre coalition, by a curious irony, on an issue which once again opposed Republican to Anti-Republican.

The resignation of the Cabinet opened the eyes of the Parliamentarians. They had in fact wasted a whole year. It was not altogether their faults, for the muddle in March in Geneva had prevented the completion of Herr Stresemann's work until September, but thereafter there had been no attempt to get on with legislation or take advantage of the victory abroad to clear up the situation in Parliament. Half the bitterness of the flag conflict, the Prince Wilhelm conflict and other similar incidents had arisen, not because of their intrinsic importance or significance, but because nothing more important or more significant was there to take up the minds of the deputies. That there was nothing was the Cabinet's misfortune and not its fault. It had no programme and it was not agreed within itself on almost any burning issue. It could not rely on its own minority, much less rely on a majority whose composition changed with the subject at issue and which was obtained usually at the cost of losing some of its nominal supporters. There was no coherence in a system which presented Fascists voting for a Communist motion, which combined Socialists and Nationalists in a majority existent for personal reasons, and which allowed an essential part of the coalition to vote against its own Cabinet.

It was urgently necessary to achieve the creation of a Parliamentary majority or sheer chaos would supervene in a Parliament of which the nation was getting critical. All the leaders feared a dissolution. They had no idea how the elector would vote, but all foresaw a defeat of the Government, and that would be interpreted abroad as a defeat for the Stresemann policy just when that policy had enabled Germany to speak again as an equal in the councils of Europe. No one saw that more clearly than the President and his advisers, and the President took a notable part in ending the crisis. He took the view, and events have proved him right, that it was highly inadvisable for the Nationalists to continue in opposition. That meant the sacrifice of a Left coalition, but the advent of a Left coalition, the President saw, would revive the opposition between Republicans and Anti-Republicans. That opposition was dying, but very slowly ; it had been the root cause of all the troubles of the Luther and Marx Cabinets, and it could only die in peace if no one had time to revive it. A Government which included the Nationalists could only be a Right Government, for the Democrats, having had painful experience, refused to co-operate with the Nationalists. But neither the Centrists nor the Populists were going to enter an Anti-Republican Government, and the President used his great influence to induce the Nationalists to enter a Republican Cabinet. Eventually he had his way. The Nationalists agreed, but characteristically nominated at least one avowed Monarchist as a minister. But the President and Dr. Marx, who had consented to lead the Coalition Cabinet, cleverly avoided the trap. The President vetoed the nominations and the Nationalists nominated less objectionable members. They entered the coalition under the shadow of a rebuff incurred by their own blunder.

Thus, at the beginning of 1927, Germany, for the first time since 1920, had a Government which fulfilled the two essential conditions. It was a Republican Government and the *régime* was safe ; it possessed a Parliamentary majority and could carry an agreed programme against a skilled compact Socialist-Democrat opposition which could look to office in its time if and when the country so decided. It was true it was not a united coalition and housed more enmities than friendships, but it imposed discipline alike on the parties who composed it and on the opposition, and discipline was above all what the parties needed.

We are too near the event to judge the results of its career. Its main achievement has been to exist and to supply the nation with a positive policy which the nation could either support or reject, but its main title to fame is that it preserved Herr Stresemann in power. During the months succeeding the entry of Germany into the League her policy under his guidance disappointed the fears of her enemies. Before the League and before Europe she has justified her permanent seat on the Council by the consistency of her peace policy, but her main endeavour has been to reassert her title to her old place in the Concert of Europe. She has done it so success-fully that the Nationalists have never been able to make an issue of foreign politics, and the formal defeats she has received are so formal and correspond so little to the realities of the situ-ation that only the irresponsibles have made trouble. There may still be French troops in the Rhineland, but there is no reason at all to stress their presence as a terrible sign of foreign domination when Herr Stresemann goes on governing Europe on full equality and amity with his Allied colleagues. In the disputes and crises that have arisen at Geneva and round Geneva all crises, as it were, crystallize. Germany has never been compelled to turn a German policy into a European one. She had always been able to interpret a German policy in Euro-pean language. She has appeared before the League as a plaintiff and acted also as a judge, and in neither capacity has she justified the forebodings of those who saw in her presence a steady source of trouble. Her spokesmen have earned her respect, and not least for the independence of their attitude. There is nothing in her reception at Geneva to suggest that she is a defeated, discredited nation. The German Republic no longer carries the sins of the Empire ; treaties notwithstanding, she stands a free and equal democracy among her peers. Nor is that equality a mere sentimental concession from her former enemies. It is a matter of practical fact. Within the League, almost inevitably, an inner circle formed of the claimants to the rank of a Great Power. Germany is admitted to that circle ; or rather admitted herself, and fully shares in its task of trying to solve crises before they get unwelcome publicity at Geneva. Thus, when trouble breaks out, her statesman participates in the secret negotiations of the all-powerful. When *démarches* are necessary she participates in them, influences policy and seeks as an equal to enforce her view. Even in affairs that do not primarily concern her she has ensured that she is consulted. When the Italo-Serb dispute threatened Europe with war, France and Britain associated Germany with their action towards preserving peace. Versailles is indeed past history when France and Germany are associated in a *démarche* intended to bring pressure on an Allied Power. That means more in the real political sense than Herr Stresemann's presidency of the League Council, though the latter may possess greater historical significance, and Freiherr von Rheinbaben stated accurately the course of the German Republic's history when he called his history of German foreign policy " From Versailles to Freedom ".. The events of last year triumphantly vindicated his choice.

CHAPTER VIII

OUT OF THE WILDERNESS

Germany a united Republic—normality and constitutionalism—
the domination of home policy—war-guilt question—the rôle of Germany in the League of Nations—peace policy of Stresemann—the
swing to the Left—grouping of political parties in the future—the
unitary State—the *Reich* and the *Länder*—future problems—triumph
of Republicanism—the strength of the Republic.

ALTHOUGH we are too near the event for final judgment, it is still possible to risk the statement that the
formation of the Marx Cabinet and the intrigues
attendant upon it mark the end of a period in German political
history. Throughout 1927 that Cabinet functioned as a normal
parliamentary Cabinet in possession of a parliamentary
majority. The *régime* is not in question. Whatever mon-
archical principles the Nationalists had had, they sacrificed
them for the solid fact of being able to carry on a conservative
policy. For the first time, Germany became a united Republic,
and President, ministers and party leaders agreed to affirm
their loyalty to the republican form of government. For the
first time also, a Right Government could be trusted not to
attempt to overthrow the Constitution, and, in spite of the
animadversions of the Left, the reaction intends to be reactionary within the limits of the Constitution. Monarchism still
survives, but it is gradually becoming the property of a sect
more respectable, but not much more influential, than the
section which has repudiated the old German god and gone
back to Wotan. A less democratic system has many adherents, but the struggle will be fought out by parliamentary
methods and change, if any, will require a national majority.

The recognition that change must be constitutional change
means that German politics have reached normality ; that is
to say, it is not the *régime* that is in question, but the measures
of the Government, and the debates on such measures become
more intense and more real in proportion as the thought of a
constitutional struggle becomes less predominant. The change

117

from previous years was the inevitable result of the change in Germany's international status. By the recovery of independence and her restoration to the ranks of the Great Powers, she ceased to be an object of policy. Her policy, therefore, except in one or two cases, no longer depended on the will of others ; it was no longer subject to the same scrutiny ; it could develop along German lines, and it was not dominated as hitherto by the international situation. Nothing is more noticeable than the rapid divorce between home and foreign politics that 1927 shows. There is no longer a cleavage in the nation on the general principle of foreign policy, no antagonism between a policy of resistance and a policy of fulfilment. The elements of such a cleavage are still there, but so long as there occurs nothing to make a dramatic appeal to the nation, they will never coalesce to become a disruptive force in the national life. The resistance still goes on, but it is a resistance of officials and does not concern the nation. The criticisms of foreign policy are party and not national criticisms, and they are based on considerations of expediency rather than of prestige. Foreign policy is stabilized and so becomes subject to party interpretation and enters normally into the general political activity.

On its broad outlines there is general agreement that it can only be a peace policy. At the moment of writing, Germany is indeed a definite force for peace in Europe. That is recognized abroad and the recognition has atoned for much. When as an equal Stresemann participated in those private negotiations that kept the peace in the Balkans and in Eastern Europe, when it was admitted abroad, and therefore could not be denied at home, that the policy pursued was a free one and that its spokesman had actually influenced, as agents of a German policy, the cause of international policy, much of the sense of humiliation passed away. The restoration of the Concert of Europe, however deplorable from the point of view of the League of Nations, restored self-respect to Germany, and the frank admissions of her former enemies have confirmed the restoration. The sense of outlawry has passed. It is true that the war-guilt clause still stands, but it is virtually a dead letter except in the eyes of legalists and reactionary politicians, for it is no use maintaining that a nation is a criminal and a pariah if her accusers co-operate with her on terms of perfect equality. Nothing is more significant in this connection than the reaction to Stresemann's experiment at the unveiling in autumn of the Tannenberg memorial. There Hindenburg read out a statement, carefully prepared by the Cabinet, formally repudiating war-guilt. It was in effect a national repudiation and could scarcely have been made more official. The consequences were curious. While certain sections abroad revived academic discussions of the issues involved and the French patriotic Press fulminated as usual, the declaration was received with sympathy where historical questions evoke interest, with indifference everywhere else. It had no international consequences. But it had all sorts of consequences in Germany. So much had the war-guilt question become a *chose jugée*—and not in the old Allied sense—that the declaration was made the occasion of violent attacks on the Government by the Opposition, not because they objected to its content, but because they considered that it might be used as a Left weapon against a Right Cabinet and for aid in the Socialist campaign against the President. Such consequences were unthinkable three years ago. When a nation can make its branding as a pariah an incident of party politics, the mark of the branding has disappeared. Stresemann had reason to be pleased with his experiment.

The restrictions imposed by membership of the League of Nations do not gall Germany—they are indeed to her advantage. She cannot challenge the Versailles settlement by force —it would be dangerous to seek to challenge it by using the policy of alliances favoured by most of the European States, and in the new era presenting more risks of failure than hope of success—but she can consistently criticize it through the League of Nations and negotiate changes by the same medium under the Covenant. Any European crisis strengthens her position as a Great Power and her right to demand change when circumstances make change possible, and whenever her services are needed to solve the crisis, she has the opportunity of using the actual terms imposed upon her as a weapon to decrease the distance that still separates her as a Power capable of action from her former enemies. Thus her disarmament has left her with a compact well-equipped force that is formidable enough and it can be used as a weapon against the refusal of her neighbours to disarm. She has all the logic of the position on her side, and the comforting knowledge that if, in the course of this or that negotiation, she forced a genuine measure of disarmament on her neighbours, her own position would grow proportionately stronger as general disarmament was achieved.

Her policy, as guided so ably by Stresemann, does not always produce successes. Thus she has been able neither to secure general disarmament nor bring the Allied occupation to an end. That is undoubtedly a defeat for the Locarno policy, but it is not reckoned a defeat for German policy, although it can be used as a weapon against the Foreign Minister by party enemies.   It does not arouse the indignation in Germany that one would expect, for it is realized that the refusal to evacuate is a confession of weakness on the part of France, and sooner or later evacuation will have to be ordered.   A foreign policy based on peace and avoiding entangling alliances, with a clear sense of the realities of the situation and of the interests of Germany, and able to identify the morally righteous with the politically wise, is a strong foreign policy and the German nation recognizes it as such.   The next Ministry may greatly vary Stresemann's language, but it will not greatly change its course.

Nothing since then has been more noticeable than the tendency on the part of the nation to leave foreign policy to the Foreign Office or to Parliament in the confidence that it will be carried on on the lines laid down in 1925 and 1926.   But it is being subtly modified to correspond with the needs of the Parliamentary situation.   Its bases remain unchanged ; its application is made with an eye to the position of the Cabinet. Foreign policy, though guided by one man, is becoming part of the Cabinet policy, and if the Cabinet falls because its majority has definitely gone, the application of it will reveal the general political tendencies of the new majority.   There is no morbid exaggeration of the importance of foreign policy as opposed to home policy.   Both are facets of a general attitude to the general mass of problems confronting a democratic State in the post-war period.   With the relegation of foreign policy to its proper place as the result of a return to the policy of co-operation in Europe, a co-operation still too much influenced by the theory of equilibrium but radically different from the co-operation of pre-war days, Germany has been set free to take a creative interest in her domestic affairs.   The issues that divide her people are no longer external or influenced predominantly by external events ; they are those that divide nations everywhere—the struggles of interests, classes and ideals within the frontiers.

It was to secure victory in these struggles for conservatism that the Nationalists agreed to accept Locarno, the League of Nations and the Republic and enter the Cabinet.   They dominated the Marx Cabinet from the beginning by their numbers : in home policy their differences with the Populists are not so much on principle as on detail ; their co-operation with the Centrists is the result of a normal political bargain ; the Centrists accepted tariffs in exchange for the Nationalists' acceptance of the Centrum's educational policy. With a good working majority and an agreed programme, the Cabinet has succeeded in getting some of its measures into law. But it has had to face a persistent and well-guided Liberal and Socialist opposition which is based on a formidable opposition in the country. Once home politics became the dominant issue, the individual citizen voted with far less restraint than when the dominant issue was a foreign one, and it speedily became evident that the Right Cabinet was scarcely representative of the country. The necessity at the time of its formation of retaining Stresemann at the Foreign Office, in view of negotiations with the Allies for an alleviation of the Rhineland occupation, has passed, and there is no reason now why a Democrat or a Socialist politician should not negotiate with equal authority in the debates of the future. A Nationalist in foreign politics is not necessarily a reactionary in home politics, and with internal issues before the electors the 1927 elections to Land parliaments and to municipalities have shown a striking swing to the Left and notoriously to the Socialist Left ; indeed, were it possible for the whole Left to reunite, the united Socialist party, if it did not secure a majority, would at least secure a commanding position as the result of a general election. In practically all these minor elections, the Communists have fared badly, although local reasons gave them a triumph in Hesse at the expense of the Socialists. Their party is threatened with disintegration. They have suffered notable defections and their activities do little more than split the Left vote. Their clear-cut extremism, dictated to them by Moscow, as well as their parliamentary tactics make co-operation with the Socialists impossible, and reunion can only come by the gradual return of the workers to Socialism as opposed to Moscow Communism. But that return will be very gradual, and the Socialists face the next election under the grave handicap of having so far to compete with the Communists for votes. The tide, however, all through 1927 flowed their way and they look to the future with a confidence that is completely lacking in the Communists. The Democrats have held their own and have even in places improved their position, but they cannot look forward to any great gains. Still they may well feel that they have sunk as far as they will sink and that they are beginning to come up again. A Democrat-Socialist coalition ministry supported by the Left of the Centrum is not outside the bounds of possibility, and that is the most significant thing about the actual political situation. The Centrum, happily buttressed

by a solid confessional voting mass, will always retain its peculiar position in German politics, and its possession of well-
defined Right and Left elements enable it to form coalitions in
either direction, while its internal discipline and the strong
sense of the necessity for protecting Roman Catholic interests
maintain it united. There are, however, signs that the opposing
wings are becoming more hostile than before, and any defection
on a non-confessional issue might change dramatically the
parliamentary party. The Right has suffered the reverses.
The Nationalists have suffered the less as the many votes lost
have been somewhat compensated for by the return of electors,
temporarily attracted to the Fascists, but the Populists have
suffered more seriously, having lost alike to the Democrats
and the Nationalists. The tendency toward a four- and even
a three-party system is growing and it is not really hindered by
the appearance of small parties representing a definite social
stratum or interest. A party representing the small or middle
bourgeois may be relied on to support either the Liberals or the
Conservatives, but once its support is pledged it disappears for
the duration of the alliance into the larger party.

Before the war only the reckless prophesied on political
futures ; now only the foolish do so, but it is not too rash to
expect a continuance of the swing to the Left and a Left victory
following on the 1928 elections. The swing is normal and is
the best evidence that the Constitution is functioning normally
and satisfactorily. It does so because very largely it has ceased
to be discussed. If it is discussed, it is rather as the essential
basis on which reform can be raised and not as a thing to be
rejected or supported, and the reform seems more likely to
come from a Liberal urge than otherwise if one considers the
action of the Liberal Land governments, the stand taken by
Prussia in the Reichsrat against tariffs and for disarmament,
and above all the growing agitation in favour of a unitary State.

This is one of the most interesting aspects of present-day
Germany and it raises a whole series of questions of historic
right, geography, economics and administration. The Right
naturally opposes it, but, on the other hand, the Right is in
favour of a proper federalism for Prussia, that is, that the
Prussian votes in the Reichsrat should be divided among the
federal parts and not regarded as a Prussian *bloc* vote. As it
is, the Prussian Government, Liberal in tendency and supported by a Liberal majority, throws the whole weight of
Prussia's vote—twenty-six out of sixty-three—in the Reichsrat against the reactionary measures of the Cabinet. Nothing

infuriates the Conservative more than to see Prussia, of all
States, posing as the defender of Liberal ideas in the Upper
House even if its action there is only delaying and not decisive.
But if the votes were divided up among federal divisions the
vote would certainly not be a solid Liberal one. The proper
federalism of Prussia would not necessarily hasten the unitary
State, but it would break up one of the unitary States that prevent the arrival of *the* unitary State. If the federal divisions
became *Reichsländer*, that is to say, territory belonging to the
Reich as a whole, and Prussia became a geographical and historical term, most of the other States would raise no rooted
objections to becoming *Reichsländer* also. But they will not
be merged in Prussia on any terms. That was made perfectly
clear by Hesse's responsible spokesmen, who at the same time
favour a unitary State. The Land parliaments would disappear
as such and reappear as provincial councils or something akin
and there would be no division of powers or duplication of
authority. The difficulties are technical as much as anything,
except in the case of Bavaria, which is violently opposed to
losing her identity. She still poses as a sovereign State, which
she is not, and maintains her rights as such, partly because she
has a greater State consciousness than any other State, partly
because she is the Catholic State *par excellence*, and because,
in her violent reaction from Communism, she is the chief centre
of Monarchism and Conservatism. She has dabbled in Monarchist intrigues which have injured the cause of Monarchism
as much as they have helped it, but she is nearer a Monarchist
restoration than any other State. But she knows that it could
only be a Bavarian restoration, and that the rest of Germany
did not suffer the expulsion of the Hohenzollerns to submit to
the rule of the Wittelsbachs. No more than any other section
of the community does she wish to disrupt Germany, and it is
doubtful if the Bavarian worker would endure action which
would lead to weaken the ties with the Reich. Her statesmen
are quite conscious of that and it explains possibly the vehe-
mence with which they insist on Bavarianism and repudiate
the unitary State. Whether they would make good their
words if it came to a definite trial of strength is another question, which one dare not try to answer.

It may betray excessive optimism, but one may venture to
declare that there is definite evidence that Germany has settled
in solidity. That implies the opinion that the Republican
system is secure unless extraordinary circumstances arise.
The first noticeable thing is that to the average German the

question of the *régime* is an academic question.   It is true that the German has a genius for treating any question academically, but, prior to the end of 1925, the academic attitude was not apparent.   To-day, an average Anti-Republican will produce one hundred and one proofs of the undesirability of the Republican system and he will applaud vigorously the orator who presents him with a hundred and second, but he will take no action against it and when he goes to the poll it is no longer the supreme issue.   Out of Anti-Republicanism of that sort it is impossible to create an Anti-Republican party, especially at a time when there is officially no Anti-Republican party and actually only one which, besides being Anti-Republican, is a lot of other things which academic Anti-Republicans dislike intensely.   It is true that there exist all sorts of Anti-Republican organizations capable of noisy demonstration, but it is doubtful if—again given the continued absence of extraordinary circumstances—they can do more.   It is equally true that an enormous amount of political and legal controversy goes on, but it is conducted mainly by the journalist.   The agitation that forced the resignation of Seeckt because of the presence of Prince Wilhelm of Prussia at manœuvres has its counterpart in the artificial agitation against the naval authorities for allowing Prince Heinrich to be entertained on board the *Berlin* on its departure for foreign waters, but, while the former controversy agitated the nation, the latter agitated mainly party politicians and journalists.   The notorious battle of the flags and the refusal of certain sections to hoist the black, red and gold of the *Deutscher Bund*, officially proclaimed the national colours by the Weimar Constitution, was waged with a good deal of bitterness, but, when it came to ministers boycotting hotels and ex-Prussian captains barricading themselves in their rooms and defiantly shaking out black, white and red flags of enormous extent, the humorous side of the affair struck the nation, which, in its vast majority, sees no insult to Germany in preferring the flag of Lutzow's riders to that of the Hansa merchants *plus* that of the Hohenzollern dukes.   The Republican *v.* Monarchist quarrel is real and deep-seated and it creates nasty incidents, but it will have dire political consequences till the Republican State fails in its duty as maintainer of order and upholder of law.   So far it has done it, perhaps not quite impartially, for the Monarchist gets more easy treatment than the Communist, but that is true of all bourgeois States, and the pressure of public opinion is beginning to force a more even treatment.

The more statesmanlike conduct of the Allies has robbed the Monarchist of his best ally.   It is no longer possible for him to complain that Germany is treated as a helpless inferior ; the evidence to the contrary is too plain.   He still indulges in polemics with his counterparts on the left bank of the Rhine, but he cannot rouse them more easily than he can his own countrymen, who have taken the measure of him and the French Chauvinist with considerable accuracy.   That does not mean that the nation has simply accepted the Peace Treaty as the eternal basis of European relations.   On the contrary, the opposition to the Treaty is as strong as ever, but the opposition to Treaty fulfilment has died away and Monarchism is no longer identical with patriotism.   It is only that the majority of the nation has become convinced that fulfilment is the quickest way to escape from the Treaty.   It has already recovered Cologne and seen the Allied Commissions of Control depart ; it knows that the rest of the Rhineland will be recovered in seven years ; it knows that its reparation payments are an irksome but not an intolerable burden and are hurting the recipients quite as much as, if not more, than the payers ; it does not and cannot forget the lost territory, but every day, that brings strength, brings the day of recovery nearer, and that strength requires unity to make it effective ; it has the feeling that it is not for Germany to make the opportunity, but to be ready to seize the opportunity when others create it, as create it they must.

Germany is working in all her parts and a nation that works has little time for barren controversies, for, in the work itself, lie controversies that affect more deeply the life of the average German than the controversies on political philosophy and political history.   Questions of tariffs, of socialization, of trustification, of the cost and distribution of food supplies, of wages, of municipal government, of housing, of general administration, education, and the Civil Service—these are the questions that fill the first place in his thoughts.

The lasting political struggle in Germany, the struggle between Left and Right, the struggle of democracy against reaction from the Right and reaction from the Left, perhaps against an unholy alliance of both, will be a severe one, but one sees as yet no reason to despair of the German Republic, to doubt of its future or to disbelieve in the possibility of a liberal Germany becoming one of the buttresses of peace in a Europe that has attained a settlement that corresponds to the deepest needs of Europe as a whole and is a beginning of the organization of Europe for the service of humanity.   It may augur well for one's power of credulity to believe at the end of 1927 in the future of Germany, but to disbelieve in its future is to disbelieve in the future of Europe.   Credulity is not necessarily a vice because it is the credulity of optimism.

BOOK II
THE NEW ECONOMIC STATE

CHAPTER IX

THE RECOVERY OF PRODUCTION : THE GROWTH OF GERMAN INDUSTRY AND THE TREATY OF VERSAILLES

The political versus the economic mentality—dissociation of industry from politics—the Ruhr-Lorraine-Luxemburg economic unit—industrial expansion of Germany after the Franco-Prussian War—the effects of the Treaty of Versailles—an estimate of the loss incurred through provisions of the Treaty.

WHILE it is true that politics and economics come together in the formation of the modern State and decide the main characteristics its development assumes, they do not always coincide either in mode of action, in principle, or in result. They may be often seriously out of phase and distort what might otherwise be a perfect perspective of the national idea ; they may come into antagonism for a moment or be dominated one by the other ; they may decide in combination or in isolation, certain national mentalities which distinguish one race from another. In the case of Germany, it has been stated, as one explanation of the recent history of that country, that the political genius, which has always been a marked trait of the British State, has still to be found elsewhere and, above all, in our principal industrial competitor. The Germans, on the other hand, trace a great part of the industrial depression ruling at present in this country to the predominance of the political sense and the disappearance of the economic, as far at least as the organization and administration of industry are concerned.

It is dangerous to carry simplification to the extreme and show an immense prodigality in labels. Nothing in the world of politics and trade can be analysed and neatly classified in an appropriate series : subtle reactions and inter-reactions, subtle shades in tone and colouring, even divergences in interpretation, may serve to weaken and render farcical the most splendid structure of theory and definite statement. In spite of this, there is some measure of truth in the conception that Germany has advanced much more rapidly in the economic than in the political field through the emergence of qualities, both national and individual, which found a more congenial soil in the former than in the latter. The peculiar ability which goes to the formation of what is regarded as a sound political view of life, with its accompaniment in a right political conscience or instinct, is not the same as the capacity to develop an immense industrial complex or carry forward a whole nation on a plan of rapid economic expansion. Politics, in the accepted meaning of the word, is an art of compromise, of conciliation, of mass-approval ; it remains fluid, infinitely elastic and opportunist ; it depends for its success on the creation and maintenance of an atmosphere of consent, in the bringing together almost within one psychological unit of a whole people. The ideals and methods it sets up can take effect only if the nation grants, consciously or unconsciously, a form of sanction, and this sanction depends on factors which belong more to instinct and emotion than to cold, clear reasoning and exact calculation.

If this definition be accepted, then the German mentality falls only with difficulty into the political category. In the midst of profound speculation as to the form and content of life, of material and moral existence, in a haze of philosophic systems all converging on the discussion of reality, modern German thought has appeared unpractical and inept, but the very act of concentration on philosophic doctrines and the very application of logic to the investigation of spiritual phenomena have induced a love of discipline which, after many years, has grown into the inner texture of the German spirit.

If this tendency towards discipline, towards acceptance of authority is diverted into the world of industrial production, the results become evident at once. Co-operation in the technique and administration of industry comes easy to a mind already attuned to system, while the rigid framework within which great industrial movements are held after an initial period of expansion yields opportunity for minute attention to detail and the careful elaboration of set methods and principles. In industry, a fixed determination, even accompanied by a narrow outlook, may lead to more effective and more spectacular achievement than perpetual experiment and perpetual compromise.

The history of German industrial expansion since the Franco-Prussian War has been a history of set design with few moments of doubt or hesitation. Politics became subordinated entirely to economic needs and, for forty years, the world could view

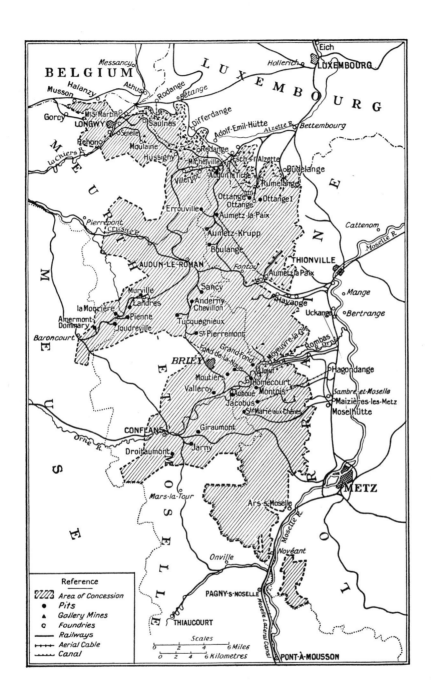

LORRAINE IRON-ORE FIELD

the efforts of a nation elaborating and perfecting the most remarkable equipment for production on a giant scale ever known. Economic histories bring fact after fact into perspective from the formation of the Customs' Union and the occupation of Lorraine, from the development of great iron and steel and chemical works in Lorraine, Luxemburg and the Ruhr to the unfolding of a powerful engineering centre in Berlin, and the evolution of a railway transport system unparalleled in Europe. The balance of power in Europe did not depend on agreements reached between diplomatic plenipotentiaries in a council-room, but on those industrialists who were welding Lorraine, the Saar, Luxemburg and the Ruhr into one productive unit and, under cover of a tariff, were building up vast organizations to control production and price and form international groups controlling the basic industries.

To understand the fundamental influences and movements which brought on the war, one must study the grouping of economic forces in Germany over the forty years preceding it. Economic domination came closer to reality in the minds of the industrialists than the dream of imperial splendour in the minds of the diplomats and politicians. The latter played still with theory, while the former had almost achieved reality. The problem of Lorraine and the movement towards specialization in industry itself decided German economic development before the war and were decisive factors, not only in the definition of the Treaty of Versailles, but also in the work of recovery which has since taken place. Other elements enter, of course, into the scheme ; the growth of finance and the extension of international trade relations with, in certain cases, international agreements, the development of administrative and manufacturing efficiency, the emergence of new interests subsidiary to the old, and the evolution of a skilled labour force in the basic industries, the conception of a new standard of living and economic wage levels, were all of significance, but the critical points were to be found in the two factors mentioned.

The iron-ore deposits of Lorraine and adjacent territory were potentially the most valuable in Europe and, as such, would have constituted a great source of wealth to France prior to 1870 if the technical conditions of iron and steel production had been favourable. The low iron content of the Lorraine minette (32–35 per cent.) required a special process before pig-iron of a satisfactory quality could be produced and, in the early decades of the industry, up to and beyond 1870, high

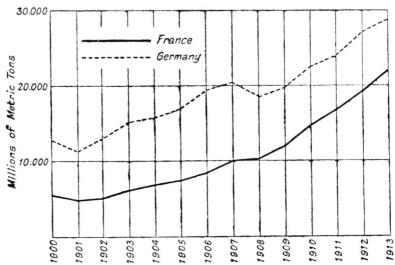

PRODUCTION OF IRON-ORE IN FRANCE AND GERMANY (1900–1913)

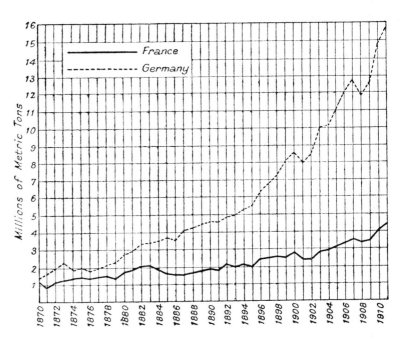

PRODUCTION OF PIG-IRON IN FRANCE AND GERMANY (1870–1911)

grade ores of 60 per cent. iron content and above alone were used. The minette fields of Lorraine had little real value until the Thomas process reached commercial development in 1890. At that time, Germany was in possession of, roughly, half the iron-ore area, as the map indicates, and entered at once on a programme of intensive exploitation. France, on the other hand, in spite of the fact that it still possessed deposits in volume not far short of those now being opened up by Germany, did little of its own initiative to expand its output of iron and steel—one factor adverse to such a policy being the necessity of importing coal and coke from the Saar and the Ruhr.

From many points of view, therefore, the defeat of France in 1871 was tantamount to an economic revolution in Europe ; it retarded, apparently for good, the industrialization of France and forced it to remain largely a country of small industries with agriculture providing the bulk of the national wealth, while those special qualities which, in time, form a highly skilled reserve of labour for industry were not allowed to develop to any extent in the French people ; it initiated the industrial era in Germany and was undoubtedly the *point de départ* for every economic movement of importance which took place in that country during thirty years.

Without Lorraine, it is difficult to see how the coal-mining, iron and steel and heavy engineering industries of Germany could have reached their state of perfection, both in volume of output and in administrative efficiency, in the first decade of this century. The German ironmasters linked up the Saar with Lorraine and Luxemburg in a closely interwoven system, whereby the Saar coal and coke could be used in the iron and steel works located in the ore-fields and the Lorraine ore be transported to the blast furnaces operating in the Saar. Community of interests meant something more than an interchange of raw materials : the Saar industrialists acquired concessions in Lorraine and built iron and steel works there, they formed working agreements with the French ironmasters operating in French Lorraine and were instrumental in developing the entire minette area. A further development lay in the penetration of the Ruhr industrialists into Lorraine in turn, with a consequent rapid expansion of large-scale production from modern plant of high efficiency, in the linking up of German interests in Luxemburg with the new productive complex to the South, and the close association of the Saar and Ruhr industries. With these developments, we associate the names of Thyssem,

Röchling, Stinnes and Klöckner on the German side and De Wendel on the French.

The work of development came to a conclusion in the few years preceding the war, and Lorraine had, as a result of the policy adopted, changed its character as an ore-producing area alone and become one of the most powerful iron and steel centres in the world. The ore-mines fed directly into blast-furnaces and the blast-furnaces into steel works and rolling mills, and the possibilities of industrial wealth were expanded accordingly. Lorraine was changing into one of the most valuable assets the German nation possessed. The Ruhr itself, as the result of these developments, tended to specialize more and more in finished steel products : the Saar and Lorraine works supplied pig-iron, steel ingots and semi-finished steel, which were worked up in the Ruhr rolling mills and machine-shops. Specialization took place very largely from area to area, and was undoubtedly a main factor causing prosperity and active trade ; one economic unit was being moulded and, when the war broke out, it was operating with a high standard of efficiency. The Ruhr sent coal and coke as well as finished steel products into Lorraine and the Saar, while it received from them iron-ore, pig-iron and semi-finished steel. The volume of trade was very considerable. Over the railway alone, the Ruhr sent in 1913 more than nine million tons of coal and coke into Lorraine, Luxemburg, the Saar and Eastern France, while it received almost four million tons of ore, slightly more than one million tons of pig-iron and one million tons of semi-finished and rolled steel. We should add to this shipments down the Rhine between Duisburg and Strasburg.

Lorraine with the New Thyssen works established at Hagon-dange, the Gelsenkirchen works at Esch, the Klöckner works at Knutange and the Rombachar works on the border between it and the Saar could show some of the largest and most modern installations in the world. Similarly, in Luxemburg, the Ruhr industrialists established great iron and steel plants—among them, the Differdange works of the Stinnes concern and the Burbach-Eich-Dudelange group. The process of linking up these areas gave to Germany a period of very great activity and laid the foundations of immense industrial wealth, which served to confer a new economic status on the whole country : it stood forth as a direct rival to Great Britain in the heavy industries and showed possibilities of expansion paralleled only by those of the United States. In 1870, its iron and steel industries were behind those of this country, both in volume of output and in equipment, and were very little superior to those of France. By the end of the century, they had moved far ahead of their French rivals and had drawn parallel with the British industries ; at the outset of the war, they were chief in Europe and had a greater output than Britain, France and Belgium combined. The United States and Germany between them accounted for nearly 70 per cent. of all the steel placed on the market by the iron and steel plants of the world.

In these circumstances, the declaration of war by Germany on France in 1914 must appear as economically unsound to the last degree ; in the industrial sphere, the victory had already been decisively won, and the wisest policy lay in consolidation of existing gains with the sure prospect of complete domination in the near future—as far, at least, as the iron and steel and engineering industries were concerned. It is difficult to believe, therefore, that industrial Germany desired the war, unless, of course, the economic positions of both countries, both Germany and France, promised the immediate defeat of France. If France lost the minette area in Lorraine as well as the coalfields of the Nord and Pas-de-Calais districts, it would be only a matter of time before she would collapse through lack of basic raw materials required for prosecuting the war. From that point of view, therefore, one of the most decisive battles of the Western Front took place in the early months, when the French thrust into Lorraine was repulsed with terrible loss and the retreating armies were forced out of the minette area back to the Couronne de Nancy. One part of the victory was won for Germany in Lorraine, while the occupation of the Nord and Pas-de-Calais coal-mining districts completed the campaign as far as materials were affected. France could depend only on a few iron and steel works located in Normandy for the supply of munitions. The first two years of the war were years of crisis, when Great Britain, aided by imports from the United States, was making good the loss of the Lorraine iron and steel works and, even into 1917, the German superiority in munitions continued. We cannot know how close was the margin between stalemate and utter defeat for France in 1914 and 1915, through this factor alone.

The creation of the Ruhr-Luxemburg-Saar-Lorraine economic unit brought great changes into the balance of industrial, financial and trade forces inside Germany. At one time, the possibilities of economic expansion on a wide front with no industry other than agriculture predominant were very real ; coal-mining, iron and steel and engineering were important sources of wealth, but they did not predominate absolutely and decide in themselves the course of national development. But the expansion of Lorraine threw the balance strongly in favour of the heavy industries, and we find the main effort of the country concentrated on them. They assumed greater and greater significance from 1882 onwards and only now are beginning to yield ground. Without them it is, of course, a matter for conjecture whether Germany could have supported easily the rapid increase that took place in its population after the war of 1870—an increase which had no parallel in the leading European industrial countries.

To give definite instances of the changes which took place, we might compare the course of population and employment in the industries affected by the movement towards specialization. In 1882, the population of Germany stood at 45,223,000 ; in 1895, at 51,770,000 ; in 1907, at 61,720,000 ; and in 1925, allowing for the ceded territory, at 62,700,000. Between 1882 and 1907, the population increased by 36 per cent., and industry accounted for two-thirds of it. Thus, industry, which supported 35 per cent. of all the German people in 1882 and 39 per cent. in 1895, expanded sufficiently during the twelve years prior to 1907 to maintain 43 per cent., and the present ratio stands at about 48 per cent. The process of conversion, which had proceeded very slowly prior to 1882 and quickened up slightly during the subsequent twelve years, came into full *tempo* towards 1907, reached its highest point at the beginning of the war, and has since slowed down. The population dependent on industry increased by 10,300,000 between 1882 and 1907, and, of this total, 4,800,000 represent the quota which the rapidity of conversion brought.

The change in the character of the German State from agriculture and small widespread industries to large-scale production concentrated in well-defined areas can be appreciated from these figures. Industry caused the expansion of population, and it was able, through the increase of wealth it brought, not only to stand this burden but also to raise considerably the standard of living and the economic status of the German people. Such a development was not general over the entire industrial field : a small number of industries held in themselves the object and justification of expansion—the industries within the coal-mining and metallurgical group. In coal-mining, iron and steel, metal-working and engineering, the number of employees increased from 1,255,000 in 1882 to 3,056,000 in 1907 and 4,060,000 in 1925 ; in 1882, 19 per cent.

of all employees in industry were engaged in this group, in 1907, 27 per cent., and, in 1925, 33 per cent.

Even more spectacular are comparisons based on manufacturing equipment.   In 1907, 34 per cent. of all motive power plant in industry was installed in the mining and metallurgical group, but by 1925 it had risen to 56 per cent.—9,946,258 h.p. out of a total of 17,656,660 h.p.   We should include also chemical production, since the German chemical industry grew up in close association with the coal-distillation plant of the Ruhr, and depended for part of its output on the utilization of waste-products from the treatment of coal in coke-ovens and similar plant.   The entire chemical, mining and metallurgical group employed 1,333,652 workers in 1882 and 4,374,000 in 1925, while the capacity of manufacturing equipment expanded to 10,894,671 h.p., equivalent to 62 per cent. of all motive power in German industry.

With the exception of Upper Silesia and certain isolated areas in Central Germany, the coal-mining, iron and steel and chemical industries have been concentrated in the Ruhr, Saar and Lorraine economic unit, and owed their development to that immense work of co-ordination which, begun slowly and speculatively after the Franco-Prussian War, had reached its first great stage in achievement in 1907 and was moving towards a culmination in 1913.   The history of German economic Imperialism dates from the time when the Ruhr ironmasters built their great iron and steel plants in Luxemburg and Lorraine, and moved forwards towards domination of the iron and steel production, not only of Europe, but of the world.   It had its moments of crisis during the eighties and in 1907, when the financial security of Germany was threatened with collapse and severe depression ruled in many important markets, but it has proceeded almost in a definite and carefully elaborated plan, conceived at the hour of victory and brought, slowly and carefully, to fruition.   The future of Germany as an economic and industrial power was bound up irrevocably to all appearances with the great industries of the Ruhr, the Saar, Luxemburg and Lorraine.

The Treaty of Versailles cut through the many links joining up the various sections of the Ruhr, Lorraine, Luxemburg and the Saar economic unit and destroyed the work of thirty years ; the German iron and steel works in Lorraine passed over to France and provided it with equipment of the most modern type for metallurgical production, while the decision of Luxemburg to enter into a customs' union with Belgium meant a

similar change in the status of German-owned plant. Compensation was paid for such transfers and the payments constituted
an important financial reserve, which was tapped by the Ruhr
ironmasters during the period of inflation when they had
definitely joined issue with the Republic on reparations. The
loss of Upper Silesian coal-mines and metallurgical works as a
result of the plebiscite of 1922 apparently completed the downfall of the German industrial *régime*. The incidence of war had
been instrumental above all in bringing a serious crisis into the
economic life of the country ; the policy of specialization in
the heavy industries, to which the nation had been committed
during thirty years at least, was seen to be wrong, and no sub-
stitute was forthcoming to make good the decline in production
and national prosperity confidently predicted by politicians
and statesmen. The Ruhr stood in isolation with its sources
of raw materials cut off and with no market for its coke production other than that created by reparations deliveries.
France could look forward to a period of intense industrial
activity and domination in iron and steel.

The Treaty of Versailles found its justification in the economic if not in the political sphere. Certain elements in the
situation escaped, however, the attention of the French and, at
first, the German industrialists—chief among them being the
character and destination of the output of Lorraine, the Saar
and Luxemburg. Paralysis of the Ruhr would entail paralysis
of the other areas as well, unless new markets could be found
to absorb the demand once represented by the Ruhr. In addition to this, the major industries of the ceded territories were
essentially raw material and not finishing industries, and the
raw materials they supplied were not their absolute monopoly.
Other areas could make good ultimately the deficiency and feed
direct into the Ruhr, while the latter could render conditions
favourable for a transfer of demand away from the ceded territories. The Ruhr possessed steel furnaces, rolling mills and
finishing shops capable of dealing with an output not much less
than that of the old economic unit ; its blast furnaces could be
developed to treat foreign high-grade ores instead of the Lorraine minette, and thus bring the manufacturing complex into
full activity again. The links joining up the Ruhr foundries
and steel works with the great engineering workshops of Berlin
and Nuremberg had not been disturbed and they could operate
at once.

While, therefore, the domination of Germany in iron and
steel had been destroyed by the Treaty of Versailles, the eco-

nomic life of the country was not vitally affected, and the policy of specialization in the heavy industries could not be declared bankrupt, even in anticipation. It is as easy to overestimate the consequences of the Treaty of Versailles and the Upper Silesian plebiscite as it is to underestimate them. Undoubtedly, the severance of the Ruhr from the Saar, Lorraine and Luxemburg and of the Central German engineering works from their raw material sources in Upper Silesia meant widespread disturbance which could not be smoothed down for a considerable time, but fundamental conditions made for recovery. The perception of this truth may have led to the invasion of the Ruhr by France and Belgium in 1923 ; the victory was beginning to lose reality in the work of adjustment and recuperation that had already set in, and only the paralysis of Ruhr production could ensure the real economic subjection of Germany. The Ruhr invasion failed simply through the determination of the Rhineland to oppose directly and indirectly all efforts made to exploit the manufacturing capacity of the area. The position was stalemate from the first hour of the invasion and stalemate it remained until the invaders withdrew. It is true, nevertheless, that Germany sustained severe injury industrially as the result of the Treaty of Versailles, and sufficient information is available at this distance of eight years to illustrate at last how great this injury was.

It is difficult to estimate with accuracy the real loss Germany sustained through the surrender of Alsace-Lorraine, the Saar and Upper Silesia. The result of the plebiscite to be held a few years hence may decide the fate of the Saar in favour of Germany, but, since the conclusion of the war, it has been possessed almost as effectively by France as Lorraine. Mere calculations regarding capital value of the ceded territory, a favourite source of propaganda against the levy of reparations, can have little value, since the earning capacity represented by capital remains always the decisive factor, and such capacity bears no consistent relation to potential wealth. The industry of a people, the vitality of trade and the activity of markets decide the real value of a territory, and they cannot always be assessed in monetary values. Certain sources of information may, however, be tapped—statistics of employment, of manufacturing equipment, of production in the basic industries and of trade exchanges—and from them we may derive some conception of the change in the economic status of Germany caused by the Treaty of Versailles.

Examination of the census returns for 1907 shows that the

ceded territories employed 858,420 workers in industry alone, and 1,109,704 in all branches of activity, industry, trade, finance and commerce. The total population supported by such a labour force would not be more than 6,400,000. The capacity of manufacturing equipment in industry alone was 891,000 h.p., while, for all activities inclusive of industry it exceeded 1,000,000 h.p. Coal-mining, iron and steel alone accounted for 434,000 h.p., the only other industry of importance being textiles with 72,960 h.p. Engineering and electrical manufacture accounted for 27,000 h.p., equivalent only to the capacity of one large works. Assuming that the ceded areas progressed at the same rate as the rest of Germany, the number of employees in industry in 1925 could be given as 1,079,000, and in all activities as 1,400,000, while the capacity of manufacturing equipment in industry might be estimated at 1,825,000 h.p., and in all branches of activity at slightly over 2,000,000 h.p. The total population of the lost territories would be 8,100,000.

We can assume, therefore, on the basis of these calculations, that the economic loss incurred by Germany as a result of the Treaty of Versailles, apart from the question of colonies and dependencies abroad, was equal to 11 per cent. of her annual productive capacity and, in all probability, 11 per cent. of her annual income. It would be dangerous to state that 11 per cent. of the national wealth had gone over to France, Belgium and Poland, since no assessment could possibly be made of the real value of the Lorraine ore deposits or the Saar coal measures. Inclusion of such elements would lead undoubtedly to a figure greatly in excess of that given. The only test, however, which can have actual economic value is that of annual earning capacity and, by that test, the loss suffered by Germany could not have been less than 11 per cent. or more than 15 per cent. —in itself a very high figure, but not quite so high as propagandists would desire us to believe. The decline in competitive power *vis-à-vis* France, Belgium and Poland would be greater than 11 per cent. through transfer of this earning capacity to them, but the reality of such a decline would depend wholly on the enterprise of Germany. The recuperative power of the country might be rapid enough and strong enough to restore a condition of balance and wipe out deficiency. As a matter of fact, the history of Germany during the last five years has been a history of recovery and of a restoration in the balance of economic power, and we shall see later how this has been effected. The main point at issue for the moment is that the

Treaty of Versailles, with all its sanctions and territorial transfers, only reduced the economic strength of Germany, taking all branches of production, by about 11 per cent.

In view of the economic development in the ceded territories, which has already been discussed, the loss in production fell specially on the coal-mining, iron and steel industries, and affected very slightly the material-consuming industries of Germany, such as engineering, electrical manufacture and textiles. Germany had in 1913 an output of 189,764,000 metric tons of hard coal and, of this total, Upper Silesia contributed 43,435,000 tons, the Saar 13,217,000 tons, Lorraine 3,796,000 tons, and Aix-la-Chapelle 3,273,000 tons. The partitïon of Upper Silesia meant a reduction of 32,000,000 tons in effective production within the German frontiers, if the 1913 statistics are used as a basis, so that, adding the Saar, Lorraine and the Eupen-Malmédy outputs, the total annual loss in coal alone may be given as about 50,000,000 tons. In iron and steel the position was even more serious. In 1913, the *Zollverein,* inclusive of Luxemburg, produced 28,000,000 tons of iron-ore, 19,300,000 tons of pig-iron, 18,935,000 tons of steel ingots and castings, and 16,699,000 tons of rolled steel products. Germany, limited to its present frontiers, represented, of this total, 7,471,000 tons of iron-ore, 11,520,000 tons of pig-iron, 13,232,000 tons of steel ingots, and 12,000,000 tons of rolling-mill products. Thus the Treaty of Versailles and the Upper Silesian partition caused an annual loss of 21,136,000 tons of iron-ore, 7,780,000 tons of pig-iron, 6,703,000 tons of steel ingots, and 4,699,000 tons of finished steel, taking 1913 as a representative year.

In coal, therefore, the decrease in productive capacity was 25 per cent., in iron-ore 74 per cent., in pig-iron 41 per cent., in steel ingots 51 per cent., and in rolling-mill products 39 per cent. If we omit Luxemburg as not being in reality German territory, the decline in pig-iron may be given as 31 per cent., in steel as 25 per cent., and in rolled steel as 30 per cent. In the basic raw materials, necessary to her engineering, ship-building, electrical and metal-working industries, which, between them, supported the greater part of her industrial population and contributed most to the favourable balance of trade, Germany had been seriously weakened, and certain industrialists and politicians, especially in France, held that recovery would never be sufficient to restore industrial pre-eminence to Germany. Yet, fundamentally, the position could not be regarded as hopeless ; the earning capacity of the country as a whole had not been impaired, a deficit of 11 per cent. could be remedied by better organization and the study of economy in materials, and the industries seriously affected were capable of expansion within very wide limits.

CHAPTER X

THE RECOVERY OF PRODUCTION (*continued*) : GERMANY AFTER THE TREATY OF VERSAILLES

The problem facing the industrialist—the significance of fuel economy—hard-coal and brown-coal production—electrical development—a super-power system—an industrial revolution—international aspects—iron and steel—the Ruhr occupation—recovery in 1927—the rôle of the large concern—the engineering, chemical and electrical industries—a general survey.

THE problem now confronting the German industrialist, if he ever envisaged it as a problem at all, was this : would it be possible to make good eventually the loss in production and restore the position as it existed prior to the war, or would he require to assume a permanent decrease in the volume of output in the coal-mining, iron and steel industries and effect a corresponding reduction through the entire range of industries branching out from the latter ? Adoption of the second principle would be, in essence, a recognition of defeat and it would be accompanied by all the dangers and disturbances of industrial depression and national impoverishment on an unparalleled scale. The most pessimistic views of the future of German industry would pale on contact with reality, and the whole of European trade and industry would be seriously affected.

It is difficult to believe that the pros and cons of the situation were weighed up so carefully, either by the German State as a whole or even by German industries. Political factors obscured the issues in the early years, inflation diverted effort into unsound speculative enterprise, the occupation of the Ruhr brought politics again into prominence, and it was only at the end of 1923 that a clear perception existed of economic realities. The problem as such lay in a state of inanition during four years, and instinct more than definite reasoning determined the course of events. It was clear, however, that it would be easier to build up, even artificially, the raw materials sections in the chain of production, coal, iron and steel, and incur perhaps fairly severe losses in doing so than to recognize the *status quo* resulting from the Treaty of Versailles.   Such a theory coincided with the urgings of a mentality which had been schooled in industry for fifty years to the conception of steady progress in technique and production, and it entered, consciously and unconsciously, into all the calculations made by the industrialists.

If we deal with coal alone at this stage and reserve discussion of iron and steel till later, the deficit of 50,000,000 tons annually had to be made good.   The most obvious method lay in importing coal to that amount, but such an importation would require at least a corresponding increase in the surplus of wealth available from industrial production to ensure an effective balance of trade, and the consuming industries would require to pay prices for their fuel far in excess of those paid in competing industries abroad, losing through this their power to maintain a strong trade position and realize a large export surplus.   The deficiency had to be made good within Germany itself.   Several possibilities might be entertained in this connection : the more intensive exploitation of existing coal areas, notably the Ruhr, where output would require to rise to 50 per cent. above the 1913 total to cover the entire deficit ; the study of fuel economy on the most thorough scale throughout the entire range of manufacturing activity ; and the discovery or exploitation of substitutes for coal.   Increased output from the Ruhr mines to the extent required would mean opening up of new coal areas, sinking of new shafts and reconstruction of surface equipment, all of which would take a considerable time, to be measured in years rather than in months, and heavy capital expenditure in excess of what the country as a whole could afford.   Prior to the loss of Upper Silesia in 1922, the situation was not critical, but, thereafter, the need for rapid development became apparent.   Success was achieved in Germany through a combination of all factors : increase in the production of the Ruhr within already exploited areas, the study of fuel economy, the development of brown coal, and the elaboration and execution of large power schemes.

The use of coal in industry remains fundamentally a power problem.   In iron and steel and metal-working, as well as in foundry work generally, coal may be valuable as fuel alone, but, even in these cases, exhaust gases or waste heat may be recovered and used for power production.   Manufacturing processes constitute the basis of industrial production under modern conditions, and these processes depend on mechanical or electrical motive power ; such power depends in turn on steam produced in boilers consuming coal. In the early decades, up to 1913 in fact, steam was translated into mechanical power with no further utilization in electricity, but modern developments have altered the situation. The substitution of electricity as a motive force and the conversion of manufacturing processes to electric drive rendered possible mass-production of power in giant stations serving wide areas, and allowed great economies to be made in the technique and distribution of output ; such economies led in turn to savings in fuel.

In few other industries has scientific and technical progress been accompanied by more spectacular economic results than in electricity supply ; the design and performance of generating machinery have improved so consistently from year to year that one ton of coal can now produce twice as much electric energy as it did in 1913. If we take note of the fact that in 1925 66 per cent. of all manufacturing processes in industry were driven by electrical power, that in iron and steel 74 per cent. were so driven, while the figure now is over 80 per cent. and that in a number of basic industries, such as chemicals, engineering and electrical manufacture, it fluctuated between 72 and 100 per cent., the influence of electrical development in the coal situation in Germany may be appreciated. It should, of course, be remembered that generating stations consuming coal (both hard and brown coal) accounted for 81 per cent. of the entire national production, water-power, gas and oil-plant being responsible for the remainder. Any improvement in the technique of electricity generation would, therefore, be reflected at once in the consumption of coal.

The national output of electrical energy in 1925 would have required at least 18,000,000 tons of coal, inclusive of brown coal translated into hard coal values, whereas, in 1913, 36,000,000 tons would have been required for an output equivalent to that of 1925. To this should be added the very considerable power savings caused by electrification itself and by the introduction of the large-scale principle into power generation ; these savings would, on a moderate estimate, be not less than half of the saving in coal consumption. Over the period 1913 and 1925, fuel economy in this direction alone meant a reduction in the national coal requirements of about 27,000,000 tons. Against this, however, should be balanced the growth of industry itself, which would serve to neutralize to some extent the apparent economies as translated into aggregate coal-consumption returns.

Other examples of fuel economy may be quoted. According

to Dr. Benhold, German locomotives had now reached the pre-war standard of consumption per locomotive, but their efficiency was 16 per cent. higher. The consumption per 1,000 locomotive kilometres was in 1913 14·4 tons, but in 1926 it had fallen to 12·59 tons. In 1920, each ton of potash represented a coal consumption of 3·7 tons, but in 1926 the average had fallen to 2·0 tons, and is now even less than that figure. Similarly each ton of steel, calculating from the blast furnace onwards, meant about three tons of coal in 1913, but in 1926 two tons sufficed. One can go through the entire range of industrial production and find exactly the same changes taking place. Fuel economy in itself has practically made good the loss on coal resulting from the Treaty of Versailles and the partition of Upper Silesia. One cannot ignore the fact that the high degree of electrification recorded in 1925, which led to an effective saving of 27,000,000 tons of coal from the 1913 total, was in very great measure the work of the four preceding years, and, as such, testified to the reality of the achievement which the policy of recovery had inspired in the minds of German industrialists and business men. This process continues and is, in itself, one reason why coal-consumptioin statistics are not reliable indices of the state of industrial production.[1]

In addition to fuel economy, the exploitation of the brown coal deposits on a large scale contributed very largely towards economic independence. The plains of Central Germany and the district south of Cologne began to assume fantastic contours as the surface excavations spread over a wider and wider area. In certain parts, the deposits lay over a depth of forty to eighty feet under a surface layer of thirty feet and more, so that miniature mountains with valleys and lakes were moulded and the monotony of the plain yielded to a picturesque disturbance, where the dark brown colour of the coal gave a strange tone to the landscape. This element of the fantastic and strange was probably instrumental in creating the legend of a country saved through brown coal.

Brown-coal production has increased steadily from 1913 to 1927, but the real value of this increase, measured in hard coal, has been only 13,500,000 tons—or an average, over fourteen years, of one million tons a year. Its significance lies, above all, however, in the functions it performed ; it represented fuel at a price lower than that of coal, even allowing for differences in heating value, and was used largely for the generation of electricity and chemical production. As such, it allowed

[1] See footnote on facing page.

electricity supply companies operating in Central Germany and Cologne to distribute power to industrial consumers more cheaply than almost any other undertakings in the world, water-power or otherwise. It contributed to the expansion of the German chemical industry to a point where it stood superior to all other chemical industries in Europe and the world. Brown coal did not serve to make good a national fuel deficit, but it improved immensely the efficiency of two of the basic industries of Germany and, through them, exerted a favourable influence on the economic development of the country as a whole.

The *Badische Anilin und Soda-Fabrik*, to give a definite example, consumes annually 2,250,000 tons of brown coal and brown-coal briquettes, while coke and hard coal between them account for about 950,000 tons. The brown coal is used for

[1] A comparison of the consumption of coal in Germany as supplied by the Rhenish-Westphalian Coal Syndicate in 1912, 1926 and 1927 may give some indication of movements in fuel economy and the shifting balance of industry.

CONSUMPTION OF RHENISH-WESTPHALIAN COAL

(METRIC TONS)

Industry or Service	1912	Per cent. of Total	1926	Per cent. of Total	Jan.–June, 1927	Per cent. of Total
State Railways	8,217,289	12·62	7,156,295	11·65	4,724,615	12·69
Private Railways						
Water-Works . .	286,498	0·44	212,480	0·35	105,026	0·30
Gas-Works . .	2,480,814	3·81	3,561,490	5·80	1,829,191	5·19
Electrical Power Stations . . .	1,178,549	1·81	1,939,206	3·16	1,062,407	3·02
Iron and Steel * .	28,154,958	43·24	20,307,353	33·08	11,030,262	31·30
Mining and Quarrying †	3,223,105	4·95	2,679,507	4·36	1,723,415	4·89
Chemicals . . .	2,233,384	3·43	3,381,804	5·51	2,057,538	5·84
Textiles . . .	2,103,157	3·23	1,240,819	2·02	839,196	2·38
Paper and Cellulose	1,302,264	2·00	1,072,190	1·75	568,438	1·61
Food Preparation .	1,836,193	2·82	1,664,084	2·71	749,721	2·13
Other Industries .	859,495	1·32	2,891,703	4·72	3,326,805	9·44
Shipping . . .	3,477,046	5·34	4,440,399	7·23	1,565,131	4·44
Domestic, etc. .	8,809,810	13·53	10,636,691	17·33	5,537,666	15·72
Total (including army and navy supplies) . .	65,113,224	100·00	61,389,300	100·00	35,236,203	100·00

* These statistics refer only to iron and steel works not possessing coal-mines. Iron and steel works consuming coal from their own or subsidiary undertakings are not included in the sales total.

† Excluding consumption by the coal-mines.

heating purposes direct under boilers and for the production of gas required in the nitrogen-fixation works at Merseburg. In 1926, the chemical industry took 24 per cent. of the national consumption of brown coal, and public electricity supply stations 37 per cent., a total between them of 61 per cent., the only other industry of any importance being paper. In the Central German zone, 54 per cent. of the total consumption went to chemicals and electricity supply.

The recovery in production effected since the conclusion of the war is shown diagrammatically with brown coal reduced to a hard coal basis. The loss of the Saar, Upper Silesia and Lorraine has now been made good, and a heavy surplus is actually available for export. Such an achievement must be ranked with the most significant economic developments of modern times ; it has restored the power capacity of pre-war Germany with the addition of the technical advantages which the study of fuel economy and electrification on a national scale have brought. The efficiency of industry and transport measured in fuel values is to be placed to the asset side of the national balance-sheet.

The desire for a nationally co-ordinated scheme of electrical power generation and distribution was not by any means a post-war development. In the later years of war, much discussion raged round problems of transport and power, largely with a view to deciding a policy of economic expansion after the cessation of hostilities. The German industrialist, if he were prone to romantic speculation at all, may have had a vision of great rivers of energy running over the whole country, bringing industries magically to life in remote areas, revivifying existing industries, speeding up transport and opening up agricultural development ; he may have dreamt of giant reservoirs of power tapped at critical times for the provision of those elements in the national wealth which modern economic science has shown to be all-important—the capacity to produce cheaply and the strength to generate resistance to the onslaught of war ; he may also have seen those rivers of energy issuing forth from great power stations located in the heart of the coal and water-power districts, joined up with each other in an immense system whose only limits would be the national frontiers ; he may, finally, have conceived the domination of national economic, industrial and even financial forces to lie in the possession of these stations, a possession defined and rendered absolute by law.

There is no doubt that a first consequence of the Treaty of

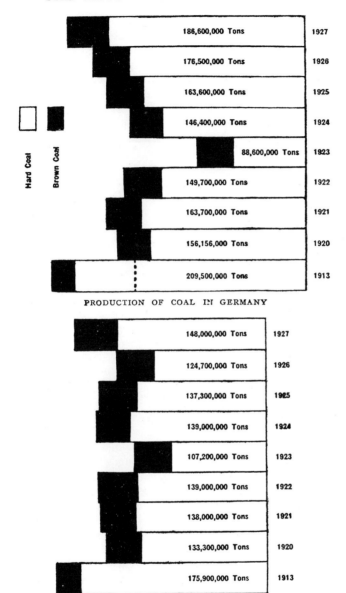

PRODUCTION OF COAL IN GERMANY

CONSUMPTION OF COAL IN GERMANY

The figures given within the rules refer to hard and brown coal together, on a hard coal basis.

The dotted line shows the production of hard coal in Germany within its present frontiers in 1913.

Versailles was the perception that only a new era of intensive industrial development could restore full economic strength to Germany and allow it to make good the losses imposed by political factors. Only scientific utilization of the national power resources could complete the work of recovery and allow Germany to take a leading part in a world where electrical energy would take the place of steam-driven mechanical energy and decide the volume and speed of production. In the early years, national ownership appeared to be the policy most certain of adoption. The Electricity Act of 1919, although it defined the national claim to control of power stations and public supply systems and merely cleared the way for ultimate legislation in this direction, might easily at that time have been converted into an instrument of nationalization and thus have constituted the first great measure of practical Socialism imposed by the new *régime*, but the forces of the opposition were sufficient to convert it into a purely optional measure with no legislative reality. The technical principles at issue, however, the construction of super-power stations, the elaboration of super-power transmission and distribution zones which would cover the whole of Germany and ultimately bring every area into a single unified scheme, remained as a guide to progress after 1919, and dictated the policy of the Government and the great power companies who were taking grip of electricity supply.

The Government itself furnished the most impressive example of the super-power principle through the creation by it during the war of the *Elektrowerke A.G.*, the largest power undertaking in Europe and one of the most important in the world. This company had generating stations located in the heart of the Central German brown coal-field, and fed from them into the engineering and electrical manufacturing works of Berlin. In 1916, one year after it was taken over by the State and used largely for the manufacture of nitrogen products, it had an output of 300 million units, but in 1926 a total of 1,472 million units was recorded, generated in the Golpa, Trattendorf and Lauta stations, which in 1926 housed 408,000 kilowatts [1] of power plant. The example of the *Elektrowerke* was decisive for the rest of Germany ; the publicly-owned undertaking conducted on the lines of an industrial privately-owned company came rapidly into existence over the period 1922–26, and many undertakings already supported by private capital changed their character and became wholly public, both in administration and finance.

[1] One kilowatt = 1·34 h.p.

An industrial map of Germany would explain in itself the course of development ; certain well-defined areas could be selected at once as centres of great power systems.   The Ruhr with its coal-mines, iron and steel, engineering and textile works, the Central Rhine district with its chemical plants, Saxony with its textile, coal-mining, paper and chemical industries, and Berlin with its group of engineering and electrical manufacturing firms would at once constitute power centres, while subsidiary areas such as Hamburg with its shipbuilding, Silesia with its iron and steel and coal-mining enterprises, Southern Germany with its engineering and locomotive construction at Nuremberg, Regensburg and Munich, and its electro-chemical, electro-metallurgical works in the Alps, on the Inn and on the Swiss frontier at Rheinfelden, could be brought into a national scheme.

Between the industrial zones stretch agricultural plains with apparently no demand for electricity, and wide gaps would be visible in a national system dependent purely on industry. Yet agriculture, with 2,500,000 h.p. of electric motors already installed, has, next to iron and steel, and coal-mining, the highest capacity of electrical power-consuming plant of any industry in Germany.   Its main disadvantages lie in diffuseness and in the low degree of utilization of machinery the very nature of its activities requires, the result being an insufficient and widely fluctuating demand for power, at the most not quite 10 per cent. of the maximum it would consume under conditions of steady load.   Yet, combined with other industries or with other sources of demand of a less irregular type, agriculture would form a sound basis for the elaboration of super-power systems covering wide territory.   The value of agriculture has already been proved in this respect in Bavaria, where a super-power zone has been built on the combination—electro-chemical, electro-metallurgical production, railway electrification, agriculture, isolated engineering districts lying to the north and south—and has been, perhaps, the most striking success of the new power policy in Germany.

Any plan of production on a national scale would aim at the creation of giant power-stations in the industrial zones and of smaller stations in subsidiary areas, with main transmission lines linking them up ; it would also aim at exploitation of cheap power resources to the maximum degree, brown coal, waste heat from iron and steel works, and water-power, and save the more valuable hard coal reserves.   Thus, we find in the Central German brown-coal-field the giant stations of the

Elektrowerke Company feeding into Berlin and supplementing the production of the Berlin Municipal Power Company, both undertakings now being responsible for an annual total of over 2,000 million units. In the brown-coal-fields south of Cologne, the Goldenberg Station of the Rhenisch-Westphalian Company, the Fortuna stations of the Rhenish Electricity Supply Company feed into the Ruhr and the Rhine province, the two companies producing annually 1,500 million units ; in the Ruhr iron and steel area, a high-pressure pipe system with special gas towers collects waste-heat from blast furnaces and coke-ovens for interchange between the leading works, with the result that the United Steel Works in Hamborn can furnish over 200 million units annually, while almost all the power requirements of the iron and steel and coal-mining industries are met from waste-heat. In Bavaria, the *Bayernwerk* has developed important water-power plant, especially at the Walchensee and, in conjunction with the *Mittlere-Isar* Company, the *Innwerk* (devoted to aluminium) and the *Alzwerke*, accounts for an annual output of about 1,200 million units ; similarly water-power schemes, as carried out and projected by the *Badenwerk*, the *Kraftübertragungswerke Rheinfelden* and smaller companies will yield annually not less than 500,000,000 units. State or municipally owned companies operate in the folowing areas : Saxony, the *Sächsische Werke* (600 million units) ; Central Germany, the *Elektrowerke* (1,500 million units) ; Berlin, the *Berliner Elektrizitätswerke* (700 million units) ; the Ruhr, *Rheinisch-Westfalisch Elektrizitätswerke* (1,400 million units) ; Hamburg, the *Hamburgische Elektrizit-ätswerke* (300 million units) ; Bavaria, the *Bayernwerk*, the *Innwerk* and the *Mittlere-Isar A.G.* (850 million units) ; Baden, the *Badenwerk* (200 million units) ; and a number of smaller areas in Hanover and East Prussia. Including the latter, public supply undertakings, State or municipally controlled, contributed not less than 7,300 million units to the national output of electricity in 1925. In other words, 70 per cent. of the output of electricity by public supply undertakings was controlled by the Reich (1,520 million units), the States (1,600 million units), the municipalities and communes (4,180 million units), in 1925—the Reich and States acting as central co-ordinating influences.

The functions performed by these central power enterprises are more important even than their effective output ; they act as central co-ordination systems for wide areas and link up other undertakings to the main scheme ; their high pressure

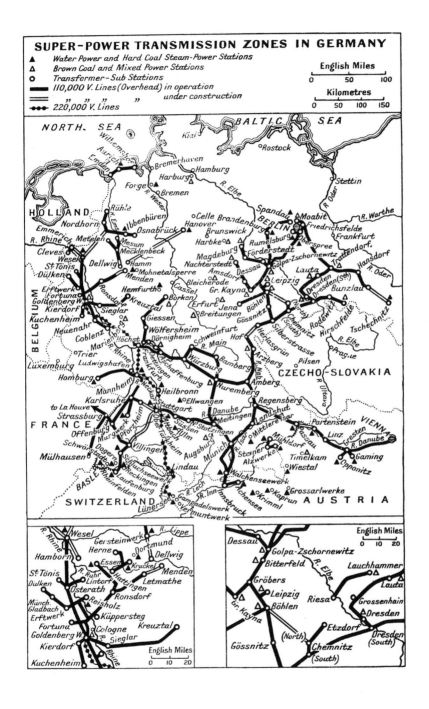

SUPER-POWER TRANSMISSION ZONES IN GERMANY

▲ Water Power and Hard Coal Steam-Power Stations
△ Brown Coal and Mixed Power Stations
○ Transformer-Sub Stations
▬ 110,000 V. Lines (Overhead) in operation
═ „ „ „ „ under construction
◆◆◆ 220,000 V. Lines

English Miles
0   50   100

Kilometres
0   50   100   150

NORTH. SEA   BALTIC   SEA

Kiel
°Rostock

Wittemsolen
Aurich
Emden
Bremerhaven
Harburg °Hamburg
Forge ○△ °Bremen
R. Elbe
Stettin
R. Oder
R. Warthe

HOLLAND
Rühle
Nordhorn
Ibbenbüren
Celle Brandenburg
Hanover
Spandau Moabit
Friedrichsfelde
Frankfurt
Osnabrück
Brunswick
BERLIN
Emmerich
Metelen
Mesum
Harbke○△
Rumelsburg
Oberspree
R. Rhine
Mecklenbeck
Magdeburg
Försterstedt
Cleves○
Wesel
Hamm
Nachterstedt
Dessau
Golpa-Zschornewirtz
Trottendorf.
St Tönis
Dellwig
Mohnetalsperre
Amsdorf
Lauta
Hansdorf
Dülken○
Menden
Bleicherode
Leipzig
Dresden(St?)
R. Oder
Erftwerk
Fortuna
Hemfurth
Cassel
Gr. Kayna
Dresden(Sth)
Bunzlau
Goldenberg W.
Kreuztal
Börken
Chemnitz
Rodewitz
Kierdorf
Sieglar
△
Erfurt Jena
Böhlen
(Spah)
Hirschfelde
Tschechnitz
Kuchenheim
Giessen
Breitungen
Gössnitz
Silberstrasse
R. Elbe
Neuenahr
Wölfersheim
Heilbsgrün
Prague
Coblenz
Marien-Höchst
Dörnigheim
Schweinfurt
Hof
Arzberg
Trier
R. Rhine
R. Main
R. Nab
CZECHO-SLOVAKIA
Luxemburg
Ludwigshafen
Frankfurt
Aschaffenburg
Würzburg
Bamberg
Amberg
R. Uttava
Homburg
Mannheim
Heilbronn
Nuremberg
Regensberg
VIENNA
Karlsruhe
Neckar-Stadtbarg
Ellwangen
Landshut
Partenstein
to La Houve
Strassburg
Pforzheim
R. Danube
Meitingen
Isar
Mittlere
Linz
Dresten
FRANCE
Offenburg
Murgwerk
Oberhausen
Süssen
R. Stötzingen
Isar
Passau
R. Danube
Schwör...
Dagen...
Villingen
Ulm
Augsburg
Munich
Steiner
Mühldorf
Timelkam
Gaming
Mülhausen
Schluchseewerk
Lindau
Alzwerke
Wiestal
Opponitz
BASLE
Meckingen
Laufenburg
Rheinfelden
R. Lech
Walchenseewerk
Grossarlwerke
SWITZERLAND
Lünersee
Gampadelswerk
R. Inn
Achensee
Kaprun
Krimml
AUSTRIA
Vermuntwerk
Innsbruck

Wesel R. Lippe
Gersteinwerk
R. Rhine
Herne Dortmund
Hamborn
Essen Kruckel Dellwig
St. Tönis
R. Ruhr Hattingen Menden
Dülken
Lintorf Letmathe
Osterath
Ronsdorf
Münch.
Gladbach
Reisholz
Erftwerk
Küppersteg
Fortuna
Kreuztal
Goldenberg W.
Cologne
Kierdorf
R. Sieglar
Rhine
English Miles
0   10   20
Kuchenheim

English Miles
0   10   20
Dessau
Golpa-Zschornewitz
Bitterfeld
Lauchhammer
Gröbers
Lauta
Leipzig
Riesa
Grossenhain
Br. Kayna
Böhlen
Dresden
Etzdorf
Dresden
(North)
(South)
Gössnitz
Chemnitz
Dresden
(South)
(South)

transmission lines, operating generally at 110,000 volts and even in some cases, as the map shows, at 220,000 volts, and above, radiate out to strategic points over their areas, and connect up with other systems.   The result of such a development is clear : electricity can be transmitted now from Holland to Switzerland and Northern Italy, from Holland to the Black Forest, Bavaria and Austria, from Bavaria to Saxony and Silesia or Central Germany and Berlin, from Central Germany back again to the Ruhr and Bavaria.   Rivers of energy are flowing along the same paths as the great rivers, the Rhine and the Danube, and know no boundary of hill or valley ; they have formed a ring of living power through the industrial zones of Germany and are bringing to reality the conception of a single national economic unit which visionaries have advocated, with little hope of achievement, since the beginning of the industrial era.

The revolution effected is much greater than a mere economy in fuel or in man-power ; it is to be found in the orientation of industry.   The textile mill operating in an obscure valley of the Black Forest may obtain its power from a high-pressure system as cheaply as a great factory located in the Ruhr ; it can tap power plants feeding into the network as far away as Cologne or Central Germany, and is sure of an absolutely constant supply.   Of all the changes effected by the post-war policy of Germany, none can have more profound significance for future economic strength.   The Treaty of Versailles failed definitely and finally as far as the fuel and power status of Germany is concerned, and the last traces of its influence on industrial development will vanish with the completion of the all-German super-power zone.

A still deeper significance attaches to the formation of super-power zones covering the whole of Germany—the international points of contact of such zones.   Thus we find French supply companies exporting energy into Germany, Swiss supply companies transmitting power north into Baden and linking up with companies feeding into Northern Italy, and the *Bayern-werk* sending energy via Passau into Austria.   In 1925, to give concrete illustrations, Germany imported from Switzerland and Alsace 247,000,000 units and exported 68,000,000 units in turn to them ; it imported also 21,000,000 units from Austria, 11,400,000 units from Poland, and exported 6,800,000 units to Czecho-Slovakia.   In 1926 export permits were issued in Switzerland for Germany amounting to an annual energy transmission of not less than 250,000,000 units, while France made arrangements for an import of about 900,000,000 units, and Italy 350,000,000 units.   It is doubtful whether these maxima were reached in the year in question, but they show clearly that the formation of something much more than a series of national super-power zones is under way—something akin to an Alpine power block radiating out to cover ultimately a European zone.   We have indicated elsewhere the future economic importance of such a development.[1]

" France recognizes, as clearly as the German industrialists of the Ruhr, that the formation of one enormous power zone from Lorraine to the Alps, from the great iron and steel areas to the electro-chemical and electro-metallurgical areas of the south, constitutes perhaps the greatest single possibility of a rapid increase in industrial wealth.   With the Ruhr connected to Switzerland and Lorraine to the Upper Rhine, a new economic unit is created, and there is little doubt that co-operation between France, Germany, Switzerland, and ultimately Italy, will result.   When this is done, the tariff problem will fade into the background ; interconnection across the Rhine and over the Alpine system will create in itself an economic solidarity beyond the control of politics or the recommendations of international conferences.   The change effected has in it all the strength of a natural economic process which nothing can stop.   The future of industrial Europe lies along the Rhine and in the Alps."

The fact that the Rhine is to be harnessed at last in a system of water-power plants stretching north from Kembs to Strasbourg illustrates in itself the reality of the change that is taking place.   The doctrine of a United States of Europe grouped together in one customs' union, which has been advocated so earnestly by British and German economists alike, may well be displaced by the reality of a European power-zone which will overleap frontiers and bring great industrial areas and great industries into contact with each other.   The way towards international agreements governing production and price, towards international peace and prosperity, may be traced by those rivers of energy borne on lofty steel towers from power station to power station.

Iron and steel is still the most impressive industry, both in volume of production and in the immense power it displays always under the effective control of man.   Seen against any landscape, a blast-furnace, steel works and rolling-mill complex has a spectacular quality not divorced from beauty, while there is a perpetual throb of creation in it, a thunder and long-

[1] *Towards Industrial Recovery*, by Hugh Quigley (Methuen), p. 116.

sustained welling of sound which has an inspiring force, even to the most materialistic observer. If, however, instead of being scattered over a wide area in isolated units, the great iron and steel works are clustered together and form almost one continuous circle of production closely connected even in space, the impression of enormous strength becomes intensified, To sense the iron and steel industry of Germany, it is sufficient to climb up the steps leading to the Rheinbrücke at Duisburg-Ruhrort, pass beneath the arcade leading out from one of the square flanking towers, and go out on to the bridge. From that point, some of the most powerful of the Ruhr enterprises may be seen—a ring of smoke stacks and blast-furnace towers closing out the horizon. To the north, the *August-Thyssen Hütte* at Hamborn, to the east, beyond the entrance to the bridge, the *Rheinische Stahlwerke* and *Phoënix* plants now joined as one, and beyond them again, in the distance, the *Gutehoffnungshütte* at Oberhausen, a faint shadow drawn across the far horizon ; farther down the Rhine, the blast-furnaces of Krupp at Rheinhausen, and innumerable smaller works engaged on the rolling and finishing of steel.

From that single point, overlooking a Rhine covered with shipping which bears the products of the Ruhr south as far as Switzerland and north to the ocean, one can see some of the greatest iron and steel works in Europe and the world, and survey an industrial complex responsible for much of the real wealth of Germany. The atmosphere, except on dull wet days, is strangely clear ; no smoke comes from the stacks other than a stray wisp or so, and only occasionally does a black smudge trail over the sky low to the horizon. Except for an uninterrupted throbbing and muttering, which may sometimes burst into a roar when the wind shifts, there is little evidence of activity. Even at night, when one would expect to view a sky suffused with flaming colour from the furnaces and coke-ovens, gases escaping into the air in a furious glow, the spectacular only comes at moments. A row of ladles bearing molten steel or slag from the steel furnaces to the ingot moulds or to the crushing mills may pass into the open and throw a flickering into the air ; intermittent flashes may occur when the roofs of the blast-furnaces move aside to allow the skips of iron-ore, limestone or coke to be discharged into the glowing mass within, or the Thomas converters belch forth roaring flame through gaps in the iron-shielded roof and tear a blinding curtain away from darkness. But the old days of flame and fury are passing away ; the waste gases from the blast-furnaces, coke-ovens and open-hearth furnaces no longer exhaust into the air, but are caught and used for the production of power or for the heating of steam, or, again, for the melting of steel.

Nothing goes to waste. Even the blast-furnace slag is consumed in cement works rumbling and crackling beside the iron and steel plants, the steel-furnace slag is ground to dust and used as fertilizer, the dust from the blast-furnace gases is forced into round briquettes and thrown back again for the iron it contains, while bricks are pressed from slag which has neither cement nor fertilizer value. The hills of slag have virtually disappeared ; here and there they still exist, but they have ceased to be ugly. At Oberhausen, where green lawns stretch even to the foot of the blast-furnaces, a grass-covered hill of slag acts as an observation post for a vast terrain of coal-mines, iron and steel, engineering and cement works owned by one group, while, at Dortmund, the *Deutsch-Luxemburgische A.G.*, hemmed in between two main railway tracks and the town, has built its new plant on a slag dump, an enterprise risen from its ashes, and from that imminence one can look down on the picturesque clumps of houses. At Essen, again, engineering works have risen on a foundation of slag. The study of local amenities may have provoked such developments, aided by the work of a special organization created with almost arbitrary powers in the Ruhr for this purpose, but the economic changes imposed by the Treaty of Versailles must have caused some part of this achievement.

Economy in fuel was essential to make good the loss of valuable coal-fields, but even as important was economy in materials. Deprived of the Lorraine minette deposits and fully determined to secure full economic independence, the Ruhr industrialist decided to obtain his raw materials from other countries and supplement in this way the production of the Siegerland. From minette he went over to the ores of Sweden, Spain, Algiers and Wabana in Newfoundland, all high-grade, expensive material, used a higher percentage of scrap and waste steel products in his steel furnaces to reduce his consumption of pig-iron, and aimed above all at securing the highest possible yield from the cycle of production—coke-ovens to rolling mills. Nothing that could be recuperated on an economic basis— gases, chemicals, oils, cement, bricks, fertilizers, even steam— was neglected and the real earning capacity of the plant was greatly improved as a result. The actual production of pig-iron and steel, owing to expensive materials, did not result in a selling price which narrowed down the market and weakened

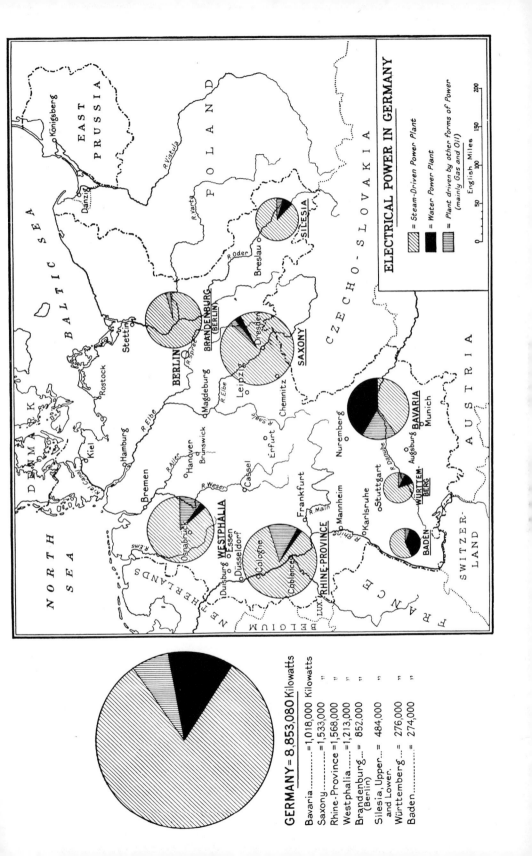

ELECTRICAL POWER IN GERMANY

▨ = Steam-Driven Power Plant
■ = Water Power Plant
▥ = Plant driven by other forms of Power (mainly Gas and Oil)

English Miles
0   50   100   150   200

GERMANY = 8,853,080 Kilowatts

Bavaria............. = 1,018,000 Kilowatts
Saxony............. = 1,533,000   "
Rhine-Province = 1,568,000   "
Westphalia...... = 1,213,000   "
Brandenburg... = 852,000   "
(Berlin)
Silesia, Upper.. = 484,000   "
and Lower.
Württemberg... = 276,000   "
Baden............. = 274,000   "

competitive power ; in certain cases, subsidiary profits furnished the margin of profit and allowed firms to quote directly at cost.[1] Through coking and by-product recovery, 13 per cent. was added to the earning capacity of all the coal-mines in the Ruhr, or, if calculation is limited to the actual coal consumption of the coke-ovens, about 40 per cent.   No estimate can be made of the total value the study of economy in fuel and materials has brought to the iron and steel industry of Germany, but it must bear now a very high ratio to the actual value of production in pig-iron, steel ingots and finished steel products.

If now we follow the course of output in iron and steel since the conclusion of the war, a measure of the recovery effected may be obtained.   The three years, 1920–22, saw a rapid recovery in steel production, possibly under the stimulus of inflation which reached its highest point in the early autumn of 1922 and thereafter began to influence production adversely. Abnormal activity in all branches of industry resulting from excessive consumption beyond the real wealth of the country accounted for the increase in steel ; export trade improved slightly, but it was neutralized by the volume of imports which reached a record high level in 1922.   The iron and steel industry, as a basic raw material industry, is always more sensitive to financial changes than the finishing industries, and reacts much more rapidly.   In a sense, therefore, the upwards curve in production corresponded only to an artificial economic condition, which the restoration of sound finance might destroy.

The occupation of the Ruhr broke up the whole manufacturing position and brought with it an interruption in the course of demand and supply.   The French and Belgian Control Commission (M.I.C.U.M.) might arrange for the transport of coal and for the collection of dues on the production marketed as well as for the supply of coke to Lorraine, but against the determined resistance of the Ruhr industrialist and the Ruhr labour

[1] It is only necessary to glance at the statistics of by-product recovery in the Ruhr from coke-ovens alone to appreciate how important this phase of economic activity has become. In 1913, the production of gas of a commercial value totalled 905,856,000 cubic metres, but in 1926 it had risen to 3,446,245,000 cubic metres, an increase of almost 300 per cent. ; ammonia liquor rose from 3,233 tons in the same period to 26,808 tons ; sulphate of ammonia fell, on the other hand, from 333,539 tons to 299,040 tons ; refined benzole increased to 138,333 tons from 86,478 tons, refined toluol to 20,503 tons from 5,773 tons, refined solvent benzole to 20,053 tons from 9,774 tons ; crude naphthalene to 18,803 tons from 13,051 tons, impregnating oil from 21,810 tons to 37,681 tons, while a number of tar products showed similar movements.

leaders, backed by the financial resources of the German State, it could do nothing.[1]   It was only towards the end of 1923 that the finances of the State yielded under the strain and the occupation began to justify itself.   The occupying forces, even accompanied by engineers and technical experts, could not work the coal-mines and still less the iron and steel works and, unwilling to hazard production on railways and waterways under alien control, the Ruhr industrialist piled up stocks of finished steel products in readiness for the time when they could be released with safety.   Such stocks came into the market in 1924 and provided a much higher percentage of the national consumption than any calculation based merely on statistics of production, imports and exports would show.

The diminution of stocks kept production at a low level during the first nine months of 1924.   The year 1923, if we transfer excess of production not marketed to the subsequent year, must be regarded as one of the most disastrous in the history of modern Germany ; even the heavy engineering and electrical firms were seriously depressed, and the industrial structure of the country came nearer to collapse at that time than at any previous period.   The year 1924 represented a

---

[1] On January 10, 1923, French, Belgian and Italian engineers, protected by a military force, entered the Ruhr and began the technical and military occupation of that territory. The Italian delegation retired in February. The German Government in April guaranteed up to 80 per cent. of the total loss incurred by industrial undertakings in making forced reparations deliveries—which was equivalent to making resistance complete ; the Government, on April 14, gave guarantees to cover the cash requirements of the iron and steel works and make good losses incurred in forced reparations deliveries. On June 12, a similar arrangement was made with the coal companies. On September 27, the German Government declared passive resistance at an end ; on October 7, the Otto-Wolff concern came to terms with the *Micum* for coal deliveries, followed on November 1 by Krupp, while the German Chancellor, during the period October 20 to November 13, entered into negotiations with the Mining Association at Essen to begin again reparations deliveries. On November 23, the *Micum* and the Mining Association came to terms regarding coal, and similar agreements covering brown coal, chemicals and other products ensued. The Ruhr occupation entered, therefore, into a new phase, and a return to normal conditions of production took place by degrees. The stand taken by General Dawes on March 21, 1924, that no good could result from the labours of the commission of experts unless the Ruhr were evacuated, contributed to a change in the attitude of France and Belgium, and the acceptance by Germany of the Dawes Report made evacuation possible. On August 10, 1924, the Herriot Government decided to terminate the Ruhr occupation. Such, in short, is the history of the Ruhr adventure.

time of swift recovery in the material-consuming and finishing industries, but of stagnation in iron and steel, though, on the whole, it showed little recession on 1922.   Imports of finished steel products dropped to 60 per cent. of the 1922 average, with a similar fall in exports—evidence that a movement towards stabilization in home demand was taking place.   In 1925, recovery both in production and consumption seemed complete, with a further fall in imports and a rise in exports to a post-war record.   The material-consuming industries, engineering especially, were inactive and were still in the midst of depression, a depression which reacted in turn on steel production in the early months of 1926.   From June 1926 onwards, the upward cycle in economic activity over the whole country, accompanied by heavy orders from the railways, shipbuilding, constructional engineering, chemical and building trades, restored full activity to iron and steel works and, during 1927, strained their productive capacity to the utmost.

The improvement in the relative position of Germany in world production effected by the boom of 1927 was very striking.   In 1913, out of a total output of 65,679,000 tons of steel by the United States, Germany, Great Britain, France and Belgium, Germany with Luxemburg accounted for 28·83 per cent. ; in 1923, out of a total of 69,388,000 tons, Germany supplied only 9·09 per cent., but, in 1927, her share of a production of 85,000,000 tons had risen to the high figure of 19 per cent., the actual volume of output being only 16 per cent. below that of 1913 within the old *Zollverein*.   Exports of finished steel products in 1926 were, at 3,600,000 tons, one-third of the total production and 1,400,000 tons greater than in the previous year, while imports reached a record low figure, so that home consumption was even less in 1926 than in 1925.   Recovery in trade generally set in towards the end of 1926 and the beginning of 1927.   Proof of such activity may be seen from the fact that imports of iron and steel in 1927 were more than twice the 1926 totals, while exports were slightly more ; consumption was more than 80 per cent. up in 1927, compared with the previous year, and represented the highest reached in Germany either before or after the war.

The iron and steel industry of Germany has been governed throughout its history by the principle of control being centralized in a few firms and the control of these firms, in turn, being vested in a single family or group of families.   In other countries, such a system would have led inevitably to inefficiency and nepotism of the worst type, but the conception of a stern duty to be discharged has always been predominant in the education and mentality of the iron and steel industrialist. Thus we find the Krupp family dominant in the affairs of the great Essen firm from the beginning of its history till now, the

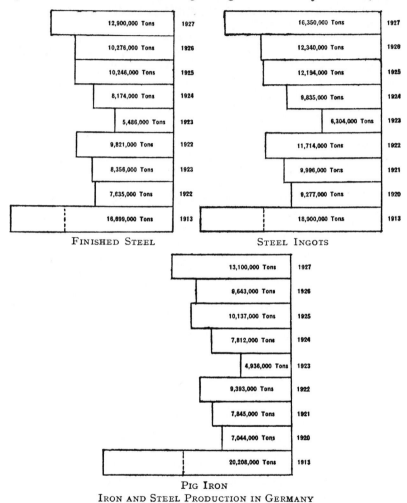

FINISHED STEEL

STEEL INGOTS

PIG IRON

IRON AND STEEL PRODUCTION IN GERMANY

The dotted line gives the output of Germany within its present frontiers in 1913.

Haniels governing the *Gutehoffnungshütte,* the Thyssens the *August-Thyssen Hütte* and affiliated concerns, the Stinnes the *Deutsch-Luxemburgische A.G.* and the Mathias Stinnes coal-mines, and the Hoesch family the *Eisen u. Stahlwerk Hoesch.*

To this circumstance may be traced the emergence of the large manufacturing group, distinguished by cautious financial policy and co-operation in marketing, and the steady expansion outwards of the entire industry, into coal-mining, engineering, shipbuilding, and electrical manufacture. The German industrialist, by the very nature of his training, was a realist first and an individualist second ; he saw, almost at once, that the development of industry might become a national process based on the principle of co-operation and high technical achievement in common rather than a wild scramble for orders in a world of frenzied competition ; he recognized also that, even with the protection of a tariff, the efficiency of the industry would decide its economic future, and that production would require to be on a basis of minimum cost and minimum price ; he appreciated, finally, the necessity for a clear definition of the value and legal status of the principle of combination and was able to impress the German Government with his views.

The shipbuilding industry, which may be regarded as part of the iron and steel group, owing to the close connection between the leading iron and steel concerns and the shipbuilding companies, was, before the war, one of the most active sections in production ; the expansion of industry and the steady upward movement in foreign trade as well as the naval policy of the Government all contributed to its prosperity. At Hamburg and Kiel, the great shipbuilding yards throbbed with activity and gradually swallowed up the surrounding acreage ; they were, in themselves, the most impressive memorials to the new spirit inspiring German industry and represented the most advanced modern technique. The Treaty of Versailles, however, with the complete disarmament of the country, affected adversely the naval builders, and, deprived of an important market, they were forced to revert to ordinary merchant construction. Even although the surrender of the mercantile fleet caused a situation of acute shortage, and, in some way, compensated for the loss of naval business, the productive capacity of the German yards was as a whole rather greater than the demand which might be laid on them. In addition to this, the policy adopted by the shipowners, of buying back the surrendered ships indirectly and recommissioning them, narrowed down the orders for new shipping, and it was only during the height of the inflation period that even moderately prosperous conditions obtained.

Thus while, in 1913, the ships under construction totalled 1,345,877 gross tons and the ships launched 458,755 gross tons, and, in 1921, the most active post-war year, a record of 1,726,399 gross tons under construction and 445,400 tons launched was reached, the curve of activity has since moved steadily downward.   In 1925, for example, 545,116 gross tons and, in 1926, 631,962 gross tons were recorded as under construction, with launchings of 280,937 gross tons and 259,281 gross tons respectively.   In other words, the shipbuilding industry, at the end of 1926, was producing at rather less than half of its pre-war average.   In 1927, a recovery to 360,000 gross tons launched took place.   Since 1921, the addition to the German mercantile fleet, as shown by the shipbuilding statistics, aggregated 1,858,424 gross tons, an annual average of only 309,700 tons, even including the two boom years of 1921 and 1922, while, on foreign account, 419,636 tons were launched, giving an annual average for all construction of 378,640 tons, equivalent to 84 per cent. of the total given in 1913.

It is obvious that the future of the industry depends on the trade situation in Germany and the competition for freights : as long as foreign trade remains at a sub-normal level the demand for tonnage will remain depressed and, even if the traffic passing through German ports has, on the whole, shown a slight tendency to rise since 1921, it has not been spectacular enough to justify enterprise.   It has only been since the autumn of 1926 that a sharp improvement can be recorded, and already greater activity has set in.   The shipbuilding industry has suffered more than almost any other industry from the provisions of the Versailles Treaty.   It is always a sure indication of the long-period economic activity of a country and it lends itself to few measures of recuperation.   Rationalization cannot be effectively applied to the production of units as large and as varied as ships, although the workshops may be laid out for scientifically regulated manufacture of accessories and standard parts ; the provision of credits, as illustrated in the experience of the German State, cannot cure the disease. Only a general revival of international trade can bring prosperity.

The story of recovery, so effectively amplified and illustrated in the coal-mining, iron and steel, potash and electricity supply industries, dies down here to a record of decline and impoverishment.   Yet, in this case, it would be dangerous to attribute such a consummation to the incapacity of the industry itself : in common with shipbuilding in other countries, it has been confronted with an array of difficulties beyond its control—

excess productive capacity on the one hand, excess carrying capacity on the other, and a world-wide trade paralysis with falling prices to complete the scene.   Even in the near future, one cannot see any prospect of change : the drama moves forward still in tragic vein and gives little promise of lightening to comedy.

In other industries, such as engineering, chemicals, electrical manufacture and textiles, the war brought few changes either in territorial or in economic alignment ; the inflation period, with its extensive re-equipment of the great iron and steel, coal-mining, and chemical works, caused a boom in engineering and electrical manufacture which continued right into 1923 ; the stabilization crisis fell severely on them and depression continued until the late autumn of 1926, when, as a result of the adoption of trustification and rationalization on an extensive scale in the basic industries and the application of credits obtained in America to productive enterprise, the demand for equipment rose very rapidly and continued at a high level all through 1927.   In 1924 and 1925, the possibility of a severe economic crisis was never absent in general engineering : one leading industrialist at the 1925 annual meeting of the Union of German Engineering Firms stated :

" A large number of firms must keep stock for months at an interest charge of 9–14 per cent., although now they could buy on short notice any amount they desired, while, abroad, with an interest charge of 3 per cent., stocks for only 8–14 days are required."

A serious shortage of capital and liquid cash resources, combined with a restricted market (the result of financial stringency) raised the price of financial accommodation and at the same time encouraged manufacturing for stock or closing down of factories.   What closing down, apart from destruction, means in overhead cost may be understood from an example given by the same industrialist :

" The Rheinmetall Company has reduced its locomotive and carriage works to scrap, because the cost of upkeep, even when closed down, meant an annual outlay of about 500,000 marks, or £25,000."

The credit position, which became impossibly difficult during the stabilization period, improved rapidly during 1926, and reached a satisfactory basis in the spring of 1927.   In electrical manufacture, the important schemes for a national system of power supply to ensure the maximum degree of fuel economy and raise the efficiency of production in industry generally, the modernization of equipment in the coal-mining, iron and steel industries, the extension of railway electrification and the natural growth of demand inseparable from the use of a new commodity and a new service, all contributed towards the maintenance of prosperity. Even here, the depression in other industries had its effect during 1924, 1925 and 1926, but the swing of production has since been determinedly upwards and will probably continue so for years to come.

The views expressed by the chairman of the largest manufacturing concern in 1927 have a peculiar interest as a comment on recent industrial developments in Germany :

"Even although electrical manufacture in Germany, in the development of certain of its branches, was affected less than other industries by the trade depression which occurred in 1926, there are few grounds for the belief that we can look forward with any certainty to the future, the possibility of many surprises and many trade setbacks being always present, owing to home and foreign political conditions. Even although we may have the greatest confidence in the wide possibilities of expansion open to the electrical manufacturing industry, the greatest possible foresight is required, since our prosperity depends on the prosperity of our main customers. The advantage for us lies in the fact that we serve practically all branches of production and consumption, and, as a result of this, are less subject to depression. A new possibility of danger lies also in the changes in manufacture caused by the adoption of rationalization of production. Such rationalization makes it more difficult to carry out adjustments to sudden changes in demand, and a decline in the market leads in a shorter time to heavy losses, since fixed charges and overhead costs represent a much greater proportion of the value of the total product. At the same time, selling costs have risen, owing to increased competition and the necessity for increasing allocations for propaganda purposes. We are, unfortunately, coming close to the American system."

Between the basic raw-material industries, however, and the material-consuming industries, electrical manufacture and artificial silk alone excepted, a distinct line of cleavage can be traced. While the former, by dint of concentrated effort and consistent improvement of manufacturing capacity, have moved towards almost complete economic recovery and are now producing at a higher rate than before the war, while industrialists are linking up in immensely powerful combines with international affiliations and striving to obtain some measure of effective control over the national and even international markets, the latter have been confronted with depression and stagnation in demand which is only now lifting.[1] Yet the very activity in the raw-material industries must betoken a widespread measure of national economic recovery since they begin the cycle of production, and we may, in time, see other evidences of increased activity.

In other countries, the tendency has been for the finishing industries to be active and the basic industries inactive, which may be due to the presence of factors inoperative in Germany, financial, administrative, or technical. In a number of industries, Germany's experience has been similar to that of other countries—depression with little possibility of rapid revival ; shipbuilding and some sections of heavy chemical production form examples of a movement practically world-wide in scope, and, in these industries, Germany has not caused significant changes or shown determined enterprise. The screen may disclose the inspiring design of great industries, like coal-mining, iron and steel, chemicals, electrical manufacture and artificial silk, moving forward in close procession, but it may show, on the reverse, a gloomy picture of unemployment and exhaustion of capital resources. The importance of the former and more prosperous group has grown, if anything, with the years : from the beginning, Germany specialized in a few basic industries, concentrated all her wealth in human effort and finance on them, and, after the vicissitudes of war and inflation of stabilization and of reparations, they stand firm—the pillars still of the national prosperity.

[1] The difference between the two groups of industries is shown by the index of production prepared by the *Institut für Konjunkturforschung.*

INDUSTRIAL PRODUCTION IN GERMANY
(1913 = 100)

Period		All Industries	Raw Material Industries	Material Consuming) Industries
1924	January	57·1	56·5	58·1
	July	72·9	80·3	59·3
	December	91·4	98·7	78·0
1925	January	94·4	101·7	81·0
	July	89·7	95·0	79·9
	December	88·1	90·6	83·4
1926	January	82·7	88·0	73·0
	July	81·9	93·7	60·1
	December	104·3	112·9	88·3
1927	January	104·3	113·3	87·7
	July	104·9	113·1	89·6
	October	108·5	118·0	92·0

CHAPTER XI

FINANCE: INFLATION AND THE WAR POLICY OF GERMANY

Finance and industry—financial policy aimed at increasing production—meeting war demands—industrial credits—currency inflation—prices of commodities—exchange fluctuations of the mark—
financing imports—towards a crisis—the reparations factor—the
loss of foreign investments—the collapse of the mark—the social
effects of currency depreciation—industry and inflation.

FINANCE played a part in the expansion of German industry even as important as the technique of production
or manufacturing enterprise. We have been accustomed
in this country to regard financial transactions as something
apart, something quite self-contained with no visible connection either with industry or politics, and, in the opinion of
some writers, an elaborate ceremonial, with all the pomp and
mystery of a cult, has grown up round the conception of finance.
The high priests remain in the temple, sacrosanct, beyond criticism, and emerge only at intervals to dispense solemn counsel
to the mob of industrialists and politicians kneeling without.
The banks deliver their views every year on the state of trade,
which are taken as irrefutable dicta. There is, of course, much
that is fanciful in such a vision ; reality may serve to show at
moments that the interests of finance and industry are not so
widely dissociated, and that the support given by finance to
industry in this country can be very substantial indeed. It is
valuable, however, as an illustration of an attitude commonly
adopted : industry has no right to question financial policy,
even as little as finance, industrial policy.

The antinomy remains and it admits of explanation. The
geographical position of Great Britain has decided the direction and utilization of the national wealth ; it was a great
trading nation before it became an industrial nation, and it had
accumulated reserves of wealth, actual and potential, which
the rise of industry, after the early decades, served to increase.
The export of capital, the allocation and exchange of credit all

over the world, the transfer of gold from the industrial markets to London and thence to other markets under development constituted in themselves a source of profit, at some periods as valuable as the surplus derived from industrial production. The greater part of the national wealth available for investment abroad came from activities which were not primarily dependent on industry, while industry itself derived advantage from the export of capital to new markets.

In Germany, on the other hand, conditions were quite different. There was no long history of trading activity to inspire policy and decide the course of economic development ; the country itself as a national unit only began to function after the Franco-Prussian War. Its experiences during the European wars, from the Thirty Years War to the Napoleonic campaigns, had been uniformly disastrous, and no real foundation had been laid for the acquisition and utilization of wealth. Germany, up to the end of the nineteenth century, was a capital-importing country—a market for industrial products rather than a competitor—and it had to concentrate all its resources on the work of national industrial and economic expansion, assisted largely by British finance. During the early years of this century, a change had taken place, a state of balance had been reached and passed in the creation of wealth, and a real surplus become available for investment abroad.

The point at issue is that finance became subordinated to industry in Germany, owing to the factors already indicated, and it strove concurrently to open up Germany as a great market for the products of the national industries and to encourage them to improve and expand their manufacturing equipment. The banks participated directly in the administration of industrial firms, arranged credits for them in London and other international money centres, and were willing to risk a high proportion of public investment in the financing of production.

The system worked with success and a high degree of efficiency prior to the war, largely owing to the principle of distribution of risk over many branches of production and the utilization of credits on foreign institutions available through a rapidly expanding export trade ; the upward movement in production continued, with a few notable interruptions, as in 1895 and 1907, when world depression forced down prices and eliminated profits. The banks could move within a fairly wide margin of safety as long as the earning assets they possessed in industry were fully valuable ; a sudden and lasting depression in the latter would have meant collapse of the structure of security on which banking transactions depended, and caused a widespread crisis. Even a slowing down in the rapidity of circulation of capital and of goods sufficed to introduce a period of crisis and, on several occasions prior to the war, disaster was barely averted.

There is no doubt, however, that, without the assistance and active co-operation of finance, the rise of German industry, which constituted the greatest single economic change in the late nineteenth and early twentieth centuries, would have been much less rapid and much less effective than it was. On the eve of war, Germany had at its disposal an industrial weapon beyond a rival in the world, but, to forge this weapon, it had weakened its capacity to tap financial resources resulting from large capital investment abroad. The banks had accumulated important reserves undoubtedly, but they were insufficient to stand a period of prolonged hostilities or carry the nation through years of readjustment after peace. The savings of the German people were not available in a liquid form: they had gone, directly and indirectly, through the banks into industry. The policy, which made for industrial supremacy, threatened also national bankruptcy in years of stress and capital shortage. The reality of the national wealth was there, in immense manufacturing units capable of producing indefinitely—with a concrete capital value and unlimited power to meet the demands of the world—and it could never be eliminated unless through deliberate destruction by an army of invasion. It was always ready to function, provided that capital could be supplied to finance its requirements and stimulate its markets.

The deadliest blow that could be levelled at Germany would be destruction of its capital resources, diversion of its capital requirements each year away from industry, and depreciation of the national credit in foreign markets. Mere interruption or even partial demolition of the industrial machine would mean little beside an attack on finance. The Ruhr incident showed very clearly that a country cannot be subdued entirely through paralysis of industry in one area, however important. If, therefore, one should desire to trace the history of the inflation crisis in post-war Germany and explain why the reparations problem is and will always be incapable of solution, one should begin with the fact that industrial development in Germany prior to the war was sufficiently rapid to absorb practically all the surplus wealth created in each year—wealth which would otherwise have been available for investment abroad and for the accumulation of reserves against a time of great national stress. A long period of capital stringency would therefore be accompanied by paralysis of the national productive capacity and, above all, of the national credit. The financial strength of Germany in 1914 was unable to stand the strain of anything but a short war with a successful issue ; a long war meant exhaustion of reserves and the elaboration of artificial credits, with the introduction, in a short time, of inflation.

The conviction that only one result could terminate the hostilities, namely, the victory of Germany, and perhaps, also, the desire to avoid any issue which would make war unpopular at home, dictated the financial policy of the State. Looking back on it now, one is tempted to designate it all as a gamble which could only end in disaster. The intention of making the vanquished pay for the war was not peculiar to the Allies : it formed part and parcel of German finance right from the beginning, and the problem of reparations would have been every whit as difficult for a victorious Germany as it was for the Allies. It is futile, therefore, to speak of a possible German ability in handling post-war financial problems compared with the muddle in which the Allies floundered, and the protestations of the German economists at the unwisdom of reparations might easily have found a parallel in British or French protests if the rôles had been reversed. There can be no monopoly in political or economic virtue ; the future, apart from this determination to recover the costs of the war from the vanquished, meant probably less to the German politician and financier than it did to the British or even French.

War finance was a singularly haphazard affair at best, with few moments of vision to guide policy. The problem to be faced was twofold : the financing of the war itself and the supply of credit and capital to industry. The method adopted in the former case was that of debt accumulation in preference to severe taxation. Thus War Loans were issued directly to meet the greater part of the demand for accommodation, while Treasury Bills, bearing no interest, were discounted at the Reichsbank. These bills represented short-term credit and were nominally supposed to be cancelled after the period, for which they were issued, came to an end. Under normal conditions, the volume of such bills would remain fairly constant, but their rate of issue and cancellation would vary with the national requirements, loans bearing in themselves the long-term obligations of the Reich. Yet the gap between the value of bills issued and the value of bills cancelled widened as the war went on, a sure sign of capital inflation, and a proportion of these bills was converted into long-term debt, while a heavy proportion was allowed to accumulate and form a constantly increasing floating debt with no apparent basis of redemption. Between September 1914 and March 1916, receipts from War Loans provided much the greater part of the State financial requirements, and thereafter Treasury Bills became almost as important as sources of supply. No real effort was made to reduce the burden of debt through taxation. At the end of the war, when the total debt figured at 147,000,000,000 marks, eighty-nine milliards of which were represented by funded debt and fifty-five milliards by floating debt (Treasury Bills), taxation had been devoted to the redemption of less than one-tenth of it. It was clear that the reduction of the Treasury Bills would entail a debt-funding operation of considerable magnitude. The State budget could not be expected to provide a surplus sufficient to clear away a floating debt of £2,500,000,000 within one year or even twenty years. All the dangers of inflation were already present before the reparations problem became acute.

The capital and credit requirements of industry were met in much the same way as the State requirements ; a special credit currency came into force to cover short-term credits, the *Darlehenskassenscheine* (Loan notes), and it soon entered into general circulation on the same basis of security as the Reichsbank note. The original gold cover of one-third, imposed by the legislation creating the new currency and defining the system under which it should be distributed, was soon abandoned as impossible. The capital requirements of industrial undertakings were met easily enough in the open market. The restriction of exports narrowed down the demand for credit to bear the initial cost of contracts and release shipments ; every industry was working for the State (which paid in cash with little margin of time between deliveries and payments) and had, therefore, at its disposal a steady cash reserve sufficient to finance production at full capacity.

There was little strain actually on the money market : capital issues averaging in pre-war years about 1,200 million marks fell to 368 millions in 1915, and in 1918 stood at 784 millions. These figures represented, in all probability, the effective capital requirements of industry under conditions of abnormal prosperity, where revenue could provide a heavy surplus for expenditure on capital account without the necessity for a public issue. On the whole, therefore, industry emerged

from the war much stronger than the State, and it had fewer
difficult problems to solve ; it could revert to peace conditions
fairly rapidly if it were successful in steering clear of boom
psychology and could pursue a conservative capital policy.

The expansion of the currency was an additional factor
making for future trouble. At the outbreak of war, the currency in circulation amounted to 7,000,000,000 marks, or
£350,000,000, and, of this, metallic currency—i.e. gold, silver,
nickel and copper coins—represented 53 per cent. at
3,700,000,000 marks. During the war, the Reichsbank absorbed practically the whole of the latter, and in 1918 it had
fallen to 100,000,000 marks (£5,000,000), while the gold holdings of the Reichsbank had only increased by 1,000,000,000
marks to 2,300,000,000 marks. Thus a real deficit of
2,600,000,000 marks had taken place, due to the necessity of
the Reichsbank to export gold both to pay for supplies abroad
and to support the mark exchange. On the other hand, the
circulation of Reichsbank notes and Loan bank-notes rose from
5,900,000,000 marks in December 1914 to 32,900,000,000 marks
in December 1918, an increase of 440 per cent. in four years.

If now we cast a glance at the course of prices of commodities, certain interesting points stand out. Under normal
conditions, currency inflation would have been followed very
closely by an upward movement in wholesale prices and,
accompanying them, a less rapid movement in the cost of
living. Currency as such represented purchasing power in the
hands of the public, and its rate of turnover would remain very
similar from year to year ; hence, unless prices were controlled,
increasing demand would bring the prices of commodities up
to a new level roughly in line with the increase in purchasing
power. During the war, the State exerted very effective control over both wholesale and retail prices. Even as late as
July 1917, the price of commodities relative to 1913 had only
risen by 60 per cent. ; in August, a rapid adjustment upwards
occurred, and control thereafter was never quite so effective.
The whole economic structure of Germany showed signs of
collapse. Even so, in December 1918 the index stood at 145
per cent. above 1913, or 96 per cent. above the level of December 1914. Retail prices followed much the same course as
wholesale prices, a few points higher up. Illicit prices reached
much higher levels still, but the volume of commodities escaping control was small and had little influence on the price situation. Comparison between currency inflation and the rise in
food prices would lead to the belief that a currency inflation

of not much more than 100 per cent. was justified, and that
the total by which this increase was exceeded should be
regarded as a net addition to war expenditure. On a gold
basis, the total currency in circulation in 1918 should have
been closer to 11,800,000,000 marks than to 33,000,000,000
marks.

The fall in the real gold holdings of the country and the excessive inflation of the currency led fairly soon to depression in the
mark exchange abroad. From October 1914 onwards, the
value of the mark fell steadily from 4·20 marks to the dollar
until in October 1916, after the battle of the Somme had died
away, a level of 5·70 marks was reached. Thereafter, until
July 1917, depreciation was less rapid, probably owing to the
intervention of the Reichsbank and the favourable news from
the battlefields ; the early autumn of 1917 showed, however, a
further decline to the lowest point in the war, 49 per cent.
below parity, but the failure of the Passchendaele offensive
brought further confidence in German victory. The collapse
of Russia and the first brilliantly successful months of the
offensive on the Western Front caused a revival in the mark,
which had recovered in April 1918 to 5·1 marks to the dollar,
but the progressive weakening of the German position during
the last few months of the war brought the mark down to
half its par value in December 1918. The gold value of the
total currency circulation was equivalent to 16,800,000,000
marks against the 11,800,000,000 marks already calculated, so
that, even allowing for currency depreciation, there was an
excess of 5,000,000,000 gold marks.

Part of the cost of the war was covered by the printing press
in Germany with no basis of redemption or security other than
the prospect of conversion to other forms of currency. The
loan bank-notes, which were intended originally to finance industry, were diverted to war purposes in 1914 and 1915 for the
greater part, but after 1915 they entered into general circulation. The total transactions recorded up to the end of 1918
in the loan bank branches, namely, 50,000,000,000 marks, were
little more than the total of the notes in circulation in each
year from 1914 to 1918, and showed that they had never
effectively carried out their function as short-term credits for
industry ; they constituted inflation pure and simple.

The financing of German imports constituted the greatest
single problem imposed by the war ; during the period August
1914 to December 1918, the total adverse balance of
trade had reached the high figure of 15,000,000,000 gold marks

(£750,000,000).   To cover this gold to the value of 1,000,000,000 marks, foreign securities valued at 3–4,000,000,000 marks and German securities estimated at 1,000,000,000 marks were exported.   The deficit of about 10,000,000,000 marks was bridged by means of loans raised abroad on the basis of securities held by the Reichsbank, the total of securities actually exported, to cover purchases of food-stuffs and war materials and to support the exchange, being 7,000,000,000 marks.

We should be justified in estimating the total cost to Germany on trade account, including securities confiscated in enemy countries and the exports of gold already indicated, at not less than 13,500,000,000 marks, equivalent almost to the entire adverse balance of trade.   Externally the position of German trade appeared to be strong at the end of the war and, in the event of victory, would have allowed German industry to move forward into a successful campaign.   As it was, the advent of peace found Germany with her holdings abroad reduced to 5,450,000,000 marks, which developments during 1919–22 brought lower still to slightly over 2,100,000,000 marks of little real value, since they represented Russian, Austro-Hungarian, Turkish and Rumanian securities.

Germany had made her gamble financially and failed, with results the ultimate spread of which could never be estimated. Her currency stood at £840,000,000, two and a half times the pre-war total, her unfunded debt was 55,200,000,000 marks (£2,760,000,000), and her funded debt 58,514,000,000 gold marks (£2,976,000,000), while the gold holdings of the Reichsbank were 2,300,000,000 marks (£115,000,000).   Funding of the entire debt would mean an annual service of not less than £380,000,000 per annum ; the currency could only be restored through drastic deflation to a level not much higher than 50 per cent. above the pre-war total, or, if the same ratio of gold cover were to be adopted, inclusive of all gold in circulation, to not much more than half.   There were no internal and no external gold reserves, no basis of credit to float an immense refunding operation at low interest rates, and the foreign credit of Germany was exhausted with the transfer of her last high-value securities.   The catastrophe was already in plain sight to all who had followed the course of German finance throughout the war ; the collapse of the mark was only a matter of time.

At this juncture, the problem of reparations assumed forbidding proportions, and the attempt to meet the demands of the Allies precipitated the crash.   It is beside the point to

discuss whether Germany deliberately forced on the depreciation of the mark as a method of avoiding payment of reparations and of liquidating her war indebtedness at home.   In
our opinion, the position at the close of war was so critical that
only a serious writing-down of the total burden of debt, virtually amounting to defalcation on a high proportion of it,
would have brought relief.   In Britain, difficulties were great
enough and the process of readjustment caused profound economic disturbance, the effects of which have not yet worn off,
but they were nothing beside the difficulties confronting Germany, quite apart from the problem of reparations.

The one determination of the Allies, to which they were committed politically as a result of elections, held in Britain and
France, immediately after the conclusion of the war, was to
make Germany pay the costs of the war and so release them
from international entanglements, into which financial policy
had led them.   Politics were in the ascendant, and clear reasoning based on sound economic doctrine played no part in deliberations.   It was a time of passions and recriminations, all
surrounded by an atmosphere of resentment at heavy losses in
men and treasure.   At this distance, the whole situation
appears artificial, a drama fought out with a multitude of
players, none of them of heroic stature and none of them capable of seeing the main issues clear—crude melodrama in places
and stark tragedy in others.   We may wonder at the display of
action and question the reality of motive, but it is impossible
to ignore the deadly earnest of the chief players.   They had to
face problems quite unlike anything they had even imagined
before, to take decisions of grave moment for the economic
future of the world, and it is not surprising that they should
burke the real issues, avoid looking into future implications of
present policy and adopt a frankly opportunist policy with
little economic or even political justification.

The cost of the war, which should be met by Germany, was
fixed in 1921 at 132,000,000,000 marks (£6,600,000,000), about
30,000,000,000 marks above the total of inter-allied indebtedness.   With the external debt regulated, some attention could
be devoted to the internal debt of each country, which actually
presented much more formidable difficulties, owing to its influence on the profit-earning capacity of industry and the prosperity of trade.   Until internal debt could be entirely funded
and reduced to manageable proportions, either through reduction in interest or partial renunciation or through inflation with
currency depreciation and subsequent stabilization at a low

level, the economic position of Europe could not be regarded as at all healthy or even promising.

Some inkling of this uncomfortable truth may have filtered through to the politicians and intensified their ardour in the search after reparations. They only fleetingly asked themselves the question : How can Germany be rendered capable of paying reparations at all under existing conditions ? Even supposing that the transfer difficulty could be overcome, the annual charges on a burden of debt amounting to 269,000,000,000 marks, including internal funded and floating debt and the reparations total, would have been not less than £850,000,000—a fantastic figure, which could be met perhaps through decline in the gold value of the mark and of international currencies resulting from an enormous increase in prices, but certainly not if a return to the gold standard were proposed.

The action of the Allies themselves made the recovery of Germany and the payment of reparations virtually impossible : territorial losses reduced the productive capacity of the country by 11 per cent. to 15 per cent., the surrender of her mercantile marine with a total gross tonnage of 2,596,000 tons, the loss of shipping aggregating 818,000 tons held in embargo and transferred to the Allies, the delivery of railway wagons, locomotives and other rolling stock, chemicals, dyes, agricultural products, coal and coke, the loss of foreign investments, and the economic disturbance caused by the disruption of the Ruhr-Lorraine-Luxemburg industrial unit were sufficient in themselves to cause a paralysis of long duration in the wealth-producing activities of Germany. The loss of all foreign investments, partly through financial policy during the war, partly through confiscation by the Allies, partly through transfer (valued at 792,000,000 marks) consequent on the Treaty of Versailles and through the flight of capital away from Germany during 1919 to 1922, meant that the whole machinery of foreign trade was out of action and that the recovery of exports within a reasonable time would be problematical.

According to Dr. Alfred Weber, German capital investments abroad before the war could be estimated at 20–30,000,000,000 marks, and they yielded in interest and dividends about 1,500,000,000 marks (£75,000,000). The real significance of such investment abroad may be appreciated from an estimate made by Franz Eulenberg. The capital investment of all European countries before the war was given by him at £7,500,000,000 and the annual income derived from it lay

between £400,000,000 and £500,000,000.   With that should be
included at least £500,000,000 on funding and other account.
The total trade of the world before the war was about
£7,000,000,000, so that capital investment was responsible for
at least 12 per cent.   In the case of Germany alone, it accounted
for well over 20 per cent. of the total export trade, and it influenced, directly and indirectly, the whole international credit
and trade position.   The loss of such investment meant decline
in exports and general impoverishment (as far, at least, as the
international trade balances were in question).

The only sums that could be transferred to the Allies without
endangering the economic stability of Germany, for reasons
which we shall discuss later, were those resulting from a surplus obtained in international trade ; the main factors contri-
buting to such a surplus would be excess of exports over imports, the earnings of shipping services and railway transport
over the frontiers, profits earned on the granting of credits and
other financial accommodation abroad, interest from capital
investment in foreign countries and tourists' remittances.   In
the years immediately prior to the war, there was a surplus
available for investment abroad, but even in exceptionally
good years it is doubtful whether it exceeded £60,000,000 to
£70,000,000, and it was actually rather less than the income
from capital already invested.   The situation after the war
was quite hopeless from this point of view : shipping services
and capital investments had gone, financial stringency of the
severest type made credit operations impossible, while the
exhaustion of food-stuffs and raw materials forced on excessive
importation.   There was not a single factor which could be
employed effectively to meet the charges for reparations imposed by the Allies, and every payment made to them provoked a crisis in the exchange and a further decline in the value
of the mark.

The payments actually transferred to the Allies, namely,
1,000,000,000 gold marks in August 1921 as a result of the
London Conference, 368,000,000 gold marks following on the
Cannes resolution and the moratorium of March 1922, and the
Treasury Bills converted into securities in favour of Belgium (as
a result of a Note of the Reparations Commission of August
1922) and valued at 254,000,000 marks, were small in comparison with the total of 132,000,000,000 marks held as Bonds by
the Allies.   But even 1,622,000,000 marks (£81,000,000) taxed
severely all the resources of Germany and were instrumental
in causing the final downfall of the mark.

We can follow the various stages in the decline of the national credit by reference to the dollar exchange. From December 1918 to January 1920, depreciation took place at an increasing rate through excessive imports required for replenishment of stocks ; from January of 1920 until August of the same year, a certain stability ensued and the Reichsbank was able to gain control of the money market with a resultant appreciation in the mark ; from August to September 1920, the mark slipped again, but the credit of 200 million gulden at 6 per cent. for ten years arranged with Holland restored confidence and conditions improved. In July 1921, the mark stood at eighty-one to the dollar, but in October, after the first reparations payment had been made, it had fallen to one hundred and eighty-one ; in April 1922, it had reached two hundred and eighty-three, and in July, after the Cannes payment had been transferred, six hundred and seventy ; in October 1922, following on the transfer of securities to Belgium in August, it lapsed to 4,500 marks to the dollar. Thereafter descent was rapid, the only check occurring in March 1923, when dollar bills totalling 50,000,000 dollars were issued by the Reichsbank and used to support the exchange. By August 1923, the mark ceased to have any value, and practically all transactions at home and abroad were carried out in foreign currencies. In November 1923, the currency was stabilized at one-billionth of its par value and the Rentenmark was introduced.

During this period of decline, the currency in circulation expanded and taxed the resources of the printing presses ; the discount rate of the Reichsbank was raised at frequent intervals to keep pace with depreciation and interpose some check on credit, but it never drew level with the rate of decline of the mark, with the result that the mere discounting of bills could be developed into a source of profit, especially for industrialists. Certain critics have stated that Germany deliberately adopted a policy of inflation to avoid meeting her obligations on reparations and on debt account generally, but to anyone who lived for a time in Germany during 1921 or 1922 or 1923 the belief must appear incredible and actually inhuman. No State, and least of all a State with a history of culture and middle-class integrity behind it such as Germany, could fall easily or willingly into a condition where the mere struggle for existence dominated every issue and the finer social qualities were abandoned to destruction. The picture is sufficiently gloomy without the addition of ignoble motive. The entire savings of the German people disappeared in the collapse of the mark ;

investment in the various loans issued by the Government, by the municipalities or public bodies ceased to have any value ; mortgages were repaid at prices only an infinitesimal fraction of their original value, and industrial stocks and debentures were liquidated for an old song.   Institutions, such as the Universities and High Schools, which depended for their income on fixed interest-bearing securities, found themselves unable to continue, and only in a few cases, the University of Munich, for example, where real estate constituted the bulk of the wealth at their disposal or industry was sufficiently interested to make special grants, could any real effort be made to adhere to the old standards of teaching and culture.

The shortage of housing accommodation made the position even more difficult, in spite of the fact that control over all dwellings was instituted and a parcelling out of all residents took place on a large scale ; no dwelling-houses were built owing to the lack of initial capital and the steady fall in values. The middle classes with fixed incomes suffered most severely, since they were unable to impose some method of adjustment in earnings which would take care of the decline in purchasing value of the mark and bring income into line with the cost of living ; labour, both skilled and unskilled, was much more successful in meeting the situation, largely owing to the profits earned by industry, and suffered less than any other section of the population.

A calculation made in 1923 by Hans Guradz and Karl Freudenberg into the minimum required to maintain a higher civil servant and his household in existence showed that, while the actual income of this official in 1913–14 was 34 per cent. above the existence minimum, in February 1923 it was 30 per cent. below.   Using the pre-war income as a basis, the higher civil servant in 1923 was only receiving in real income 53 per cent. of what he should have received under normal conditions.   In the highest grades, this ratio was actually 33 per cent.   On the other hand, an unskilled worker received in 1913–14 about 65 per cent. of the existence minimum in wages, and in February 1923, 59 per cent.—no great change !   Using 1913–14 again as a basis and making allowance for the introduction of the eight-hour day in place of the nine-hour day, we can fix the remuneration of the unskilled labourer in 1923 at 2 per cent. above the pre-war level.   This in itself was not entirely satisfactory in view of the low wages paid in 1913–14, but it does show that labour suffered much less than the middle classes.

The latter, forced down to a starvation level, under-nour-

ished, under-clothed, unable to afford education fees and
deprived of all power to enjoy the pleasures of life, went through
a period of ever-growing martyrdom ; they could not afford
books or pictures or even music, and lived in an atmosphere
of struggle without a gleam.[1] Yet they withstood the test.
Their victory was less spectacular than a victory on the battlefield enshrined in the magnificence of war, but it was not less
real, not less noble, not less worthy of lasting honour.   In those
years, when a frenzied juggling with the materials of existence
represented life in a world of cultural and social relations, the
power of thought, of abstract speculation, of artistic or literary
creation came vividly at moments to expression.   In the cafés,
the art cenacles, theory was discussed passionately and wordy
conflicts were staged round æsthetic and philosophical doctrines.
The pessimism of a Spengler, the inchoate musings of a Steiner,
the fine criticism of a Georg Simmel or a Gundolf, the social
visions of a Bernstein, the futuristic rhapsodies of an Eberz,
the clear speculation of a Rickert, and the economic or social
or religious profundities of a Weber or a Troeltsch, the logical
subtleties of an Husserl, came together to form a bewildering
and yet animated mosaic, which might in time have changed to
a marvellously vivid and compelling picture of a greatly creative
age.   The years of stress had brought some measure of insight
into the realities of the spiritual and material life, some desire
to explore deep and probe down into the heart of beauty and of
feeling, some moment of discontent akin to sublime enthusiasm, and the promise of awakening was very real.   Yet
at the time of unfolding, some frost took hold and cooled

[1] Statistics of consumption of food-stuffs illustrate the poverty
ruling in Germany during the inflation period in a remarkable fashion :

Food-stuff		1913 or 1913–14	1921 or 1921–22	1922 or 1922–23	1925 or 1925–26
Rye	. . . . (tons)	10,321,543	6,283,655	5,661,297	7,166,894
Wheat	. . . ,,	6,455,220	4,762,816	2,929,888	4,613,892
Barley	. . . ,,	7,282,183	2,175,262	1,845,873	3,601,481
Oats .	. . . ,,	8,645,547	4,598,786	3,598,643	5,377,746
Potatoes .	. . ,,	47,192,298	20,744,941	35,288,984	36,434,217
Meat (of all kinds)	,,	31,030,455	—	19,177,068*	30,124,400
Beer .	. (hectolitres)	68,847,000	33,993,000	31,233,000	48,376,000

* 1923.

In 1922, consumption was not much more than half of the total
recorded for 1913—sufficient indication of the standard of living of the
people. Potatoes alone remained the staple food.

enthusiasm, and little of final value emerged. The quickening died down through lack of sustaining fires. The years 1921–23 were of extraordinary interest in Germany from the social and cultural points of view alone.

If now we pass over to industry, a different world appears. Industry, dependent on real values as measured in production, could move its prices upwards in line, or almost in line, with depreciation in the mark. The manufacturer paid less for materials and wages on account of the time-lag in adjustment to ever-changing conditions; he could make a profit on his short-term credit transactions and reap an ever higher surplus on his costs of production. At the same time, he could discharge fixed interest-bearing indebtedness, such as bank loans, debentures, bonds, and even preferred shares, with marks at only a fraction of their gold value, and embark, as a consequence, on extensive plans of re-equipment and expansion of productive plant. The more ambitious could embark on schemes of amalgamations and absorption of allied firms, and so form vast manufacturing complexes covering more than one industry.

In coal-mining, iron and steel, engineering, electrical manufacture and chemicals, spectacular developments in this direction took place. Certain writers have held that closer co-operation between the State and industry, with a much more loyal recognition by the latter of its duties towards the national executive in finance, would have spared Germany from the worst horrors of inflation and so have brought economic recovery nearer; they have seen in the collapse of the mark the direct evidence of struggle between industry and the State. We shall deal with this aspect in a later chapter covering industrial organizations, but it is sufficient at this juncture to adhere to the conviction that financial policy in Germany during and immediately after the war would have led inevitably to the fall of the mark, and that reparations precipitated the crisis.

CHAPTER XII

FINANCE (*continued*) : STABILIZATION AND THE DAWES PLAN

The introduction of the Rentenmark—a crisis of confidence—tackling the reparations problem—the impossibility of reparations without the economic recovery of Germany—principles necessary to success—the Dawes Plan—criticism of the Plan—the difficulty of transfer—foreign loans—the policy of the Reichsbank since 1924—effect of stabilization on industry—revaluation of balance-sheets—recovery of production.

WITH the introduction of the Rentenmark, a new period opened in the financial history of Germany, or, rather, the post-war financial crisis came to a settling-point prior to the development of a new and sounder policy and the elaboration of a new currency. The reparations problem moves again into the foreground and occupies the limelight during 1924, but the very conditions which rendered possible the miracle of the Rentenmark were also favourable to a more realistic treatment of reparations. The occupation of the Ruhr, which had lasted all through 1923 and contributed to the financial collapse of the State, produced no results of immediate cash value to France or Belgium and showed that force could do nothing. The evacuation of the Ruhr, which occurred at the end of 1924, actually caused a clearing of the political and financial atmosphere, and inspired better understanding between the Allies and Germany.

Proposals for reform of the German currency had been advanced all through the inflation period, but it was generally recognized that, until the reparations problem were solved, no plan could have any prospect of lasting success. Throughout the early months of 1923, reform was discussed by German economists and industrialists, and two definite movements could be distinguished—the movement towards return to the gold standard, headed by Julius Hirsch, the Federation of German Industries, and, later, Hjalmar Schacht, when it was thought that it would be possible to introduce a gold currency based on

181

the gold holdings of the Reichsbank combined with the foreign securities in the possession of the banks and of the country as a whole—and the movement towards substitution of some new basis of security other than gold for a stabilized currency.   In the opinion of the group at the head of the latter movement, namely, Helfferich and Minoux, there was not enough gold in the Reichsbank nor sufficient foreign securities in Germany to act as cover for the proposed gold mark, and the failure of the plan would involve in it the collapse of the Reichsbank and, ultimately, of the whole German financial structure.

Helfferich suggested something much more revolutionary in character, something which would bring industry and agriculture directly into the work of financial reorganization. Real estate or material values should act as a basis for a new currency, and these values would in themselves constitute sufficient security.   Land and its yield of crops, industry and its productive capacity were elements which would remain good when everything else had lost its value, and they could not be transferred outside of Germany.   In August, Helfferich put forward a plan with a rye-pound (Roggenpfund) and later a rye-mark (Roggenmark) as units of currency, agriculture representing the security behind them, but the final scheme included industry as well, and on October 15, the Bank Law creating the Rentenbank and the Rentenmark was passed through the Reichstag.   In December 1923, the new currency had entirely displaced the old mark.

The Rentenbank was founded by representatives of agriculture, industry, trade and commerce as well as the banks, with a capital of 3,200 million Rentenmarks.   Of this capital agriculture subscribed one-half and industry, trade, commerce and the banks the remainder ; the Rentenbank should acquire mortgages, defined in gold marks, equivalent to 4 per cent. of the rated value of agricultural properties, and these mortgages would bear interest at 6 per cent.   Industry, trade, commerce, and the banks would furnish mortgages on the same conditions to a value equivalent to those supplied by agriculture.   Neither the capital of the Bank nor the mortgages could be transferred, either in whole or in part, and the Rentenbank would issue bonds, bearing interest at 5 per cent., of a value of 500 marks, or multiples thereof, on the security of the mortgages lodged with it ; the bonds in turn would act as cover for the Rentenmark currency.   The maximum circulation of Rentenmarks should not be greater than the capital of the Bank, namely, 3,200 million marks.

The most striking characteristic of the reform proposed and carried out was exactly the pledging of the fixed capital and vested wealth of the German nation—in itself a hazardous innovation, since the earning capacity of the country was tied up with the currency circulation, and any serious increase in the latter, beyond the limit of 3,200 million marks, would mean increase in the total value of the mortgages levied on agriculture, industry and trade. The most optimistic could scarcely regard a currency circulation of £160,000,000 as at all adequate for the needs of a country which, before the war, required £350,000,000, and the Rentenbank would undoubtedly have found itself under the necessity to double its capital, double its commitments and double its mortgage holdings within a comparatively short time. In addition to this, the nature of the security for the note issue made the new currency valid only within the German frontiers ; the bonds could not be exchanged for a negotiable value, such as gold or foreign securities ; they were fixed in Germany and had no real exchange value. The Rentenmark could not be used to finance foreign trade and, even within Germany, any serious move towards the realization of the security behind the bonds would have jeopardized at once the existence of the whole plan.

The crisis was, therefore, one of confidence, of the confidence of the German people in the future of their country as a great industrial and trading power in the world, and the success of the Rentenmark proves beyond all question that this confidence was held. Since that dark period at the end of 1923, when disaster menaced the industrial and financial structure of Germany, the note of confidence and trust has been maintained and has been one main factor causing the recovery which has since taken place. Of the currency raised by the Rentenbank, namely, 3,200 million Rentenmarks, 1,200 millions at 6 per cent. were to be placed at the disposal of the State for two years to allow it to get over budgetary difficulties and provide it with funds during the period of transition, while 1,200 millions could be granted to the Reichsbank and to the four private-note banks for the supply of credit to industry. The State received at once 300 million Rentenmarks to cover its floating debt. On October 26, the Reichsbank received authority to issue gold mark notes, which should have one-third cover in gold or gold securities, and the date of application of this authority would coincide with the issue of notes by the Rentenbank. Thus, in November 1923, both the Rentenbank and the

Reichsbank issued notes of a gold denomination to replace the paper marks now valued at one-billionth of a gold mark, and the conversion of German industry and trade to sound currency conditions had begun.

The position of industry itself was peculiarly difficult ; through foreign trade, it had been able to acquire a considerable holding of foreign currencies, and had used them to finance production and even, in some cases, to pay wages.   The imposition of a legal gold currency made it impossible for the industrialist or trade to use directly such financial resources, and a serious shortage of cash was felt very soon.   There was practically nothing available to keep the machinery of production in operation, while the maintenance of foreign trade, even at the level of 1922 or 1923, appeared improbable in view of the absence of any central institution for financing international transactions.   Unemployment in December 1923 and the early months of 1924 assumed alarming proportions, and considerably over 2,800,000 workers were out of work.   Towards the summer of 1924, however, the situation lightened and the critical period was over.

The currency in circulation, Reichsbank and Rentenbank notes and metallic currency combined, had risen from 1,998,000,000 marks at the end of November 1923 to 2,929,000,000 marks at the end of June 1924, and 3,750,000,000 marks at the end of December.   At that point it was moving towards equilibrium and was sufficient for the cash requirements of industry, while the restoration of confidence had eased the credit position.

Looming in the background menaced still the reparations problem.   Without some final settlement, no work of currency reform could be lasting in Germany, and the recovery of German credit depended on the moderation of those who were responsible for financial policy on the part of the Allies.   Four years' juggling with economic facts had shown that mere political legerdemain could achieve nothing, and that the constantly proclaimed determination to extract gold from Germany might sound very impressive to a gullible public, but had little force against inexorable economic laws.   The difficulty, as always, lay in creating a situation favourable to the payment of reparations by Germany and the transfer of large sums from one country to another other than by the ordinary processes of trade and finance.   The full complexity of the subject only began to dawn on politicians and statesmen towards the period of stabilization of the mark, and even economists and financial experts were not quite certain in their minds regarding the ends to be achieved and the means by which the suitable consummation should be reached.

There were few illusions left at the end of 1923 regarding the value or even need of reparations—in Britain and the United States at least ; but France, committed to enormous expenditure on the devastated territories and dissatisfied with the various agreements regarding deliveries in kind made with German industrialists (those associated with the names of Rathenau and Bemelmans and Stinnes, above all), held fast to the idea of reparations. A condition of financial security in France was exactly the levy of reparations on Germany. Yet if we analyse the position at all carefully, the difficulties confronting any lasting settlement appear enormous. The actual burden of reparations, if we accept the total of 132 milliard marks (£6,600,000,000) as established by the Allies, would have represented about £350,000,000 annually without any allowance being made for funding operations, and, in meeting this, Germany would pay almost the equivalent of what is now disbursed in Britain for the annual service of debt. Apparently, therefore, the reparations problem meant imposing an annual charge on Germany not much more than that being met already by the British people, but the analogy ends with the figures. Germany had no public debt to speak of after the collapse of the mark, and alone among the European nations could move forward to a clear-swept balance-sheet ; it could budget, therefore, for a substantial service of reparations debt. If, however, the financial complications underlying the heavy disbursements in Britain are examined, and there is no doubt that the main cause for depression in British industry has been exactly the annual debt levy, the position becomes less hopeful for success in Germany. The British debt service represented almost a circular transaction, from the public to the State and from the State again to the public ; those in receipt of interest and dividends from the State repaid a large part of it directly through income tax and indirectly through other forms of taxation bearing on the debt service. The latter could be and was used to finance production and economic activities within Britain, and constituted the main source for the realization of new capital required each year for industry, transport and, in some cases, for foreign investment. Even so, it represented a form of financial inflation which increased the manufacturing costs of industry and kept prices of home-manufactured products above a level where they could be sold against international competition in the markets of the world, and encouraged excessive importation. Its worst effect was to be found in the paralysis of the competitive power of the great export industries, which still constituted the foundations of the national wealth and, as such, it was instrumental in forcing down wages below an economic level, in eliminating profits on capital investment, in introducing a period of reorganization, financial and technical, to improve competitive efficiency—but it only weakened the financial strength of the country when it began to be exported in excessively high volume abroad, either to finance imports or to bring greater profits to finance houses.

In Germany, on the other hand, the total of £350,000,000 would represent a direct burden on the industries of the country, with no possibility of repayment through taxation of recipients which had served to reduce the real total paid in Britain and, as such, it was definitely beyond the capacity of Germany to pay. Without considering the transfer problem, and assuming that the German budget could be debited with a total corresponding to the real total met by the British budget after deduction of income and other taxation (probably about £200,000,000), we should regard the financial position of industry itself as precarious in the extreme. All this debt charge, instead of being retained in the country and subjected to circular transactions, from the State to the public and vice versa, necessary to the maintenance of internal credit, would be transferred to the Allies and could only be recovered from them through increased exports or through services capable of yielding to Germany an equivalent of the sums transferred. Otherwise, the perpetual transfer of reparations would mean a progressive diminution of German capital, a long-drawn-out selling-up process accompanied by economic ruin, a complete exhaustion of the resources which kept in existence a population of sixty-three millions. The disturbance of economic conditions in Germany would react at once on the industry and trade of the world and cause universal depression.

The success of reparations depended, therefore, on four great developments, none of them very satisfactory to the Chauvinists :

1. The recovery of German industry to a point where it could contribute to the favourable trade balance of Germany. This meant that the competitive efficiency of German industry would again be high enough to allow it to occupy a dominating position in world

exports, and that British, American and French industry would require to yield ground.

2. The restoration of the subsidiary services which made for improvement of German credit, above all, of the mercantile fleet, and the reorganization of transport with a view to increasing its profit-earning capacity.

3. The development of foreign investments by Germany abroad, resulting either from export of capital, from a heavy excess of exports over imports, where such excess would be available for investment, or from both.

4. The restoration of German credit, so that the capital required to finance production in the early years of recovery could be obtained abroad and foreign trade and exchange transactions be carried out on the basis of credits obtained in the international money-market. With this would come the formation of a bank to finance foreign trade and build up again trade connections through the medium of finance.

Other factors enter, of course, into consideration—the balancing of the budget, the raising of taxation within Germany, the adjustment of rates for transport and of tariffs, but they affect predominantly the internal situation and only bear indirectly on the reparations problem.

To make Germany into a goose capable of laying golden eggs indefinitely appeared to be an exceedingly intricate business, even to those who were responsible for the framing of the Dawes Plan and, even now, the problem comes no nearer solution. Germany, in order to pay reparations, without dissipation of fixed capital and the collapse of the mark exchange, would require to become the most prosperous and most active industrial country in the world, with a steadily increasing export trade yielding a large favourable balance, with industries superior in efficiency and marketing success to those of Great Britain, America and France, with unlimited credit to finance transactions in the most distant markets, and with investments abroad of sufficient value to allow it to secure a strong hold on the economic development of many important markets. After this consummation had been reached, it would be possible for Germany to pay reparations, but they would be reparations won from the defeat and decline of the industrial countries that had emerged victorious in a military sense from the war. Under no other conditions could the reparations problem be solved, and its solution would spell disaster, above all, for the industries of Great Britain.

With these reflections as a criterion, we may pass on to consideration of the first real move to deal with reparations on a rational basis—the Dawes Plan—and discuss some of its benefits and inherent weaknesses. The Dawes Committee proposed to render Germany capable of paying reparations with the minimum disturbance of the economic *status quo* ; they aimed at securing some basis inside Germany itself for the creation of funds which would be available for transfer and decided on the maximum which Germany could pay annually under normal conditions. The essentials were the balancing of the State budget, the severance of the Reichsbank from the Government so that political factors would not be allowed to interfere with financial, and the realization of a certain contribution from industry and transport to ensure co-operation of all the economic forces of the country. There could then be no possibility of a struggle between the State and industry, such as could be observed during the inflation period.

The changes determined were the recovery of German credit, the elimination of the political factor as far as possible from the main public services contributory to reparations and to financial control, namely, the railways and the Reichsbank, and the maintenance of the gold standard with a stabilized mark in Germany. The reorganization of the Reichsbank was perhaps the most significant development. The Reichsbank became specifically independent of the State with the right to control the circulation of currency in Germany, to facilitate financial transactions and to utilize capital placed at its disposal. For fifty years, it would have sole right in Germany to issue bank-notes, but the notes already issued by the four private banks remained unaffected. The Reichsbank was empowered to raise its capital to 400 million marks, but its present capital transferred to the new gold basis should not exceed 100 million marks. Other regulations dealt with the ordinary discount business of the bank on the usual lines, with the important proviso, however, that the Reichsbank could grant working credits to the State only for a maximum period of three months at a time within a limit of 100 million marks and, at the end of the financial year, State indebtedness towards the Bank should be liquidated. All financial transactions of the State should pass through the Reichsbank, which could grant credits to the German railways and the German post not exceeding 200 million marks for both. The Bank was not permitted to advance credits to the Reich, the various

CARL VON SIEMENS
(CHAIRMAN IN 1927 OF THE GERMAN STATE RAILWAYS COMPANY)

States, communes or foreign governments, but it would have a special reparations account which could not go beyond 2,000 million marks without the consent of the Bank. The currency in circulation should have a gold cover of 40 per cent., three-fourths of which should be actually gold. In the event of a lower ratio being adopted, the Bank would require to pay duty to the State and raise the discount rate. The government of the Bank itself was to be vested in a Direktorium, the President of which was elected by the General Council composed of fourteen members, seven German and one each nominated by Britain, France, Italy, Belgium, United States, Holland and Switzerland. The voting arrangements permitted of special consideration being given to German interests and, in this way, the international element was toned down. The Reichsbank became, as a result of this scheme, the main element in German financial policy, and its very constitution made inflation for political purposes impossible.

The functions of the Gold Discount Bank, commissioned in March 1924 to finance trade and deal with commercial credits, passed into the hands of the Reichsbank and, from October 1924 onwards, we can see in operation one banking policy carried out by one all-powerful institution removed effectively from the control of the State. In much the same way, the control of the State railways was taken away and vested in a private company in which the Allies would be represented, but the action of the State in acquiring all the shares of the company was tantamount to renewal of national control within the form of a private industrial undertaking. In the latter case, the main preoccupation of the Dawes Committee lay in abolishing a *régime* of waste, in restoring efficiency to administration and in realizing more satisfactory profit margins, while, in the former, the recovery and the consolidation of the national credit were held to be more than anything else fundamental to the economic salvation of the country.

Other changes of less importance were envisaged, but the two already indicated were decisive. A special Reparations Commission, under the chairmanship of Mr. Parker Gilbert, an American representative, came into operation to collect reparations dues and exert some advisory control over German financial policy, especially where it affected the delivery, actual or future, of reparations. Under the Dawes Plan, Germany had to pay in reparations in a full year 2,500 million marks (£125,000,000), but for the first years of the scheme lower contributions would be exacted—1,000 million marks in 1924–25,

1,220 million marks in 1925-26 and in 1926-27, 1,750 million
marks in 1927-28, and 2,500 million marks thereafter.   In the
first year the new Reichsbank was set up, the German budget
balanced, the railways transferred to a private company with a
capital of 15,000 million marks, with 11,000 million marks in
bonds bearing interest at 5 per cent. with 1 per cent. Sinking Fund, and industrial debentures created to the value of
5,000 million marks under similar interest and sinking fund
conditions.

Contributions from the budget began in 1926-27, when
130,000,000 marks were paid to reparations account ; in 1927-
28, 500,000,000 marks, and from 1928-29 onwards, the full
quota of 1,250,000,000 marks would be due from this source.
For three years, therefore, a partial moratorium existed, in
order to lighten the financial difficulties of the State and allow
it to establish its budget on a sound basis.   The moratorium
also affected to some extent the railway bonds and industrial
debentures, since 125,000,000 marks were derived from interest
on the latter in 1925-26 and 250,000,000 marks in 1926-27,
instead of the maximum of 300,000,000 marks levied thereafter, while the sinking fund of 1 per cent. began to operate
with the railway bonds from 1927-28 onwards, bringing the
total in this case from 550,000,000 marks in the previous year
up to a maximum of 660,000,000 marks.   A further source
of revenue, the transport and traffic tax, completed the
payments.

It is unnecessary to go into the matter in fuller detail, since
the actual method of collection and allocation bears a purely
technical significance, but we can touch on certain principles
which emerge from contemplation of the scheme.   The favourite
criticism made on publication of the Plan was that German
economic recovery would take more than the three years estimated and that the most critical period would be exactly the
first year, when the launching of an international loan of
800,000,000 marks would find few foreign investors willing to
risk so much on the revival of German credit.   Events have
proved these prognostications vain.   The main weakness,
however, of the scheme lies in concentration of receipts on the
budget revenue rather than on other financial resources which
would contribute more directly to the favourable balance of
trade.   The problem of transfer weighed less with the authors
of the Plan than the collection of revenue and, even now, the
attention of the Agent-General for Reparations has been devoted
more to budgetary movements than to changes in the general

financial and capital situation.[1] The difficulty cannot be
cloaked by the fact that deliveries in kind represented a high
percentage of the reparations received by the Allies and that
receipts from the Reparations Recovery Act satisfied almost the
entire British claim to a percentage of the Dawes payments.
Even subtracting these items, the sum remaining to be transferred in a full year would not fall far short of half of the total
to be paid by Germany and, as such, would represent a problem
of the most formidable type.

The purchase of currencies and securities for transfer on a
very large scale would cause a decline in the exchange value of
the mark. One proviso in the scheme is destined to remove
this danger or, at least, to obviate it : when the exchange
position makes it impossible for transfer to be made, the Agent-
General is allowed to accumulate funds derived from reparations up to 5,000,000,000 marks, but he may not exceed this
total and, in the event of a higher accumulation being necessary, he must relieve the German budget accordingly. Under
these conditions, the Agent-General will probably strive to
avoid reaching the maximum and use his power to influence
German financial policy in the direction of internal credit
restriction and the furtherance of exports. Even so, there is a
limit to credit-rationing and to the stimulus of exports through
financial factors, and it is almost certain that the maximum
will be reached within a few years after the entrance into operation of the standard scale.

With Germany capable of developing a strong export trade
and of financing its internal capital requirements without
having recourse to foreign loans or foreign credits, there would
have been a clear possibility of the Dawes payments being met

---

[1] It is interesting, in this connection, to compare the expenditure
of Germany on public services other than those which enter into the
productive category in 1913 and 1925–26. The total expenditure in
1913 was 5,408,000,000 marks (£270,400,000), the army and navy
accounting for 32·16 per cent., education for 20·74 per cent., social
welfare (i.e. hospital, unemployment, housing and other activities
of a social nature) for 10·56 per cent. In 1925–26, the total expenditure stood at 11,871,000,000 marks (£593,550,000), slightly more than
twice the pre-war figure. In this case, however, the army and navy
only accounted for 5·26 per cent., education for 17·39 per cent., but
social welfare had risen to 23·96 per cent., owing to unemployment
and building grants, while war costs, pensions, etc., accounted for
22·77 per cent. There was little ground, therefore, for the complaint
made by the Agent-General for Reparations in 1927 that Germany
was spending too much on education and similar services and that
any increase in the allocation for such purposes would not be justified.

and transferred without danger to the mark : the real surplus to be transferred in cash would probably not have exceeded £70,000,000, and the right of the Agent-General for Reparations to accumulate balances up to £250,000,000 would have sufficed to avert a crisis. We should not expect any serious changes for five years at least. But the collapse of the mark exhausted all the capital reserves of Germany and left industry without any resources to draw on to finance production. The cupboard was swept bare when stabilization took place, and the introduction of balance-sheets on a gold basis meant writing-down of existing capital to the lowest possible figure and the disappearance of reserves. This capital scarcity, not in industry alone but in every section of economic life, meant recourse to foreign loans until a position of balance had been reached. The framers of the Dawes Plan made no allowance for excessive capital imports and had no provisions for the control of internal credits based on foreign indebtedness. Otherwise they might have created an instrument for regulating the interest rates on the capital requirements of Germany and so removed all danger of borrowing too expensively—a factor of importance in the adverse annual balance of payments.

The combination of the Dawes payments and the interest due on borrowings abroad must be such as to jeopardize the future of the Plan and make the transfer problem one of the most difficult economic propositions of our time. Again, the influence of borrowing abroad on the balance of trade itself must be unfavourable, since it tends to stimulate home consumption and encourage imports. The history of Germany since 1924 vividly illustrates the process. It may be perfectly clear, as some writers have stated, that loans raised by the German States, municipalities, public institutions and industrial firms abroad since the entrance into operation of the Dawes Plan have actually exceeded the total payments due under the latter. The American investor, who has advanced much the highest proportion of these loans, may have been paying indirectly Germany's total for reparations each year. Even now, we cannot be sure that the annual capital accretion of Germany, estimated at about 4,000,000,000 marks, will be met in the near future from the internal resources of Germany alone. The future of the Dawes Plan, in the opinion of many observers, depends on the willingness of the American investor to advance money to Germany virtually *in perpetuum*. This, in our opinion, is an overstatement of the case. The American investor, if only to maintain the status of existing loans to

Germany and to ensure the security of capital already invested, will no doubt continue to advance loans to Germany until the country is in a position to dispense with them. If, however, a panic should occur and the constant stream of credits from the United States cease within the next three or four years, then undoubtedly a serious crisis will at once ensue.

There is little prospect of the inflow of foreign capital ceasing within an appreciable time. The total debt of the German State, quite apart from industry, has risen from 2,406 million marks in 1924 to 4,487 million marks in 1927, an increase of 2,081 million marks in three years, due partly to compensation for the old debt eliminated by the collapse of the mark and partly to an internal loan of 500 million marks raised in the spring of 1927. This alone would indicate a shortage of capital in Germany. The long-term foreign loans raised by Germany (almost wholly in the United States) in 1924, inclusive of the Dawes loan, totalled 900 million marks, in 1925, 1,249·7 million marks, in 1926, 1,575·4 million marks, and, in 1927, 1,383·9 million marks, or 5,209 million marks in four years. Short-term loans and credits bring the aggregate up to about 7,000 million marks, which would require an annual service of interest of 480 million marks, with an additional 140 million marks at least to cover funding operations—a grand total, therefore, of 620 million marks (£31,000,000). This should be added to the Dawes payments as forming part of the transfer problem. Again, the balance of trade has become seriously adverse : in 1924, it reached 1,940 million marks, in 1925, 2,959 million marks, changed to a favourable balance of 314 million marks in 1926, and in 1927 showed a deficit of 3,300 million marks, so that for four years a deficit of 8,885 million marks was reached. While long-term and short-term credits together accounted for 7,000 million marks and should be regarded as cover for excess of imports, even then a net deficit of almost 2,000 million marks was incurred over the four years 1924–27, before the full payments, as required by the Dawes Plan, were made.

These statistics, forbidding as they may appear in a general survey of the economic situation, are necessary to appreciation of the complicated and enormously difficult issues confronting German economists and statesmen. Owing to the changes that have characterized production and trade since 1924, the condition essential to the well-being and prosperity of the country is that the flow of capital into Germany should not be interrupted : interruption would mean collapse of the insecure building housing the national credit, the emergence of new and dangerous elements beneath the elaborate artifice of foreign trade and international credits, which have hitherto governed every development. Yet the increase in such indebtedness must serve to bring into play again all the factors making for complexity and difficulty, the excess of imports, the problem of transfer, the lack of symmetry and balance in production, and so the vicious circle continues.

The question arises : at what point in this circle can it be broken or diverted so that a healthier state of affairs financially will result ? At production, possibly, or at transfer of payments, or at foreign trade ? The abolition of reparations would probably suffice to restore solidity of credit and permit of exact adjustment of ingoings and outgoings ; the creation of a great export surplus through the improved competitive efficiency of German industry would avert a crisis, but such an expansion in exports would depend on restriction of home consumption, credit rationing to force liquidation of stocks and an immediate advance in world demand. Control of finance might have forced German industry to concentrate on exports entirely, and there is little doubt that, on various occasions, a determined effort was made by the Reichsbank to further this aim.

Few chapters in financial history are more interesting than those through which the Reichsbank and industry alike passed since 1924—a period of recovery and readjustment, of revaluation and expansion culminating in a boom year, 1927, when records were established in industrial activity. From October 1924 onwards the currency increased steadily, practically without remission, from 3,610 million marks (inclusive of metallic currency) to 4,777 million marks in October 1925, 5,180 million marks in October 1926, and 5,806 million marks in October 1927. Since the end of 1923 it had more than doubled : in the spring of 1924 there was a short pause, while some effort was made to keep credit movements in check, and a similar movement took place at the beginning, and in December, of 1925. The serious depression that set in during the spring and summer of 1926, largely owing to severe credit restriction by the Reichsbank with a view to encouraging exports and consequently improving the balance of trade, forced a change in policy and the currency moved rapidly upwards. Towards the end of 1927, again, a tendency towards decline could be noted, but the upswing in trade has forced on expansion and there is apparently no limit to the process.

Some writers have looked on such a development as pure

inflation, destined to force on home consumption and bring prosperity to industry, but the pre-war currency had a circulation of 7,000 million marks, fully 1,000 million higher than the maximum reached in 1927, and, in view of the post-war rise in prices, there would still be room for expansion up to 10,000 million marks. The only check to such a tendency would be the security available at the Reichsbank for such a note issue. As a matter of fact, the position was not entirely reassuring in this connection : the gold cover for the Reichsbank notes, which was as high as 64 per cent. in 1926, fell steadily during 1927 and reached 47·6 per cent. in October. As such, it was still above the minimum of 40 per cent. prescribed in the constitution of the Bank. For the total currency in circulation (inclusive of Rentenmark notes), however, the gold cover fell from 40·3 per cent. in October 1926 to 34·3 per cent. in October 1927. Unless, therefore, the Reichsbank were to purchase gold and foreign securities in large quantities during 1928, the limits of expansion would be reached in the early spring of 1928 and a period of deflation would necessarily ensue.

The credits and advances granted to industry showed similar movements in 1924 and 1925, a period of recovery, but a serious fall took place all through 1926 and, even in 1927, with an upward swing in the trade barometer, the level of October 1925 had not yet been reached. On the other hand, the cash and credit position was so much more liquid in 1927, owing to the higher profit-earning capacity of industry and the inflow of funds from the foreign loans, that we would not expect a repetition of the credit curve of 1925. The continued fall in the discount rate of the Reichsbank to a minimum of 5 per cent. in May 1927, with a sharp upward movement thereafter to 8 per cent. in November 1927, corresponded to the improvement in the trade position and showed that the Reichsbank, during 1926 especially, was bent on improving the employment figures rather than on narrowing credit with a view to liquidation of stocks and lowering of prices. Its action in the summer and autumn of 1927 would point to a desire to impose some check on financial developments and realize some effective control over both credit and currency circulation. Towards the end of 1927, in spite of these measures, the balance of trade had become less favourable, imports were still in excess of exports, and the gap was widening. Industry gave indications of a slowing-down, while the volume of employment declined ; wholesale prices moved, however, in sympathy with prices in the United States and Britain and were higher than at the

beginning of the year, while the cost of living remained stationary at the high level reached in the spring.

The effect of the discount policy of the Reichsbank was less
pronounced than might have been expected ; the resistance of
the market increased and no repetition of the Stock Exchange
crisis of the early summer took place ; industrial securities
were quoted still at abnormally high figures on the Exchange,
even after comparatively unfavourable reports had been published by leading iron and steel firms and, if the value of new
securities listed can be taken as a guide, the year 1927 represented easily the most active in recent German history. By the
end of 1927, the Reichsbank had become effectively the final
source of credit of the State as envisaged in its constitution
of October 1924 ; the circulation of Rentenmark notes had
declined from a maximum of 3,200 million marks recorded at
the end of 1923 to 896 million marks in November 1927, while
the private note-issuing banks accounted for only 180 million
marks. The centre of control was vested now almost completely in the Reichsbank, and it had powers superior even to
those exerted by the Bank of England in Britain ; it was the
arbiter of German economic and industrial prosperity ; its
policy decided whether industry should be fed with abundant
credits or forced to liquidate its production at all costs to secure
credit ; deflation, if carried out by it, could be more drastic
even than in Britain.

While, therefore, the vitality of industry during the year
prior to the first full payment of the Dawes Plan inspired admiration in many observers and induced gloom in those who witnessed at the same time the struggles of British industry, the
possibility of crisis could never be absent from thought, and
anxiety was more and more deeply felt regarding the solution
of a problem which loomed menacingly in the immediate foreground—the problem of reparations.

The effect of financial changes on the course of industrial
production could be followed with reference to employment or
output in the basic industries. During the years of inflation
up to September 1922, immense profits in marks were earned,
and the cost of re-equipment on the most extensive scale could
be met easily out of current revenue; if credits were obtained
directly or through the medium of special bills discounted at
the Reichsbank or through the creation of specific bonds as
security, repayment could easily be undertaken. The persistent fall in the mark served to reduce even short-term indebtedness to a fraction of its initial gold value, while the dis-

count rate imposed by the Reichsbank lagged seriously behind this rate of decline in the mark, and repayment could actually be made at a profit by the industrialist.   It is well known that, from the autumn of 1922 onwards, German industrialists were accumulating heavy balances abroad, held as payment for exports, and were allowing these funds to remain in Holland, Switzerland, America, and even Britain ; the financial needs of production were met by the wise manipulation of short-term credits and bills discounted at the Reichsbank.

At that time, a few outstanding figures appear—Rathenau and Stinnes chief among them—who devoted profits to the realization of control over the most varied industrial, commercial and financial undertakings—a form of industrial imperialism at low capital cost.   The inflation period meant prosperity for industry, but it was wholly artificial, dependent on exhaustion of the capital and financial resources of the country.   When, however, the position became critical and the bottom of the sack appeared, the profit-earning capacity of industry swiftly declined ; inflation, after the autumn of 1922, became even as great a curse to German industry as it was to the German State and the German people ; the invasion of the Ruhr completed the process of disillusionment and, at one time, the Ruhr coal and iron magnates dreamed of elaborating their own bank with their own currency to stop the rot.   The advantages of inflation had been overshadowed by its disadvantages, and the stabilization proposals put forward by Helfferich and subsequently incorporated in the Rentenbank found industry on the whole in a chastened and favourable mood.   No end, other than economic ruin, attended a policy of further inflation, and the substitution of foreign currencies for the mark could only be a makeshift, since it tended to bring the selling prices of German goods out of phase with world prices, make German goods for export too expensive, shorten the range and the period of credits necessary to finance imports of raw materials and food-stuffs, make discount rates incredibly high, paralyse the competitive power of industry, and make it unable to maintain a large volume of exports necessary to the use of foreign currencies.   It was a vicious circle which could break up only in a general disaster.

Stabilization brought with it, as everyone had foreseen, a period of adjustment accompanied by serious depression : unemployment in the early months of 1924 exceeded 2,800,000, and even then a collapse was imminent, but the policy pursued by the Reichsbank in rapidly increasing its note issue and thus stimulating purchasing capacity at home brought relief, and a period of genuine recovery set in. Finance and the State dominated industry for the first time since the conclusion of the war, but it was essentially a domination by consent and not by force. Industrialists were still able to interpose effective resistance to excessive deflation or control of credit imposed by the Reichsbank, as events during the late autumn of 1924 and the spring of 1925 showed, and the restoration of the national credit allowed them to borrow abroad on the security of the plant and equipment which they had perfected during the inflation period and converted into a real capital asset immune from currency fluctuations. Revaluation of balance-sheets in accordance with legislation, so that every item should be recorded in gold marks, meant a change in the liquid assets owned by industrial firms. Inflated capital, as expressed in paper marks, was written down to gold marks, but, in a number of industries, chemicals and electrical manufacture especially, a cautious capital policy, assisted by considerable cash balances held abroad, allowed a change to be made with very little adjustment in value ; the process was not drastic and a few companies transferred their share capital to a gold basis without alteration in its nominal amount.

The greatest change took place in fixed-interest bearing shares and debentures ; revaluation meant in this case elimination from the balance-sheet, and the majority of companies emerged nominally clear of loan and mortgage debt. The first gold-mark balance-sheets dealt with the interim period ending October 1924 and were largely tentative and experimental ; the following year saw adjustment completed and a return to normal conditions achieved, while 1926 and 1927 were years of capital accretion with a view to increasing the earning capacity of industry and extending its financial resources so that it could embark on more ambitious export plans.[1] There is no doubt

[1] In a statistical survey covering all public companies entered on the register, the increase in the total working capital from 1924-25 to 1925-26 was stated as 5,231,000,000 marks (£261,500,000). Of this increase, long-term indebtedness accounted for 1,015,000,000 marks (£50,750,000), and other indebtedness, mostly short-term credits, for 3,873,000,000 marks (£193,650,000). The paid-up share capital had expanded slightly from 17,871,000,000 marks (£893,550,000) to 18,214,000,000 marks (£910,070,000) ; production had not yet reached a stage where it could justify new capital, but it required to be financed very considerably in other ways. Out of the total working capital of 38,250,000,000 marks (£1,917,500,000), no less than 20,000,000,000 marks (£1,000,000,000) represented financing of production through loans and credits and advances. The average

that, during 1924 and 1925, industry suffered from acute capital shortage ; the rates levied for short-term and long-term credits alike were excessively high and made production correspondingly expensive ; the internal resources of Germany were so depleted that capital issues were doomed to failure ; the banks, subjected to a more drastic pruning operation even than industry as a result of revaluation, had no funds available for investment on any basis, short-term or long-term. They were carrying on with exceeding difficulty and had not yet recovered even a fraction of their international connections, so necessary for the realization of credits for German industry abroad.

The inflow of foreign capital during 1925 and 1926 improved conditions very greatly ; the coal strike in Britain caused a demand for mining and metallurgical products at high prices and allowed the banks to strengthen both their cash and credit positions as well as to accumulate heavy balances abroad. The result was that money became plentiful during 1926 and the first half of 1927, discount and interest rates went down, credit could be obtained easily by industry, especially short-term, and something like a boom took place in industrial shares on the Stock Exchange. The average market rate of discount fell from 8·5 per cent. in December 1925 to 5·5 per cent. at the end of 1926, and at one time during 1927 had fallen below 5 per cent. In the autumn of 1927 it moved up again almost to the 1925 level, for a reason different from that obtaining in 1925 ; *then* actual capital and credit shortage due to under-production caused severe stringency, but in 1927 production had risen to such a volume that it imposed a strain on financial resources and led to a demand for accommodation. The recovery of industry was complete in 1927, but the banks had still considerable lee-way to make good. Stabilization of 1924 had reduced their holdings in industry and weakened considerably their power to finance reconstruction and prepare the way for a policy of expansion in production. The Dawes Plan also served

dividends paid amounted to 4·41 per cent. in 1925–26, a slightly lower figure than in the previous year : the iron and steel industry, on a share capital of 1,834,368,000 marks, earned 2·26 per cent. ; engineering, on a share capital of 1,586,723,000 marks, 2·28 per cent. ; chemicals, on 1,446,599,000 marks, 5·8 per cent. ; textiles, on 983,704,000 marks, 5·01 per cent.; electrical manufacture, on 533,167,000 marks, 5·46 per cent. ; mining, on 1,946,710,000 marks, 3·73 per cent. ; electricity supply, on a capital of 1,106,556,000 marks, 6·90 per cent. In the finishing industries profits were higher than in the raw material industries, in chemicals especially, owing to the successful results achieved by the *I.G. Farbenindustrie* with its subsidiaries.

to extract every year the real surplus of wealth rendered available by industry, narrowed down the sphere of operation of the banks, as far as internal economic and trade activities were concerned, and forced them to rely to a greater degree than formerly on international credit and discount transactions. The securities and participations held by the ten principal banks fell from 1,094,000,000 marks in 1913 to 219,000,000 marks in November 1926, a fairly accurate indication of the dissociation of the banks from the administration and direct financial control of industry, but their success in linking up with great American and British financial institutions, especially in 1927, as well as the ease with which they have been able to resume activity as capital issuing houses and to launch new capital expansion schemes to supply industry with the resources necessary for increase of production and development of trade, are sufficient guarantee that the new German State will meet all its financial problems without serious danger of overstrain.

We can distinguish three phases in the financial policy of Germany since 1913, all of them interesting as illustrating some national characteristics of significance for anyone who would understand the mentality and psychology of Republican Germany. First of all, the war finance phase, where the entire effort of the nation was concentrated on the business of achieving victory and the claims of sound finance were subordinated to the desire to win without excessive strain on a people already burdened to the utmost, should be regarded as one of consistent optimism. The result of hostilities was never in doubt to those responsible for financial policy, or, if they felt any doubt, it would have been dangerous to afford any inkling of it. The end of the war showed German finance to be in a critical position.

The second phase covered the years of inflation, of quarrelling over reparations, and the Ruhr invasion. The nemesis of war finance had come, but the exhaustion of the country in materials and in human labour brought also its share of depression and made recovery (under conditions of free development without interference from the victorious Allies) a matter of some doubt at least for years to come. The collapse of the mark brought into play all those qualities of obedience to a national ideal, of determined resistance to misfortune, of corporate action, which had distinguished the German people since the Napoleonic wars ; the future of the Republic was never in doubt after those years of poverty were surmounted. Its testing period came at that time when nothing solid remained of the financial structure on which the credit and the trade of Germany had been built, when the Ruhr adventure had jeopardized the authority of the national executive, and the nation emerged victorious. The stabilization of the mark, which certain writers have entitled the supreme " confidence trick " since no real security of a negotiable nature existed for the Rentenmark, was undoubtedly a " confidence trick ", but not in the sense they meant—it was the first triumphant affirmation by the German people of the faith they had in the future of their own country. The Rentenmark will always remain as a record of those qualities which brought Germany into first place among the great European nations.

The third phase has not yet come to an end, but there are indications of change that may betoken a crisis. The Dawes Plan, the recovery of German credit, the adjustment of the economic complex to the conditions imposed by a return to gold and the sudden up-swing of industrial production have brought new problems to finance, which must be solved if disaster is to be avoided. Even as in the war, finance is not omnipotent and may again be overshadowed by industry, and certain grave defects are already visible in the edifice of national and international credit. The collapse of the Dawes Plan will involve with it not merely the hardly-won financial stability of Germany, but the stability of all the European countries ; it will be a disaster for international trade and international economic prosperity. Yet, in its present form, it cannot be carried out by Germany and the difficulties intensify with the capital demands of expanding industry. A crisis may again intervene unless some modification is made. In any case, the rapidity with which recovery has taken place in German production and the thorough fashion in which reorganization of industry has been effected point again to constructive qualities in the national character and to administrative capacity such as few countries have shown in post-war years.

No one can see what lies in the future, or even estimate the course of economic progress or decline. Perhaps a fourth phase will come, after all the wrangling and mutual recrimination over reparations have died down and a higher conception of international co-operation in finance and trade has taken the place of a frenzied counting of marks. The history of reparations has not been pleasant or edifying ; it has been instinct with the least worthy passions and cupidities of man, and it has coincided with a tale of misery and disaster blacker than that of the war. The domination of the little man will pass, no doubt, and an era of international goodwill open, where the fundamental things will be clearly understood and policy be inspired by a desire to achieve prosperity rather than maintain a shadowy prestige or an equally vague security. Before that occurs, however, the Dawes Plan and German finance will be once more in the melting-pot, and a transition period will intervene, fraught with all the possibilities of disaster.

CHAPTER XIII

THE ORGANIZATION OF INDUSTRY : THE NATIONAL BACKGROUND

German national psychology favourable to organization of industry —recognition of State authority—the large productive unit and the cartel—organization for war production—the theories of Rathenau —the economic State—Max Weber—Socialist conceptions—rationalization—legislation of 1919 for the control of coal, electricity, potash, iron and steel—the vertical combine during the inflation period— the effects of the Ruhr occupation—stabilization.

THE economic development of Germany, especially since the annexation of Lorraine, was bound up very closely with the cultural and even psychological. Perhaps the determination to evolve a powerful manufacturing system with every element fixed tightly into place may have imposed a discipline which affected every stratum of the German people, and so induced a philosophy of co-operation, of obedience, of compliance in a common endeavour. It is true that, as far as the organization and control of industry are concerned, the achievement of Germany has not been paralleled by that of any other country. Certain individualists may doubt the final value of, or even the necessity for, the particular forms industrial organization took, and may advocate the doctrine of personal effort alone as essential to lasting success and effective progress in any sphere of life. Certain other critics of the opposite school have held up examples of co-operation between producers to control production and prices as worthy of adoption in this country, and have argued that co-operation of this type must be common to the entire German industrial complex.

We must go deeper if we are to strike against a vein of truth and perhaps see in industrial movements and changes some expression of the spirit and inner thought of a people. The processes of reason are not confined to logical subtleties or argument in a vacuum ; they come ultimately into the world of reality and decide an attitude towards external manifestations, political or economic.   Conceptions held to be purely philosophical and, therefore, incapable of practical application, may be shaped to include real events and guide the course of life.

The German mentality has always been philosophic in the sense that it could enter into the discussion of modes of thought, of psychological states and revel in the elaboration of philosophic and æsthetic systems ; it gave to philosophy something of a popular and universal appeal and to philosophers at times almost a legislative sanction.   Such a condition may appear strange in this country, where we are wont to relegate philosophic schools to the Universities and dialectic societies and avoid warily any implications in theories which cannot be translated immediately into action or into personal profit.   Yet it was possible, even in the darkest moments of the inflation period, to enter a café in Munich and listen to a closely-reasoned debate on the idealism of the Neo-Kantians or the Hegelians, held in a constant roar—from the orchestra and the audience itself—which would have sufficed elsewhere to drown the most enthusiastic speculation.   At Stuttgart, one could attend conferences on philosophic subjects in crowded auditoria and listen to discussion in a railway compartment, some of it crude, but all of it sincere.

I have instanced these occasions as evidence that the German mentality had, perhaps through natural causes, a leaning towards philosophy which distinguished it in the economic as well as in the political or scholastic world, and this characteristic explains in great measure the success of the principle of co-operation and combination in German industry and, in recent years, the preservation of the Republic.   To generations imbued with the doctrines of Fichte and Hegel, the omnipotence of the State was more than an abstract theory to be paraded at election times and then carefully hidden away in the cupboard for occasional future use ; it was part of existence itself, an instinct accepted and obeyed almost without question. Individualism remained at a discount as far as politics were concerned, and the habit of obedience to a central authority was deeply ingrained.   Such a training had its significance for industry ; the industrialist himself became accustomed to the idea of the industry in which he was engaged rather than the prosperity of the single undertaking under his control ; he recognized that, granted a uniform policy in administration, in production and price, as well as stability of manufacturing and trading conditions, co-operation and the establishment of a central executive or advisory body would mean prosperity. The latter in turn required obedience to the main principles laid down as well as a recognition, on the part of the public, that combined action was morally and economically justifiable. The public itself, in turn, saturated already with doctrines that advocated unity of control, mass-psychology and mass-action under an intelligent central force, and, above all, obedience to the conception of authority, saw no reason to criticize the organization of industry on a central idea—either the control of production or of price or of both—and acquiesced in the formation of great manufacturing units, trusts and cartels. The effect of tradition was valueless beside the teaching of philosophy and the clear processes of reason.

On the other hand, the German industrialist knew that usurpation of excessive power *vis-à-vis* the State and undue exploitation of a monopoly or a specially favoured position would mean reaction and the formation of a hostile body of opinion exceedingly difficult to shift. He saw also that his power to justify combination through the stimulation of production depended on an enlightened conception of the relations between industry, finance and the State. Throughout the economic history of Germany since the Franco-Prussian War, the reality of a closely-knit economic unit served by industry, finance and politics together has always been envisaged by philosophers, economists, financiers and industrialists alike, and there has been no real antagonism between the interests of finance and industry or between industry and the State. Several points of difference might arise at periods of strain, such as the revolution, the invasion of the Ruhr, or the stabilization crisis of 1923, but, fundamentally, a very considerable measure of unity was achieved.

It is not our purpose to analyse in detail the various theories which accompanied and perhaps inspired many of the changes that took place in the industrial organization of Germany ; in the mass, they constitute the most important and most suggestive body of economic theory put forward in any country, and have been instrumental in justifying the special position occupied by Germany in the history of economic thought. It is sufficient to single out a few outstanding conceptions as advanced by men whose influence was most powerful during the post-war period and, from them, deduce perhaps the guiding principles underlying the movements that have since taken place in industrial organization and in the attitude of the public towards such movements. Theoretically, we may be justified

in ignoring human values entirely in discussing the administration and technique of industry, since it is possible apparently
to treat the subject in isolation without carrying out an elaborate dissection, but we cannot ignore them in practice. They
may decide important issues affecting the future of industry.
The truth of the matter is still that the real function of industrial production is not to enrich stockholders or add to the
power of a few captains of industry, but to develop the resources
in materials and human labour vested in the State as the single
political unit, and, thus, contribute to the maintenance of this
unit. Social and even, at times, æsthetic factors enter into
consideration ; the social enthusiasms of a Rousseau may do
more to upset the industrial balance of the State than the
ponderous musings of an economist or technician bent on perfecting a manufacturing process or developing a new industry.
It is difficult, therefore, to draw the line between what should
be and what should not be discussed.

On this foundation—namely, the recognition that the prosperity of the State depended on obedience and acquiescence on
the part of the individual and that obedience and the sense of
order, both in action and thought, came closer to the ideal
enshrined in the conception of the State than excessive individualism—industrial organization and industrial relations
were elaborated during the fifty years prior to the war. The
inspired teachings of Fichte and his vision of an all-powerful
State, justified in action and in thought, sanctioned mass-obedi-
ence to, and mass-support of, the doctrine of a central executive,
representative of only a limited proportion of the people, but
vested with full powers. The absolutism preached by Nietzsche, with his scorn of political institutions and his advocacy
of a domination removed from all idea of parliamentary institutions and the elective power of the masses, was an extreme
version of the theory of obedience to the State and, as such,
obtained only a narrow measure of approval. It showed,
however, that the return to individualism might well result
from excessive elaboration of the supreme individual, the all-
powerful dictator conception, but only once, during the revolution of 1918, did some inkling of this possibility enter into
political consciousness.

The main point at issue is still that the ground was prepared
for three great movements which dominated economic and
industrial changes prior to and after the war—the movement
towards greater authority on the part of the State ; the application of the central executive principle to industry, and the

growth of Socialism which, in some lights, might appear a continuation of the same movement to its logical conclusion.   The movement towards more effective control over production and price through the establishment of central groups, cartels, or great manufacturing units had been a much more important factor in the economic expansion of Germany than the development of socialistic theory, and it was only during the last two years of the war and the five years after the war that the latter enjoyed public support sufficiently strong to permit of legislative enactments.   Yet the struggle between the two conceptions of industry has never been entirely quiescent, and has assumed at times all the qualities of a pitched combat with the issues hanging in the balance ; at some moments, labour has asserted itself with considerable force, and, at other moments, the State, when industry threatened to become too autocratic and to challenge the authority of Government.   We can follow through many years the actions and interactions of industrialism and socialism, the advances and retreats of capital and labour, but we never find any real advocacy of undiluted competition, of *laisser-faire*, of the abandon of control over the forces active in production.

The basic industries of Germany, coal-mining, iron and steel, engineering and chemicals, were brought together in a series of central associations with power to determine quotas, fix selling-prices and co-ordinate, or rather guide, technical progress. The cartel was firmly entrenched during the years preceding the war, and it was one of the principal factors making for the expansion of production and the strengthening of competitive power in the markets of the world ; it functioned with the consent and loyal co-operation of its members, but it had legislative sanction for the principle of combination and could enforce at law its agreements, the only exception being agreements directed against the authority and integrity of the State. Secure behind a tariff, which was designed originally to encourage the formation of such central associations, it eliminated internecine competition, was instrumental in ensuring stability in production and in marketing, and, where wisely administered, did much to raise the level of technical achievement.

One objection to the cartel system has been its tendency to preserve the *status quo* and arrest the process of elimination of the inefficient, necessary to the realization of sound economic and industrial progress.   But there are more ways of getting rid of the inefficient than by cut-throat competition.   We have seen recently in this country with reference to the coal-mining and textile industries that the inefficient firms are not killed off at all easily and that, if they are numerous enough, they may end by reducing an entire industry to their own level of inefficiency.   The beneficent function of competition in industrial organization has yet to be proved, but the value of the cartel in German industry has been demonstrated through the history of great expansion in production and material prosperity.   The vision and enterprise of the German industrialist were active enough in the growth of immensely powerful industries, and it is significant that, in those industries where the cartel principle has been most firmly established, coal-mining, iron and steel, shipbuilding and engineering, production became more and more concentrated in a few great firms of high efficiency and with an international reputation.   *Krupp, Thyssen, Gutehoffnungshütte, Allgemeine-Elektrizitäts-Gesellschaft, Siemens-Schuckert, Klöckner, Röchling* and *Linke-Hoffman* were all firms of more than local importance, and they contributed in no small measure to the development of German trade at home and abroad.   With few exceptions, they formed complicated industrial units covering coal-mining, iron and steel, shipbuilding and engineering, and were linked together in a number of cartels governing each branch of production.

The large manufacturing unit with one central control, the cartel formed by association of such units with a central executive appointed by them, and the association of cartels to cover closely-allied industries, especially in the mining, metallurgical and engineering group, these were the moulds into which German organization for production fell, and they served to place Germany in the first rank of great industrial countries. In other countries, such a consummation would probably have been impossible, owing to differences in the national psychology and national training, and it might have been equally impossible in Germany if the trend of philosophic and even religious teaching had not been towards the suppression of the individual and the predominance of the State, towards the acceptance of control from above rather than the excessive cultivation of the ego.   Reflection showed quite clearly, especially to minds intent on order and clearly outlined administration, that the application of reason to industry could only be beneficial.   Instinct might have brought some moments of brilliant success, which the careful processes of logic might have overlooked or recognized too late for effective use, but logic would have a cumulative effect far beyond the powers of instinct.

The determination to advance industrial development in

HUGO STINNES (on left)

Germany was also a factor making for co-operation and unity in control : in a rising market, producers could work more successfully than in a falling, and, from 1870 onwards, Germany, with the exception of a few periods of interruption, was emphatically a rising market with every possibility of unlimited expansion.   In a number of industries, however, the cartel principle did not operate effectively, possibly owing to wide territorial diffusion—among them, textiles, wood-working, paper-production may be mentioned—and they were, as a rule, much less prosperous than other industries.   The large manufacturing unit had not developed to any great extent among them, and they presented at once a problem for the statesman determined on ensuring the most effective co-operation between industry and the State and an example of the dangers of uncontrolled production and price conditions.   Textiles, especially, could not keep pace with the national economic advance and remained in a state of constant depression.   The real danger of the situation, as far as these industries were concerned, became apparent at the outbreak of war, when all the forces of the country, economic and industrial, were concentrated on the immense task of meeting the requirements of a nation at arms.   The value of the cartel at this crisis was recognized.   In the industries where it had been established and was functioning smoothly, it constituted a central control which could be employed directly by the State to co-ordinate production and to ensure the maximum concentration of effort without waste and without friction.

The main problem confronting the German public at the outbreak of the war—namely, the diversion of the entire productive capacity of the nation into satisfaction of war needs —was rendered comparatively simple through the strength of the cartel system.   The basic industries upon which the success of the campaign depended, coal-mining, iron and steel and certain branches of heavy engineering, were already organized in large manufacturing units and worked together in cartels. The Government could, in this case, arrange direct with the cartel executive for the allocation of production quotas, for the control and stimulation of output, for the adjustment of labour conditions with a view to elimination of excess labour which might be available for military service, for the determination of manufacturing costs and the exact regulation of prices.   The cartel became an essential part of the national organization for war and it received, through this circumstance alone, the prestige and legislative sanction necessary to its continuance in time of peace. The Government might conclude separate agreements with the principal armament firms regarding special branches of production, which technical peculiarities necessarily kept secret, but, in the main products, the cartel functioned with almost complete authority.

In this way, direct Government control was avoided, except where production was carried out on a cost basis and a certain percentage was added to cover capital charges and profit margins. In this case, a State representative or group of representatives was present on the board of the great industrial undertakings and the cartel itself. Nationalization in the sense of complete State control of administration and manufacturing policy meant inefficiency at best and could only be justified in extreme cases ; any possible alternative which would avoid the elaborate machinery and complicated staff-work inevitable in the event of nationalization and preserve the full force of private initiative would be welcomed as directly contributory to the national efficiency and ultimately to the success of the war.

From every angle, therefore, the war period represented the triumph and the conclusive justification of the cartel system. But a number of industries essential to war were not fully organized in cartels ; the story was not complete with coal-mining, iron and steel, potash, shipbuilding and engineering. Other industries of vital importance, notably textiles and leather, remained without a central organization which could be used by the State, and in others, again—chemicals, electrical manufacture, the preparation and marketing of food-stuffs—a few large firms held together in a community of interests dominated the situation. In their case, it was comparatively simple to promote the formation of a trust and deal, therefore, with one executive. Textiles and leather, and, to some extent, paper, constituted the greatest difficulty, and an effort was made to create central associations for them with functions very similar to those exerted by the great cartels.

We can distinguish four forms of industrial organization active during the war : the trust pure and simple with control over practically the entire output of an industry—chemicals being a good example—or the direct association of a few firms, not more than five as a rule, to form a merger for the purposes of war production, electrical manufacture being perhaps the most important illustration of this system ; the cartel as at present existing, notably in the mining, metallurgical and engineering industries, with, however, conversion of the central association into a nominally State-controlled federation where it would assume certain of the characteristics of a great public service ; the compulsory cartel which included badly organized industries, such as textiles, and was administered by an association called into being by the State, adopting the character of a public service again ; and, lastly, special undertakings or companies dealing with branches of production outside the range of interests of the three types of organization recorded.   In this last case,'a real weakness appeared in the national scheme, since the special character of these undertakings tended to render them speculative, inefficient and excessively difficult to control.

It is quite clear from the survey already made that the mobilization of industry in Germany became almost as perfect in its degree as the mobilization of transport and of the fighting forces.   At this distance of time, the whole plan may appear simple, with few obstacles to rapid and effective operation, but it passed through many critical moments, when success was more than doubtful and only the organizing ability of industrialists like Walther Rathenau and Georg Klingenberg, aided by economists like Dr. Brück, overcame the difficulties.   The final form of the national organization for war lay in the elaboration of central executive boards for the principal industrial groups culminating in one board for the entire industrial complex.   German industry was welded together, therefore, into one immensely powerful cartel governing the machine and responsible only to the State.   The State itself entered more and more directly into the organization and administration of the individual cartels and was instrumental in creating purchasing, manufacturing, price-fixing and distributing associations, where the industries concerned represented one section and the State the second section in control and administration.

The tendency was, therefore, to bring the cartel principle closer and closer to the conception of the trust with one executive and unimpeachable control, and the war period was characterized by far-reaching experiment in this direction.   Theory could be translated into practice and practice in turn be tested in the light of theory.   The result of such experiment was undoubtedly favourable to the trust, first of all, where it could be formed without excessive strain on the organization and economic strength of the producers, and, secondly, to the cartel, as the most effective alternative to the trust.   The justification of the individual firms as such disappeared in the necessity to co-ordinate and direct the national effort, and it never afterwards assumed even a modified significance as a factor in the industrial situation. Even after the war, when the State moved clear of the cartels and granted them independence again, a central economic council composed of representatives from the latter remained in existence as an advisory body : coal-mining, iron and steel, engineering, textiles, chemicals, potash and other industries had each a separate council reporting to the central State council. The substance of the war organizations was retained with the State less in evidence. The trust movement, encouraged by the latter, affected industrial firms within the old cartels and syndicates, inspired them to form mergers or, where a trust pure and simple did not emerge, close associations of firms with a view to unifying manufacturing and marketing policy. The intention, as always, was to gain control of the market. All the possibilities of a more scientific grouping of industries and groups of manufacturers into something like a national system without national control were present, when the Socialist conception of the State and industry came into prominence during the revolution.

If, however, we desire to gain some clear idea of the course of industrial theory after the war, we should discuss the systems propounded by Rathenau. For Rathenau the outstanding characteristic of industrial civilization, as it had evolved from the beginning of the nineteenth century until the war, was rationalism—the substitution of exact deduction and practical achievement for intuition and instinct. Science predominated and, with it, mathematical calculation and design. Industry, society, the State had become concrete entities with nothing mystical or ideal (in the symbolical or philosophical sense) in their composition ; they were the work of a precise, exquisite and soulless technique. The transition from the contemplation of nature to the exact observation of natural phenomena, from the individual enterprise inherent in many small undertakings, each governed by a personal and entirely human conception of wealth, to the inhuman and impersonal efficiency of the large manufacturing firm conducted on joint-stock principles, from local government to centralized rule in the State, could be regarded as a vast work of mechanization.

The bureaucratic age was for him a mechanical age where emphasis was laid on increase of production accompanied by economy in materials and labour, on the most minute division of labour and the concentration of activity in a few areas, on standardization of processes and design and on the greatest possible utilization of mechanical methods. The capitalist system could be regarded as a phenomenon forming part of a much greater complex, the product and not the cause of the mechanical age.   The concentration of population had led to a change in the character of the people ; mechanization gave new force to the uncultured races, such as the Slavs, and deprived the more cultured, such as the Germans, of their principal advantages in organization and intelligence ; it destroyed the seigneurial types of the pre-industrial eras and allowed an essentially decadent bureaucracy to triumph.   At this point, Rathenau comes very close to Nietzsche, especially in the glorification of the daring, dominating seigneur and in the scorn of the intellectually-minded bourgeois intent on avoiding risk through anxious calculation.

The war brought the mechanical epoch to an end, and in this " middle-class war of the Europeans " the old capitalist arrangement of industry and trade was in danger of burning down to ashes.   What then should be created in its place ? Socialism was merely the opposite of Capitalism on the same plane of intellectual and philosophic achievement.   It could be no alternative if the doctrines of Karl Marx were adopted.   A new form of social idealism could be evolved, where social liberty might be finally achieved.   The rationalization of the means of production and the elimination of excessive profit above the bare costs of production in favour of the State could alter fundamental conditions not at all : the return on invested capital had more than a national, it had an international significance, since it determined the flow of capital into productive enterprise and constituted a reserve necessary to the conduct of world trade.

Social freedom could result only from increased production and, to achieve this, Rathenau projected a grandiose scheme for the organization of industry and trade on a new basis.   The theory that industry and trade were not a private but a public matter could not be accepted entirely, but that did not mean either advocacy of uncontrolled and unrestricted private enterprise or absolute Communism.   The ideal lay in planning private enterprise from the sole point of view of efficiency of production, and Rathenau proposed to concentrate all the energies of the nation on production of the most essential and most valuable kind.   He condemned a state of trade where the principal factor in production was the satisfaction of consumption stimulated by fashion, publicity and the desire for luxuries, where millions of labour force and production values were squandered and enormous waste occurred in expensive and extravagant distribution.   Control over imports and exports should be established with a view to limiting the supply of superfluous and luxury goods and safeguarding provision of raw materials. Excessive consumption, responsible for the loss of valuable effort in unnecessary production, should be combated, and all theory favourable to the dissemination of luxuries as essential to the national welfare should be brushed aside. The essential was economy of effort and the highest possible production of real wealth. Through virtual abolition of the laws of inheritance, to be accomplished by means of death duties verging on confiscation, the accumulation of property and material wealth would give way to the creation of a higher general standard of prosperity. No place existed for the speculator, the large property-owner and the monopolist in the new State. As a last stage of all, the State itself should have some power of control and the only monopoly permitted should be that of the State as representative of all the citizens in it.

In a later writing, *Die neue Wirtschaft*, fuller detail is given of the ideal organization for production. Concentration of manufacturing plant producing similar or closely allied goods could be effected, so that the transition from raw material, semi-finished product and thence to the finished article would follow the shortest way. Elimination of intermediate trading and excessive publicity allocations during supervision and calculation of the market requirements, grouping of manufacturing units within a great industrial complex to bring saving in power and labour were essential, while close association could be carried out between industry and industry. In the same way, the labour force employed in advancing production should be organized in special associations for the whole of industry, these associations would be grouped together in guilds, and the employers would form, in turn, corresponding groups. Capital and labour working together through these associations would avoid dispute and ensure the highest efficiency in production.

Rathenau envisaged, therefore, a form of cartel where capital, labour and the State would be represented—not nationalization, but national co-ordination on a basis of private enterprise. The scheme, as translated into reality, meant control of consumption even as much as of production, and it had features in it which commended it to all shades of economic opinion, with, however, little possibility of enthusiastic acceptance by any school. Industrialists looked with suspicion on the socialistic aspects, and Socialists deprecated his advocacy of private enterprise : yet the main theories running through it all, the necessity for the more scientific organization of industry, the concentration of effort on production with the greatest economies in labour and power, and the insistence on some form of central control, were of moment for German industry and influenced very markedly its development.

Max Weber as a thinker belongs to a different category. He was less concerned with the reform of existing economic and industrial conditions than with the necessity for clear thinking. A capacity to think out problems and get to the heart of economic changes had a greater value to his mind than vague theorizing about the functions of industry in the State or the future of the State itself. The rational contemplation of social reality had developed in close conjunction with modern science and bore a close similarity to the latter in its logical structure ; the essential lay in divesting the knowledge of reality of all individual characteristics, and in creating a system of concepts which could be recognized as mathematically true. In other words, it would be dangerous in the extreme to take any section of economic life, of industry, of trade, evolve certain laws from close investigation of it and apply them to the whole of economic and industrial reality ; they could not be considered as other than abstractions, ideal types, until the whole of historical change and present reality were known. The authority of any economic principle depended on the scientific analysis of its structure and its associations, and such analysis could at best be only relative. Industrial theory might concur in formulating ideal types and in defining the possible range of application of such types, but the application to reality of principles derived from observation of them would only mean the translation into practice of an idea of capitalist culture, the introduction of Utopia. Such an attitude might betoken pessimism, since it connoted rejection of all theories such as those propounded by Rathenau, which were essentially of a practical nature with a narrow range of application.

Weber, however, was intent on clearing away uncertainty and mugginess in thought ; he desired the clear-cut image, the logical synthesis, if only to obtain some secure hold on speculation during a time of extravagant ideals. If the methods he proposed could be adopted, if the recognition were general that the laws and tendencies enunciated by Marx and other thinkers, in Socialist and opposing camps, were only relative and referred to ideal types which could not be compared with reality, much of the danger attendant upon social and economic change would be removed. Views of the world could never be a product of the science of experience transmitted and

strengthened from epoch to epoch, but would be a creation
of ideals brought into existence through conflict with other
ideals even as holy. "The middle way comes no closer to
scientific truth than the extremes on either side." In one fine
passage, he says:

" The stream of immeasurable events swirls endlessly into eternity.
Ever-fresh and always different in colour, arise those problems of
civilization which influence men : the circle of that which has
meaning for us in the endless stream of individual moments remains fluid, and fluid also the historical individual. The processes
and associations of thought, which govern contemplation and decide
perception, change perpetually. The end and aim of the social
sciences remain changeable in a boundless future and will remain
so if a form of Chinese paralysis of the spirit does not deprive
humanity of the power and the desire to ask new questions of
inexhaustible life."

Weber penetrated more deeply into psychological, ethical,
æsthetic and philosophical motive than Rathenau, and viewed
industry and the economic world generally as part of a much
wider cosmos including all reality, but he had many points of
contact with the latter. He shared Rathenau's attitude towards the mechanization of the State, the rise of bureaucracy
and the emergence of the calculating machine as predominant
in modern industrial civilization ; he questioned even as bitterly the function of politics in a modern State, and insisted
on a more scientific regulation of production and consumption ; he was sympathetic to the "Planwirtschaft" advocated
by Rathenau, if only as an example of reasoned control, but
at many points he differed. He pointed out the danger of a
syndicated *régime* resulting from rationalization of consumption. The determination of a given consumption and the
satisfaction by the producer of an equivalent demand meant
a policy of assured nourishment—i.e. stationary condition of
production and trade and abolition of the economic rationalization process. Adjustment to demand should not come from
the formation of syndicates and monopolies on the part of the
producer, but exactly the opposite—from the organization of
the consumer. The organization of the future should not be
on the lines of compulsory cartels, associations, trade unions
arranged by the State, but should come closer to a gigantic,
State-organized consumers' co-operative, which would determine the course of production in accordance with its needs.
Weber, therefore, moved farther towards Socialism than even
Rathenau, and bridged in some measure the gap between the

MAX WEBER

purely Socialist and the Capitalist economic theorists who fought over the problem of industrial organization immediately after the war.

The Socialist theories came to full blossom in the first year of the Republic, when the soldiers' and workers' councils dominated the State ; the war mentality, with its glorification of strength and power, strove for some outlet when the long-expected hour of victory did not arrive and a disappointed army crept back over the frontiers ; the sacrifices of the war years, the bitter recollections of struggle in a world where war-profiteers battened on the misery of the civilian population and the martyrdom of the fighting forces, came to upset old traditions and destroy cherished ideals. At that time, the structure of obedience to the State and of distinction between class and class, on which the Imperial conception rested, fell down and brought with it in ruin all the plans for industrial and economic recovery which had already been proposed during the war.

Yet the revolution was composed of two fundamentally different classes, or rather conceptions : the Army desired a continuance of the war conditions where its organization could be adapted to peace-time requirements, and it would be predominant and exact some measure of revenge against the war profiteers ; but the Trade Unions aimed at elimination of a system which could include an army and recognize the superiority of a whole series of classes. The truce lasted, therefore, only as long as the enthusiasm for change possessed everyone. When the business of settling down to ordinary economic conditions took place, the two groups split asunder, and for a moment the future of the Republic was in doubt. At that time, the recovery of power by the middle classes saved the situation and weakened the prestige and authority of Socialism.

During the war, industry was freed from all risk ; the need for supplies kept demand constantly active with an increasing possibility of profit ; labour had every possible security, living was assured, and the sense of responsibility and effort had been effectively delegated. But a condition of success for a purely Socialist *régime* was a return to co-operative effort with acquiescence in the workings of the machine, a desire to increase production and build surely the foundations of a new economic and industrial order, where effort rather than the cloudy vapourings of idealism would be the prime motive. Under effective control, such a consummation might have been reached, but no central control could be established. As Otto Bauer said :

" We cannot cut adrift from the labour masses, but we cannot be led blindly by them." It was impossible to decide what was the will of the masses, and no real leadership could be established. Politically, therefore, Socialism failed; yet, in the sphere of industrial organization, the theories advanced by it exerted very considerable influence in Germany and dictated important changes in the organization of industry and the participation of the State in industrial production.

The measures adopted by the German Government to control production during the war were regarded as pure Socialism by the protagonists of Socialist theory, and the latter concentrated all effort on the continuation of these measures. Lensch, in his *Drei Jahre Weltrevolution*, published in 1918, stated : " The State has undergone a socialization process, and social democracy a nationalization process." The path to co-operation and the creation of a true democracy lay over economic and industrial Socialism. The destruction of class warfare and class distinction, the cessation of exploitation of man by man, the realization of a common ideal of civilization for all peoples, and the maintenance of the rights of the people, could only be effected through Socialism applied to industry and trade.

During the war, developments moved steadily towards the translation into practice of guild Socialism, although the policy inspiring them had not the slightest connection with it : the production and distribution of raw materials, the control of production in a definite series of goods arranged in accordance with the needs of war were in the hands of central organizations, and, where the latter had not been operating already in the form of cartels in many industries, new associations were created to carry out this system. The guild Socialists advocated an economic grouping of industry not markedly dissimilar from the theory of Rathenau, who was responsible for the reorganization for war production of German industry. Heimann advocated the principle of the guild, the unified central body, self-organized, for each industry, and in this way prepared the way for the application of the theory of evolution to existing organizations : the incorporation of the principles underlying the formation of cartels and syndicates in one great body which would cover the needs of all industry and of all participants in production instead of the needs of one isolated group of employers. The management of such cartels, syndicates or central associations should include representatives of various industrial and economic interests (labour and the staff, the State and the consumer). As these representatives might be in turn associated with other industrial groups and could bring their ideas and desires to bear on any other group, the possibility of a national system based on association of all interests could be envisaged.   The will of the whole nation would then find expression without the necessity for nationalization.

Such a policy could only be carried out gradually ; it would begin with industries already closely organized and ripe for socialization and extend to others less well organized.   The present form of industrial company with share capital was to be retained with a definite return on the capital invested, but with less representation afforded to the shareholders on the board of management.   Production itself should be reorganized on a more scientific basis, should be rationalized.   Rationalization meant the adjustment of a productive undertaking, in the closest degree possible, to its economic function ; the elimination of waste, excess power, excess labour and the coordination of all elements in manufacture to ensure the lowest cost.   Such, of course, has always been theoretically the purpose of any industrial enterprise where profit-earning capacity decides the issue and, for such a purpose, capital was invested. By this criterion—namely, the return on capital—the choice of manufactures, prices and methods of manufacture as well as the investment of new capital were determined.

For Socialism, however, the issue could not be so simple : innumerable other interests must be considered under a *régime* of socialization, as conceived by the guild theorists—the observation of the interests of the consumer and his purchasing power in the determination of prices, the claims of the labour employed in production to decide on the methods of production.   Such elements would serve to weaken very seriously the capacity of industry to earn profits and would dam the flow of new capital required to finance production and distribution.   The Socialists argued that the realization of any profits or any surplus would represent a form of taxation of the consumer and should be obviated through reduction in price, but, as Rathenau pointed out, such profits represented a form of security, of reserve necessary for the efficient prosecution of trade, and the capitalist system was based on it.   One could not eliminate profits and still retain the capitalist system.

From this broad conception of rationalization as the introduction of order into the anarchy of production under a capitalist *régime*, a further step was made towards the more definite application of the theory to the industrial workshop or manufacturing enterprise.   In this case, it meant only the perfecting of manufacturing processes, the grading of production from the raw material to the finished article to ensure the maximum utilization of machinery and so cut down factory costs ; it had no connection with the effective control and administration of industry implied in the broader conception, and had no *raison d'être* when the necessity to earn profits was abolished, as the Socialists proposed. From many points of view, rationalization meant restriction of consumption : the consumer under a Socialist *régime* would find his requirements met but not exceeded ; he would never be able to pick and choose and his mode of life would tend to become standardized. Such an objection had little influence with Rathenau, who was at one with the Socialists in aiming at controlling the direction and volume of consumption and, unlike them, proclaimed the necessity for doing so in the interest of the State. The Socialist conception of organization for production rested on a given volume of consumption, and this factor removed one important consideration making for increased enterprise and efficiency— the adjustment of production and the means of production to an ever-varying demand.

Max Weber proposed the opposite, namely, the adjustment of production to consumption, with no effective limit to consumption, to avoid the solidification of enterprise. Complete socialization with statistical determination of the total demand ignored dynamic forces making for changes in demand and the power to stimulate demand through price adjustment or through variety of product, while the possibility of rewarding labour according to output, and thus ensuring some form of competition in labour efficiency and purchasing power, struck against the limitation of total output imposed by a definite volume of consumption. We find Plenge proclaiming in 1915 : " Act as part of the whole ! Act from the sum-total of the organization ! "

" For the 1914 conception of organization means not so much the aim and desire of the generality as the state of conscience resulting from experience. It is not composed of single, isolated will atoms with definite claims and with joint action in prosecuting them. It is much more the actual life of the State as a whole, conceived as a greater self-contained unit where each member contributes its experience, where each member can grow out of its own circle of perception and knowledge, and where each member can enjoy increased strength and a more certain inner security."

In this tumult of ideas, in this constant discussion of the function played by industry in the State, by the individual in

the nation, by the capitalist system in a future economic cosmos, the German revolution and the early years of inflation
were passed, and much of what was then discussed has passed
into history.   Yet a residuum of great value and of lasting
significance remained and served to inspire schemes of industrial organization, which have since been carried out.   The
Socialist theories did not survive the attack of hard economic
fact, least of all the demands made on the German State for
reparations, but, at one time, there was every possibility of an
orientation of political and State policy generally towards
Socialism.   Legislation bearing on labour conditions in a
definitely socialistic sense was passed, and an effort was made
to introduce State control over essential public services and
utilities other than the railways and communications.

Yet the forces of the opposition had sufficient authority
still to divert the movement away from nationalization pure
and simple towards recognition of the need for co-operation
between private enterprise and the State in running essential
industries.   The Act dealing with the national reorganization
of electricity supply (December 31, 1919) merely provided
that, until April 1, 1921, control of electricity supply on a
national basis might be undertaken.   Similarly, Acts covering
the production of coal, iron and steel, potash and coal by-products came into existence with largely permissive functions.
For the coal and potash industries, a central organization equivalent to a State-controlled cartel was set up in 1919, followed in
1920 by a central control body for iron and steel termed the
Eisenwirtschaftsbund.   The latter was composed of thirty-
six producers, twelve merchants and twenty-four consumers,
and the Minister of Industry and Trade had the right of veto on
resolutions which, in his opinion, were against the public weal.
The coal and potash organizations worked effectively, decided
prices with full authority and other matters affecting the industries they represented and have been functioning ever since,
but the iron and steel body lost power during the Ruhr invasion
and became inoperative.

These Acts foreshadowed a time when the State could proceed towards full control after negotiation with industrial interests had failed.   In the coal industry, a council might be
formed, with representatives from mine-owners, labour and the
consumer, which would advise the State in its policy—a revived
form of the war cartel or company created by Rathenau.
The danger of future action could not be ignored entirely by the
industrialists, and there was no guarantee that the post-war

reconstruction enthusiasms might not flare up again at a critical moment and commit the State to a wholesale plan of nationalization.

The struggle between the economic interests of the State and private interests began in 1920 and continued with varying success on the part of the latter until the invasion of the Ruhr and the period of stabilization. Certain writers have held that the lack of co-operation between industry and the State was responsible for the catastrophic fall of the mark, that the industrialists desired to break down for good the authority of a national executive, which had still definite Socialist leanings, and withheld their support from it, in its time of stress, preferring to maintain their funds outside of the country and provoke a flight from the mark. There is undoubtedly a grain of truth in this theory, and it may be that the industrialists, intent on consolidating and improving their position, lent themselves to a policy of encouragement of inflation without actually working for the complete depreciation of the mark. As we have shown in a previous chapter, other factors were at work beyond the control of either German industry or the State. Inflation revived the economic condition of war-production with the wealth of the country thrown into production to meet consumption. Consumption had been stimulated out of all balance both by artificially increased purchasing power and by the force of the conviction that monetary values were a declining quantity and that the only method of retaining wealth or even property lay in acquisition of goods. In this way, the internal capital resources were depleted, enormous profits were made by the industrialists, part of which was used to carry out a policy of concentration and vertical combination, and part was transferred abroad to improve cash resources. Inflation meant, therefore, confiscation of the liquid capital resources of Germany and the introduction of economic imperialism into industry.

The scientific organization of industry within the State, as proposed by Rathenau, was adopted, with the proviso that both the State and the consumer should have no control over, or connection with, the new combinations that were being formed. The justification for the vertical combine was simple : the market was expanding so rapidly in the early years of inflation that every element in such a combine could produce to full capacity and swell to overflowing the coffers of the controlling firm or industrial executive. The combine, if strong enough, could cut adrift from the cartel system where restriction, in the interest of all members, might be placed on the profit-earning capacity and production of the most powerful ; it could absorb subsidiary companies manufacturing goods outside of the range of one cartel, and avoid duplication of restriction through a number of different cartels ; it could effect standardization and specialization through allocation of orders to works producing one series of articles and obtain technical and administrative advantages through economy of effort and limitation of waste ; it could link up such special firms with other firms of a similar nature and so avoid intermediate profits and duplication of the turnover tax ; it could aim at independence of temporary market fluctuations through control of output and the rationing of the consumer ; it could ensure for itself a certain demand for finished products and a certain supply of raw materials within its own organization.

The vertical combine developed very rapidly, especially in the group—coal-mining, iron and steel, shipbuilding, engineering and electrical manufacture. Under both Rathenau and Stinnes, the two enormous industrial combines, the *Allgemeine-Elektrizitäts-Gesellschaft* and the *Siemens-Rhein-Elbe-Schuckert-Union*, came into operation to control the iron and steel, engineering, electrical manufacturing and electricity supply industries and dominate the national economic situation. Other combines functioned beside them, the *Haniel, Krupp, Stumm, Klöckner* and *Röchling* companies with their subsidiaries, but they were overshadowed by the organizations operated by Rathenau and Stinnes. Stinnes, in a vision of industrial imperialism, extended his range of interests in iron and steel and coal-mining to important firms located in Central Europe, Italy and Spain, brought in railways, banks, insurance companies, shipping lines, importing and exporting agencies, hotels and film companies, printing presses and newspapers, forests and paper works, oil-wells and refineries, and so elaborated a vast system of connections and alliances ranging through the whole of German industry and touching on many of the leading industrial countries of the world. He used the capital reserves of an exhausted country to embark on a scheme of world domination of industry. It is difficult to find in this any motive other than ambition ; the vertical combine in one series of industries had swollen into a huge combine covering other combines located in other industries, and no limit appeared to the policy of expansion other than those imposed by economic conditions. A collapse in the market, for example, would have thrown the machine out of action and, through reduction of earning power, have engendered a financial crisis beyond the power of any single industrialist, even with the resources of Stinnes. As long as inflation could allow the industrialist to redeem loans, bonds and credits with a constantly depreciating currency, to borrow readily with every prospect of gain in the borrowing, to remunerate labour below a reasonable level, to reduce the standard of living of the workers and to amass great profits, the industrialist would be favourable to an inflation policy.

The occupation of the Ruhr came into the imperialist schemes of the great industrialists and cut away their foundations. The vertical combine, which depended on close and rapid co-operation between the raw-material firms and the finishing firms, found itself cut in two at iron and steel production ; coal-mining, coke-production, iron and steel works were concentrated in the Ruhr in close proximity, but the engineering subsidiaries were located outside of the occupied territory, while electrical manufacture had its centre in Berlin. It is possible that, if purely economic principles had been at stake alone, the Ruhr industrialists would have come to terms at once with the French and Belgian Control Mission and so kept the existing organization precariously intact for such time as the invasion lasted. But the economic issue was of little consequence beside the political and the psychological : the war psychology had returned, the determination to uphold the prestige of the Reich at any sacrifice and so confound the plans of the usurpers. In this struggle of a nation, the interests of the industrialists became subordinated to those of the State, but the subsidy granted by the latter atoned in some measure for the resistance offered by the Ruhr industrial complex. Paralysis of production and the refusal to entrust stocks to the French and Belgian agents were compensated to some extent by the Reich, but, as far as industrial organization was concerned, the days of the vertical combine in its extreme form were numbered.

The exigencies of the moment proved beyond any doubt that, if the vertical combine were to disappear, something much more concentrated and much more powerful in action would require to take its place The coal cartels were disbanded and a new form of joint-stock undertaking was substituted to undertake the sale of coal ; similarly, pig-iron and steel associations ceased to operate within the Ruhr proper, and much of their equipment was transferred to centres farther in Germany, where an attempt might be made to concentrate effort on areas outside of the occupied zone.

The Ruhr invasion, therefore, struck a severe blow both at the cartels and at the vertical combines, but, on the whole, it brought very real advantages to the German State. The growing power of industry, especially in the hands of unscrupulous adventurers like Stinnes, who had no hesitation in sacrificing everything to their own interests, threatened to undermine the authority of the State and break down the Republican form of government ; industrialists rose on a wave of reaction from the Socialist theories of the revolution and post-revolution years, and the end of the movement was not yet in sight. It might easily have culminated in a severe struggle, with a second revolution towards the Right, and a country bled to exhaustion. The discomfiture of the industrialists made them much more willing to co-operate with the Government and so uphold the authority of central rule ; they recognized the organization brought into existence to govern prices and manufacturing conditions under State advice in the coal-mining, potash, iron and steel industries, and were ready to acquiesce in any scheme of national reconstruction, both financial and industrial. The final collapse of the mark and the chaotic conditions of price fixation in gold currencies made them still more amenable to conversion.

The determination was general, therefore, to abandon over-ambitious plans of expansion and devote effort to the improvement and intensification of the means of production within the heavy industries, so that an instrument might at least be created for the rapid penetration of German industrial products into world markets after the conclusion of the Ruhr adventure and the return to normal trade conditions. The lesson taught was wholly salutary : it brought industrial policy back to realities and allowed the State to recapture lost ground. A movement contrary to lasting economic progress had been arrested and reaction had set in, reaction which coincided with the introduction of stabilization and the new legislation bearing on cartels—in essence, a movement again towards modified Socialism, which even the Dawes Plan has not been able to arrest.

The position prior to stabilization is to be found in the description given in the preamble to the Cartel Law of November 1923 :

" The production and price policy of the cartels and conventions has been the object of violent attack (for several months) on the part of the consumers and, to some extent, on the part of the producers. The Government has deemed it its duty to test for accuracy the complaints made and to adopt measures of a general economic nature to meet them. It is an indubitable fact that, under the influence of currency depreciation and the changes in manufacturing and market conditions caused by it, many disputes have developed among producers' organizations leading to abuse of their power. At a time of crisis, such as industry and trade have gone through since the summer of this year, when the price of several German products were forced up high above the world level, there is a general interest in combating, as strongly as possible, any measure tending to control production artificially, to exact excessive supplementary charges to cover exchange risks and establish selling prices beyond a level justified by the costs of production. The recovery of genuine freedom in trading and the restoration of a feeling of responsibility towards the nation are aims to be achieved."

The stabilization of the mark, with the consequent reduction in the currency and in the supply of capital, caused a serious temporary decline in production, made the burden of overhead expenditure excessive and forced up prices in every branch of industry, in many cases above the world level ; it tested severely the structure, both financial and technical, of the cartels and the great industrial combines and accelerated the process of rationalization ; it did not affect fundamentally the organization of the basic industries. Mr. H. G. Daniels, in a recent book, *The Rise of Republican Germany*, stated :

" Even those undertakings which, by a process of absorption, had obtained control over whole branches of industry from raw material to the finished article, together with the allied transport and distribution—familiarly known as the vertical trust—had the unsoundness of their methods rudely brought home to them the moment they were forced back upon the principles of legitimate finance. Indeed, the great Rhineland and Westphalian trusts, such as those formed by Hugo Stinnes and his many imitators, shook to their rotten foundations and, in the long run, failed to survive."

This, in our opinion, is a complete distortion of the facts ; there was never any doubt regarding the technical and administrative efficiency of the large industrial concerns, and their use of finance was, if anything, too clever for the security of the German State. The vertical trust was not destroyed as a form of industrial organization ; all that stabilization did was to clear away unnecessary connections from the main groups, wipe out unnatural growths ; the combines, such as the *Siemens-Rhein-Elbe-Schuckert-Union*, the *Thyssen*, *Gutehoffnungshütte*, *A.E.G.-Linke-Hoffmann*, the *Krupp* and *Klöckner* concerns, remained practically intact, and the recovery in German production since the end of 1923 must be attributed in great measure to the fact that they had withstood the crisis.   Smaller firms, of a purely speculative nature, which had battened on inflation, were reduced to liquidation through the complete disappearance of their market, and an intensive purifying operation was carried out through the whole of industry, but the main lines of development in organization and technique were little affected.

The time of adjustment to the economic conditions imposed by the war came to the end with the introduction of the gold mark and the Cartel Law of November 1923, and we can trace now four main lines of development in contemporary industrial organization, which will probably continue for a number of years before a stage of equilibrium will have been reached :

(a) the strengthening of the cartel through co-operation between the large producers, the State and the cartel organization ;

(b) the growth of large-scale enterprise, as represented by the horizontal trust :

(c) the formation of international cartels and trusts in the basic industries ; and

(d) the increasing participation of the State in the administration and control of industry.

In all of these developments, the influence of the theories propounded by Rathenau, Weber, the Socialists and other schools of economic thought may be followed, but the changes even now effected bear no resemblance in nature to any one body of thought, but constitute an amalgam wherein many theories have been fused together.

CHAPTER XIV

THE ORGANIZATION OF INDUSTRY (*continued*): CARTELS AND THEIR FUNCTIONS

Definition of the cartel—criticism and justification—expansion of cartel system—Cartel Law of November 1923—the Ruhr invasion —coal cartels—functions and legal position—Pig-Iron Association— Steel Ingot Syndicate—*Stahlwerksverband*—consumers and the cartels.

THE cartel has been regarded as a peculiarly German institution, the principal contribution of Germany to the world advance in industrial organization. But no one can determine with any measure of accuracy what a cartel really is. It remains a designation incapable of final definition and, as such, has been employed in the most varied contexts. The nearest approach that we can make to a definition is that of an association of producers or distributors to control in some way or other marketing conditions—sufficiently vague, but safe. Marketing control can be effected from the production or distribution end or both ; it may take the form of control of production alone throughout an industry with a view to maintaining a healthy state of demand and, as a result of this, a satisfactory level of prices ; it may take the form of control of selling prices without regard to the state of production, the price factor being ultimately a controlling factor in production through the introduction of a stable rate of demand ; it may cover control of production and price at the same time, and it may exist merely to delimit markets or spheres of influence.

Again, an entire industry may be held in one cartel or separate cartels be formed to deal with production and price under the jurisdiction of a central association ; the various sections of an industry may each possess cartels, sometimes working in co-operation with each other, sometimes in antagonism, and a number of cartels may control production and determine quotas in the main branches of an industry, with one central association determining prices throughout the entire series. Elimination of competition and the realization of a high profit-earning capacity are motives inspiring all cartel-formations, and they provide as a rule the key to the maze.   Variety both in constitution and in power is infinite and has resulted from the technical and administrative conditions peculiar to each branch of production.   At first sight, such variety might lead to inefficiency and excessive duplication, but few sections of economic and even of mathematical science have been so far advanced as those dealing with the organization and functions of cartels, and it is still true that, with this network of associations controlling in some form or other both production and consumption, the final price and quality of goods to the consumer have always borne favourable comparison with those tendered in countries where cartels do not exist.

Many decades have served to strengthen the cartel form of industrial organization and justify it in the eyes of the industrialists and the public ; it must be regarded as an element of primary importance in the industrial and economic expansion of Germany.   The main argument against it has been that, by stabilizing both price and production, it has served to retain and protect the inefficient firm, to bring the efficient firm ultimately down to the level of the inefficient, as far as selling prices and the determination of basic production costs are concerned, and so force industry to standards of mediocrity leading to declining enterprise and, ultimately, to economic incapacity. To some extent, such an accusation may be justified, but the advantages derived from the cartel must be weighed in the balance and they are by no means insignificant.   Elimination of uneconomic competition and stability of market conditions, as well as the realization of a steady, if sometimes exiguous, margin of profit, have encouraged the industrialist to work out schemes of rational development whereby he might improve his competitive position, especially in export markets beyond the range of control of the cartel, and so strengthen his bargaining power *vis-à-vis* the cartel.   The latter made, therefore, for improved export trade as well as for a higher standard of productive enterprise at home.   It is significant also to note that the industries enjoying a high level of efficiency and competitive advantage both in Germany and abroad were those where the cartel had been most scientifically developed, namely, coalmining, iron and steel and engineering, and that, in these industries, the movement towards large-scale production in a limited number of works had always been far advanced.   In other industries, where more open conditions obtained and the cartel was relatively weak in its control over the range of production

—textiles, leather and the rubber trades—the opposite was the case, and these industries expanded much less rapidly than iron and steel and engineering.

It is impossible, therefore, to generalize about the advantages and disadvantages of the cartel; the balance would certainly appear to lie in favour rather than against. In certain industries, however, the cartel was never entirely in control; the principle of the trust or the large firm controlling (directly or in association with one or even several firms of similar calibre) both production and marketing in one industry was adopted fairly soon in chemicals, electrical manufacture and other branches requiring high standards of technical and manufacturing achievement. Such firms adhered nominally to a central association, but they acted through and not in obedience to the dictates of such an association.

Again, we must draw a distinction between industries where the cartel organization was complete and spanned the whole range of production, with the industry organized as one complex formed of many units working harmoniously together, and those industries where no such compact organization existed and the various branches of production merely decided their own conditions without reference to other branches. To the former belong the raw-material industries very largely, where the range of products is narrow and adjustment consequently simple, where one producer may supply all the varieties listed in production and link up easily with other producers in similar conditions—coal-mining, both hard coal and brown coal, pig-iron, iron and steel, potash, cement and paper; to the latter, the material-consuming industries, where specialization may take place on a very extensive scale with no links binding up the various sections of production—engineering, textiles, printing, leather, wood-working.

Dr. Metzner has estimated the number of cartels operating in Germany at 1,500, while a still later estimate gives 3,000. Accepting the lower figure, we can distinguish about one hundred and fifty in engineering, textiles, iron and steel, about twenty-five in the wholesale trades and a wide diffusion in smaller numbers through all other industries, both on the production and distribution sides. In 1905, an investigation carried out by the Ministry of the Interior fixed the number at four hundred, which was probably two hundred less than the real total. Since 1905, therefore, the number of cartels has increased by 150 per cent. at least—in itself a sufficiently remarkable economic development. Some conception of the real extent and influence the cartel was assuming in the national life led undoubtedly to the promulgation of the law against the " Misuse of Economic Powers " in November 1923.   The cartel alone did not come under the new regulations ; with it were grouped trusts, *Interessengemeinschaften* (mergers or associations of manufacturers to preserve common interests), and other forms of industrial combination, so that the Act dealt with the whole problem of industrial organization and the part played by the State in relation to combination in industry.   All forms of market control, including conditions of contract and manufacture, price fixation and production were affected. The policy of industrial associations should come under restraint where it conflicted with the common interest and the general economic welfare of the State, or where " production or sales were restricted without economic justification, prices raised or maintained at an unduly high level, or where freedom of trade was adversely affected by barriers in sale or purchase or by the determination of discriminatory prices or conditions ".

While, however, British law does not recognize the principle of association or combination in industry and insists on the fullest possible freedom of trade, German law does grant legal authority for combination or association with a view to carrying out trade policies and conditions, and declares as illegal all measures which restrict this freedom or hinder it in any way. Restraint of trade is permissible, therefore, according to German law, and all that the legislation of November 1923 tried to establish was that some guiding motive should be given to association in industry, so that the economic prosperity of the country should be advanced.   It was now possible for public action to be taken in the name of the community without the necessity for a definite case of injury to a firm or individual to be cited.   The guardians of the national economic welfare were, first of all, the central executive, as represented by the Minister of Trade and Commerce or the Minister of Food and Agriculture, and, secondly, the governments of the States within the Reich through their central executives.   Such bodies could refer complaints to a special Cartel Court, an independent legal tribunal brought into being by the new legislation.   The Court should consist of five members, three of them lay judges chosen by the Minister of Industry and Commerce from a panel supplied by the President of the Court, one to be a specialist in the matter at issue, and two representatives of the conflicting parties.   Such a Court would have a permanent President, but its constitution would change to suit the question at issue and thus ensure some measure of accurate and unbiased opinion. The conditions under which appeal could be made to this Court are interesting as showing that the Court itself had full power to call all agreements governing and constituting cartels into question and, if necessary, to override them. A member of a cartel or any directly interested person could appeal against cartel decisions and agreements, when they restricted adversely the economic and trading freedom of the appellant, in the production, sale or pricing of goods. The Court sat on the validity of the claim and its judgment was final, even if theoretically it were possible to appeal to the usual judicial tribunal ; failure to establish a claim meant failure of the appeal and, contrary to opinion at the time, the Cartel Court has not made the denunciation of cartels or the disturbance of cartel agreements at all easy. It has, on the other hand, shown a high degree of impartiality and forced appellants desirous of evading agreements they had signed to adhere to them, and, in this way, strengthened the legal position of the cartels.

The Government itself, instead of taking advantage of authority to initiate an inquiry into the operation of cartels on its own account through appeal to the Court, has contented itself with furtherance and support of the unofficial arbitration councils created by the central associations representative of industry, wholesale and retail trade, and the co-operatives to make good differences between cartels. The actual investigation of the accuracy of and justification for any appeal to the Cartel Court produced in itself sufficient criticism of the cartels in question to clear up many disputes, and an important body of case law of permanent value was established for the definition of the legal status of the cartel. The new Act gave further powers to the President of the Cartel Court ; he could decide, for example, the appropriation of securities lodged with the cartel executives within the cartel itself and the formation of barriers or other trading obstacles against non-members. The Act could not apply to associations formed according to law or definite decrees, nor to conditions of production or price, where such were determined by the Government or State executives in accordance with the powers vested in them—i.e. to associations in the coal-mining, potash and other industries which had the character of publicly controlled cartels.

The opponents of trustification and combination in German industry regarded the new legislation as a German version of the American Sherman Anti-Trust legislation, where the Ministry of Industry and Commerce would control the policies of the great firms or groups of companies, which were then being formed in the basic industries, and the industrialists themselves were alarmed.   But there was little real intention of interfering with existing conditions, probably owing to the reflection that the large industrial enterprise would easily enough adjust its agreements or even its constitution to neutralize the effects of the new ordnance, and defeat it in the letter and in the spirit.   The German Government had no intention of entering, with a flourish of trumpets, on an anti-trust campaign : it desired above all to regularize the position of cartels, guide the course of industrial organization, while legally conceding the principles of combination, and use the instruments already in existence for the improvement of the economic position of Germany ; it even narrowed down the limits imposed on industrial firms in the preparation of balance-sheets and gave them a greater margin of secrecy during the restoration of their financial statements to a gold basis.

The new legislation came at a difficult moment in the history of the cartels and served, in some measure, to consolidate their position *vis-à-vis* the powerful trusts which had been developed throughout the inflation period.   The invasion of the Ruhr affected adversely the great cartels operating in the coalmining, iron and steel industries.   The Rhenish-Westphalian Coal Syndicate, which had been renewed for one year from April 1, 1922, was prorogued first of all until September 30, 1923, then to December 31, 1923, and finally until January 15, 1924, until some decision would result from the discussions carried out towards the end of 1923.   The original syndicate was dissolved and replaced by a limited liability company with the designation of Association for the Distribution and Sale of Ruhr Coal.   It held 98 per cent. of the output controlled by the former, a number of firms having seceded.   The Association came into effect on January 5, 1924, with validity until December 31, 1924, members being allowed to denounce the agreement under certain conditions during the whole of June. There had been a marked tendency since 1922 for the member-firms to increase their individual powers and thus weaken the authority of the central association—in itself a cause of perpetual disturbance.   One group representing 85 per cent. of the total production controlled by the syndicate was formed to deal with the sale of coal in Holland, while all members, including this group, could contract direct under certain provisos with their customers.   In this way, the central selling policy of the Syndicate, on which its existence depended, threatened to disappear in excessive concessions to individual mines or groups of mines. The thirteen selling companies commissioned by the syndicate to cover Germany were replaced by thirteen limited liability companies constituted by the commercial organizations of the mining companies which became the shareholders in those companies and received direct the proceeds of sale.

The invasion of the Ruhr and the agreements made between individual firms and the Franco-Belgian Control Commission (M.I.C.U.M.) for the supply of coal were responsible in great measure for this partial return to free trading conditions, and only the intervention of the State to form compulsorily a coal cartel kept the syndicate from dissolving without possibility of renewal. In the same way, the Steel Union (*Stahlbund*) and the Sales Association of the Upper Silesian Steel Industry (*Verkaufsgemeinschaft der oberschlesischen Stahlindustrie*), as well as the Shipbuilding-Steel Association (*Schiffbau-Stahlkontor*), were dissolved, while the Pig-Iron Association experienced difficulties very similar to those already noted in the Rhenish-Westphalian Coal Syndicate. In cement again, owing go the action of large firms determined on asserting their power, a state of crisis occurred.

The Cartel Law came, therefore, at an opportune moment for the preservation and development of the cartel system in Germany and, while its jurisdiction did not extend to coal-mining or potash, its findings were of value to all cartels. Thus it defended the position of the smaller firm in the cartel against the trust, which might become sufficiently strong and possess sufficient voting power through absorption of other firms to run the cartel and dictate its policy. In such an event, the smaller firms, finding themselves threatened by the trust or large concern to their economic disadvantage, could denounce the restrictions imposed on them by the cartel agreement and resign from it. It was sufficient for the firms to prove that a change had taken place in the balance of voting power and that decisions in favour of the concern had been made and the Cartel Court would then allow them to break the agreement. In potash, for example, the struggle between the Wintershall concern and the smaller firms almost led to disruption of the syndicate ; the Wintershall group, through a drastic process of rationalization, had been able to reduce its costs of production, and was trying to force selling prices down to correspond with this change, and so drive the smaller firms out of business. In this attempt it failed, and the higher level of prices was maintained under State support of the cartel.

After the stabilization crisis had been surmounted and production increased, the cartel situation became much easier and
progress could be realized in more effective internal organization and central control.   The growing trustification of
industry, which at one time might have led to dissolution of
the cartel system, only served, in many cases, to strengthen it :
the large producers recognized that the maintenance of stable
conditions of price and production meant a higher margin of
profit for them, and would allow them to carry out extensive
re-equipment with a view to penetrating more deeply into the
world market.   The Dawes Plan was a factor contributory to
such a development.   It would be interesting, therefore, to
examine in some detail the constitution of certain typical
cartels—in coal-mining, pig-iron and steel—and, from them,
illustrate some part of the structure of German industry.   It
is customary to take the Rhenish-Westphalian Coal Syndicate
as the finest example of the cartel in Germany, but the Rhenish
Brown-Coal Syndicate comes closer to the ideal, and by it we
should measure similar cartels operating in the coal, potash and
cement industries.

All coal and potash cartels have common characteristics
with a few variations from cartel to cartel ; they have been
legally constituted and must be a person or a company with
full responsibility at law in much the same way as an industrial
company.   The State, through the Coal Association or the
Higher Coal Council, has power, in the case of disputes leading
to dissolution, to form compulsory cartels and force on combined action in the interests of the economic well-being of the
State.   On many occasions, this power has been used to retain
the Rhenish-Westphalian Coal Syndicate and the Potash
Syndicate in existence, and so avoid the return to unrestrained
competition.   The legislation of 1919–20 entrusted to the
State Coal Association (*Reichskohlenverband*) and the Principal
Committee of the Coal Council (*Grosser Ausschuss des Reichs-
kohlenrats*) the duty of determining the prices to be charged
by the cartels, and all price schedules prepared by the latter
had to be approved.   At the end of 1923, however, the price
control exerted by the State was virtually abandoned, and the
syndicates had almost complete freedom to determine prices.
They had still to go through the formality of submitting price
schedules for approval, and these prices were not prices at the
mines only, but those to be charged by wholesale merchants to
their customers.   The right of approval was never waived by
the State, and, during the brown-coal strike of the autumn of

1927, the firm stand taken by the Coal Council against any increase in brown-coal prices was a factor in causing and prolonging the strike.

The Rhenish-Brown-Coal Syndicate was created in the form of a trading company with a central selling bureau ; the members, or rather shareholders, in the company signed agreements transferring their production to it. Under this form, the cartel has operated since 1915. The syndicate agreements are valid until March 31, 1930—a lengthy period, but necessary to the establishment of smooth and effective working conditions. The functions and purpose of the cartel lay in the control of production, of consumption by the individual mines, and of marketing ; the distribution of quotas and the sale of coal were the main objects of its foundation, and agreements covered the production, stocking and marketing of fuel as well as the creation of special selling agencies, wherever necessary. The syndicate had a nominal capital of 2,122,000 marks and did not exist to earn profits ; its expenses were met from the production sold by it on the basis of a royalty per ton, generally fixed at about 10 pfennig. A compensation fund might be established to make good losses incurred by members, the maximum levy for this purpose being fixed at 5 pfennig per ton of briquets. The voting at the meetings of the association was based on the percentages of the total production granted to each member with a correction for calorific value. Thus one ton of briquets counted as 2·5 tons of raw brown coal in the Rhineland and 2 tons in Hesse ; the production was the net quantity delivered for sale to the syndicate. Twenty-six members (nine of them public companies, eleven mines, and six limited liability companies) constituted the syndicate ; the nine companies had 76·93 per cent., the eleven mines 12·28 per cent., and the six liability companies the remaining 10·79 per cent. of the total quotas. For infringement of agreements heavy fines could be exacted.

The four main branches of activity referred to control of production itself, control of sales and marketing, the organization of sales and the determination of prices. In production, the functions of the syndicate were to regulate output to market requirements in order to avoid excess production and price-wars ; the individual firms had to place their entire output at the disposal of the central association, which was entitled to accept production to the total of the quota allocated to each firm. The technique of production remained the affair of the individual members, but co-operative research and development could be and were financed by the syndicate, with the result that considerable economies and improvements in technique took place.   In addition to this, dwellings for miners to the number of 1,230 were built, so that the cartel might avoid the reputation of being interested merely in capital and not in labour conditions.

Control of sales and marketing took the form of collection and allocation of all orders.   The sale of fuel remained the function of the syndicate alone ; it decided the distribution and destination of orders, invoiced shipments to consumers and transmitted payments to members.   It had power to pass on to the firms legal difficulties regarding delivery dates, accuracy of weight and quality of material.   Every member had the right to uniform employment of its mines as far as possible, and orders were allocated on this basis.   Each quota was established in relation to the annual total and all other quotas, while the syndicate could decide on a uniform restriction or increase of production to correspond with the state of the market.

The determination of a fixed quota allowed certain firms owning a number of mines to concentrate production on the most profitable and to close down others ; such a procedure would permit of economic operation during a period of restriction. A further development, the increase of quotas through the purchase of mines belonging to other members with a view to fuller employment of mines already worked, could be followed, as in the case of many firms within the Rhenish-Westphalian Coal Syndicate.   It was impossible, on account of legislation, to sell a quota without the corresponding mine or mines, but members could claim a revision of the quota percentages every three years.   At the end of each year, members were asked to submit a return of the excess production they could supply beyond their quota and, in the event of a rapid increase in demand, this excess could be tapped proportionately to the quotas.   No provision might be made to compensate irregularity in the allocation of orders.

The consumption of fuel by the members themselves, in the Rhenish-Brown-Coal Syndicate, was not included in the quota or sales totals, but in the Rhenish-Westphalian Coal Syndicate and in the Central German Brown-Coal Syndicate a special rubric included this consumption.   Consumption also by undertakings of an auxiliary type, chemical works, iron and steel furnaces, or power stations, owned by the firms was also omitted, but such omission required the approval of the syndicate.   Ownership meant possession of at least 81 per cent. of the working capital of auxiliary and allied companies ; exemption led to unification, security and cheapening of supplies in the event of a vertical combine being formed. The total capacity exempted, however, was taxed with its proportion of the expenses of the central organization to avoid victimization of the firms producing wholly for sale. The syndicate controlled sales directly and distinguished clearly two types of consumer—the large consumer represented by the wholesale merchants, the railways and a number of industrial firms supplied direct, and the small consumer dependent for supplies on the wholesale merchant. Severe selling and delivery conditions were imposed, with a view to standardizing, simplifying and cheapening distribution ; special concessions in price were made to encourage a constant demand during the summer months and so ensure more regular production throughout the year ; decline in the quantities taken by wholesalers under the limit fixed by agreement during the summer months brought with it the danger of a corresponding restriction during a period of intensive demand. Such action might be regarded in Britain as " restraint of trade " of a flagrant kind, but the syndicate had legal authority for its action.

The central selling organization fed into several distributing companies owned by it, and these companies dealt with selling areas arranged according to railway stations ; mines nearest such stations met the requirements of the area as far as possible. The Rhenish-Westphalian Coal Syndicate, as we have already seen, possessed its own selling branches, but it also permitted a number of coal-mines to have their own agencies, and the existence of both types together meant perpetual strife within the syndicate, since the mining companies demanded special preferences for their selling agencies, both in deliveries and in quotas. Wholesale merchants could not purchase coal from mines which did not belong to the Brown-Coal Syndicate, or supply associations of merchants, peasants' unions, co-operative or similar unions of consumers ; the main intention was to eliminate intermediaries and interest the merchants directly in the syndicate. Non-compliance with these conditions brought fines equivalent to 25 per cent. of the shipments. Prices were fixed on a basis agreed with the State Coal Association, and covered the total production costs at the mines inclusive of depreciation and profits, turnover tax, working expenses of the syndicate and distribution margins allowed to the merchants. The final price paid by the consumer supplied from the wholesale merchants' stocks allowed for freight costs and handling charges in addition to the standard price.   Such additions were defined by local coal merchants' associations for each sales region and permitted a surplus for profit to be taken by the merchant.   Such, in short, is the character of a typical cartel in the German coal-mining, potash, cement and other raw material industries.

The Pig-Iron Association experienced greater vicissitudes since the war than even the coal syndicates ; the Treaty of Versailles cut through its sphere of operation and separated compulsorily from it many important firms located in Luxemburg and Lorraine, while the partition of Upper Silesia affected adversely its hold on the eastern German producers.   The Iron Industry Law of April 1, 1920, introduced State control into the iron and steel industry to ensure reconstruction of the old associations and the more effective organization of the producers with a view to creating more stable conditions of trade. The Iron Trade Union (*Eisenwirtschaftsbund*) came into existence to ensure the provision of iron and steel for the home market, to determine maximum prices and selling conditions, to regulate imports and exports, and control the trade in scrap. Two groups of products were affected :   (1) pig-iron, ferro-manganese, ferro-silicon and scrap, and (2) semi-steel products, railway material, iron shapes, bar iron, wire and wrought-iron tubes.   A number of committees dealt with these subjects, with the addition of an Export Committee and a Saar Committee.   The regulations of the Iron Trade Union were not intended to apply to those branches of the industry where cartels were in operation and the Pig-Iron Association soon achieved independence, while the abolition of maximum prices for steel and rolling-mill products on July 27, 1923, destroyed the *raison d'être* of the Union, and it ceased to function.   On July 15, 1920, the Pig-Iron Association was renewed for three years, on July 1, 1921, for five years, i.e. until December 1926 and, in December, for a further five years until 1931.   With the coal syndicates, it was one of the few cartels to pass through the war and the post-war period without a breakdown, and it served to keep the producers together in one of the most severely hit industries of Germany.   Its range of effectiveness has, however, declined with the growth of vertical combination, which reached a first point of expansion early in 1921 and increased further in strength during 1927.

Since the association dealt only with the surplus remaining after the needs of the producers and their allied firms had been satisfied, the absorption of blast-furnaces into great iron and steel combines, where the raw material could be worked up into the finished article inside of the one complex, meant a serious diminution in the quantity of pig-iron available for sale in the market.   The formation of the *Siemens-Rhein-Elbe-Schuckert-Union* in 1920 and 1921, the expansion of the Stumm interests and the absorption by the Mannesmann Tube Works of blast-furnaces to meet their requirements, the dissolution of the *Siemens-Rhein-Elbe-Schuckert-Union* in 1926, followed by the amalgamation of the *Thyssen, Rheinische Stahlwerke, Phoenix, Bochumer Verein, Stumm, Dortmunder Union, Gelsenkirchen* and *Van der Zypen* interests in the *Vereinigte Stahlwerke*, where the greater proportion of the pig-iron production of the Ruhr went direct into consumption with little surplus, were all factors weakening the influence of the Pig-Iron Cartel and diminishing the range of its activities.

The pig-iron required for consumption by the firms or their subsidiaries themselves was subject to the control of the association and statistics had to be submitted monthly of the tonnage thus used, but it would not be reckoned as part of the quota. Members of a firm for the purposes of this calculation could be

Trustification has virtually taken the place of the cartel in pig-iron production.   It is doubtful, however, whether it will be allowed to disappear entirely.   As established in the main agreement of 1914, modified slightly in 1920 and 1921, the cartel has existed to carry out functions almost exactly the same as those already recorded for the Rhenish Brown-Coal Syndicate, and the administrative details bear a singularly close resemblance to each other.   Both cartels have elaborated what may be a standard form of agreement covering production, marketing, selling and price-fixation in their respective industries. The main differences lie in the definition of price itself, in the determination of the level of the quotas and, to some extent, in the status of the cartel *vis-à-vis* the large consumer who is also a producer.   The relations between the central organization as unique selling agency for the pig-iron industry, the producers, and the wholesale merchants or distributors are exactly the same as in the Brown-Coal Syndicate, with the proviso that the central organization may purchase pig-iron from foreign or even non-member firms in the event of the market demand being much greater than the supply.   All orders should be passed on by the producers and allocated in accordance with the quota percentages, care being taken to ensure regular employment of the member-firms and to eliminate excessive freight dues through supply to the consumer from the nearest works.

firms linked up in an *Interessengemeinschaft* or loose merger. The recognition of such an *Interessengemeinschaft* and its validity would be decided at a general meeting.   The prices were based on a standard price ex-works with a slight addition or a subtraction as determined for certain types of pig-iron ; special supplementary prices for high-quality deliveries to definite specifications could be made, but where, in the face of competition from foreign makers, such a supplement could not be levied, the syndicate might indemnify the producer accordingly.   From 1921 onwards, the quotas were fixed on a quarterly basis—on November 1 for the first quarter of the following year, on February 1 for the second quarter of the same year, on May 1 for the third quarter, and on August 1 for the fourth quarter.   The average output during the six months, April 1 to September 30, of the previous year determined the volume of participation in the first quarter of the year, and on this six-monthly figure, beginning from July 1, October 1, and January 1, the succeeding quarters were decided.   In October 1925, the quotas for the whole of 1926 were fixed on an average of the twenty-eight months between July 1, 1924, and March 31, 1926.

These regulations may give some idea of the complicated procedure required to bring some elasticity into the cartel control of production, especially during a time of fluctuating demand.   Unlike brown coal, pig-iron had not a constantly rising market, even if the producers entertained at one time that conception in view of the economic changes caused by the Treaty of Versailles and the partition of Upper Silesia ; imports, especially from France, were an important factor in the situation, and the cartel had to adjust its machinery to meet these conditions.   The growth of vertical combination reduced the total available for sale by the syndicate, and we may regard such a reduction as an indication of better organization and improved competitive efficiency in the iron and steel industry as a whole.   Thus, in 1922, we find the total shipments of the association given as 2,083,630 tons out of a national production of 9,396,000 tons, in 1921 1,670,042 tons out of 7,845,000 tons —roughly 20 per cent. in each year, but in 1924 and in 1925, this proportion had fallen to 17 per cent., and is now even less. The Pig-Iron Syndicate affords a good example, therefore, of the adverse influence trustification as such may have on the cartel and of the fundamental antagonism between the cartel conception of industrial organization and the combine or trust.

In the steel industry, an association very similar to the Pig-

Iron Syndicate in constitution and function was formed in
1904, the *Stahlwerksverband*, renewed in 1907 and in 1912 for
periods of five years, and, during the war, came directly under
Government control.   At the beginning of 1920, the creation of
the Iron Trade Union under State supervision rendered unnecessary the revival of the special activities of the *Stahlwerksverband*, and it was only late in 1923 that an effort was made
to bring the steel industry into line with coal and pig-iron as
far as production was concerned.   Price-fixing was undertaken
by the central Association of Iron and Steel Industrialists
working in conjunction with the *Stahlwerksverband*, which has
now assumed its pre-war functions.   The production cartel
alone, however, has dominated activities in crude steel since
1924, and no effort has yet been made to combine production
and price-fixing in one great organization on the terms of the
coal, potash or pig-iron syndicates.   Such a development will
probably materialize in time, provided that one trust or group
of trusts does not control the entire industry.

The Steel Ingot Syndicate (*Rohstahlgemeinschaft*) was
founded on November 1, 1924, with validity for five years.   A
test period of eleven months would intervene, at the end of
which members could denounce the agreement and retire from
the association.   Other members had to declare their adhesion
or non-adhesion to the scheme at the time of denunciation,
and if they elected to remain in the cartel, it would continue in
operation for the remaining four years.   The only further
possibility of dissolution would occur when a reduction of 40
per cent. or more had been declared in production for three consecutive months.   In view of the fact that the total production
fixed originally by the syndicate was 13,641,904 tons for practically the whole of Germany, a figure below the consumption
of the country under active trade conditions, the eventuality of
a reduction of 40 per cent. was remote and, to all intents and
purposes, the syndicate had a sure four years' life in front of it
after November 1925.   Its functions were simple : to determine the annual production and the quotas of the firms signing
the agreement, to ensure adherence to these quotas by imposing fines for over-production and compensate for under-production, to decree increases or reductions in the volume of
production to correspond with market conditions, and to represent the industry in a national capacity.   Three Commissions
would sit : one on sales which would study home and export
markets, assess demand and make recommendations regarding
legislation or expansion of production to the General Meeting ;

a second on associations which would consider the possibility of national or international agreements between producers ; and a third which would represent the syndicate in negotiations of an international nature.   The purely administrative functions would be undertaken by the *Stahlwerksverband* at Düsseldorf.   Each member would receive a quota equivalent to the output of any month during the period January 1922 to October 1924 multiplied by twelve, and these quotas would be increased or reduced by the percentage fixed by the General Meeting. If production were left uncontrolled for two consecutive months or more, new annual totals might be determined by multiplying the output of three uncontrolled months by four.

The formation of the Steel Ingot Syndicate gave an impetus to similar developments throughout the entire range of the steel industry.   The *Stahlwerksverband* was reconstituted as a central selling and price-fixing organization on April 23, 1925, working in co-operation with the Steel Ingot Syndicate ; between them, they represented, in their functions, the steel equivalent of the Pig-Iron Association or the Rhenish-Westphalian Coal Syndicate.   One section dealt with steel ingot quotas and the other with the prices of semi-products, railway constructional material and shapes.   The Tube Syndicate came into operation on March 11, 1925, with a duration of five years to cover quotas and act as a selling and price-fixing cartel ; on July 1 in the same year, the Heavy Wire Association, and at the beginning of August, the Bar Iron Association, the Steel Plate and Sheet Steel Association, and, in December, the Fine Wire Association, Rivet and Rolled Sheet Selling Cartels were formed, the majority of them working in close co-operation with the *Stahlwerksverband*.

The latter, adopting perhaps the analogy of the Rhenish Westphalian Coal Syndicate, established three great selling syndicates, one with its head-quarters at Düsseldorf, for the Ruhr, one at Leipzig for the North, West and Centre, and a third at Berlin for the North-East.   These organizations included selling agents controlled by the firms as well as independent wholesale merchants, and had the sole right to deal with the *Stahlwerksverband* and sell its products with a supplement of 4 per cent. above the cost price.   Certain large consumers continued to receive their supplies at the standard price, while four categories of merchants were distinguished, entitled to a rebate of 4 per cent., 2 per cent., 1 per cent., and 0·5 per cent. respectively.   Price conditions were the same as those indicated already in the Rhenish Brown-Coal Syndicate.   The Steel

Ingot Syndicate had already made agreements with the Union of Steel-Consuming Industries allowing them substantial reductions on the selling price of steel products, provided that they purchased only from its members, and these agreements were continued by the *Stahlwerksverband*.   Certain other groups of consumers, notably in engineering and electrical manufacture, were able to obtain special concessions from the iron and steel producers : the Central Association of Electrical Manufacturers, for the period March to July 1927, obtained rebates averaging 13·53 per cent. of the selling price of the iron and steel products consumed by its members.   This percentage was greater than any conceded previously.   Thus, from March to August 1925, only 6·4 per cent. was allowed.

While, therefore, the coal-mining, iron and steel industries could tighten up their organizations sufficiently to ensure practically complete control over production and price, and so co-ordinate national development, other industries dependent on them for raw materials had also improved their organizations, and were able to exert considerable influence on the prices quoted to their members and modify conditions of delivery in their favour.   In potash and cement, the cartel followed closely the type already described, but in more complicated industries, such as engineering, shipbuilding, chemicals, textiles, porcelain, and wood-working, the price-fixing group with no control over production predominated : its function lay primarily in determining minimum prices for certain standard products, eliminating cross tendering for important contracts and arranging for the distribution of important contracts. In certain cases, they formed export associations to open up demand in foreign markets and negotiate with producers in other countries.   At the end of 1926, Germany presented a complicated but orderly arrangement of associations of producers working together to maintain stable economic conditions and co-ordinate the national effort, and it was at this time that the development of the horizontal trust assumed considerable proportions.   Since 1926, trustification with its consequence in rationalization of production has attracted attention above all.

CHAPTER XV

THE ORGANIZATION OF INDUSTRY (*continued*) : TRUSTS AND INTERNATIONAL CARTELS

The trust and its place in the cartel—main factors causing trustification—the United Steel Works—the chemical trust—electrical manufacture—artificial silk, cement, potash, linoleum—international groups—the significance of international agreements to regulate competition—electrical manufacture, aluminium, potash, artificial silk, linoleum, chemicals, magnesite—the International Steel Cartel— other iron and steel groups—the future of the trust.

THE movement towards trustification becomes intensified, as a rule, during a period of trade depression or uncertainty regarding the market situation ; the efficient producers are able to absorb, at comparatively low cost, the smaller, less active firms, and are, in fact, encouraged to do so in order to keep down uneconomic competition. Even the cartels with their agreements governing production and price are not always able to force adherence to those agreements, and producers, confronted with a shrinking demand and heavy overhead expenses, often show remarkable ingenuity in breaking the spirit of an agreement while nominally adhering to the letter. Again, the large concern may switch orders over to a limited number of factories, keep them operating at full pressure and close down the superfluous factories ; it can produce fairly cheaply in times of poor demand and keep earning profits at a time when the smaller undertakings show heavy losses. In recent economic history, the large industrial enterprise has weathered depression much more effectively than the small, and has shown a much greater recuperative power.

In Germany, certain factors contributed above all to the growth of the trust : inflation made the vertical combine possible on the most extensive scale, and even a return to normal currency conditions, while it shook out a number of superfluous undertakings, did not entirely destroy the vertical combine or seriously weaken the case for the large manufacturing

245

unit. The Colossus elaborated by Stinnes displayed a mighty torso after the death of its founder and formed the substance of the *Vereinigte Stahlwerke*, the greatest single trust in the European iron and steel industry. The foundations remained after the inflation period had passed. The Dawes Plan, through the impetus it gave to the realization of higher competitive efficiency on the part of German industry—as essential to the development of a favourable trade balance—forced on amalgamation of small firms and gave prominence to the conception of the trust. In addition to this, the revival of the cartel and the establishment of quota and price-fixing systems in practically every section of industry led to the acquisition of quotas by the more enterprising firms and the steady absorption of other producers in order to improve the economic status and the voting power of the large concern.

In a number of the more important cartels, one firm might occupy the leading position and thus control an entire industry. Thus the *Vereinigte Stahlwerke* had a quota of 21·8 per cent. in the Rhenish-Westphalian Coal Syndicate, 43·14 per cent. in the Pig-Iron Association, 41·08 per cent. in the Steel Ingot Syndicate, 40·96 per cent. in the semi-products, railway material and shapes cartels attached to the *Stahlwerksverband*, 34·37 per cent. in the Bar Iron Association, 44·55 per cent. in the Heavy Plate Association, and 50·2 per cent in the Tube Association. In the cartels where its quotas were higher than 40 per cent., the *Vereinigte Stahlwerke* could decide the voting and eventually impose its own conditions. The recovery in German production since the formation of this trust has, however, made action within the cartel unnecessary, and the issues have not yet been joined.

In the same way, the Wintershall concern, with its allied firm, the *Kali-Industrie A.G.*, had a participation of 39·3 per cent. in the Potash Syndicate, and, in conjunction with the Burbach concern, could command a majority of the voting power. In cement, the *Wicking'sche Portland-Cement Industrie A.G.*, had a quota of 53·9 per cent. in the Western German Cement Syndicate ; the *Schlesische Portland-Cement Industrie A.G.* 16·87 per cent. in the North German Cement Association, and 50 per cent. in the Selling Union of Eastern German Lime Firms, while a similar position was occupied by the *Portland-Cement-Werke Heidelberg-Mannheim-Stuttgart A.G.* in southern Germany. In jute, the *Vereinigte Jute-Spinnereien und Webereien A.G.* was responsible for 45 per cent. of the national production. The list can be extended to cover the most diverse industries, glass, porcelain, electrical manufacture, chemicals and pottery, and, in each case, we find the large concern breaking through, abrogating more and more executive power. Already the Cartel Court has had to deliver restraining decisions regarding the rights of the large undertaking, with strong voting percentages, to use the cartel organization to further its own ends, and the position is certain to become more and more difficult as the growth of trustification spreads out farther and affects more and more branches of industry.

The last main incentive, from many points of view the most important, has been the reduction in the costs of production, coupled with increase in profit margins, which rationalization on the most thorough scale may bring with it. To make such rationalization fully effective, it is not sufficient to improve organization and tighten up methods of works' control to ensure the greatest possible economies in labour and materials and, in this way, make the single manufacturing unit fully efficient : the industrialist looks farther than this—he aims at specializing in the various products of an industry or even industries, at obtaining sufficient control over demand to permit of concentration of production in modern, well-equipped factories destined for one range of articles. In this way, production costs fall to the minimum, the competitive position of the trust is improved enormously, and a virtual monopoly realized for the supply of the products in which it specializes. This motive was predominant in the formation of the *Vereinigte Stahlwerke,* the great steel trust of the Ruhr. Other intentions inspired the formation of the *Interessen-Gemeinschaft Farben-Industrie,* the chemical trust, the *Vereinigte Glanzstoff A.G.* in artificial silk, the *Deutsche Linoleum Werke A.G.* in linoleum ; in their case, the desire to obtain a strong control over the home market without any reference to cartels and, on the basis of this control, to establish international groups to eliminate competition dictated policy. A similar design has been behind the expansion of the interests of the two electrical manufacturing concerns, the *Allgemeine-Elektrizitäts-Gesellschaft* and the *Siemens-Schuckert-Werke.* There is no doubt that the individual company can move much more effectively than the Cartel in the linking up of interests with foreign producers, while it can manœuvre for place much more rapidly.

An additional factor making for trustification has been finance—the actual shortage of working capital in Germany and the need to borrow new capital abroad as well as to arrange short-term credits to finance production. Only the large industrial company, with a definite statement of assets, manufacturing equipment and profits, could hope to borrow on reasonable terms in America, and the trust could act in this capacity most effectively of all.   The success attending the issue of loans for the United Steel Works (*Vereinigte Stahlwerke*), the great electrical manufacturing companies, the potash and chemical concerns in New York, has been due to the fact that they promised concrete security for the loans, and in their organization appealed to the mentality of a country which was the home of the trust idea.   The cartel had no power to undertake such operations, even if legally it could do so, and finance contributed, therefore, its quota to the reorganization of German industry on the basis of the large productive concern.

The model for the formation of the *Vereinigte Stahlwerke* in May 1926 was undoubtedly the United States Steel Corporation, the most powerful combination of iron and steel producers in the world, while the inspiring motive might be found in the determination to create for Germany an efficient organization, which would, through progressive reduction in manufacturing costs and through concentration of financial and technical strength, assume first place in the European iron and steel industry, and develop German export trade in volume greater than hitherto recorded.   Three great manufacturing groups constituted the trust—the *Rhein-Elbe Union*, associated with the *Siemens-Schuckert* electrical manufacturing concern, the *Thyssen* works, and the *Phoenix* concern associated with the *Allgemeine-Elektrizitäts-Gesellschaft*.   The *Rheinische Stahlwerke*, the *Vereinigte Stahlwerke van der Zypen*, the *Rombacher Hüttenwerke* and the *Stumm* concern completed the number of constituent firms.   Of these companies, the *August-Thyssen Hütte* at Hamborn, the *Dortmunder Union*, the *Bochumer Verein*, the *Rheinische Stahlwerke* at Duisburg and the *Phoenix* works at Hörde had equipment of the most modern type and were capable of embarking on a policy of mass-production without limit.   The *Thyssen* works alone could produce 2,000,000 tons of steel annually, and it was followed closely by the combined *Rheinische Stahlwerke-Phoenix Werke* at Duisburg.

These undertakings were marked out at once for the supply of iron and steel products in universal demand, such as billets, bars, rails, wire and blooms ; the position of the *Thyssen* works with their port on the Rhine made them peculiarly suitable for export at low freight charges and they concentrated on foreign markets almost entirely.   The *Gelsenkirchen Bergwerks*

A.G. specialized in tubes and plate, the *Dortmunder Union* in steel forgings, castings and constructional engineering, the *Friedrich-Wilhelm-Hütte* at Mulheim (associated with the *Dortmunder Union*) in tubes, castings and engineering, the *Bochumer Verein* in the manufacture of high-grade steels, railway tyres, springs, rails, bolts, rivets and nuts, as well as tubes, and the *Stumm* group in wire.

The trust could, therefore, allocate the various branches of production to the firms most capable of dealing with them and ensure the highest possible degree of specialization ; it could close down the older plants, as in the case of the *Rombacher Hüttenwerke* and certain sections of the *Phoenix* and *Stumm* concerns, transfer their quotas in the various cartels to the more efficient plants and keep the latter in full activity. It carried out reorganization on a horizontal basis, leaving to the member firms subsidiary undertakings unnecessary to the production of steel : thus the *Gelsenkirchen Bergbau A.G.*, the *Phoenix Werke* and the *Thyssen Werke* retained coal-mines other than those required for the purposes of the trust, the *Thyssen Werke* transferred their interests in the engineering firm *Thyssen & Co. A.G.* to the *Demag* of Duisburg and the *Siemens-Schuckert* company, which took over the mechanical and electrical sections respectively.

As we have already indicated, the *Stahlwerksverband* and other associations were formed to act as selling organizations for the iron and steel production of Germany on much the same basis as the Rhenish-Westphalian Coal Syndicate, but the Steel Trust possessed its own selling companies, especially *Raab Karcher & Co.* in coal, the *Stahlunion Export G.m.b.H.*, and ten other agencies in iron and steel, so that, in this respect at least, it could act independently. Such a development might be regarded as logical, since there was no guarantee that the cartels would remain in existence indefinitely, and collapse of the latter would bring with it disruption of the marketing system. The trust could act also with a fuller measure of independence and power in the elaboration of a manufacturing and selling policy.

The annual productive capacity of the *Vereinigte Stahlwerke* is now 37,188,000 tons of coal, 9,189,000 tons of coke, 10,000,000 tons of pig-iron and 9,000,000 tons of steel ingots, while, in the year ending September 1927, the actual output aggregated 26,081,000 tons of coal, 8,205,000 tons of coke, 6,351,000 tons of pig-iron and 6,837,644 tons of steel ingots. The total number of employees, inclusive of staff, was, in September 1927,

198,410, while the turnover reached 1,419,888,000 marks
(£71,000,000). Allowing for the reduction in total capacity
caused by the closing down of the older, less efficient plants,
we can estimate that, in its first full year, the trust was working
at over 90 per cent. capacity ; it accounted for over 40 per cent.
of the national production of steel and 50 per cent. of pig-iron,
assuming the same position *vis-à-vis* other producers in Germany as the United States Steel Corporation in America.

Not content with this achievement, the *Vereinigte Stahlwerke*
was instrumental in forming a Central German Steel Trust
(*Mitteldeutsche Stahlwerke*), which, in turn, with the *Oberschlesische Eisenbedarfs A.G.*, created an Upper Silesian trust
(*Vereinigte Oberschlesische Hüttenwerke A.G.*). These three
enterprises, with a combined share capital of 1,005,000,000
marks, and debenture, loan and mortgage capital of 500,000,000
marks, or a total working capital of 1,505,000,000 marks
(£75,000,000), form the most powerful association of producers
in Germany, or, for that matter, in Europe, but, side by side
with them, other firms have been able to exist in iron and steel
and maintain their position intact, chief among them being
*Krupp, Klöckner, Eisen u. Stahlwerke Hoesch, Gutehoffnung-
shütte,*[1] and the *Mannesmann* Tube Works. We illustrate on
page 251 the comparative strength of these undertakings by
reference to their quotas in the various syndicates.

The *Vereinigte Stahlwerke*, although, in conjunction with the
Central German and Upper Silesian trusts, it covers the greater
part of production in the majority of iron and steel products,
is not yet in a position to dominate the market entirely, but its
voting power in the various cartels remains strong enough for
it to decide the direction of cartel policy. The favourable state
of the market has rendered unnecessary any movement towards
restriction, and the testing period has yet to come. It is
obvious, however, that any further move towards trustification
in iron and steel would bring with it the inclusion of firms like
Klöckner and the *Eisen u. Stahlwerke Hoesch. Krupps,* the
Gutehoffnungshütte and the *Mannesmann* concerns are largely
self-contained with important engineering subsidiaries and an
international reputation for certain specialities ; it is doubtful
whether even the *Vereinigte Stahlwerke* would be willing to
absorb these firms in view of their economic situation and the
strength of their organization ; it should form with them rather

---

[1] The *Gutehoffnungshütte* produced in 1926–27, 4,229,000 tons of
coal, 930,490 tons of pig-iron, and 1,031,144 tons of steel ingots.

PARTICIPATIONS OF IRON AND STEEL FIRMS IN SELLING
SYNDICATES
1927

Syndicate	Total Production assessed for Quotas (Metric Tons)	Vereinigte Stahlwerke Per cent.	Klöckner Per cent.	F. Krupp A.G. Per cent.	Eisen u. Stahlwerke Hoesch Per cent.	Mannesmann Per cent.
Rhenish - Westphalian Coal Syndicate .	164,000,000	21·82	3·52	6·31	1·73	3·72
Pig-Iron Association . .	2,260,000	43·14	6·42	5·77	0·44	—
Steel Ingot Syndicate . .	16,600,000	41·08	5·37	10·50	5·00	2·44
A. Products Association .	4,320,000	40·96	3·92	14·19	6·38	—
Bar Iron Association . .	3,900,000	34·37	14·20	11·37	5·00	—
Heavy Plate Association .	1,620,000	44·55	5·22	5·17	2·70	9·10
Rolled Wire Association .	1,550,000	29·88	10·30	14·27	5·04	—
Drawn Wire Association .	825,000	23·57	—	—	5·05	—
Tube Association	—	50·20	—	—	—	45·0
Hoop and Strip Association .	955,000	48·44	7·10	—	10·05	—

an *Interessengemeinschaft*, where the great firms would retain their individual character. The iron and steel industry has already moved far enough forward on the road to make these speculations more than theoretical ; they may in the near future find a material illustration in a great steel trust covering the entire German production.

The chemical industry shows a similar movement towards concentration of production in one concern, in this case, the *Interessengemeinschaft Farben-Industrie*, which was constituted in October 1925 by the fusion of thirteen leading manufacturers. Chief among them stood the *Badische Anilin u. Sodafabrik* with its subsidiary, the *Ammoniawerk Merseburg*, the *Farbenfabriken vormals F. Bayer & Co., Meister Lucius & Bruning, Leopold Casella & Co.,* the *Chemische Fabrik Griesheim-Elektron,* the *A.G. für Anilinfabrikation* and the *Chemische Fabrik vormals Weiler ter Meer*. The range of its interests is very great, and it has been estimated that associated firms in all branches of chemical production at home and abroad now exceed eighty-six in number. The main policy behind these participations has been the control and supply of raw materials, the control of production with a view to elimination of competition at home and the realization of an efficient distributing system.

In raw materials, it is interested in brown coal, hard coal, lime, sulphur, crude oil, petroleum and textile companies capable of meeting the greater part of its requirements ; in heavy chemicals, electro-chemistry and electro-metallurgy, mineral dyes, compressed gas, artificial silk, celluloid, explosives, wood distillation, photographic materials, it has subsidiary and associated firms feeding into the central organization or controlling special sections of the market, while it maintains a number of development companies to stimulate the use of artificial fertilizers in agriculture and carry out extensive research. Recently, it has embarked on the production of oil from coal by the Bergius processes, and has developed very rapidly the output of artificial silk by the viscose and acetone processes, the companies dealing with this being the *Agfa-Viscose Fabrik*, the *Aceta G.m.b.H.* and the *Köln-Rottweil Konzern*. At this point, it constitutes the only great manufacturing group in artificial silk in Germany outside of the *Vereinigte Glanzstoff* combine.

The *I.G. Farbenindustrie* does not control the entire chemical production of Germany, but it has been in a position to dominate and initiate technical development, a factor of importance in chemicals above all, and so, through the possession of initiative, has exerted almost complete control over the market. It has made profits consistently at a time when other chemical firms have showed unsatisfactory results, and was able to surmount the stabilization crisis with ease. In 1927, its share capital, exclusive of preference shares, totalled 1,100,000,000 marks, with reserves at 173,155,000 marks and debentures and loans at 257,729,000 marks, while its net profit was, for 1926, 70,500,000 marks.

The two principal chemical concerns operating in Germany independently of the *I.G. Farbenindustrie* are the *Kokswerke Schering*, with a capital of 90,300,000 marks, and the *Rütgerswerke*, with a capital of 80,000,000 marks—specializing in coal by-products. Neither of them recorded satisfactory financial results in 1926.

In electrical manufacture, the growth of trustification is not a post-war phenomenon, since, even before the war, the two combines, the *Allgemeine-Elektrizitäts-Gesellschaft* and the *Siemens-Schuckert Werke*, were responsible for about 60 per cent.

of the national production.   A special characteristic of these firms has been their close association with the iron and steel, engineering and electricity supply industries, all of which were important consumers of electrical plant.   The *A.E.G.* had interests in shipbuilding through the *Deutsche Werke A.G.*, in locomotive construction through the *Linke-Hoffmann* concern, and in iron and steel through the *Phoenix-Werks* prior to the formation of the *Vereinigte Stahlwerke* and lately through the *Mitteldeutsche Stahlwerke* ; and it has recently formed associations with the *I.G. Farbenindustrie*.   The *Siemens-Schuckert* concern is now, through its acquisition of the *Thyssen* electrical engineering shops, principal supplier to the *Vereinigte Stahlwerke*, and remains connected with the firms constituting the *Rhein-Elbe-Union* before they were amalgamated in the Steel Trust.

Both firms control in common a number of companies supplying a monopoly, the *Accumulatoren Fabrik* in batteries and accumulators, the *Osram G.m.b.H.* in lamps, the *Vereinigte Lausitzer Glaswerke* in glass, the *Deutsche Fernkabel G.m.b.H.* in cables, and, from many points of view, we may consider them as a loose *Interessengemeinschaft*.   The output of both firms is now in excess of 1,200,000,000 marks (£60,000,000) ; the share capital of the *A.E.G.* totals 155,000,000 marks, loan and debenture capital 61,800,000 marks, and reserves 16,120,000, giving an aggregate working capital of 232,920,000 marks ; the *Siemens-Schuckert, Siemens u. Halske* combine now has 187,500,000 marks share capital, 107,620,000 marks loans and debenture capital, and reserves of 57,071,000 marks, a total working capital of 352,181,000 marks.

In three trusts affecting the iron and steel, chemical and electrical manufacturing industries, we can fix in 1927 a working capital, inclusive of reserves and loans, exceeding 3,550,000,000 marks (£177,500,000).   The greater part of the long-term loans and debentures has come from the American investor, and the financial strength of these great undertakings is a certain proof in itself that the economic recovery of Germany will be maintained and supported as far as the basic industries are concerned.   In other less important branches of production, artificial silk, where the *Vereinigte Glanzstoff* company, associated with Courtaulds, predominates, cement, potash (*Wintershall-Kali-Industrie*), aluminium, pottery (*Deutsche Ton und Steinzeugswerke*), jute (*Vereinigte Jute Spinnereien und Webereien*), linoleum (*Deutsche Linoleum-Werke*), and a number of the luxury trades—trustification is already far advanced, and, as

such, has imposed new problems on cartel executives desirous
of maintaining some balance of power between the large and
small producers.

A further development arising out of trustification has been
the linking up of manufacturers in the principal industrial
countries with the object of eliminating competition and stabilizing market conditions. The mentality active in the formation of the trust on a national or even regional basis is the
mentality which sees in international affiliations, the most certain method of obtaining the maximum security, both against
financial and political developments. Industry leaps over frontiers through the fact of international trade : tariff walls of the
most forbidding dimensions cannot close out production entirely
and make a country economically self-sufficient. They narrow
down the interchange of goods and encourage national industries to extend their manufacturing equipment under a pro-
tective system which eliminates competition from without ;
such equipment in time becomes too extensive to be fully
employed on the national requirements alone, and the need for
outlets becomes urgent. When, as in Europe, a group of industrial countries, Germany, France, Belgium, Austria, Czecho-
Slovakia, Italy, Switzerland and even Poland are all seeking
outlets at the same time for industries very similar in character
over more than one country—coal-mining, iron and steel,
engineering, chemicals and electrical manufacture chief among
them—the danger of chaotic trade conditions, severe price-
cutting and widespread depression is never absent. The productive capacity of the basic industries of Europe remains
considerably in excess of demand and will remain so until
the world market expands sufficiently to absorb all the surplus production available. No one can foresee when that
event will take place ; it is shrouded still in a dim future.
The international association of producers, either in the form
of a cartel or a trust, owes its existence to the desire, first of
all, to control competition, stabilize the market, and neutralize the worst effects of tariffs. A firmly constituted, fully
representative international trust can have little interest in
tariffs ; it can adjust prices to correspond with production
costs and knows that the consumer will pay those prices with the
addition of the tariff ; it has control over the national production
within the tariff walls and can raise the national prices to the
maximum justified by the tariffs, creating powerful financial
reserves of value in the event of independent producers mate-
rializing. The tariff, therefore, tends to force on international

agreements and, through the reality of such agreement, to recoil on those responsible for framing it.

In addition to this, and perhaps a less obvious development, the international trust aims at restoring some balance of power between the financial and productive sections of trade. Finance has always been international in its major transactions, such as the exchange of credits to cover shipments or goods in transit from one country to another, the determination of currency conversion ratios and the allocation of long-term or short-term credits for purposes other than foreign trade ; it has established what amounts to an international capital market served by New York, London, and, to some extent, by Berne and Amsterdam, and is generally prepared to divert funds to the countries or industries most capable of yielding a high return ; it can carry out a general policy, such as the return to the gold standard, on its own initiative without consulting either industry or trade. The result has been violent fluctuation in trade itself through the operation of factors over which industry has no effective control in any country alone ; prices are not stable and move in accordance with financial policy. A severe downward movement may take place as a result of revalorization of a currency or a return to a gold standard with limitation of credit and currency in circulation to make the return effective, while the industrialist remains helpless. If, however, through international agreement, production and marketing can be controlled by the industrialist, he can interpose a strong body of resistance to financial factors making for disturbance of price conditions and can ensure stability. On such a basis the prosperity of industry rests ; the speculative element is eliminated, and a steady forward movement can be made in full security. Few trusts are in such a position, however, but an inspiring motive in their formation has been undoubtedly the desire to achieve stable conditions both of production and finance.

In Germany, the growth of trustification has been followed in practically every case by extension of the interests and sphere of influence of the trust beyond the frontiers : the *Vereinigte Stahlwerke* was the prime mover behind the formation of the International Steel Cartel, the *Wintershall-Kali-Industrie* concern behind the Franco-German quota and price-fixing potash cartel ; the *I.G. Farbenindustrie* has been the initiator of discussions with British and French chemical combines ; the *Vereinigte Glanzstoff* linked up readily with the Courtaulds and *Snia Viscosa* concerns. The *A.E.G.* renewed its technical and manufacturing relations with the General Electric Company of America, and *Siemens-Schuckert* with the Westinghouse Company. Both undertakings have developed their power finance methods to ensure close connection between electricity supply companies in Germany and important foreign markets, in South America, Europe and Asia especially, and, through their associations with American firms, have been carrying out power projects in Central and Eastern Europe. It is not a case precisely of international trustification, but rather of agreement with the possibility of an international trust being formed in the near future between American, German, French, Swiss, Belgian and Italian producers. The *Deutsche-Linoleum-Werke* has affiliations on much the same basis as the leading American producer. The International Lamp Cartel comes closest of all to the German model : practically all electric lamp manufacturers possessing a monopoly in the national markets, British, German, French, Swiss, Belgian, Dutch, Italian and American, have formed agreements delimiting markets and spheres of influence, so that the national monopolies may be maintained. Manufacturers may export to markets already dominated by other manufacturers protected by a marketing agreement only up to a certain percentage : beyond that they must pay compensation to a central fund held at Geneva, which is distributed at the end of each year. There is no attempt to fix international minimum prices or control production directly.

The aluminium industry has been brought together in a cartel covering the world production, its functions being to stabilize prices, develop markets, exchange technical information and experience tending towards reduction in manufacturing costs. The main constituent firms are the German State-owned *Vereinigte-Aluminiumwerke A.G.*, the Bitterfeld works controlled by the *I.G. Farbenindustrie* and the *Metallbank* of Frankfurt, the *Aluminium-Industrie* of Switzerland, the Aluminium Company of America, *L'Aluminium Français* and British producers. In cement, the Southern German cartel has linked up with Swiss and Austrian organizations, and the Northern German cartel with Scandinavian, while, in magnesite, Austrian, German, Czecho-Slovakian, British and Italian producers under the leadership of the *Veitschs-Magnesitwerk A.G.* in Vienna control 99 per cent. of European production. In potash, German and Alsatian mines came together in 1924 to regulate market conditions in France and Germany and to eliminate competition in the United States and Sweden. In 1925, agreements covering the world were made on the basis of 30 per cent. for the Alsatian works and 70 per cent. for the German, with the exception of America, where the ratios were 33·3 per cent. and 66·7 per cent. Beyond a total sales quota of 840,000 tons, however, both countries bear the same proportion. In other products, bottle-glass, mirrors, vinegar, soda, superphosphates, copper, dynamite and explosives, similar movements could be observed after the war, and international price conventions are now in operation.

It is in the iron and steel industry, however, that the most spectacular progress has been made. The formation of the International Steel Cartel in 1926 must be regarded as one of the most significant economic developments of the post-war period; it represented the first real effort to make good the disturbances and dislocations caused by the Treaty of Versailles in production and to recreate the Ruhr-Luxemburg-Lorraine-Saar economic unit which had formed the basis of industrial expansion in Germany. In character and functions it resembled very closely the Steel Ingot Syndicate in an international setting, and was a pure production cartel with no control over price. As such, it could be only partially effective in stabilizing market conditions, since a state of demand below the total fixed by the quota in any country linked in the cartel would mean intensive competition in the export market. Stability both in production and price could only be reached when each country was producing up to its quota strength or exceeding it in a uniform ratio. Such an event would presume a general upward movement in European prosperity and a rapidly expanding demand in the world markets. The essence of the agreement was that, out of a total production to be determined annually according to the state of the market, each of the four constituent countries, Germany, France, Belgium and Luxemburg, should receive a quota corresponding to its relative output at a given period.

The cartel, therefore, recognized as permanent the economic grouping imposed by the Treaty of Versailles, and showed that German industrialists had, temporarily at least, admitted the *status quo*. Yet the changes in relative position since 1913 were sufficiently startling : Germany with Luxemburg accounted before the war for 71 per cent. of the iron and steel production of all four countries, but, in 1926, its share had fallen to 36 per cent. in pig-iron and 44 per cent. in steel. Taking 1926 as a basis, Germany was entitled to a quota, therefore, of 44 per cent., but the basis of assessment, namely, the first quarter of 1926, when production was subnormal, gave only 40·45 per cent. to Germany, compared with 38·43 per cent. for France with Lorraine and the Saar, and 21·12 per cent. for Belgium and Luxemburg.   If the general average for 1926 as a whole had been taken, the German quota should have been 44 per cent., or, if 1925 had been taken, 47 per cent.   The German industrialists made substantial concessions, chiefly to Belgium, in order to obtain international agreement, but their proportion was 4 per cent. to 7 per cent. too low with reference either to productive capacity or to demand.   The total production assessed for quotas stood at 25,287,000 tons, but, in the event of the figure reaching the standard maximum, 29,250,000 tons, the German percentage could rise to 43·18 per cent.   Once at this level, it could not be reduced, even if the total production were to fall back again to the original basis.

Subsidiary agreements covering the relations between Germany, Lorraine and Luxemburg weakened the position of the industrialist further : 3·75 per cent. of the Lorraine production and 2·75 per cent. of the Luxemburg production had to be imported into Germany, while the Saar should be allowed to export duty-free to Germany.   In other words about 15 per cent. of the German home market was to be supplied by Luxemburg, Lorraine and the Saar, in itself a heavy sacrifice both in production and in price, since such a volume of importation, thrown direct on the home market, would tend to keep prices, as determined by the *Stahlwerksverband* and other cartels, down to the same level as those ruling outside of the country. On the other hand, France and Luxemburg were committed to the principle that they should not export to Germany more than $6\frac{1}{2}$ per cent. of the home demand.

A fine of four dollars was originally imposed for every ton in excess of the quota and one dollar was paid into the central fund for every ton of output.   Each country producing below its quota received two dollars from the central fund per ton within the limit of 10 per cent. of the quarterly quota.   If the deficit continued for several quarters at 10 per cent. or more, the compensation was reduced each time by 2 per cent.   Accounts would be cleared every three months and fines or compensations made, while, at the end of every six months, the pool would be distributed.

Owing to the effect of the coal strike in Britain in 1926, Germany and Belgium exceeded their quotas in the first quarter of the agreement, namely, October to December 1926, and the revival of home demand caused Germany to go far beyond its quota every three months during 1927.   In the first quarter,

Germany, Belgium and the Saar were debited, in fines, with 2,784,000 dollars, and France credited with 192,000 dollars. Alteration in the rules, made at the request of the German industrialist, who found himself paying four dollars per ton on production absorbed entirely by the home demand, and, therefore, outside of international competition, reduced the fine per ton of excess production on home demand while retaining the original four dollars on export demand. The new rules were valid from April 1927 onwards. In the quarter April–June 1927, home demand accounted for about 80 per cent. and export 20 per cent. ; on the former, there was an excess of 1,020,687 tons, and on the latter, a deficit of 46,961 tons. In the following quarter, the proportion stood at 70 per cent. and 30 per cent., home demand causing now an excess of 736,244 tons, and export 401,848 tons. Altogether, Germany in one year paid out in fines 46,105,281 marks, the equivalent of over eleven marks per ton exported. Since October 1927, the home-demand fine of two dollars has been reduced to one dollar. Even so, the situation cannot fail to dissatisfy the German iron and steel industrialist, and the collapse of the cartel may well take place. A number of additional countries have been absorbed, namely, Austria, Czecho-Slovakia, Poland and Hungary, so that the cartel, as at present constituted, is completely representative of European producers. Competition between France and Belgium especially has brought down prices almost to an uneconomic level, and the position of the German exporter, weighted already with a fine of eleven marks per ton, cannot be regarded as very reassuring.

Certain leaders of the industry affirm that only the formation of international price-fixing associations to deal with the various steel products marketed can preserve the cartel from collapse. Already progress has taken place in this direction : a European Rail Manufacturers' Association (Erma) came into being in 1926, with a sales office in London, to control European, inclusive of British, prices. A Wrought-Iron Tube Association had also been formed with German, French, Belgian and Czecho-Slovakian co-operation ; a Rolled Wire Syndicate was in process of elaboration between German, French, Belgian and Luxemburg industrialists ; a Pig-Iron Cartel on the lines of the International Steel Cartel was evolved by German, Lorraine and Luxemburg producers, while, in bar iron, negotiations had been begun. The main lines of development are already clear —trustification wherever possible, international agreements covering production and price, and the progressive stabilization of trade conditions.   On these lines, we may expect important developments within the next few years.

To one enamoured of philosophic systems, the thought of Germany creating and adjusting its industrial organization to the economic changes and fluctuations of the time must have a keen fascination.   By adding here, eliminating there, emphasizing the significance of a movement at one time and throwing it back into obscurity at another, one might elaborate a theory which would have all the surprise of a discovery and the substantial reality of an industrial cosmos vitalized into an æsthetic or a logical philosophical entity.   It all appears so easy and so perfectly graded : industry and the State, convulsed by the conflicts of Socialist and anti-Socialist doctrines, which melt into a conception of economic welfare beyond the range of any doctrine or set of doctrines ; the entire industrial complex held together in a series of cartels covering the whole of production and the cartels yielding in turn to powerful amalgamations of producers, either organized as trusts or as more effective cartels within one industry or group of industries, and the trusts again linked up with other trusts in foreign countries to form international cartels.   If, at every stage, full co-operation could be achieved, the central associations become entirely representative and all-powerful with no secessions, the trusts could dominate production and marketing within the industry which maintains them, and the International Cartels could enter into possession of a world monopoly, then a philosophic system might be evolved which would trace with great precision the economic future of Germany and the world.   Industry would fall into the category of exact science, where formulae might express natural processes and reaction be carefully noted in advance, where the art of prophecy would be the art of assembling the proper formulae and assessing the value of reactions, actual or potential ; cause could be bracketed with effect and the future encased in immense calculations, held within a precise mathematical system, interpreted and amplified in the light of philosophy.

Such speculations rise inevitably to the mind when the progress achieved by Germany in industrial organization is surveyed, but they are immaterial ; they have no real application or illustration in reality.   The cartel system has passed through a series of bitter conflicts between producers and survived with difficulty periods of economic stress.   The State, determined to maintain some order in the industrial world, has intervened on many occasions and compelled co-operation ; it has been forced to enter the system itself through its ownership of electricity supply, aluminium, potash and shipbuilding companies, and use its influence to preserve at least the appearance of unity ; the international cartels are still in the experimental stage with an uncertain future. The outlines are promising, but the substance changes and shifts and will do so as long as the human factor—human ambitions, human velleities, human pettiness —remains. Individualism cannot be wholly stifled, even if, by all the laws of clear thinking and sound reason, its actions at times appear to be inspired by stupidity or madness ; the waste of effort and of happiness continues and will continue as long as social relations are conceived as the work of individuals coming only at moments into contact with each other.

Yet, in Germany, there has been a stronger determination to follow the dictates of reason and ensure effective co-operation, even at the price of State supervision or control, in the organization of production and marketing, in the contribution of industry to the economic development of the State, than in any other country. Theorists like Rathenau or Max Weber may differ in their conception of the economic and industrial cosmos and approach the problem of the individual within the nation from different angles, but they unite in recognizing that pure individualism, the doctrine of undiluted *laisser-faire*, has no place in the modern world. Order out of chaos, co-ordinated progress within the State in the place of anarchy and internecine competition—these are the first articles in the German industrial and social creed. We may find magnificent visions distorted and confused by warring groups and fierce moments of passion, but the vision persists : it is the inspiration of the social philosopher as well as the industrialist, even if, in the latter case, it can be obscured by the thought of temporary gain and bitter struggle with labour. The recovery of German industry may be seen as the victory of a mode of thought, of an industrial and social philosophy which worked in an atmosphere far removed from that of *laisser-faire*, even as much as in the technical and manufacturing enterprise of the great industries.

CHAPTER XVI

LABOUR AND THE TRADE UNIONS

Labour in the national economy—cartels, trade unions and the employers' federations—the power of labour—policy of trade unions —principles enunciated during revolution—the collective agreement and the abolition of the " open shop "—Works Councils—National Economic Council—conciliation and arbitration—unemployment insurance—eight-hour day—the constitution and membership of the trade unions—co-operation between capital and labour.

THE rapid forward movement which took place in the organization for production of German industry, spectacular at moments as it may have appeared, had the vitality and force of a machine coming into action. It would be dangerous to enumerate every constructional detail, follow the play and inter-play of the moving parts and admire the efficiency of the machine alone. Or if a drama were to be elaborated on the theme and magnificent scenes of lifeless machinery working in symmetry with no human control visible anywhere—a new version of " Metropolis "—were to fill the stage, the sense of incompleteness, of stiffness, of alienation would persist and ruin its æsthetic or even moral effect. The story of German industrial organization is not ended with the elaboration of trusts or the evolution of cartels : the most powerful trust or the most closely united cartel would cease to function if the human forces in it were to become paralysed or refuse to co-operate ; one cannot, even in this age of advanced mechanical experiment and of automatic control, dispense with labour or inspired leadership altogether.

While, therefore, the machine was being perfected and assembled in an immense productive unit, the human element was also being organized on a basis of corporate effort. Employers' associations came into being at the one end and trade unions at the other, with the organization for production held in position between them ; a struggle between capital and labour meant paralysis of the latter, while effective co-operation was essential to smooth working. The motives inspiring employers' federations, such as the Central Association of Employers in the Metal-Working Industries, the Coal-Owners' Association, the Textile Employers' Union, the Union of Iron and Steel Industrialists, were the same as those active in the formation of trade unions. Strength brought into balance with strength, co-operative effort against co-operative effort, power held in place by power, capital against labour—such is the impression given by German industry.

The organization for production covered, therefore, three groups, each complementary to the other and very similar in constitution, and industry became an organization of three members working together. In the cartels, capital was alone represented, with the exception of the central councils created by legislation for the coal-mining and potash industries, and dealt, without interference from labour, with problems of marketing and price, but it bore a definite responsibility to labour ; its success was dependent on stable and prosperous working conditions, its failure might be the occasion for strife and industrial unrest leading to economic ruin. The analogy between the cartel and the trade union or the employers' federation remained. Friedrich von Weiser, in his *Theorie der gesellschaftlichen Wirtschaft*, has given the true definition of the relation between all three forms :

" Through the elimination of competition, the workers' organization has the outer appearance of a monopoly, none other than a cartel covering all the workers in the branch of production in question."

" When we compare, however, the workers' organization in function and effect with a selling cartel which stands in a monopolistic relation to the consumer, we discover profound differences. The cartel stands opposite to the unorganized consumers, but the workers' organization is confronted by employers who, with reference to labour questions, have organized themselves into a monopoly ; the workers' organization has no control and no say in the matter of expansion or contraction of production, it has no power to divide up the market and classify the consumers, it must reckon with the conditions of production established by the employers ; while, finally, the cartel deals with the whole of production, the workers' organization deals with one only out of the many factors governing production. Through refusal to co-operate, it can paralyse the course of production and throw complementary factors out of gear, injuring consumers and employers in their most tender place, but the weapon it uses cuts in two ways and wounds labour itself. The strike does not only shut off wages from labour and make it difficult for labour to hold out, but labour is refused the limiting policy of monopoly, which allows employers to exact the highest possible margins of profit—it must reduce its entire selling effort as represented by its organization into terms of wages. It may divert part of its selling effort to other less-stocked areas, but it cannot reduce the volume of labour on offer, and its monopoly is definitely restricted."

Limitation of effort through reduction of the number of working hours would simply lead to limitation of earning capacity with no compensation in increased wages resulting from intensified demand. Shortage of labour might restore some version of a worker's monopoly as effective as that of the employer's and the cartel, but such a shortage could scarcely ever occur in a State like Germany, and labour would depend for its success merely on its capacity to cause severe loss to the employer through interruption of the course of production.

The perception that organization was essential to success and safety as much in the world of labour as of capital, and the knowledge that industry itself had evolved effective systems of production and price-control, led fairly soon to the formation of trade unions in Germany; the mentality that acquiesced in the cartel or trust without advocating the indissoluble rights of unfettered competition and free trade was the mentality that inspired the co-operation of workers in powerful groups. Yet we find that the recognition of a definite limit to bargaining power was also active in the labour world; the trade unions knew that the monopoly they had was built on foundations which never could be made secure, even under the most favourable conditions; that, compared with the cartel, they must always regard their organization as defective. They strove, therefore, to a greater degree than the British trade unions to avoid trials of strength and pitched battles, and relied more on peaceful negotiations with the possibility of direct appeal to the State for arbitration. They had direct interest in politics, since industry, through the growth of cartels and trusts, was fast becoming a State concern to be controlled as much as possible without elimination of private enterprise, and the State might justifiably use its power to clear away disputes— but they belonged to no one political party. Their officials, as deputies in the Reichstag, could well be members of parties radically opposed, but they would form a solid body of opinion when labour questions were discussed and State action was demanded, and serve to prevent union of all parties in the Reichstag against labour.

Through these characteristics, German trade-unionism distinguished itself from British; it was less aggressive and depended almost wholly on conciliation and arbitration, it desired industrial peace even at the price of a lower standard of wages than that obtaining in Britain, and it belonged to no set political party. It was able to send a considerable number of representatives to the Reichstag on more than one party ticket, but in industrial matters it eschewed political action and remained, in appearance at least, non-political.

When, therefore, the revolution broke out at the end of the war, the structure raised by a triumphant and all-powerful bureaucracy had fallen shattered, and all limits of control imposed by a capitalist system had been swept aside, the great body of trade-union labour was quite unprepared either in spirit or in desire to adopt a revolutionary policy and go forward on a campaign of insensate destruction. Even then, it was prepared to concur in some measure of constructive reform, where the old order would be retained with a greater measure of power granted to labour. It did not envisage the destruction of the capitalist system.

The main principles at issue during the revolution period, as they were enunciated by the People's Commissaries in November 1918, bore on three reforms which should be covered by legislation:

(a) The right of association on the part of labour and the legality of the strike weapon, even in the hands of civil servants, and, with it, the recognition of labour's claim to rank on the same level as capital;

(b) the fuller participation of labour in the administration and control of industry and the State, and, with it, the realization on a national scale of collective agreements affecting wages and the hours of labour;

(c) the introduction of the eight-hour day into all branches of production.

On these three principles the cause of labour has been fought, not unsuccessfully, since 1919. They represented a first great effort to achieve some organization which should be a parallel to the powerful organizations called into being by the employers and defend the position of labour against capitalist extremists, especially in the basic industries, where the employers, adhering to tradition, acted on the assumption that they also should be masters in the house without question or interference from labour. It is significant, however, that labour never entertained the idea of becoming predominant, of striking out for itself with the consequent dethronement of the employers;

although certain trade unions carried on their banners the motto—Nationalization of the means of production—they had no real desire to enter into the lists against capital.   They preferred to maintain some semblance of peace while they encompassed victory ; they preferred to retain the capitalist system, but to mould it to their own ends.   In the midst, therefore, of a wild period in the affairs of labour and the State, when political strikes were the order of the day and the official strike was (apparently) a thing of the past, we should rather search for achievement, for reality, in the elaboration of the new relation between labour and the State on the one hand and between labour and capital on the other.

Even before the war, of course, labour was already fairly well organized in trade unions, and had a close measure of unity, especially when the question of wages was under discussion. The " open shop " as understood in America had only a narrow range of application in Germany, although certain coal and ironmasters, like their Scottish compeers, imported cheap foreign labour to swell the ranks of surplus workers and keep down the level of wages.   During the war, something approaching to " open shop " conditions obtained, trade-union rights and restrictions were temporarily abolished, distinctions between unskilled and skilled workers were brushed aside, and effort was concentrated wholly on production without reference to hours of labour or wage margins.   It is significant that one of the first actions of the People's Commissaries was to abolish these war-time measures and restore all the liberties and privileges enjoyed by labour prior to the war.   The trade unions had had sufficient experience of the " open shop " system to hate it very thoroughly even in a modified form, and the employers themselves had little sincere liking for it ; they had been accustomed to co-operative action and orderly progress within their own organizations, either as cartels or as employers' federations, and recognized that the main advantages of the cartel as against unrestricted competition lay above all in stability and co-operation.   There was little necessity to cut down production costs merely to obtain individual advantages, such as might have occurred in a world of open competition ; the tariff and the cartel between them made for solidarity of interests.

While, therefore, employers as a class had no particular interest in satisfying entirely the claims of labour, they had less interest in attacking labour piecemeal.   It was simpler and easier to bring labour into contact with the employers in one organized group throughout an entire industry or branch of

industry.   During the revolution, the absolute independence
of labour was not a main debating issue as much as the attri-
bution of greater authority to organized labour, so that it
would rank *pari passu* with organized capital.   The employers,
in turn, recognizing that politically labour was in the ascendant
and must be conciliated, lent itself to the principle of more
effective co-operation with it.

The foundations of the new order were provided by the
collective agreement as arranged between employers and
workers in a national or regional system rather than an individual or local, and by community of administration and control of industry between capital and labour.   The collective
agreement could only be made between representatives of the
workers, with sufficient authority to act on behalf of an entire
industry, and the corresponding employers' federation.   As
such, it was the most powerful weapon in the hands of the
trade unions in their campaigns to extend their membership
and include all ranks of labour, both manual and salaried employees, and the fact that no agreement which would have legal
sanction could be made except between the unions and employers' federations was sufficient inducement for the worker
to join the central organization and remain loyal to it ; the collapse of the trade unions would bring with it the collapse of the
collective agreement and all it meant for stable conditions of
wages and employment.   The introduction of the principle led
at once to expansion and consolidation of the trade-union
movement, and it has never since been seriously challenged.

Every industry has been organized, as far as labour conditions are concerned, on the collective agreement system, and
virtually the entire labour force employed in industry and
commerce depends on collective agreements with employers.
According to statistics compiled by the Federal Statistical
Office, the number of employees held in collective agreements
governing wages, hours of labour and other conditions totalled
11,139,863 at the end of 1926.   When we consider that the
health insurance returns gave for all persons insured a figure of
about 16,500,000, the margin remaining outside of the collective
agreement system is not very great ; the latter has been welded
into the national industrial life and will probably defy all
efforts to force it out.   The actual agreements dealing with
wages or hours of labour, as concluded in each industry or
section of industry, are not here in question.   The main point
at issue is the system on which such agreements have been
made.   So far, therefore, developments have been entirely

logical : production is fully organized, employers are fully organized, while labour has been able to move forward towards complete organization.

A further development has lain in the principle of co-operation with capital in production (*Arbeitsgemeinschaft*), also advocated with great enthusiasm after the revolution. On November 15, 1918, the General Committee of the trade unions, in association with the representatives of the most important trade unions outside of its control, concluded with the main federation of employers an agreement dealing with co-operation in production for the future. The essentials of the agreement were :

(*a*) Recognition of the trade unions ;

(*b*) Complete freedom of association ;

(*c*) The Works Association (i.e. of employers and employees) should be self-sufficient without support from outside ;

(*d*) Engagement of all demobilized workers ;

(*e*) The common regulation and administration of employment on a basis of equality ;

(*f*) The determination of collective agreements covering labour conditions ;

(*g*) The formation of a Labour Council in works employing more than fifty workers to supervise the fulfilment of agreements ;

(*h*) The introduction of the eight-hour day ;

(*i*) The creation of a Central Council of employers and employees to control demobilization and deal with economic problems, and the conclusion of similar agreements between employers and salaried or staff employees.

The agreement was signed by the central association on both sides, by the trade unions and the federations of employers, such as the Coal-Owners' Association, the Association of Iron and Steel Industrialists and the Textile Employers' Federation. Certain writers have regarded it as the Magna Carta of German labour.

The organization of industrial and trade employers and employees, " imbued with the knowledge that the reconstruction of industry required the active co-operation of all economic and spiritual forces ", came together in a Central Joint Council (*Zentralarbeitsgemeinschaft*), which should aim at the " solution in common of all problems of an economic or industrial nature affecting the industry or trade of Germany ". The representation on the council was on an equal footing for capital and labour, and the leading industries, mining, iron and steel and engineering, chemicals and paper chief among them, would have each their Joint Councils, which would be united in turn in a State Joint Council (*Reichsarbeitsgemeinschaft*). The practical significance of the latter would lie in the determination of collective agreements and the application of arbitration to all disputes " when provision for this course was made in collective agreements ". For the trade unions, the new organization was the logical conclusion of the collective agreement principle, and, working out from this basis, the Central Joint Council began to deal with all economic questions, appointing special committees to deal with legislation and workers' insurance, the supply of raw materials, coal-production and transport, taxation and reparations.

The nucleus of all the developments recorded later, Works' Councils, National Economic Council (*Reichswirtschaftsrat*) and arbitration tribunals, is to be found in this conception of the Joint Council, and it has, therefore, much more than a purely temporary importance. In its original form, it suffered from the obstructionism of the employers, the irruption of a new type of trade union favourable to the employers and supported by them in its claim to representation on the Joint Councils, and the recognition by the trade unions that any programme of nationalization or socialization would strike immediately against such an association of capital and labour. We find, therefore, the Metal Workers' and Textile Workers' Unions dissociating themselves entirely from the Joint Council, which ceased to have any real functions. Its place was taken by a new movement with a different orientation. While the Joint Councils worked from the representation of industry by industry with a central State organization, the Works' Councils began with the individual firms and thence moved towards a regional organization, with its final representation in the National Economic Council.

The German Constitution provided for the creation of some system where wage-earners and salaried employees should co-operate with employers in fixing conditions of work and wages and in developing the economic strength of the country ; the workers' councils should combine to form district councils, which would join with corresponding employers' institutions to set up district economic conferences and a National Economic Council. There were thus three links in the chain, each necessary to the other, but, hitherto, only the first and third links have been forged, while the central and connecting link is missing.

The original conception held by the workers' councils during the revolution, namely, the participation of labour in the administration of industry and in the national executive when questions of an economic or industrial nature should be under discussion, became weakened and distorted in the process of conciliating all interests, and both the Works' Councils, as constituted by the Act of 1920, and the National Economic Council have remained almost wholly advisory and, therefore, largely ineffective.   According to the Act of 1920, two grades of representation were allowed : in small undertakings, the statutory Works' Council should have a labour representation of one or several works' stewards, but, in other undertakings, the number of labour members would be based on the labour force employed.   Both types of employee, the wage-earner and the staff, have each a group representation, small councils within the main Works' Council, and they form the negotiating body of labour as against capital.   In composite undertakings, such as a blast-furnace, steel furnace, rolling mill and engineering productive complex, located in the one area, a Joint Works' Council (*Gesamtbetriebsrat*) may be formed to protect the interests of all employees, in addition to the councils operating for each branch of production.

The main purpose of the Works' Council, as such, is to protect the interests of labour and ensure the fullest recognition of its claims, particularly in matters bearing on shop conditions, disputes between employees and the management, dismissals, sickness and accident and, in certain cases, wages and collective agreements.   The Works' Council has no power, however, to deal directly with collective agreements on wages or hours of labour, where such have been arranged through negotiation between the employers and the trade unions, but it may act in an advisory capacity, especially in relation to the trade unions.   In addition to this, members of Works' Councils have a right to nominate one or more directors on the board of management of a joint-stock company, a registered co-operative society, a medical insurance association, a State-controlled cartel as in coal or potash, and may also be represented on the board of a limited liability company.   These representatives act *pari passu* with other directors and have a voice in the management of the concern, but they remain necessarily in the minority and have no claim to function on special administrative or technical committees appointed by the board.   In this respect, capital and labour have not equal representation, and the Works' Council remains in a subordinate position. It has still, under the Conciliation Order of October 1923, the power to bring an action in the labour courts against the employers and, at the instance of the workers, demand arbitration. In the latter case, it has delegated very largely its powers to the trade unions.

The trade unions viewed the legislation of 1920 at first with no great favour ; they were afraid that such Works' Councils would tend to unite labour in a new organization apart from them, force them to abrogate their principal functions and reduce them to ineffectiveness. At the very beginning, in 1919, they claimed that the Works' Councils should be linked up with the trade unions and, supported by them, carry out the new democratic administration of industry. They recognized that all the labour employed in production was not organized in trade unions, and that the representation of all labour on the Works' Councils would tend to divorce the latter from them and encourage employers to negotiate direct with them to the exclusion of the trade unions. They demanded, therefore, that the selection of the Works' Councils should take place only in works where a collective agreement was in force (i.e. in trade union shops), and that in small works, a trade union official should act on behalf of the workers. Later, however, the trade unions formed loose associations with the Works' Councils, organized an alliance with them, and set up organizations of Works' Councils corresponding to the main groups in the trade-union movement. Thus central Works' Councils Federations (*Betriebsrätezentrale*) affiliated to the latter came into existence. The General Federation of Trade Unions and the Federation of Free Unions of Salaried Employees (*Allgemeiner Deutscher Gewerkschaftsbund* and *Allgemeiner Freier Angestelltenbund*) have been most active in this direction ; they have created district federations of Works' Councils and linked them up in turn in a Central Works' Council Committee for the whole country. The district federations are divided into groups corresponding with the main industries, and, in this way, a national organization to cover the whole of industry, horizontally and vertically, has been evolved. Similar policies have been adopted by the other great trade-union groups, the Christian and Hirsch-Duncker Unions. The Works' Councils, instead of being a cause of weakness, have developed into a powerful instrument in the possession of the trade unions in their struggle for equality with the employers' federations.

The creation of the National Economic Council followed on that of the Works' Council, and the Government, in the nomination of representatives, strove as far as possible to maintain a balance of strength between workers and employers, both in industry and agriculture, to ensure protection for the independent middle classes and include all forms of economic activity. A parliament of three hundred and twenty-six members came into operation in accordance with the order of 1920, agriculture and forestry accounting for sixty-eight members, industry for sixty-eight, commerce, banking and insurance for forty-four, handicrafts for thirty-six, transport and public works for thirty-four, civil service and the clerical profession for sixteen, while twenty-four members were appointed, half by the Government and half by the Reichstag, as legal, economic and technical experts. Since the Council represents, not only occupations, but also economic and social groups, the principle of equal representation of capital and labour has been adopted in the purely industrial and commercial groups, while the representatives of the clerical professions, the middle classes and social science constitute a third main division, nominally independent of both capital and labour in the narrow meaning of the terms.

The Council, from the beginning, was divided into three groups, capital, labour, and an intermediary professional group, instead of being brought into line with the conception of joint debate and joint action in the solution of important problems, and the proviso that, in all discussions, an individual vote should be followed by a group vote intensified the movement towards separatism. A group vote could only be a formal gesture dependent on the co-operation of capital and labour and, as such, it was possible only in cases where no vital principles were at issue. Consequently differences arose almost at once between capital and labour, and only the conciliatory action of the third professional group was able to restore order and give an air of reality to the proceedings. The delegation of powers to separate committees of investigation has provided one method of avoiding unnecessary and time-destroying discussion : two main committees, each of thirty members, exist to deal with economic affairs and social policy respectively, but, in addition to them, other committees have been formed from time to time to deal with specific questions, and the transactions of the National Economic Council represent important contributions to the study and knowledge of German industrial and economic conditions.

The fact, however, that this parliament has no real constitution at law with definite powers, that its functions are wholly advisory and that it cannot enforce its decisions on the Reichstag, tends to weaken seriously its status and render it ineffective. Even its right to examine and approve all Bills or Reichstag proposals bearing on industrial and economic questions has not always been recognized by the State Departments, such as the Post Office, and Government officials as well as members of the Cabinet have often referred questions of an economic or technical nature to independent experts instead of consulting the experts associated with the Council. Like the Works' Councils, the national body has little real executive power, and it is only indirectly in touch with national conditions or national feeling : the district economic councils contemplated in 1919 as connecting links between local and national organizations have not been created.

The danger of the situation has been recognized by the trade unions especially, and they have aimed at completing the scheme as well as determining the exact legal status and functions of the National Economic Council. The resolutions passed at the Breslau Conference in 1925 are peculiarly significant in this connection. Six among the eleven resolutions passed bear directly and indirectly on the subject :

" The Congress demands of the Federal Government, the States and the communes :

(1) Full recognition of the trade unions which, as representing the labour forces active in the national economy, shall have equal rights with employers in the economic development and in the management of industry as laid down in Article 165 of the German Constitution (i.e. the Article creating Works' Councils and the National Economic Council) ;

(2) Earliest possible reorganization of the provisional National Economic Council into a definite and legally constituted economic parliament, and the speedy formation of District Economic Councils as laid down in Article 165 of the German Constitution ;

(3) The granting of facilities to workers to attend higher schools and participate in scientific and economic research, especially the study of the causes of economic crises ;

(4) The maintenance and increase of the public services owned and operated by the Reich and the State and the communes ; improvement of the standard of living and the supply of necessaries to the public by the aid of such services operated without profit ;

18

(5) The systematic support of consumers' co-operative societies, especially co-operative societies formed to increase production ;

(6) The strengthening of the rights of Works' Councils to share in the management of industry."

The trade unions have abandoned the more revolutionary articles of their creed, as elaborated during the revolution, and now insist on realization, by the State, of the advantages they obtained for themselves when the Constitution was being formed. Progress for them has meant consolidation of gains achieved rather than advocacy of Utopia, and they still see in the Works' Council principle, in the association with capital on an equal basis of strength and function, the surest possibility of growth in the future and the realization of a higher standard of prosperity for the whole country.

In many ways, the progress effected has been remarkable. Thus the Central Association of Consumers Co-operatives had affiliated to it, at the end of 1926, 1,071 Consumers' Co-operatives with a total membership of 3,180,723, while the total number of Consumers' Co-operatives registered stands now at 1,942. Dr. Loewenstein, Director of the Coal-Owners' Association, in his annual speech of 1927, gave interesting statistics relating to consumers' organizations connected with the coal-mines. At the beginning of 1924, thirty-three consumers' organizations with two hundred and seventy-three shops or branches were operating in the Ruhr, twenty-eight of them with one hundred and sixty-seven shops connected with the mines. In 1927, twenty-five of the mines' organizations with one hundred and seventy-five shops were in existence, with a total turnover of 30,000,000 marks. The two main co-operatives operating in the Reich, according to the same authority, had a turnover of 516,000,000 marks in 1913 and 1,000,000,000 marks in 1926, while the savings deposited with their associated co-operatives rose from 73,000,000 marks in 1913 to 170,000,000 marks in 1926. Even the employers were beginning to be alive to the significance of these figures.

In the adjustment of disputes through arbitration, Germany has advanced much farther than any other country in Europe, and we can attribute progress in this direction again to the ideas put forward during the revolution. It was inevitable that the principle of collective action and collective agreement, with its extreme form in the co-operation of labour and capital in the administration and control of industry, should have led to direct negotiation rather than to a bitter trial of strength.

Two powers did not contend here for mastery, but for some method of adjusting themselves to economic conditions. The Council of People's Commissaries ruled in December 1918 that collective agreements, which had become of paramount importance in the development of production within an industry and had covered certain districts, could be declared binding on all employers or workers in those districts engaged in the industry under survey, whether they were parties to the original agreement or not. Collective agreements made voluntarily between capital and labour could be given legal sanction.

Under the order of 1918, conciliation boards were set up in a number of districts to deal with disputes arising out of the interpretation or application of collective agreements ; each board consisted of six members, three representatives of capital and three of labour, nominated by the State from panels submitted by employers' and workers' organizations. Two representatives from each side were permanent and one temporary ; the temporary representatives were experts in the matter at dispute, and were chosen for their special knowledge. The chairman was permanent and neutral, nominated generally by the State. The jurisdiction of the board applied only to the district in which the dispute occurred, but in the event of an entire industry being involved and the disputes assuming national importance, the Ministry of Labour could carry out the work of arbitration direct. Proceedings by the conciliation boards might be initiated on appeal from one side, either by capital or labour, or, in special cases where serious economic disturbance was threatened, the board might take up the matter of its own accord and summon witnesses or experts to give evidence on the industry or firm in question. The conciliation board was bound to make an award when one of the parties at dispute refused to appear after being requested to do so, or to negotiate or to recognize the authority of the board. The award could not be legally enforced except where it was recognized by both parties ; awards made, however, regarding shop rules had legal force and had to be carried out.

The decrees of October 1923 abolished these conciliation boards, and established a new system with main points of similarity with the old ; the district principle was retained, but the districts were much larger and bore closer relation to the economic and industrial configuration of Germany ; the various States could combine and form joint arbitration boards and avoid the expense of separate organizations. Prussia had sixty-six boards, with the Ruhr entitled to ten, Bavaria thirteen, Saxony six, Thuringia six, Württemberg five, Baden four, Hesse three, Mecklenburg two, Bremen two, and Hamburg, Lubeck, Lippe, Waldeck and Strelitz one each. The chairman of each board was appointed by the State, without reference to the members of the board, and the old distinction between permanent and temporary members disappeared. Each district had, in addition, one permanent arbitrator, assisted, if necessary, by temporary arbitrators ; Berlin, the Ruhr, Upper Silesia, Lower Silesia, East Prussia and Pomerania constituted districts served by one arbitrator each.

The duties of the boards were to deal with disputes affecting groups of firms, entire industries or all the employees in a firm, but not with individual grievances, which could, as before, be handled by the Works' Councils. Proceedings could be initiated in the same way as in the old boards ; the chairman or the arbitrator tried, first of all, to bring both parties to agreement and, if this failed, set up a board with two members from each party under his chairmanship. The membership of the board could be extended if circumstances demanded. The presence of both parties was not essential to action being taken, and the example of the old boards was followed in this respect. Awards were not legally binding unless accepted by both, but, "if the settlement appeared just and reasonable with due consideration for the interests of both parties, and if its application was desirable for economic and social reasons," it could be declared binding ; it might not be modified or cancelled. Enforcements of awards, if they deal with wages or hours of labour, could be realized on appeal to the ordinary courts of law, since, as such, they could form part of collective agreements, but some method of evasion could be adopted, either by delaying tactics or by discovery of technical flaws. To make the new arbitration machinery fully effective, special labour courts were to be created which would deal with all matters arising out of industrial disputes without delay.

The importance of the arbitration system introduced by the Order of October 1923 lies above all in the fact that it is, in the last stage, compulsory, and, therefore, encourages agreement between capital and labour outside of arbitration boards ; it provides a weapon for use by the Government in enforcing industrial peace and maintaining a balance in equity between employment and trade conditions.

It is difficult to measure the benefits accrued from arbitration and conciliation since it came into force in 1919 in the old form and since 1923 in the new. Comparison of strikes and working days lost in strikes and lock-outs in Britain and Germany may afford some illumination :

STRIKES AND LOCK-OUTS IN GERMANY AND GREAT BRITAIN

Year.	Number of Working Days Lost :	
	Germany.	Britain.
1920	17,702,800	26,570,000
1921	26,316,390	85,870,000
1922	28,894,434	19,850,000
1923	14,583,907	10,670,000
1924	36,360,134	8,420,000
1925	17,113,886	7,950,000
1926	1,404,875	162,230,000
Total . .	142,376,426	321,560,000
Annual average	20,339,489	45,937,143

It is quite clear that Germany has suffered much less from labour disturbances than Britain. Adjusting the annual average to correspond with the number of employees, we find that Germany had less than one-third of the British loss.

Whether such a result can be attributed to conciliation methods alone, or to the influence of collective agreements, or to more effective co-operation between capital and labour, or to all three, remains a matter for speculation, but the achievement stands before us. The General Federation of Trade Unions stated that, in 1921, out of a total of 55,000 claims affecting 17,000,000 workers, 80 per cent. were settled through negotiation without intervention, and 20 per cent. through the action of the conciliation boards. The labour arbitration courts dealt in 1925 with 4,269 appeals, and, of this total, judgment was required in 1,213 cases, negotiations of some form or other accounting for the balance. In 1926, the corresponding figures were 3,801 and 1,153. About 30 per cent. of all appeals, therefore, were submitted to judgment and award. Conciliation and arbitration have taken firm root in German industrial life, and they form a guarantee for economic prosperity ; a trial of strength fought out with all the bitterness and misery of strikes and lock-outs can only mean loss both to employers and employees, and the truth of this affirmation has long been recognized.

A further move towards the close co-operation of capital and labour can be seen in the Unemployment Insurance Act of July 7, 1927, which came into force on October 1, 1927. Unemployment insurance has never been satisfactorily regulated in Germany, and a state of temporary repair has characterized legislation since 1919, when efforts were made to provide employment for demobilized soldiers and maintain them in some standard of existence. It was recognized even then that the State as such was responsible for the relief of unemployment and, in conjunction with the individual States and communes, it strove to administer relief ; it met one half of the cost and the States and communes the remainder ; the communes in turn were responsible for the administration of relief. A special Ministry of Labour was created to deal with the situation, and the Act of 1922, dealing with the formation of Labour Exchanges and the adoption of measures to combat unemployment, made the national position somewhat clearer. The Ministry of Labour controlled all the machinery used by the Reich, the States and the communes to regulate the labour market—the provision of labour, the placing of unemployed, educative measures, the elaboration of schemes of a productive nature destined to provide work, the supervision of closing-down or restrictive movements in factory employment as well as the local machinery created to deal with the unemployment problem. The Labour Exchanges controlled by the States were required to investigate the labour market, and they were founded for States, provinces and other large areas. Subordinated to them in turn were local exchanges, whose duties lay in bringing the supply of labour into line with demand and maintaining a state of balance as far as possible. Later legislation in October 1923 confirmed the position and duties of the Labour Exchange and devised a more reliable system of unemployment statistics.

With the new Act of July 1927, however, a genuinely national scheme was determined. A single State organization under the control of the Minister of Labour came into existence to deal with unemployment and unemployment insurance at the same time, and thus bring the national effort into one closely-knit system. The new body, the *Reichsanstalt für Arbeitsvermittlung und Arbeitslosenversicherung* was composed of three main groups—the local labour exchanges, the county or regional exchanges, and the central office. Each group was administered by central boards composed of representatives of employers, employees and public authorities in equal ratio. The last-named were nominated by the local council in the case of the communes, by the highest county or regional administrative bodies in the case of the States, and the two former groups by central organizations of employers and employees. The Board of Management in the State Organization (*Reichsanstalt*) consisted of a President assisted by ten representatives each of employers, workers and public authorities (States, provinces, communes), the two former to be chosen by the employers' and employees' section of the National Economic Council, and the last by the Minister of Labour at the suggestion of the Cabinet. The Central Council of the State Organization, which governed the entire system, were composed in turn of a President and five representatives each of employers, employees and public authorities, the last to be selected from special panels prepared by the Board of Management. The public authorities had no voice (in any group, local or national) in unemployment insurance ; they were confined to questions arising out of the relief and notification of unemployment alone.

Beside these organizations functioned legal appeal bodies, attached to the local exchanges, county or regional exchanges respectively, which would hear claims against the findings of the committee in charge of administration. Provisions for special sections or committees dealing with salaried employees as well as technical or professional questions might be made. To avoid as much disturbance as possible, the system elaborated in accordance with the Act of 1922 was taken over and made to function in accordance with the principles laid down in the legislation of 1927. Relief or prevention of unemployment was covered by the measures already adopted, but certain additional proposals were incorporated—namely, the granting of travelling expenses to unemployed and their dependents to allow them to take up work outside of their home district, the provision of equipment and tools, the allocation of special assistance during periods of training, the construction of institutions for technical and commercial education, the development of productive undertakings to absorb labour, and other measures aiming at the prevention rather than the financial relief of unemployment.

Unemployment insurance applied to all those registered under health insurance legislation as well as salaried employees who had an annual income of less than £300. The latter, in the event of their exceeding this salary, had the right to contract into the scheme. Apprentices with indentures covering at least two years were exempt, as well as workers not constantly employed in one job or employed in factories where an unemployment insurance scheme with higher benefits than those allowed in the national scheme was in operation.

The main point in the new Act, of very great ethical significance, lay in the legal recognition of the right of the worker to unemployment grants, provided, of course, he came into the category of legally unemployed as defined in the Act.   Eleven classes of wage-earners were defined : the lowest class with a weekly wage of less than ten marks entitled to unemployment benefit of six marks, and the highest with over sixty marks entitled to twenty-two marks.   Dependents were entitled to grants amounting to 5 per cent. of the standard wage in each class, but the total sum drawn could not exceed 80 per cent. of the standard wage of the two lowest classes, or 60 per cent. in the four highest.   A worker with more than sixty marks per week would be able to claim a maximum of 37.8 marks.   The period of benefit could not exceed twenty-six weeks, but, in special cases, it might be extended to thirty-nine weeks : contributions of at least twenty-six weeks in the twelve months previous to the application were necessary to recognition for benefit.

The funds for insurance were provided wholly by the employers and employees with no assistance from the State, the total contribution not to exceed 3 per cent. of the wages earned.   A reserve fund equivalent to the maintenance of 600,000 unemployed for three months was established through direct grant from the Reich and the States, and it had to be maintained at that level.   Certain other provisions dealt with short-time grants (where wages, in the event of short-time working, could be made up to not more than five-sixths of the full-time value) and with the control of unemployment, but the essence of the legislation is given.   As such, it constitutes one of the most important developments in the relations between capital and labour in Germany, and forms, perhaps, the most effective recognition of the part played by labour in the economic development of the German State ; it puts an end to the uncertainty and jerrymongering of eight years and defines in clear terms the responsibility of the State *vis-à-vis* both capital and labour.

Much had, in fact, been done since 1920 both in relief of unemployment and in the provision of labour, and a very considerable measure of success resulted.   According to Dr. O. Heinemann, the cost of social insurance, inclusive of health, accident, salaried employees and unemployment, was 1,248,000,000 marks (£62,400,000) in 1913 and 1,855,000,000 marks (£92,750,000) in 1924. Unemployment accounted in 1924 for 220,000,000 marks, but, in 1925–1926, it had risen to 439,000,000 marks (£21,950,000), and may be given as slightly less than this for 1927—not high figures by British standards, but sufficient to cause intensive study of the means by which unemployment should be prevented. In addition to the payment of relief direct, the prosecution of public works, such as the construction of roads and the elaboration of power systems, was adopted as one method of absorbing surplus labour : during the five years, April 1, 1920, to April 1, 1925, Prussia alone provided work equivalent to 80,344,000 days. At an average wage of six marks a day, this meant a total disbursement of 482,000,000 marks and the employment of at least 40,000 workers annually. In view of the fact that the winter of 1923 and early spring of 1924 represented the worst period, the Prussian State was probably giving employment at that time to not less than 150,000 workers. The guiding principle has been rather the preservation of the morale of the workers through effective assistance than the soulless dispensation of a few marks weekly over a counter in a labour exchange. The positive rather than the negative side of unemployment has borne special emphasis, both in policy and in action. In all these directions, the development of the collective agreement system, the nomination of Works Councils and the National Economic Council and unemployment insurance, labour has been able to record a very considerable advance, but in the important subject of hours of labour it has scored only a moderate success.

The question of the limitation of the working-day is closely bound up with the expansion of industry, and the strength of this industrial expansion in turn depends on the close co-ordination of labour and capital in a scheme of production based on the most effective system possible, both in economic utilization of economic resources and in satisfaction of social needs. The theory that production is the one dominating force in industry to which everything should be sacrificed—labour, capital, material and spiritual resources—has gradually given way to a greater belief in the power of scientific management to bring every factor in industry to bear on the development and expansions of the needs which industry alone can satisfy. In other words, the relation between industrial production and social needs is becoming more and more evident ; the possibility of exhaustion of labour in intensified production and the progressive deterioration of the main force within labour through this has now shown how important the conservation of labour itself is. The main tendency within industry has been towards greater specialization in certain branches and substitution of mechanical for human force where heavy labour is required. The workman tends to become less a manual labourer than a nerve labourer : he must be in a position to exercise constant nerve control and bring muscular effort into direct line with very delicate nerve excitation. Under such a system of specialization, the strain becomes intensified beyond the mechanical effort required in manual labour, and the efficiency of the worker remains at a maximum for a much shorter time. The old twelve or fifteen-hour day has become an impossibility under modern conditions, and the increasing specialization, consequent on scientific development and the application of methods of exact calculation and registration to machinery in almost every industry, requires greater intensity of work over a much shorter period. This intensity becomes only possible through limitation of the hours of labour.

The truth of this had long been apparent to the trade unions, and the eight-hour day formed perhaps the main article in their creed. Even before the war, they had striven through various agreements to limit the extent of the working day, but their efforts were not altogether fruitful. An analysis in 1913 of the various collective agreements in force showed that only 3·7 per cent. of the workers concerned had a working week of 50 hours or less ; 6·6 per cent., 50–52 hours ; 33·3 per cent., 52–54 hours ; 11·7 per cent., 54–56 hours ; 12·2 per cent., 56–58 hours ; and 32·5 per cent. over 58 hours. The introduction of the eight-hour day would be tantamount under these conditions to an industrial revolution. The order made by the Council of People's Commissaries in November 1918, signed by Ebert and Haase, introduced the eight-hour day into German industry and trade, and it was followed by legislation in 1919. According to it, the working day should not exceed eight hours for all workmen and forty-eight hours per week. Night work should be kept at a minimum, and the half-day system on Saturday be introduced. In each week a rest of thirty-six hours, preferably between Saturday and Monday, was advocated, while, in works with continuous operation, regular shifts should be arranged, with extra pay for night work and work on Sundays. In dangerous trades a working day of less than eight hours was advisable in the interests of health and security. Women workers and youths between 15 and 18 years of age should not be employed more than six hours a day, without night work of any kind, and with a half-day free on Saturdays.

No legislation devoted entirely to detailed application of the eight-hour day between that date and December 1923 was formulated in Germany, and it is necessary to trace the movement through isolated agreements. In coal-mining, the working-shift was reduced to seven and a half hours and ultimately to seven hours ; in the railways, to eight hours, contained in a maximum of two hundred and eight hours per month. A Bill, presented to the Reichstag in August 1921, aimed at co-ordinating the various agreements made in different industries into a national scheme based on legislation. Although this project had not found direct application from the State, it described fairly closely the application of the shorter working day to German industry as a whole. In essentials the Washington proposals were retained, but exceptions and amplifications of considerable interest were made. In factories with continuous operation, where the sixteen-hour double shift was retained, the work should be arranged in such a way that an average of fifty-six hours per week for three weeks on end should not be exceeded. The working day for youths under 16 and female workers should not begin before 6 a.m., in double shifts before 5 a.m., and not go beyond 8 p.m. and in multiple shifts 10 p.m. Youths under 16 should not be employed between 10 p.m. and 5 a.m. Regular rest intervals after four hours' continuous work were recommended : in the case of workers under 16 years of age employed six hours daily, half an hour ; beyond six hours, one hour ; in the case of women beyond 16 years, half this period. According to pars. 12 and 18, youths over 18 might be employed during night shifts in coal-mines, but a rest of fifteen hours had to interpose between shifts. This exception applied also to iron and steel works, glass factories, and paper works, where interruption of operation was impossible. In supervision, in clearing away and putting into working order, or in carrying out of work preliminary to full operation, in the event of unusual accumulation of work (especially in seasonal industries, in industries dependent on the weather or agriculture) in certain branches of industry where night work was required to prevent decay of raw materials, to make good accidents or repair faults in manufacture, the working day might be prolonged practically *ad lib.*, provided the local *Gewerbe und Bergaufsichtsbeamte* (Factory and Mine Inspector) granted his approval.

The gradual neutralization of the shorter day can be seen

in this proposal, and its main clauses were adopted in German industry. The change towards a more fluid interpretation of the eight-hour day could be seen in the arrangement concluded between the German railwaymen and the State on August 5, 1922. The waiting period prior to actual work, previously calculated on a direct time basis, was reduced in calculation to a percentage of the working period—i.e. the eight-hour day became almost entirely eight-hours' work. This arrangement coincided with legislation on the same subject in France and Spain. The meaning of such a clause was obvious : the eight-hour day might conceivably in some cases extend to ten or even eleven hours. In mining, the demands made by the Reparations Commission led fairly early to prolongation of the working day in the Ruhr. A special agreement made on February 18, 1920, between the Ruhr miners and the State allowed for two extra half-shifts per week in addition to the daily shifts seven hours. The miners of Lugau-Olsnitz in May 1920 voluntarily surrendered the seven-hour day and adopted the eight-hour day to meet the scarcity of coal obtaining then in German industry, while, in August 1922, this arrangement applied to all mines.

The perception that the growth of the eight-hour day would cause less production and weaken the competitive power of German industry led to an attack on the whole principle by the leading industrialists, notably Stinnes and Thyssen. The opinion that imposition of a longer day on German labour against the will of the trade unions would be economically unsound enjoyed the support of Robert Bosch in an article contributed to the *Soziale Praxis*. It would be impossible to carry through a law directly, but an arrangement similar to that made between employers and employees in the mines and railways, where the eight-hour principle became adjusted to meet special conditions, could well be applied to other industries. In this case, co-operation between capital and labour in the elimination of the eight-hour day in all but name would be carried out with the consent of the trade unions. Such a system would give the union leaders themselves a feeling of responsibility not only towards the State but also towards capital.

The party most opposed to the eight-hour day applied indiscriminately has been undoubtedly the Majority Socialists. While advocating retention of the eight-hour principle, Kaliske, one of their leaders, advocated abolition of the indiscriminate eight hour during a discussion round the proposal to extend the eight-hour day till October 31, 1922, while there were some noteworthy passages in an article contributed to the *Sozialistische Monatshefte* :

" We are working now on an exhausted and impoverished land, with a productive apparatus limited in development and scope, in spite of apparent dividends and profits, and with a labour capacity much below that of 1913."

The loss of time involved in the imposition of the eight-hour day is estimated by Schippel:

" Merely taking industrial workers into consideration, the number of whom was given by the Census of 1907 as 8·59 millions, and can now be estimated as about 9 millions, the daily loss amounts to 18 million working hours or 5,400 million working hours per year. This equals two and a quarter times the reparations levy calculated by Rathenau, i.e. 1·5 milliard gold marks."

Such a method of reasoning was based on too many assumptions, chief among them being the direct reduction in the quality and volume of production to correspond with the reduction in working hours. When we consider that many works located in the Rhineland reached a total production equalling, if not surpassing, the pre-war level, and that the efficiency of the more highly-skilled workmen in certain industries, especially electrical engineering, was fully as good as during any previous period, the objection put forward by Schippel had scant validity.

The opposition made by the great industrialists, especially Thyssen, rested on a surer basis. The example of the Ruhr in increasing its output from 305,000 tons to 340,000 tons per day and in supplying German industry with its most essential material at a time when reparations were depriving it of its life force could well be adopted in other essential industries. It was no longer a question of capital and labour, of industrialists and trade unionists, but of the integrity of the nation under a crushing burden of debt imposed on it from outside ; German capital did not in itself desire restoration of the longer working day, but this was alone the safest and most effective method of restoring the national credit and rendering the position of the worker himself more endurable. No indication was given, however, of the way in which this sacrifice could become immediately beneficial to the State and not to a large industrial combine.

The Stresemann Cabinet towards the end of 1923 declared that the order of 1918 and the legislation of 1919 would cease to be valid as from November 17, 1923, and would be replaced by a new Act regularizing the position, which came actually into force on December 21, 1923. During this month, however, radical changes occurred in many industries, employers taking advantage of the serious trade depression to force the trade unions into compliance with their demands. In mining, as a result of negotiations terminating at the beginning of December, the shift of eight hours was taken as exclusive of the winding periods, and the effective working day became, therefore, nine hours. On December 13, the North-Western Group of the Association of German Iron and Steel Industrialists came to an agreement with the three trade unions, whereby the three eight-hour shift system in the Ruhr iron and steel industry was replaced by the two twelve-hour shift system, as it existed before the war. In blast-furnace operation, pre-war conditions were resumed.

The legislation of December 1923 constituted a revival of the proposals of 1921, weighted more heavily on the side of capital. Its main provisions were :

(1) In case shorter time than eight hours has been worked in an establishment on individual days, this loss of time may be made up by overtime work on other days of the same or a subsequent week.

(2) The eight-hour day may be exceeded in branches of industry or trades which regularly and to a considerable extent require mere presence on duty on the part of the worker (*Arbeitsbereitschaft*). In such cases, the hours of labour may be regulated by collective agreement, or, in the absence of such agreement, by the Federal Minister of Labour.

(3) The eight-hour day shall not be applicable to temporary work that must be performed in emergencies or to prevent deterioration of raw materials or the spoiling of products.

(4) Without prejudice to the exceptions provided under No. 3, employers may, after a hearing of the Works' Council, have their employees work overtime not to exceed two hours per day on thirty days, chosen by the employees, during one year.

(5) Male workers over 16 years of age may work two hours' overtime daily, and female and juvenile workers one hour daily, if employed in guarding the establishment, in cleaning or maintenance work necessary for the regular operation of the establishment or for the re-

sumption of full operation, in the loading or unloading of vessels or railroad cars, and in the switching of such cars (provided that the overtime is necessary to prevent traffic jams or to observe loading-time limits).

(6) If a collective agreement provides for daily hours of labour in excess of eight hours, the provisions of the agreement shall be binding upon those workers to whom the agreement applies.

(7) In establishments in which the hours of labour are not regulated by a collective agreement, overtime may, on application of the employer, be permitted by the factory or mine inspection service, subject to revocation, if such overtime is considered necessary owing to technical reasons, especially interruptions of operation due to *force majeure*, accidents, etc., or owing to general economic reasons.

In all the cases in which overtime work is legally permissible, the daily hours of labour may not exceed ten. In branches of industry or in occupations involving special danger to the health and life of the workers (such as hard-coal-mining below ground), or in which the workers are exposed to the effects of heat, dust, poisonous substances, etc., or to danger from explosives, overtime work shall be permissible only if it is urgently required in the interest of the public or if long experience has shown that it is not harmful, and if it does not exceed half an hour per day.

In mines below ground, in shafts with a temperature of over 28° C. (82° F.), shorter hours of labour are to be fixed by collective agreement or by the mine-inspection service if no agreement is reached.

On the coming into force of the present decree, collective agreements which fix shorter hours of labour than those provided in the decree may be denounced on thirty days' notice.

The decree provides fines for first violations of its provisions and fines and imprisonment, or both, for repeated violations. Employers may not be punished, however, if they allow adult male workers to work in excess of the legally permissible hours of labour, provided that the employees work overtime voluntarily, that overtime is required owing to special circumstances and only temporarily, that the employer is not exploiting the necessity or inexperience of the worker, and that the overtime work in question manifestly does not injure the worker.

To all intents and purposes, the eight-hour day ceased to exist, and the action of the German Government in agreeing to wide deviations from the principle, especially in 1924, made the forces of reaction more powerful still. Collective agreements enacted in that year show the course of development : in Ruhr coal-mining, the eight-hour shift without allowance for winding time underground and the eleven-hour shift on the surface were determined ; in the Ruhr iron and steel industry, a week of fifty-eight hours, in Berlin and Central Germany, of sixty hours, in textiles, fifty-four hours, and in printing fifty-four hours, were fixed as the basis. Hours worked beyond these totals were counted as overtime and paid accordingly.

An investigation carried out by the General Association of Trade Unions in 46,122 works, employing 2,454,000 workers, showed that, during the period May 12–17, 1924, 45·3 per cent. of all employees were engaged on a basis of 48 hours or less ; 8·3 per cent. from 48 to 51 hours ; 33·4 per cent. from 51 to 54 hours ; and 13 per cent. above 54 hours. The position at that time could not be regarded as hopeless, but it had few reassuring characteristics, since, of course, trade depression cut down the range of the working week in many factories, which would have otherwise transgressed the forty-eight hour limit.

The first important step in the direction of progress was taken by the Social and Economic Committee of the National Economic Council on January 10, 1925, when they recommended that the Minister of Labour should issue an order classifying workers in blast-furnaces, coking and coal by-product plant among those employed in dangerous occupations and should require the introduction of the eight-hour shift principle as authorized by the legislation of December 1923. Such an order should come into force on January 1, 1926. The Minister of Labour decided on this course, as a result of consultation with the Cabinet, fixing the actual application of the new order at April 1, 1925. Even then, the resistance interposed by the iron and steel industrialists sufficed to make the order a dead letter, but the agitation against the sabotage of the eight-hour day continued, and on April 14, 1927, a new Act was passed amending and strengthening the Act of 1923. As such, it represents a victory for labour and brings German labour legislation practically into line with the aspirations of the trade unions. It was recognized quite frankly that existing measures allowed too much evasion and required stiffening up, and the economic reasons which justified in part the special exemptions allowed in 1923 no longer applied. The new Act practically restores the principles incorporated in the order of 1918 and the legislation of 1919 with the same range of validity. Coal-mining, iron and steel come under its jurisdiction as well as all other industries, and the Act provided, therefore, for the enforcement of the three eight-hour shift system in blast-furnace, coking and coal-by-product plant, as demanded two years previously by the National Economic Council. The iron and steel industrialists again resisted the new ordinance with the proclamation that, from January 1, 1928, they would close down their works. The Minister of Labour refused, however, to be shaken and adhered to the order that, from January 1, 1928, the three eight-hour shift must be introduced into the blast-furnaces and, ultimately, into iron and steel. Only in special cases could an additional six months be granted for the change-over, and the works requiring that concession would have to submit to supervision.

In principle, the eight-hour day is restored, the main exceptions being those noted in the 1921 proposals, and the labour situation may now become much more stable. With hours of labour, representation on Works' Councils, and the National Economic Council, unemployment insurance and the collective agreement firmly established, the German Trade Unions could regard the ten years elapsing since the Berne Congress of 1917, where the programme of German labour was first indefinitely elaborated and discussed, as years of difficulty and varying fortune—culminating, however, in a real measure of success. The more reactionary elements in the ranks of capital might look on such an achievement as the beginning of industrial and economic ruin, but the main mass of German capital as well as labour must be relieved at the prospect of a measure of genuine industrial peace. Strikes will undoubtedly occur, since reason is not always in the ascendant and the forces of tradition are not always acquiescent, but, in the labour as in the industrial sphere, the future bears promise.

The organization of labour in the trade unions must be regarded as a logical development in modern industry. Even if the workers had little inclination towards joint action and had preferred the old personal relations between employer and employed to continue with the delightful feeling that he was co-operating in the success of productive enterprise, the growing impersonality of the industrial undertaking, the diffusion of ownership and the delegation of responsibility caused by the introduction of joint stock and limited liability companies forced him into more effective organization.   Labour recognized that, confronted with the huge industrial concerns, only united effort could make good its claim to fair treatment in wages and in conditions of production generally, that employers had already come together in the cartels or trusts and were no longer in competition throughout an industry.   Again, federations of employers could only be met by federations of workers with a common policy and a united front.

Trade Unionism was already fairly well developed before the war, and the three main groups of trade unions counted in 1913 over 6,000,000 members spread over all industries ; the war itself, with its special legislation abolishing all restrictions and limiting severely the range of action of the unions, reduced their number, but the reaction of 1918, accompanied by enthusiasm for a new social order, swelled enormously both the authority and the strength of the trade unions and made them, for a short time, the dominant force in the new Republic. Such they might have remained, if internal differences in political and economic opinion had not split the main groups asunder and caused them to neutralize each other as far as the exercise of political power was concerned.   At that time, the inherent weakness of trade-union policy and of trade-union structure became apparent.   The three groups—Free Trade Unions, Christian Trade Unions, and the Hirsch-Duncker Unions—did not correspond to any natural economic, political or territorial discussion ; they had affiliated to them unions dealing with a number of industries, some of them overlapping. Thus all three groups had mining and metal-working unions, and a strike in any of these unions might involve one group without the co-operation of the other two.   The differences are fundamental and are caused by the principles governing the constitution of each group.

If we examine them in turn, we may be able to explain more accurately the position.   In each case, the year 1919 constituted a year of reorganization and expansion ; the association of manual workers and brain workers, so long advocated as necessary to the solidarity of labour, became possible, though a change in the attitude of the organizations representing the salaried employees, and each main group had affiliated to it its organization or organizations of salaried employees.   Thus, from 1919 onwards, it. was possible to link up both sides of labour in one concerted movement.   The principal trade union group, the *Allgemeine Deutsche Gewerkschaftsbund* (General Trade Union Federation) represented perhaps the most extreme form of labour policy ; it stood for Socialism as against the capitalist system and supported the socialization plans put forward in the legislation of 1919 for the coal-mines, potash and iron and steel industries ; it worked strongly for the introduction and extension of the collective agreement principle as a first stage towards socialization. At the end of 1920, it counted fifty-two unions, and 8,032,057 members compared with 2,515,042 members in 1913. During 1921, the Central Association of Salaried Employees (*Zentralverband der Angestellten*) seceded from the union and crossed over to the General Free Union of Salaried Employees (*Allgemeiner Freier Angestelltenbund*), which became affiliated to the main group. A further move in the same direction lay in association between the latter and the General Union of German Officials (*Allgemeiner Deutscher Beamtenbund*) : all three groups were pledged to work together to further all social and economic developments touching on the interests of manual and salaried employees. At the end of 1921, all three groups counted seventy-four unions and 8,692,163 members—7,751,957 employees, 690,206 salaried employees and 250,000 officials.

A similar grouping of interests could be found in the second principal trade-union group, the Central Association of Christian Trade Unions. Its policy, as outlined in 1919, lay in preserving the industrial, professional and social rights of the workers and in overcoming " the materialism destroying our people, through the cultivation of social, Christian and national ideals ". It was essentially conservative in its outlook, and believed more in the peaceful solution of employment problems than in direct action ; it opposed the socialization laws of 1919, regarding them as a form of " capitulation to the general strike apostles of Berlin and Central Germany " ; it advocated more gradual methods of socialization and regarded the coal-mining Act as merely a nationalization of the Coal Syndicate, which would bring no benefit to the consumer or the public as a whole. The three main sections of employees, manual, salaried and officials, are represented in it by the Central Association of the Christian Trade Unions (*Gesamtverband der christlichen Gewerkschaften*), the Central Association of Unions of Salaried Employees (*Gesamtverband Deutscher Angestelltengewerkschaften*), and the Central Association of Officials (*Gesamtverband Deutscher Beamten-Gewerkschaften*). It contained forty-eight trade unions with a combined membership of 2,012,000 in 1921, the manual employees accounting for 1,029,000 members.

The third group, the Association of German Trade Groups (*Verband der Deutschen Gewerksvereine*), known generally as the Hirsch-Duncker Unions, issued its manifesto in 1919 to the effect that the Hirsch-Duncker Unions "distinguish themselves from the Free Trade Unions through their independence of all political groups and through their rejection of the social-democratic class-warfare idea, from the Christian Unions through their adherence to the principle of religious neutrality which they observe at all times, and from the yellow trade unions through the recognition that employers and employees are essentially different and must be organized in full independence of each other." They advocated free initiative wherever possible and were against socialization, although they recognized that the State must ultimately be the decisive factor in economic and industrial development. In the same fashion as the other groups, they absorbed, in addition to the trade unions proper, other unions of salaried employees and officials, forming with them the Ring of Workers', Salaried Employees' and Officials' Trade Unions (*Gewerkschaftsring Deutscher Arbeiter-, Angestellten-und Beamten-Verbände*). At the end of 1921, they had a total membership of 621,000 employees, among them 224,597 manual workers.

Beside the three main groups, other purely political unions existed—the revolutionary and communist organizations affiliated to the International, the Free Workers' Union, representative of the syndicalist movement, the National Association of German Unions or yellow associations created to maintain peace in industry and regarded with complete suspicion by the workers as instruments created by the employers to break up trade unionism. Inclusive of all trade union organizations, the number of workers organized in Germany at the end of 1921 could be estimated at 12,700,000, held in one hundred and fifty-eight unions or central organizations, the three main groups accounting for 11,325,000 members.

In 1922, when the trade-union movement had reached its highest point of development, over 70 per cent. of the employees engaged in industry, transport, commerce and public administration (if we can use the health insurance totals as a basis) were organized ; in industry alone, the proportion reached 80 per cent. The power of the trade unions appeared to be unshakeable and the future was bright. Changes in trade, however, defied optimism ; unemployment figures which, from a total of 1,076,368 in February 1919, fell, with certain seasonal fluctuations, notably in the winter of 1920 and the early spring of 1921, to a record low figure of 11,700 in September 1922, and connoted, therefore, a period of rising prosperity for labour, began to increase rapidly from that time onwards. Inflation had stimulated the market beyond the economic point of balance ; the exhaustion of the capital of the country and the loss of financial reserves resulting from the depreciation of the mark began to affect adversely the demand for industrial products, and labour suffered. The invasion of the Ruhr at the beginning of 1923 intensified the movement towards depression, while the introduction of gold currency in September prior to the foundation of the Rentenbank and the issue of Rentenmarks brought unemployment to a critical stage.

In November 1923, 28·2 per cent. of all the members of the trade unions were unemployed. From January 1924 onwards, a slight improvement set in and continued until June 1925, when only 3·5 per cent. were wholly unemployed, but the situation grew worse again, and by January 1926 the high figure of 22·6 per cent. was reached. All through 1926 the depression continued and made that year, from the trade union point of view, the most disastrous in German post-war economic history. It was only in April 1927 that the cloud lifted. During almost five years the trade unions had to face abnormal industrial conditions, their funds reached exhaustion and they were unable to meet the strain placed on them as fully as the workers expected ; unemployed, on resuming work, made little effort to renew their membership of the unions surrendered during the depressed periods, and there was little surplus available to cover trade-union contributions. In addition to this, much that trade-union policy stood for, namely, the Works' Councils, the National Economic Council, the eight-hour day and unemployment insurance, had already been granted by the State, albeit in a modified form, and the trade unions were divided on the question of nationalization of essential services and the basic industries. There could be little left for active discussion and propaganda which would infuse life into the trade-union movement and allow it to retain its hold on German labour.

The three main groups, which had a total membership of 11,325,000 at the beginning of 1922, could show at the end of 1925 only 6,075,101 ; the revolutionary and syndicalist unions had declined from 250,000 in 1922 to 63,586 at the end of 1925 ; the yellow associations had, however, increased slightly from about 190,000 members at the end of 1920 to 247,173 members at the end of 1925, while the independent federations had lost over 50 per cent. of their membership during three years—i.e. from 340,000 in 1922 to 166,690 in 1925. During 1925 a slight downward movement took place, but the situation is now practically stable, and the beginning of prosperity during 1927 may well mean a new period of expansion. Organized labour is now numerically less strong than disorganized labour, but it still dominates the leading industries, and the disputes at the end of 1927, when the employers refused to introduce the three eight-hour shift principle into the iron and steel industry and were forced to conform to the new legislation, is proof that the unions can still maintain a strong fighting effort ; similarly, in the Central German Brown-Coal and the Ruhr textile disputes of the autumn of 1927, the workers showed complete solidarity.

The fact, of course, is that labour conditions are rapidly improving ; wages, as a result of collective agreements, have risen in a straight line since January 1924 ; the average weekly wage of a skilled worker was, in 1927, 50 marks, compared with 28·45 marks in January 1924, and skilled labour, which remains essentially trade-union labour, has improved its position much more effectively than unskilled. Thus the latter averaged about 37 marks per week in the autumn of 1927, compared with 23·2 marks in January 1924 ; the balance of remuneration is becoming more just as between the two types of worker.

It is possible to elaborate still further the study of labour conditions in Germany ; wages alone constitute an infinitely varied and intricate problem ; the relations between employers and workers, the special forms employers federations and trade unions should take, and the part they should play in the development of cartels and trusts will always be a subject of discussion and careful investigation ; the problems of labour efficiency, of vocational education, industrial psychology and hours of labour have not yet met an economic solution ; the effect of rationalization on unemployment and wages must always be open to controversy, while the purchasing power of wages, as expressed in commodities, and, with it, the function played by high-wage levels in stimulating consumption, will provide experts with innumerable theses.

We have outlined those developments which contributed above all to the economic expansion and consolidation of the German Republic, those formative elements which were active in the world of labour as much as in the world of capital, those enthusiasms and far-reaching plans of reform which inspired the nation even during periods of severe crisis and brought it through with no loss of morale or constructive vision.   The days of Rathenau lie far behind, and his conception of a scientifically ordered economic state has been overshadowed by the achievement of years of compromise, but the intention remains. Even at their worst moments, neither the industrialist nor the worker obeyed blindly a shibboleth or surrendered reality for a cloudy perfection ; to the extremist on either side, the history of labour in the post-war years has little of the dramatic or the spectacular in it, it thrills with no struggles for existence between capital and labour, such as we have witnessed in Britain in the coal industry, but, on the other hand, it has never fallen to the dullness and stupidity of inaction.   The German State, industry and labour together, have striven to realize some conception of economic progress resulting from co-operation rather than from strife.   The influence of reparations may have contributed in no small measure to such a result, and the collapse of the mark brought the whole nation into contact with bare realities.   It was tried in a furnace and emerged stronger and more determined ; it had shed all inhibiting traditions and shown prejudice to be mere tinsel with no permanent worth. The love of organization has persisted and has already welded the economic forces of Germany, capital, labour and finance, into one powerful complex, which, in time, will act with complete efficiency.   In that lies the hope of Germany and of the labour and capitalist forces active in it.

CONCLUSION

THE NEW GERMAN ECONOMIC STATE

Towards prosperity—social service—national duty and welfare—
the State and *laisser-faire*—economic recovery—finance and reparations—industrial organization and labour—science and research—
the future.

FEW things are so complicated and so difficult of comprehension as those changes which take place in the economic life of a country. One may, in the spirit of a
scientific investigator, place phenomena beside phenomena and,
in this way, form a pattern bearing some resemblance to reality.
Yet such a method may have its drawbacks, since, of course,
analysis can never be entirely adequate for what is, in essence,
dynamic. The mere registration of events may serve one purpose, but it is at least doubtful whether such a purpose can
correspond with our ideas of scientific accuracy. It is, of
course, a comparatively simple method of surveying vast subjects without being implicated in an immense complexity of
cause and effect, and facts, as such, must always come to the
rescue, sooner or later, of theory.

In surveying, however, political and economic changes that
have occurred in a country like Germany, one must look for
certain fundamental movements beneath the intricate texture
of fact, as recorded either in statistics or in political speeches
or in the relations between capital and labour. The whole life
of a nation is coming into expression, and only by the capacity
to appreciate every subtle change of purpose or of meaning in
such an expression can the historian do justice to his theme.
This, of course, is not a new point ; it has been elaborated in
great detail by Max Weber. No one can even pretend to assess
at their proper value all the factors which have gone to the
making of Republican Germany. Politics in isolation represent
only one phase, and not, at times, a particularly important
phase, while economics may also deal with only one phase, at
times even less important than the political. In addition to
this, intellectual, philosophical, æsthetic and artistic qualities

296

are at work, creating and modifying both the individual and the national mode of life.

At best, therefore, even the most carefully detailed study can be merely a bridge to knowledge, and not knowledge itself ; its significance is relative in the widest sense of the word, and the conclusions derived from it are almost wholly speculative. Even paraded with all the splendour of authority and apt quotation, it can only be regarded as a shadow obscuring reality —reality which will always escape us. We may trace out certain fugitive silhouettes and follow certain lines in the hope that a picture will ultimately emerge ; we must content ourselves still with the suggestion, and hope that it has some measure of balance and of artistic truth.

Germany, of all the great industrial countries, represents perhaps the most intriguing problem of to-day ; it has gone through vicissitudes which have had no parallel in those experienced by other countries ; its future remains a cause of keen interest and, in some cases, of anxiety to all the countries comprised in the European economic unit. It remains, therefore, an object of speculation not unmixed with envy or with fear ; efforts made at the Treaty of Versailles to arrest the strong upward movement in industrial and economic Germany have been shown, after six years, to be wholly futile. The bankruptcy of the war mentality and the war conception of international relations has coincided with the economic recovery of Germany and the entrance of that country as an equal into the League of Nations. What then remains ? Is it of advantage, both politically and economically, to the rest of the world that Germany should be once more fully productive and fully prosperous, or is such a consummation to be avoided as entirely unwise and dangerous ? At one time, the answer to this question might have been decided without reference to Germany, and, until the entrance into operation of the Dawes Plan, there was strong evidence for the belief that the recovery of Germany was not desired.

Now, however, the situation has changed. Any attempt to arrest such an upward movement must involve practically the whole economic and trading system of Europe and the world. Germany is now in a much stronger position than it has been since the outbreak of hostilities, and it is a position which cannot be easily shaken. It would be advisable, therefore, to take cognizance of the fact, and study, step by step, not only factors or methods which have contributed to such a result, but also the possibilities of active co-operation between the great industrial countries in the furtherance of the economic prosperity of the world as a whole.

Certain elements in the development of Republican Germany, as illustrated in its political and economic history, may be distinguished as of special significance. First of all, the conception of the part played by the individual and the State itself taken as an economic and industrial entity has assumed a different complexion in Germany to that in almost any other country. Emphasis on individual effort, on individual enterprise, on the absolute liberty of the individual, has never been a factor of importance either in German political or economic life. The social state has been regarded as effective co-operation of all individual effort which will make for a higher standard of living and material prosperity. Organization and progress within order have higher values than the genial efforts of an individual striving to create a world in his own image ; everything is reduced to calculation and infinitely patient research, but, through combined effort, progress is achieved on a wide front and the strength of the country is increased. With this entrance of corporate effort has come the realization of economic and industrial values, clearly outlined and clearly interpreted for themselves alone ; tradition and prejudice may still play a part, especially in the older industries, where something like a dynastic rule has obtained for many generations, but such factors are not allowed to interfere fundamentally with the proper conduct of industrial and economic relations. There is no triumphant affirmation of a will to conquer at all costs, at least inside Germany, and the fight to a finish is regarded as an anachronism in industry.

All through the economic complex of Germany, as represented by organizations of employers and of labour, by cartels and trusts and central economic councils, we find this recognition of definite values. To our mind, the German Republic, as represented by a highly organized industrial State moving forward, with every section carefully mapped out, with all disruptive forces neutralized, has something repellent in it ; it comes too close to the machine and lacks soul. Viewed from certain standards, there may be justification for such a feeling of repulsion ; organization may coincide with the solidification of those dynamic forces which make for progress. It may cause a static condition, but this can only occur if the spirit within the organization has lost vitality and the power to measure consequences. There are certainly no signs of a failing in this spirit in Republican Germany. There are limitations to German ability in the economic and political world, both in politics and in finance, where organization is not so much a factor of importance as intuition and the lessons of experience.

The German Republic has known moments of weakness verging on crisis. The mentality, which finds in industrial and technical problems a sympathetic range of effort, is not generally the mentality suited to political or financial manœuvring. In finance especially, international complications enter very soon, and no national organization can be capable of dealing effectively with changes or developments, either adverse or favourable, in international financial markets. A high degree of intuition is required as well as a capacity to adhere to precedent. The economic situation of Germany did not lend itself to specialization in purely financial transactions; effort was always directed towards expansion of industry, and the result of such effort was the realization of a peculiar ability in dealing with industrial problems. Finance has been subordinated to industry and has been conceived as a direct aid to the latter rather than as an independent force existing by virtue of its own right.

Few of the formulae or even practices rendered favourable through constant application in the world of finance survived the period of inflation and of stabilization in Germany. Certain observers have regarded the financial policy of the German Government as a remarkably bold adventure, which belonged more to the world of speculation pure and simple than to the world of solid fact. The methods adopted bore some resemblance to those satirized in Hilaire Belloc's novel of a company promoter, " Emmanuel Burden," and they ended in loss. There is, however, an element of special pleading in such a situation; every combatant during the war banked on the possibility of victory and threw everything into the scrum; the losing side had nothing left to compensate for its losses, no reserves, and no real incentive to create reserves to cover the charges forced on it. Finance in Germany has always been admittedly an unsatisfactory feature in the economic situation, but one must regard the whole matter as highly artificial. Reparations obey political sentiment, but have no connection with economic laws or principles; on the contrary, they cut across all conceptions of international economic progress and are, in essence, a survival of a barbarous age in common with war itself.

The Dawes Plan, therefore, must always remain a centre of discussion and contention; no principles can be applied to its interpretation, at least in a future sense ; no one can tell whether it will continue in existence or collapse. Logic and clear reasoning based on examination of the facts at our disposal would lead us to the belief that reparations in any form cannot be incorporated in an international economic system ; they raise difficulties beyond control and they open up possibilities of crisis beyond computation. They are still purely a gamble and tend, therefore, to cause uneasiness in international trade. Reparations remain the most critical problem confronting Germany, but it would be a mistake to assume that the economic future of Germany is bound up entirely with the future of the Dawes Plan. A few years ago such an affirmation could have been made with a certain amount of reason, but the economic recovery of Germany has been so rapid and it has been able to bring to the realization of such a recovery so many elements of an international character (such as credits, loans and industrial participations) that, in the last resort, reparations would require to be sacrificed to the economic solidarity of Europe and the world. In this possibility of a struggle arising between the maintenance of reparations and the economic interests of Germany lies one of the most dangerous political situations of the near future.

In every direction we can find evidence of national effort : in science and research, in the application of technical developments to industrial production, in the closer union of labour and capital within the German economic system, in the prosecution of higher education and in the elaboration of international connections, both in the world of industry and of finance, important movements have taken place and will probably continue for a very considerable time to come. We have passed the stage where we can estimate the industrial prosperity of Great Britain merely in terms of the industrial inertia of Germany. The greater the activity and the sounder the industrial position is in that country, the greater the possibility is for Britain also to be prosperous. In a number of industries, such as coal-mining, iron and steel and chemicals, competition between the two countries is very keen, and the advantage has lain with Germany owing to the strength of its organization both for production and marketing. Certain authorities, following the traditional conception of Germany *vis-à-vis* Great Britain, have regarded it as the most powerful competitor confronting us in the markets of the world, and have been inclined also to regard Germany as an immensely powerful enemy in the industrial sphere which must be overcome.   Whether such a view will have any justification in the future remains to be seen.   Co-operation, as the experience of Germany has shown, is to be preferred to unrestricted competition, and co-operation between the two countries would, in the opinion of certain leading industrialists in the Republic, lead to a fuller measure of industrial and economic prosperity, not only for Great Britain and Germany, but for the world.

These are speculations which arise inevitably from any survey of the forces active in creating Republican Germany, as we know it now.   Behind the terse and, at times, arid commentary may be seen a background of intense effort, and this effort gives tone and significance to the whole scene.

BIBLIOGRAPHY

SOURCES OF INFORMATION

To supply a complete bibliography dealing with political and economic developments in Germany over the period 1914–1927 would require more space than the entire content of this book. At best, only a selection can be made. We can indicate, however, certain main sources of information which might be of value to those who desire to examine conditions much more thoroughly and in closer detail than we have done in our survey.

In the political sphere, the main sources of information are :

(*a*) Memoirs and sectional histories published by those public men who were responsible, both in the military and political spheres, for the policy of Germany.

(*b*) The political trials and investigations held by the *Reich* and the States into certain occurrences, such as those associated with Kapp, Hitler, and Kurt Eisner, as well as the war-guilt action, which took place in Munich.

(*c*) The official publications of the *Reich* and the States dealing with the war.

(*d*) Special studies published in the leading German reviews and newspapers, and certain documents given in foreign papers such as *L'Europe Nouvelle*.

(*e*) The *Geschichts-Kalendar*, published by Felix Meiner of Leipzig, and various *Handbücher* such as *Handbuch für Staatswissenschaft* and *Handbuch für Finanzwissenschaft*, etc., a feature of historical, political and economic survey, generally very well done, peculiar to Germany.

In economics, a similar arrangement of sources can be made. In this case, however, much more importance must be placed on direct documentary and statistical evidence, since any economic survey must be largely a chronicle of fact with a certain flavouring of theory. In addition to special studies which are enumerated later, the following sources are of value :

(*a*) Statistics published by the Federal Statistical Office, by the great industrial associations, trade unions, and by individual industrial companies. The *Statistiches Jahrbuch für das Deutsche Reich* constitutes each year a central storehouse of information dealing with every economic activity in Germany.

(*b*) The Transactions of the National Economic Council, the reports of the proceedings at the Cartel Court and the new Labour Courts.

(*c*) The annual reports of industrial companies, banks, railways, trade associations and cartels ; the annual reports of the Agent-General for Reparations, and the various committees appointed to deal with the German railway bonds, industrial debentures and the transport tax.

(d) Leading economic reviews and journals, such as :
    Weltwirtschaftliches-Archiv.
    Archiv für Sozialwissenschaft und Sozialpolitik. Neue Folge des Archivs für Soziale Gesetzgebung und Statistik.
    Jahrbuch für Gesetzgebung, Verwaltung und Volkswirtschaft im Deutschen Reich.
    International Labour Review.
    Der Deutsche Volkswirt.
    Wirtschaftsdienst.
    Wirtschaft und Statistik.
    The Economist.
  Technical journals, such as :
    Glückauf.
    Stahl und Eisen.
    Elektro-technische Zeitschrift.
    Elektrizitäts-Wirtschaft.

(e) Commercial and industrial sections of newspapers, such as :
    Deutsche Bergwerks-Zeitung.
    Berliner Tageblatt.
    Berliner Börsen-Courier.
    Frankfurter Zeitung.
    Hamburger Fremdenblatt.

(f) The publications of the International Labour Office, as well as the papers and monographs submitted to the Finance Conference at Genoa, the International Economic Conference at Geneva, and the Washington Conference.

There are other sources of information, in addition to these, bearing on the subject of the economic development of Germany, but the foregoing should suffice to provide all the material necessary for the most minute study.

HISTORICAL AND POLITICAL

Adler, M. : Politik u. Moral. (Leipzig, 1918.)
Allen, H. T. : The Rhineland Occupation. (Indianapolis, 1927.)
Angell, N. : The Fruits of Victory. (London, 1921.)
Aubert, L. : The Reconstruction of Europe. (Newhaven, 1925.)
Aulneau, J. : Le Drame de l'Allemagne. (Paris, 1924.)
Auschütz, G. : Die Verfassung des Deutsches Reichs. 6th ed. (Berlin, 1927.)
Max von Baden, Prince : Erinnerungen u. Dokumente. (Berlin, 1927.) English ed., 1928.
Bardoux, J. : De Paris à Spa. (Paris, 1921.)
Barth, E. : Aus der Werkstatt der deutschen Revolution. (Berlin, 1920.)
Baument, M. } L'Allemagne. (Paris, 1922.)
Berthelot, M. }
Becker, O. : Deutschlands Zusammenbruch und Auferstehung. (Berlin, 1922.)
Bergsträsser, J. : Geschichte der politischen Parteien in Deutschland. (Mannheim, 1926.)
Bernstein, E. : Die deutsche Revolution. Vol. I. (Berlin, 1921.)

Bethmann-Hollweg, T. v.: Betrachtungen zum Weltkriege. 2 vols. (Berlin, 1919–21.)

Bredt: Der Geist der deutschen Reichsverfassung. (Berlin, 1924.)

Brunet, René: The German Constitution (translation from the French). (London, 1923.)

Caillaux, J.: Où va la France? Où va l'Europe? (Paris, 1922.)

Cambon, V.: L'Allemagne Nouvelle. (Paris, 1923.)

Celtus: La France à Gênes. (Paris, 1922.)

Clarke, C. H.: Germany Yesterday and To-morrow. (London, 1923.)

Daniels, H. G.: The Rise of the German Republic. (London, 1927.)

Delbrück, H.: Krieg und Politik. (Berlin, 1918.)

—— Krieg und Politik. Vol. II. 1916–1917. (Berlin, 1919.)

Ebert, F.: Schriften Aufzeichnungen Reden. 2 vols. (Dresden.)

Erzberger, M.: Erlebnisse im Weltkriege. (Stuttgart, 1920.)

Fabre-Luce, A.: La Victoire. (Paris, 1924.)

Finger, A.: Das Staatsrecht der Verfassung des deutschen Reichs von August 11, 1919. (Stuttgart, 1923.)

Geutizon, P.: La Revolution Allemande. (Paris, 1919.)

Giese, F.: Verfassung des Deutschen Reiches. 7th ed. (Berlin, 1926.)

Glasgow, G.: From Dawes to Locarno. (London, 1925.)

Gooch, G. P.: Germany. (London, 1925.)

Gumbel, E. J.: Zwei Jahre politischer Mord. (Berlin, 1921.)

—— Verschwörer. (Berlin, 1921.)

Haenisch.: Die deutsche Sozialdemokratie vor und nach dem Weltkrieg. (Berlin, 1916.)

Hartmann, M.: Revolutionäre Erinnerungen. (Leipzig, 1919.)

Hatschek, J.: Institutionen des Deutschen Staatsrechts. 3 vols. (Berlin, 1926.)

Helfferich, K.: Die Politik der Erfüllung. (München, Berlin and Leipzig, 1922.)

—— Der Weltkrieg. 3 vols. (Berlin, 1919.)

Hertling, K. v.: Ein Jahr in der Reichskanzlei. (Freiburg, 1919.)

Hohlfeld, J.: Geschichte des Deutschen Reiches (1871–1926). (Leipzig, 1926.)

Honnorat, A.: Le Désarmement de l'Allemagne. (Paris, 1924.)

House, E. M. ⎰ What really happened at Paris.
Seymour, Ch. ⎱ The story of the Peace Conference, 1918–1919. (London, 1921.)

Jellinek, W.: Die Deutschen Landtagswahlgesetze (includes the Reich's Electoral Law). (Berlin, 1926.)

Kjellen: Die Ideen von 1914. (Leipzig, 1915.)

—— Die politischen Probleme des Weltkrieges. (1916.)

Klotz, L.-L.: De la Guerre à la Paix. (Paris, 1924.)

Kraus, H. ⎰ Chronik der Friedensverhandlungen nebst einer Übersicht
Rödiger, G. ⎱ über die Diplomatie des Weltkrieges. (Berlin, 1920.)

Lichtenberger, H.: L'Allemagne d'aujourd'hui dans ses relations avec la France. (Paris, 1922.)

Liefmann, R.: Vom Reichtum der Nationen. (Karlsruhe, 1925.)

Linnebach, K. ⎰ Die Sicherheitsfrage-Dokumentarisches Material. (Ber-
Montgelas, M. ⎱ lin, 1925.)

Maercker: Vom Kaiserheer zur Reichswehr. (Leipzig, 1922.)

Mann, R.: Mit Ehrhard durch Deutschland. (Berlin, 1921.)

Mehrmann, K.: Locarno, Thoiry, Genf—in Wirklichkeit. (Berlin, 1927.)

Meissner : Das neue Staatsrecht des Reiches und seiner Länder. (Berlin.)
Michaelis, G. : Für Staat und Volk. (Berlin, 1922.)
Milhaud, A. : La Reconstruction du Monde. (Paris, 1924.)
Mills, J. S. : The Geneva Conference. (London, 1923.)
Müller, R. : Vom Kaiserreich zur Republik. (Berlin, 1925.)
—— Der Bürgerkrieg in Deutschland. (Berlin, 1925.)
Niemann, A. : Revolution von oben—Umsturz von unten. (Berlin, 1927.)
Noske, G. : Von Kiel bis Kapp. (Berlin, 1920.)
Oppenheimer, H. : The Constitution of the German Republic. (London, 1923.)
Payer, F. v. : Von Bethmann-Hollweg bis Ebert. (Frankfurt, 1923.)
Pernot, M. : L'Allemagne d'aujourd'hui. (Paris, 1927.)
Pinon, R. : Le redressement de la politique française, 1922. (Paris, 1923.)
—— La bataille de la Ruhr. (Paris, 1924.)
Preuss, Hugo : Deutschlands republikanische Reichsverfassung. (Berlin.)
—— Reich und Länder. (Berlin, 1928.)
—— Das deutsche Volk und die Politik. (Jena, 1915.)
Quaatz, R. G. } Deutschland unter Militär-, Finanz- und Wirtschaft-
Spahn, M. } Kontrolle. (Berlin, 1925.)
Raab, F. : Die Verpflichtungen Deutschlands. (Berlin, 1927.)
Rathenau, W. : Briefe. (Berlin, 1924.)
—— Die neue Staat. (Berlin, 1919.)
—— Cannes und Genoa. (Berlin, 1922.)
—— Zur Kritik der Zeit. (Berlin, 1922.)
Reichert, J. W. : Rathenaus Reparationspolitik. (Berlin, 1922.)
—— Von Wilson bis Dawes. (Berlin, 1925.)
Rheinbaben, W. v. : Von Versailles zur Freiheit. (Berlin, 1927.)
Runkel, F. : Die deutsche Revolution. (Leipzig, 1919.)
Ruthenberg : Verfassungsgesetze des deutschen Reiches und der deutschen Länder. (Berlin.)
Salomon : Die deutschen Parteiprogramme. Vol. III (1918–1925). (Leipzig.)
Scheidemann : Der Zusammenbruch. (Berlin, 1921.)
Schmidt : Das neue Deutschland. (Berlin, 1925.)
Severing, C. : 1919–20 im Wetter u. Wattensinkel. (Bielefeld, 1927.)
Stier-Somlo : Deutches Reichs-u. Landesstaatsrecht. (Berlin, 1924.)
Stresemann, G. : Reden u. Schriften. 2 vols. (Dresden.)
Ströbel, H. : The German Revolution (English translation. London.)
—— Die Sozialisierung. (Berlin, 1923.)
Stümke, B. : Die Entstehung der Deutschen Republik. (Frankfurt, 1923.)
Temperley, H. W. V. : A History of the Peace Conference of Paris. (London, 1920.)
Toynbee, A. J. : Survey of International Affairs, 1920–1923. (London, 1925.)
Das Werk des Untersuchungsaussachusses. 4 vols. published. (Berlin, 1925.)
Die Ursachen des Deutschen Zusammenbruches im Jahre 1919. (A series of special studies.) (Berlin, 1926.)
Vanderlip, F. A. : What next in Europe ? (New York, 1922.)

Vermeil, E. : La Constitution de Weimar. (Strasbourg, 1923.)
Weber, A. : Die Krise des modernen Staatsgedankens in Europa. (Stuttgart, 1927.)
Wertheimer, F. : Deutschland, die Minderheiten und der Volkerbund. (Berlin, 1924.)
Willmayer : Die Weimarer Reichsverfassung. (Tübingen, 1923.)
Wirth, J. : Reden während der Kanzleizeit. (Berlin, 1926.)
World Peace Foundation Pamphlets : Reparations. (Boston, 1922–25.)
Young, George : The New Germany. (London, 1926.)

ECONOMIC AND INDUSTRIAL : GENERAL HISTORIES AND SURVEYS

Ausschuss zur Untersuchung der Erzeugungs-und Absatzbedingungen der deutschen Wirtschaft. (Berlin, 1927.)
Bonn, M. J. / Palyi, M. : Die Wirtschaftwissenschaft nach dem Kriege. (A series of essays by leading economists on the development of economic study and research). (Munich, 1925.)
Bruck, W. F. : Deutschlands weltwirtschaftliche Stellung in der veränderten internationalen Arbeitsteilung. (Leipzig, 1926.)
Dawson, Sir Philip : Germany's Industrial Revival. (London, 1926.)
Dis, Arthur : Wirtschaftskrieg und Kriegswirtschaft. (Berlin, 1920.)
Dresdner Bank : Die wirtschaftlichen Kräfte der Welt. (Berlin, 1927.)
Grundriss der Sozialökonomik. (Tübingen, 1920–1927.)
Kock, P. : Der Wirtschaftskrieg. (Berlin, 1919.)
Mercator : World Trade and World Recovery. (London, 1922.)
Price, M. P. : Germany in Transition. (London, 1923.)
Rogowski, E. : Das deutsche Volkseinkommen. (Berlin, 1926.)
Schmidt, A. : Das neue Deutschland in der Weltpolitik und Weltwirtschaft. (Berlin, 1925.)
Schmidt-Essen, A. : Die Kriegsbilanz für Deutschlands Industrie. (Essen, 1919.)
Schultze, E. : Ruhrbesetzung und Weltwirtschaft. (Leipzig, 1927.)
Statistisches Reichsamt : Deutschlands Wirtschaftslage unter den Nachwirkungen des Weltkrieges. (Berlin, 1923.)
Weber, Max : Wirtschaftsgeschichte. (Munich, 1923.)

REPARATIONS.[1]

Angas, L. L. B. : Reparations, Trade and Foreign Exchange. (London, 1922.)
Auld, G. P. : The Dawes Plan. (New York, 1927.)
Batsell, W. R. : The Debt Settlements and the Future. (Paris, 1927.)
Bergmann, C. : Der Weg der Reparation. (Frankfurt, 1926.)
—— History of Reparations (English translation). (London, 1926.)
Calmette, G. : Recueil de documents sur l'histoire de la question des reparations (1919–5 mai 1921). (Paris, 1924.)

[1] A bibliography of Reparations up to the end of 1925 has been compiled by Hermann Curth and published in *Weltwirtschaftliches Archiv.*, January, 1926, pp. 27–65. The books listed here are largely complementary to the bibliography and bring the subject up to the end of 1927.

Dawes, R. C. : The Dawes Plan in the Making. (Indianapolis, 1925.)
Fossati, E. : Il problema delle reparazioni nei suoi rapporti coll' economia germanica. (Pavia, 1926.)
Heinicke, G. E. : Die volkswirtschaftliche Erfüllbarkeit der Reparationsverpflichtungen. (Berlin, 1923.)
Keynes, J. M. : The Economic Consequences of the Peace. (London, 1920.)
—— A Revision of the Treaty. (London, 1922.)
Kuczynski, R. : Deutschland und Frankreich. (Berlin, 1924.)
Marsal, F. : Les Dettes Interalliées. (Paris, 1927.)
Meier, Ernst : Handbuch der deutschen Reparation. First Section (to be continued.) (Leipzig, 1927.)
Moulton, H. G. : The Reparation Plan. (New York, 1924.)
—— The Report of the Dawes Committee. (Chicago, 1925.)
Moulton, H. G.⎫
McGuire, C. E. ⎰Germany's Capacity to Pay. (New York, 1923.)
Parvus : Aufbau und Wiedergutmachung. (Berlin, 1921.)
Respondek, E. : Grundlagen u. Kritik des Reparations—Gutachtens. (Berlin, 1924.)
Simon, H. F. : Reparation und Wiederaufbau. (Berlin, 1925.)

SOCIAL HISTORY AND THEORY

Bauer, Otto : Der Weg zum Sozialismus. (Vienna, 1919.)
Beckerath, H. v. : Probleme industriewirtschaftlicher Sozialisierung. (Berlin, 1919.)
Bendix, L. : Bausteine zur Räteverfassung. (Berlin, 1919.)
Bernstein, E. : Der Sozialismus einst u. getzt. (Berlin, 1923.)
Heimann, E. : Mehrwert und Gemeinwirtschaft. (Berlin, 1922.)
—— Die Sozialisierung. (Tübingen, 1919.)
Kautsky, K. : Kriegsmarxismus. (Vienna, 1918.)
Kelsen : Wesen und Wert der Demokratie. (Tübingen, 1920.)
Liebknecht, K. : Grundzüge einer Marxkritik. (Tübingen, 1919.)
Luxemburg, R. : Gesammelte Werke. (Berlin, 1925.)
Meinecke, F. : Weltbürgertum u. Nationalstaat. (Munich, 1919.)
Plenge, J. : Der Kriege und die Volkswirtschaft. (Hildesheim, 1915.)
—— 1789 und 1914. (Berlin, 1915.)
Pohle, L. : Kapitalismus u. Sozialismus. (Berlin, 1919.)
Popper-Lynkens, J. : Die Allgemeine Nährpflicht als Losüng der sozialen Frage. (Vienna, 1923.)
Radek, K. : Die Liquidation des Versailler Friedens. (Hamburg, 1922.)
Rathenau, W. : Die neue Gesellschaft. (Berlin, 1919.)
—— Kritik der dreifachen Revolution. (Berlin, 1919.)
—— Autonome Wirtschaft. (Jena, 1919.)
—— Gesammelte Schriften. (Jena, 1918.)
Scheler, M. : Vom Umsturz der Werte. (Leipzig, 1919.)
—— Vom Ewigen im Menschen. (Leipzig, 1921.)
Schiff, E. : Vergesellschaftung. (Stuttgart, 1919.)
Spengler, Oswald : Der Untergung des Abendlandes. (Munich, 1920.) English edition, 1926.
—— Der Untergang des Abendlandes. Vols. I and II. (Munich, 1919–1921.)

Steiner, R. : Die Kernpunkte der sozialen Frage in der Lebensnot-
wendigkeiten der Gegenwart u. Zukunft. (Stuttgart, 1919.)
Troeltsch, E. : Der Historismus und seine Probleme. (Tübingen,
1922.)
Weber, Marianne : Max Weber. (Tübingen, 1926.)
Weber, Max : Gesammelte Aufsätze zur Sozial- und Wirtschafts-
geschichte. (Tübingen, 1924.)
—— Wissenschaftslehre. (Tübingen, 1922.)
—— Wirtschaft und Gesellschaft. (Tübingen, 1925.)
—— Gesammelte Politische Schriften. (Munich, 1921.)
Wilbrandt, R. : Sozialismus. (Jena, 1919.)

FINANCE

Benfey, F. : Die neuere Entwicklung des deutschen Auslandsbank-
wesens (1914–1925). (Berlin, 1925.)
Cassel, G. : Des Geldwesen nach 1914. (Leipzig, 1925.)
Dalberg, R. : Die Entwertung des Geldes. (Berlin, 1918.)
—— Finanzgesundung aus Währungsnot. (Berlin, 1920.)
—— Deutsche, Wahrungs- und Kreditpolitik 1923–1926. (Berlin,
1926.)
Eulenberg, F. : Inflation. (Tübingen, 1919.)
Feuchtwanger, L. : Die Darlehnskassen des Deutsches Reiches.
(Berlin, 1917.)
Helfferech, H. : Money. English ed. 2 vols. (London, 1927.)
Hirsch, J. : Die deutsche Währungsfrage (Kieler Vorträge). (Jena,
1924.)
Kastl, L.
Liefmann, R. } Das Transferproblem. (Leipzig, 1926.)
Kuczinski, R. R. : American Loans to Germany. (New York, 1927.)
Moriès, V. de : Misère et Splendeur des Finances Allemandes. (Paris,
1925.)
Olphe-Galliard, G. : Histoire économique et financière de la guerre
(1914–1918). (Paris, 1923.)
Preyer, W. D. : Roggenpapiere u. Roggensteuern. (Jena, 1923.)
Schacht, Hjalmar : Die Stabilisierung der Mark. (Stuttgart, 1927.)
Schoenthal, J. : Deutsche Währungs- und Kreditpolitik seit Wäh-
rungsfestigung. (Berlin, 1926.)
Statistisches Reichsamt : Die Deutschen Banken 1924 bis 1926.
(Berlin, 1927.)
Steiner, F. G. : Die Banken und der Wiederaufbau der Volkswirt-
schaft. (Leipzig, 1920.)
Schultz, Hans Otto : Devisenhandelspolitik. (Stuttgart, 1918.)

INDUSTRY AND INDUSTRIAL ORGANIZATION (SPECIAL
STUDIES)

Adler, D. W. : Die Organisationsbestrebungen in Stabeisen-Fabrikation
und Stabeisen-Handel. (Bonn, 1920.)
Bauer, F. : Die Rechtliche Struktur der Truste. (Mannheim, 1927.)
British Electrical and Allied Manufacturers' Association (Beama) :
The Electrical Industry in Germany. (London, 1926.)
Combines and Trusts in the Electrical Industry. (London, 1927.)

Bruck, W. F. : Geschichte des Kriegsausschusses der deutschen Baum-woll-Industrie. (Berlin, 1920.)

Buchmann, Mathesius, Petersen u. Reichert : Zur Frage des inter-nationalen Eisenpreisvergleichs. (Berlin, 1927.)

Dehne, G. : Die Deutsche Elektrizitätswirtschaft. (Stuttgart, 1926.)

Deutsch, P. : Die Oberschlesische Montanindustrie vor und nach der Teilung des Industriebezirks. (Bonn, 1926.)

I. G. Farbenindustrie A.G. und ihre Bedeutung. (Berlin, 1927.)

Frank, E. : Wandlungen in der syndikatlichen Organisation des Ruhrkohlenbergbaus in der Zeit von 1919–1925. (Wattenscheid, 1926.)

Friedlander, H. : Konzernrecht. (Mannheim, 1927.)

Fritsch, K. : Das Deutsche Eisenbahnsrecht. (Berlin, 1927.)

Isay, R. : Kartellverordnung. (Berlin, 1925.)

Klotzbach, A. : Der Roheisen-Verband. (Düsseldorf, 1926.)

Kruger, Walter : Die moderne Kartellorganisation der deutschen Stahlindustrie. (Berlin, 1927.)

Liefmann, R. : Die Unternehmungen und ihre Zusammenschlüsse. (Stuttgart, 1928.)

—— Die Unternehmerverbände. (Freiburg u. B., 1897.)

—— Kartelle, Konzerne u. Trusts. 7th ed. (Stuttgart, 1927.)

Deutscher Metallarbeiter-Verband : Konzerne der Metallindustrie. (Stuttgart, 1923.)

Metzner, M. : Kartelle u. Kartellpolitik. (Berlin, 1926.)

Musold, W. : Die Organisation der Kaliwirtschaft. (Berlin, 1926.)

Pinner, F. : Emil Rathenau und das elektrische Zeitalter. (Leipzig, 1918.)

Priester, H. : Der Wiederaufbau der deutschen Handelsschiffahrt. (Berlin, 1926.)

Reichert, J. W. : Die Lebensbedingungen der deutschen Eisen-und Stahlindustrie. (Berlin, 1927.)

Schneider, H. J. : Zur Analyse des Eisenmarkts. (Berlin, 1927.)

Statistisches Reichsamt : Konzerne, Interessengemeinschaften und ähnliche Zusammenschlüsse im Deutschen Reich. (Berlin, 1927.)

Storm, E. : Geschichte der deutschen Kohlenwirtschaft von 1913–1926. (Berlin, 1926.)

Terhalle, T. : Freie oder gebundene Preisbildung ? (Jena, 1920.)

Tross, A. : Der Aufbau der Eisen- und eisenverarbeitenden Industrie-Konzerne Deutschlands. (Berlin, 1923.)

Tschierschky, S. : Neuaufbau der deutschen industriellen Interes-senorganisation. (Berlin, 1919.)

Ufermann, Paul : Der deutsche Stahltrust. (Berlin, 1927.)

Ungewitter, C. : Ausgewählte Kapitel aus der chemische, industriellen Wirtschaftpolitik 1877 bis 1927. (Berlin, November 1927.)

Vereinigte Stahlwerke A.G. : (Spezial-Archiv der deutschen Wirt-schaft). (Berlin, 1927.)

Vorstand des Deutschen Metallarbeiter-Verbandes : Die deutsche Elektrizitätsversorgung. (Stuttgart, 1927.)

LABOUR

Berthelot, M. : Les Conseils d'Entreprise en Allemagne. (Geneva, 1924.)

Brigl-Matthiass, K. : Das Betriebsräteproblem. (Berlin, 1926.)

Büsing, H. : Der Gruppenarbeitsvertrag. (Altona, 1926.)
Cassau, T. : Die Gewerkschaftsbewegung. (Halberstadt, 1925.)
Diehl, K. : Arbeitsintensität u. Achtstundentag. (Jena, 1923.)
Eckert, Otto : Die Finanzwirtschaft der Gewerkschaften in Deutsch-
      land. (Berlin, 1927.)
Lechtape, H. : Die deutschen Arbeitgeberverbände. (Leipzig, 1926.)
Rohmer, G. : Die Verordnung über die Arbeitzeit. (Munich, 1927.)
Seidel, R. : Die Gewerkschaften nach dem Kriege. (Berlin, 1925.)
Spliedt, Franz ⎱ Gesetz über Arbeitsvermittlung und Arbeitslosen-
Broecher, Bruno ⎰ versicherung. (Berlin, 1927.)
Weber, A. : Der Kampf zwischen Kapital und Arbeit. (Tübingen,
      1920.)
Willeke, E. : Das deutsche Arbeitsnachweiswesen. (Berlin, 1926.)
Wolbling, Paul : Das Arbeitsgerichtsgesetz. (Berlin and Vienna, 1927.)

INDEX

* refers to footnotes.